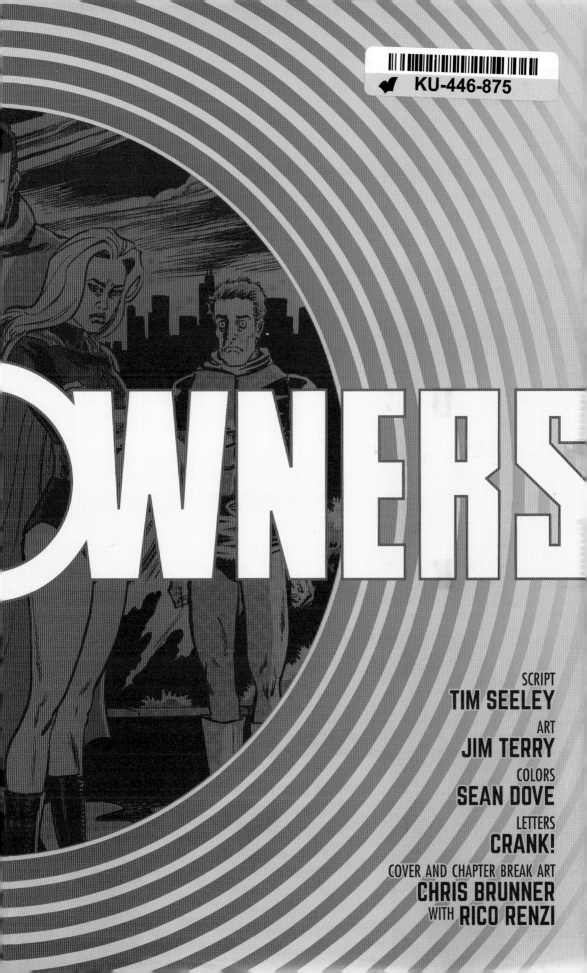

OWNERS

SCRIPT
TIM SEELEY

ART
JIM TERRY

COLORS
SEAN DOVE

LETTERS
CRANK!

COVER AND CHAPTER BREAK ART
CHRIS BRUNNER
WITH **RICO RENZI**

PRESIDENT AND PUBLISHER
MIKE RICHARDSON

EDITOR
DANIEL CHABON

ASSISTANT EDITOR
IAN TUCKER

DESIGNER
JIMMY PRESLER

DIGITAL PRODUCTION
RYAN JORGENSEN

NEIL HANKERSON EXECUTIVE VICE PRESIDENT • TOM WEDDLE CHIEF FINANCIAL OFFICER • RANDY STRADLEY VICE PRESIDENT OF PUBLISHING • MICHAEL MARTENS VICE PRESIDENT OF BOOK TRADE SALES • SCOTT ALLIE EDITOR IN CHIEF • MATT PARKINSON VICE PRESIDENT OF MARKETING • DAVID SCROGGY VICE PRESIDENT OF PRODUCT DEVELOPMENT • DALE LaFOUNTAIN VICE PRESIDENT OF INFORMATION TECHNOLOGY • DARLENE VOGEL SENIOR DIRECTOR OF PRINT, DESIGN, AND PRODUCTION • KEN LIZZI GENERAL COUNSEL • DAVEY ESTRADA EDITORIAL DIRECTOR • CHRIS WARNER SENIOR BOOKS EDITOR • DIANA SCHUTZ EXECUTIVE EDITOR • CARY GRAZZINI DIRECTOR OF PRINT AND DEVELOPMENT • LIA RIBACCHI ART DIRECTOR • CARA NIECE DIRECTOR OF SCHEDULING • MARK BERNARDI DIRECTOR OF DIGITAL PUBLISHING

Published by Dark Horse Books, a division of Dark Horse Comics, Inc., 10956 SE Main Street, Milwaukie, OR 97222

First edition: May 2015 ISBN 978-1-61655-645-7

10 9 8 7 6 5 4 3 2 1 Printed in China

International Licensing: (503) 905-2377   Comic Shop Locator Service: (888) 266-4226

This volume collects *Sundowners*
#1–#6.

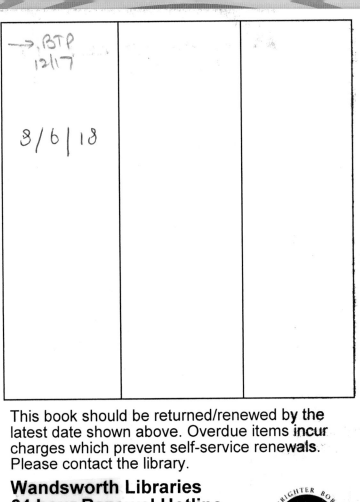

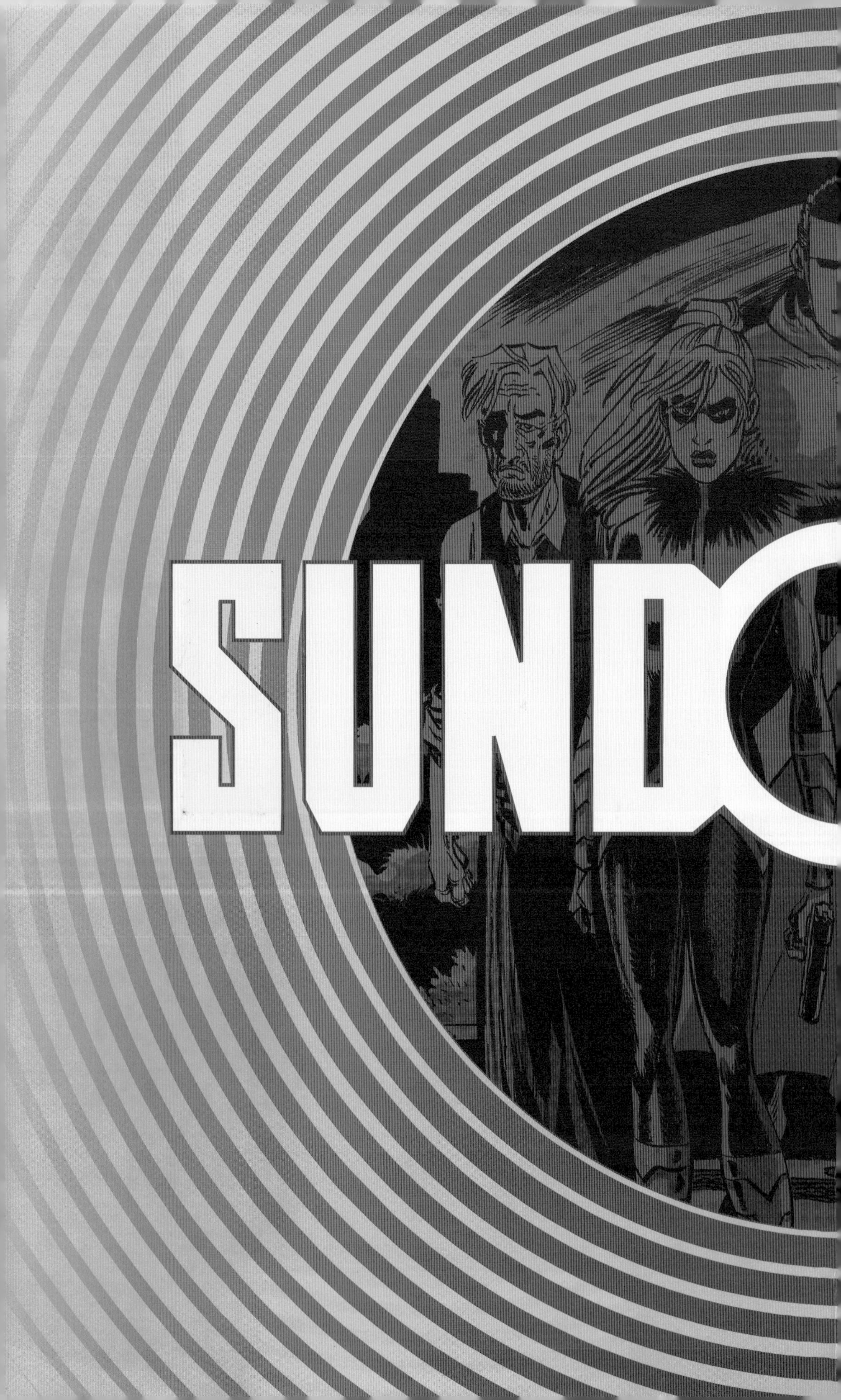
SUND

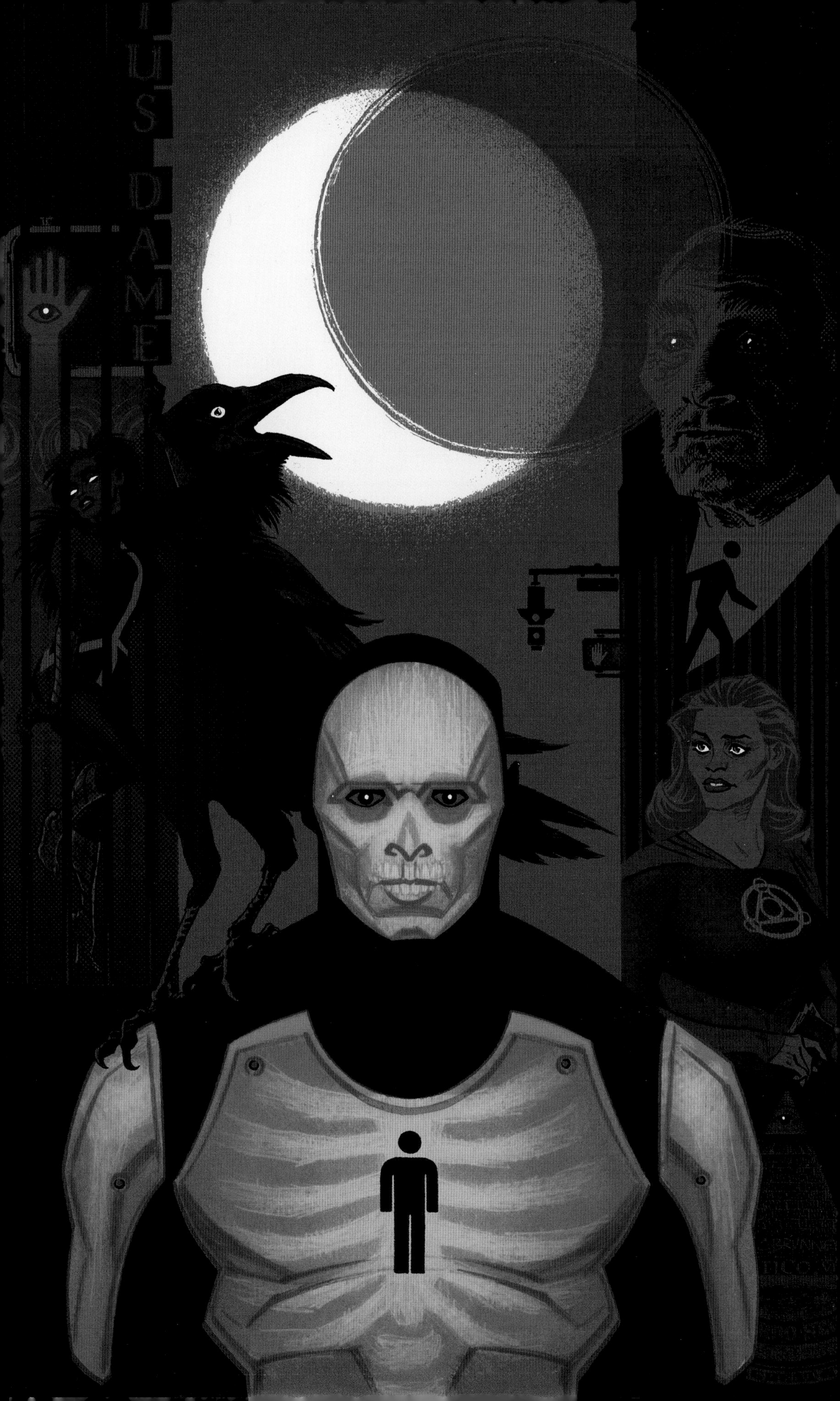
IUS DAME

SUNDOWNERS™

1

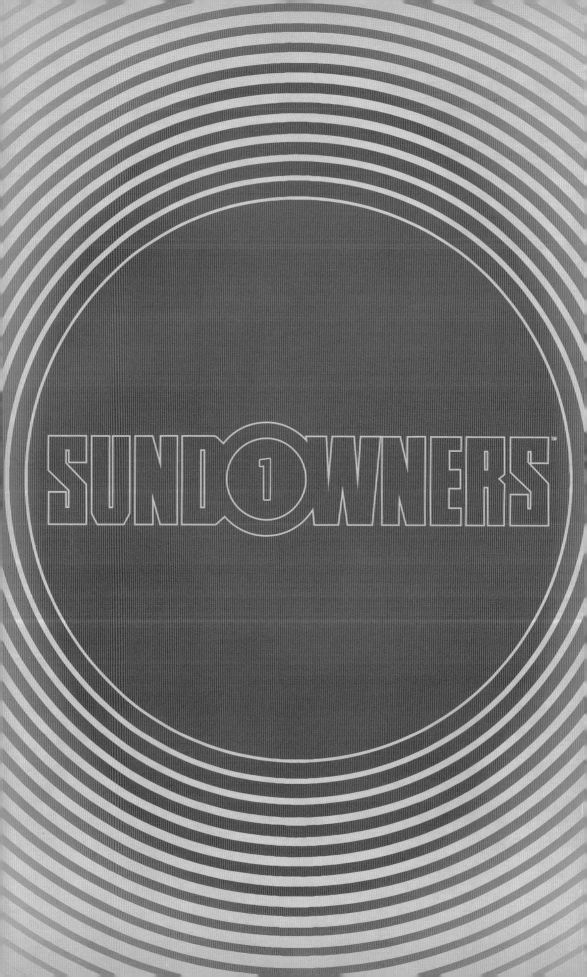

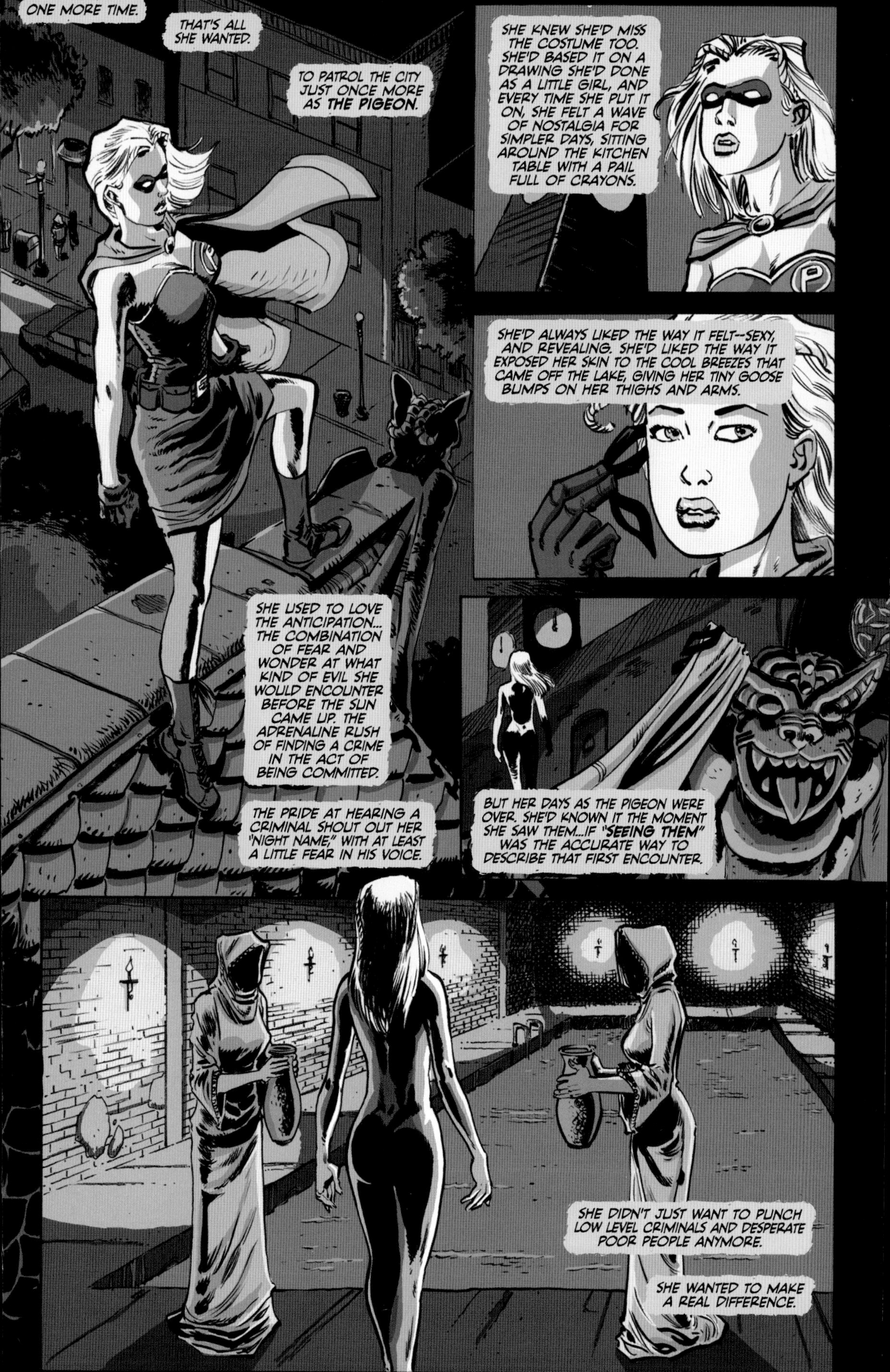
ONE MORE TIME.
THAT'S ALL SHE WANTED.
TO PATROL THE CITY JUST ONCE MORE AS THE PIGEON.
SHE KNEW SHE'D MISS THE COSTUME TOO. SHE'D BASED IT ON A DRAWING SHE'D DONE AS A LITTLE GIRL, AND EVERY TIME SHE PUT IT ON, SHE FELT A WAVE OF NOSTALGIA FOR SIMPLER DAYS, SITTING AROUND THE KITCHEN TABLE WITH A PAIL FULL OF CRAYONS.
SHE'D ALWAYS LIKED THE WAY IT FELT--SEXY, AND REVEALING. SHE'D LIKED THE WAY IT EXPOSED HER SKIN TO THE COOL BREEZES THAT CAME OFF THE LAKE, GIVING HER TINY GOOSE BUMPS ON HER THIGHS AND ARMS.
SHE USED TO LOVE THE ANTICIPATION... THE COMBINATION OF FEAR AND WONDER AT WHAT KIND OF EVIL SHE WOULD ENCOUNTER BEFORE THE SUN CAME UP. THE ADRENALINE RUSH OF FINDING A CRIME IN THE ACT OF BEING COMMITTED.
THE PRIDE AT HEARING A CRIMINAL SHOUT OUT HER "NIGHT NAME," WITH AT LEAST A LITTLE FEAR IN HIS VOICE.
BUT HER DAYS AS THE PIGEON WERE OVER. SHE'D KNOWN IT THE MOMENT SHE SAW THEM...IF "SEEING THEM" WAS THE ACCURATE WAY TO DESCRIBE THAT FIRST ENCOUNTER.
SHE DIDN'T JUST WANT TO PUNCH LOW LEVEL CRIMINALS AND DESPERATE POOR PEOPLE ANYMORE.
SHE WANTED TO MAKE A REAL DIFFERENCE.

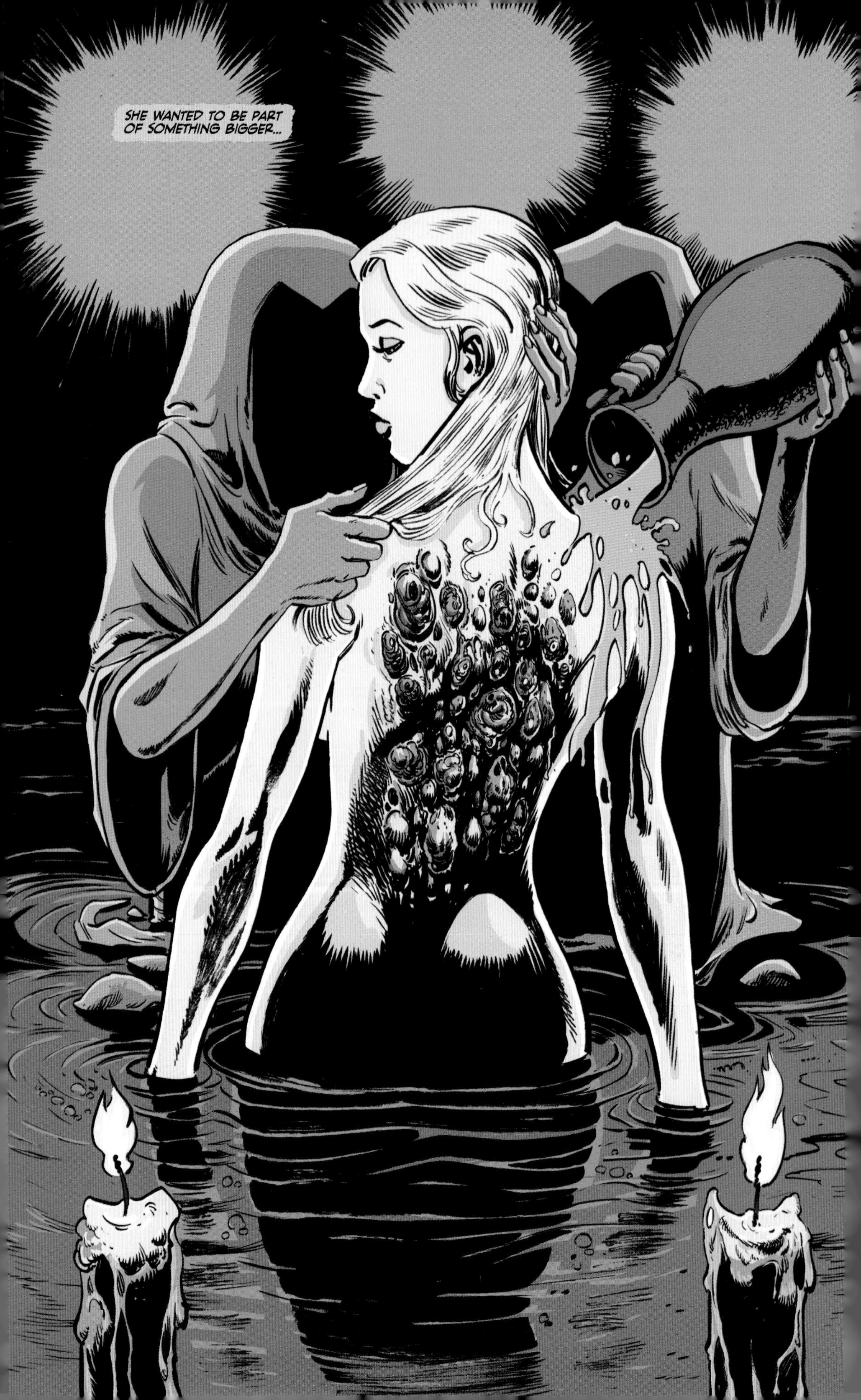
SHE WANTED TO BE PART OF SOMETHING BIGGER...

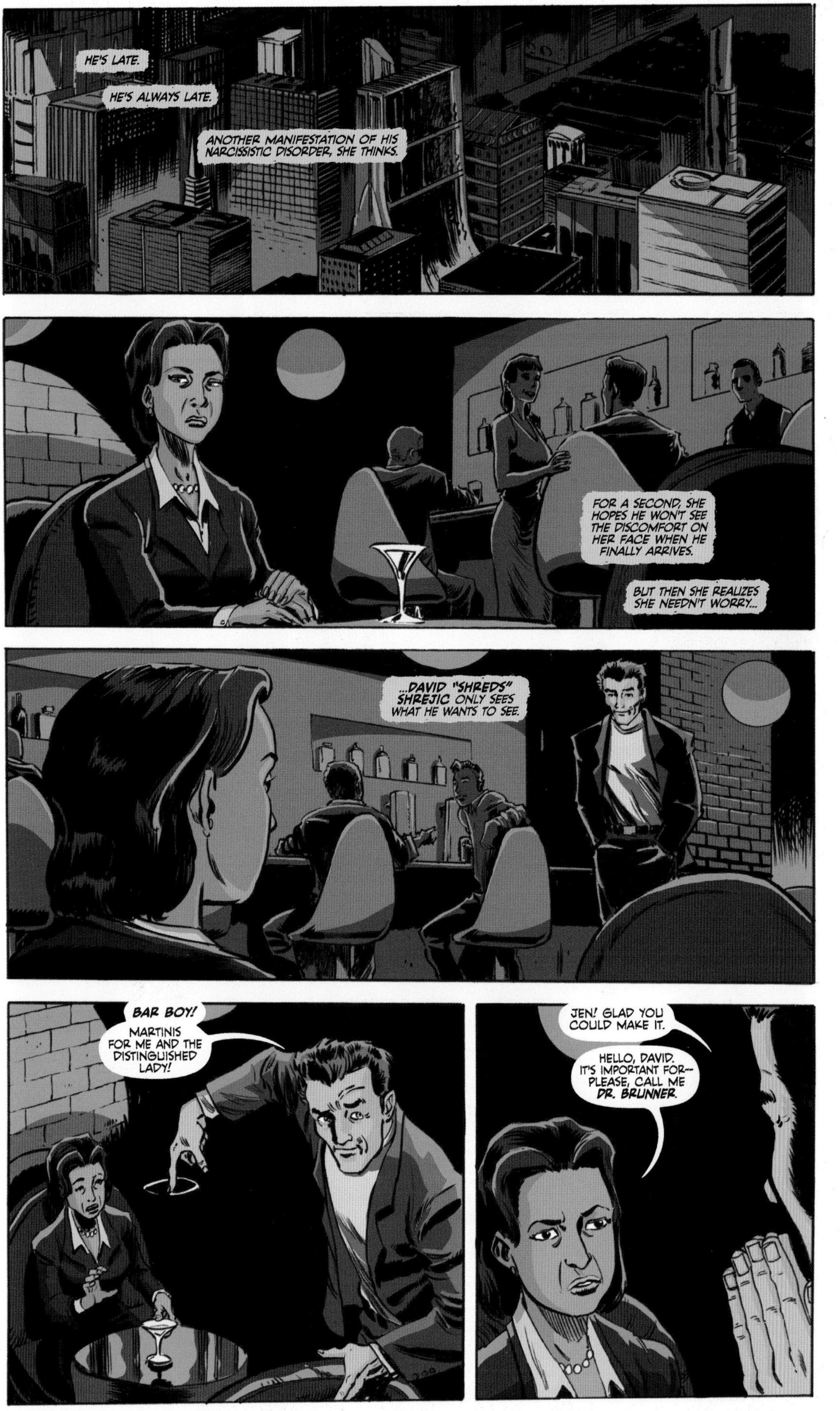
HE'S LATE.
HE'S ALWAYS LATE.
ANOTHER MANIFESTATION OF HIS NARCISSISTIC DISORDER, SHE THINKS.
FOR A SECOND, SHE HOPES HE WON'T SEE THE DISCOMFORT ON HER FACE WHEN HE FINALLY ARRIVES.
BUT THEN SHE REALIZES SHE NEEDN'T WORRY...
...DAVID "SHREDS" SHREJIC ONLY SEES WHAT HE WANTS TO SEE.
BAR BOY! MARTINIS FOR ME AND THE DISTINGUISHED LADY!
JEN! GLAD YOU COULD MAKE IT.
HELLO, DAVID. IT'S IMPORTANT FOR-- PLEASE, CALL ME DR. BRUNNER.

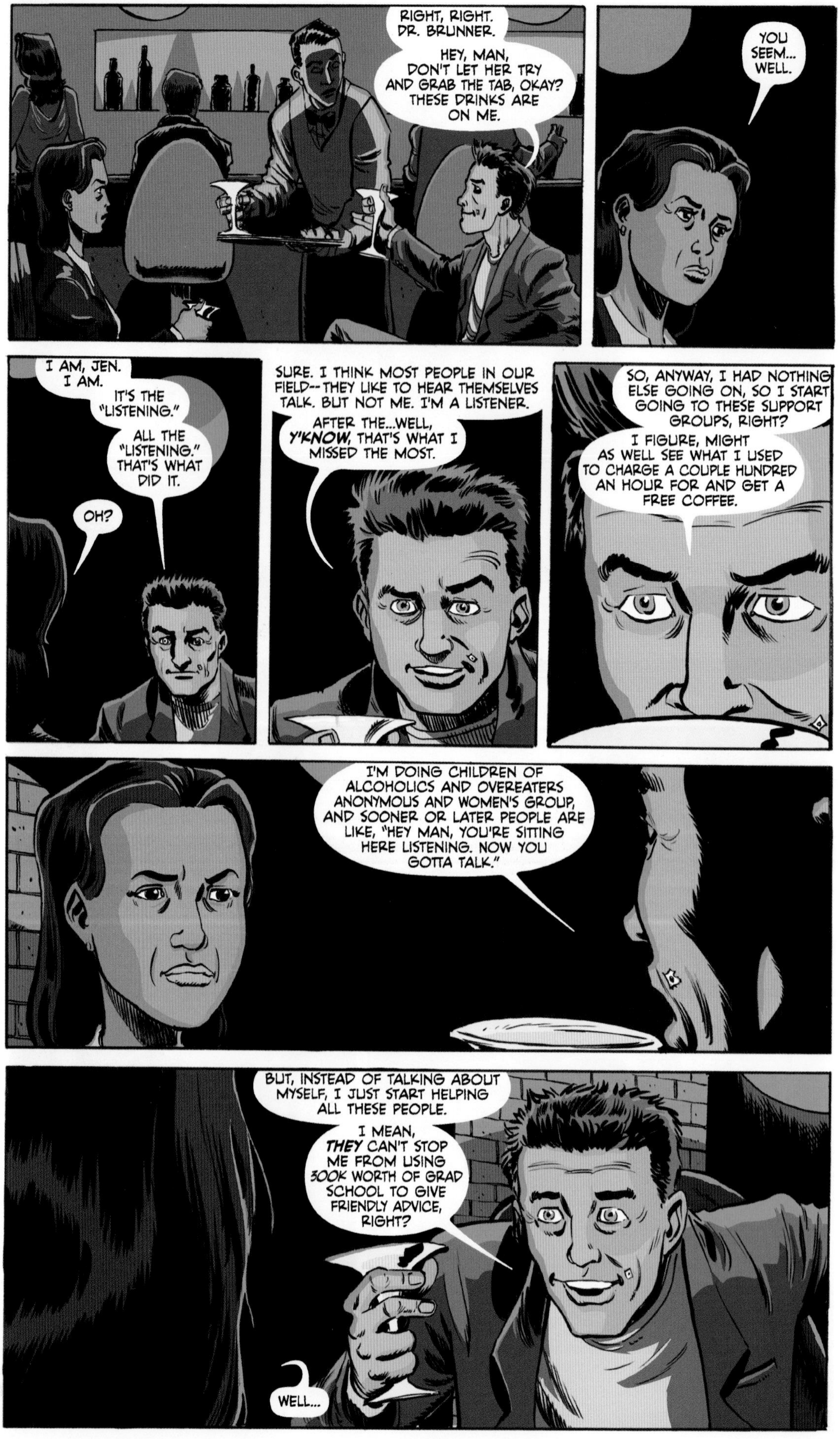
RIGHT, RIGHT. DR. BRUNNER.
HEY, MAN, DON'T LET HER TRY AND GRAB THE TAB, OKAY? THESE DRINKS ARE ON ME.
YOU SEEM... WELL.
I AM, JEN. I AM.
IT'S THE "LISTENING."
ALL THE "LISTENING." THAT'S WHAT DID IT.
OH?
SURE. I THINK MOST PEOPLE IN OUR FIELD--THEY LIKE TO HEAR THEMSELVES TALK. BUT NOT ME. I'M A LISTENER.
AFTER THE...WELL, *Y'KNOW,* THAT'S WHAT I MISSED THE MOST.
SO, ANYWAY, I HAD NOTHING ELSE GOING ON, SO I START GOING TO THESE SUPPORT GROUPS, RIGHT?
I FIGURE, MIGHT AS WELL SEE WHAT I USED TO CHARGE A COUPLE HUNDRED AN HOUR FOR AND GET A FREE COFFEE.
I'M DOING CHILDREN OF ALCOHOLICS AND OVEREATERS ANONYMOUS AND WOMEN'S GROUP, AND SOONER OR LATER PEOPLE ARE LIKE, "HEY MAN, YOU'RE SITTING HERE LISTENING. NOW YOU GOTTA TALK."
BUT, INSTEAD OF TALKING ABOUT MYSELF, I JUST START HELPING ALL THESE PEOPLE.
I MEAN, *THEY* CAN'T STOP ME FROM USING *300K* WORTH OF GRAD SCHOOL TO GIVE FRIENDLY ADVICE, RIGHT?
WELL...

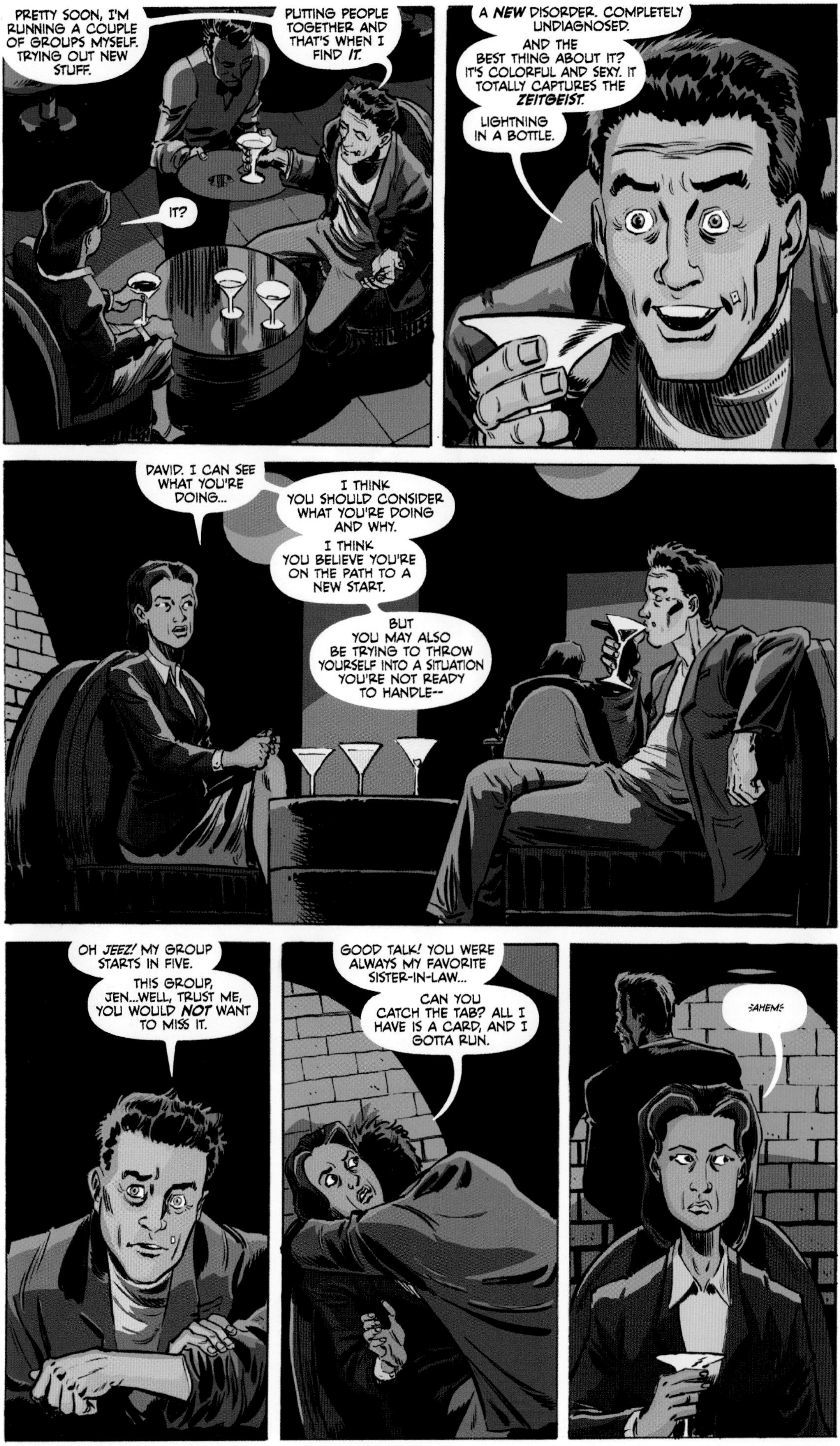
PRETTY SOON, I'M RUNNING A COUPLE OF GROUPS MYSELF. TRYING OUT NEW STUFF.
PUTTING PEOPLE TOGETHER AND THAT'S WHEN I FIND *IT*.
IT?
A *NEW* DISORDER. COMPLETELY UNDIAGNOSED.
AND THE BEST THING ABOUT IT? IT'S COLORFUL AND SEXY. IT TOTALLY CAPTURES THE *ZEITGEIST*.
LIGHTNING IN A BOTTLE.
DAVID. I CAN SEE WHAT YOU'RE DOING...
I THINK YOU SHOULD CONSIDER WHAT YOU'RE DOING AND WHY.
I THINK YOU BELIEVE YOU'RE ON THE PATH TO A NEW START.
BUT YOU MAY ALSO BE TRYING TO THROW YOURSELF INTO A SITUATION YOU'RE NOT READY TO HANDLE--
OH *JEEZ!* MY GROUP STARTS IN FIVE.
THIS GROUP, JEN...WELL, TRUST ME, YOU WOULD *NOT* WANT TO MISS IT.
GOOD TALK! YOU WERE ALWAYS MY FAVORITE SISTER-IN-LAW...
CAN YOU CATCH THE TAB? ALL I HAVE IS A CARD, AND I GOTTA RUN.
AHEM

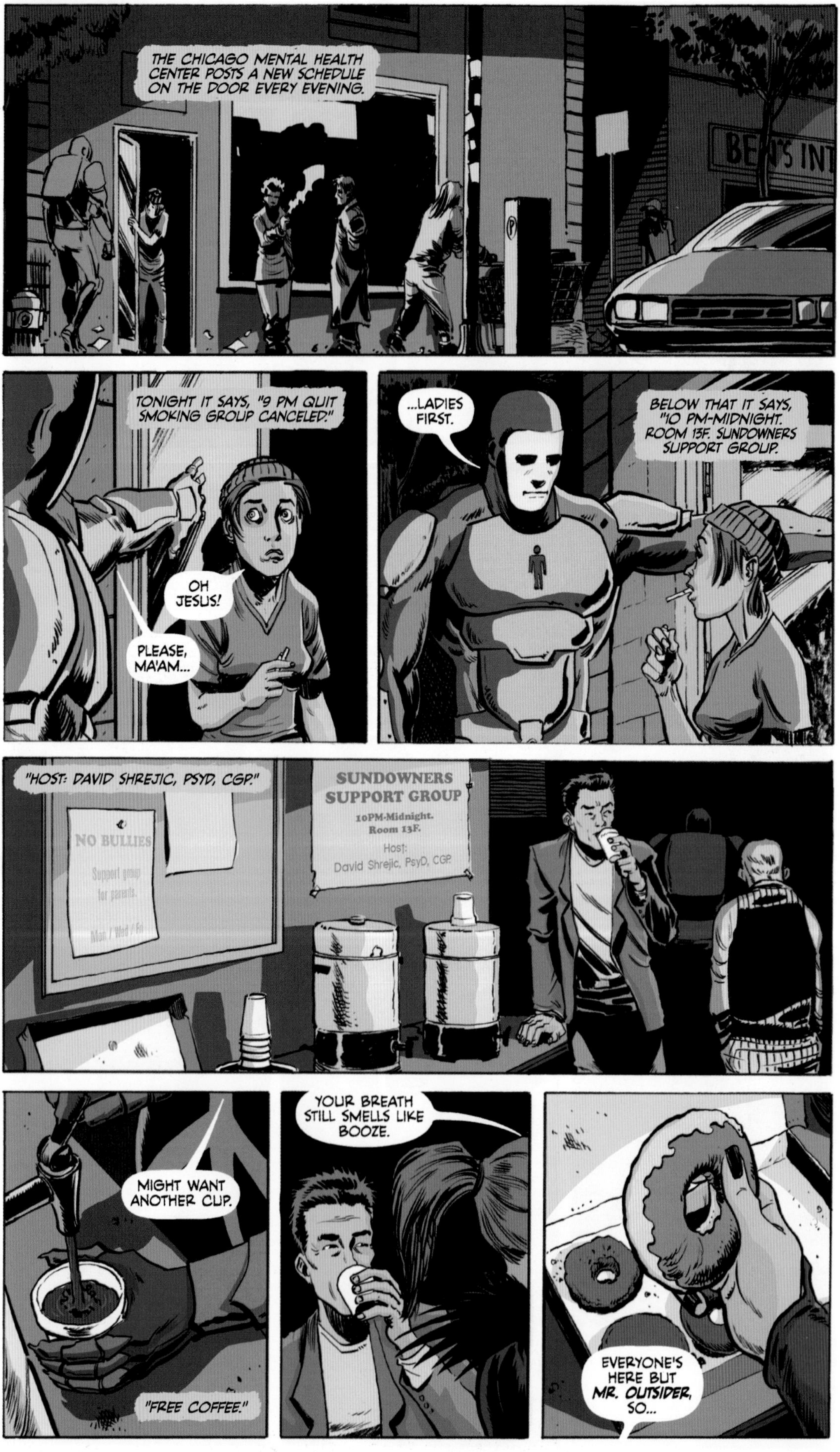
THE CHICAGO MENTAL HEALTH CENTER POSTS A NEW SCHEDULE ON THE DOOR EVERY EVENING.
BEN'S INT
TONIGHT IT SAYS, "9 PM QUIT SMOKING GROUP CANCELED."
OH JESUS!
PLEASE, MA'AM...
...LADIES FIRST.
BELOW THAT IT SAYS, "10 PM-MIDNIGHT. ROOM 13F. SUNDOWNERS SUPPORT GROUP.
"HOST: DAVID SHREJIC, PSYD, CGP."
NO BULLIES
SUNDOWNERS SUPPORT GROUP
10PM-Midnight.
Room 13F.
Host:
David Shrejic, PsyD, CGP.
MIGHT WANT ANOTHER CUP.
"FREE COFFEE."
YOUR BREATH STILL SMELLS LIKE BOOZE.
EVERYONE'S HERE BUT MR. OUTSIDER, SO...

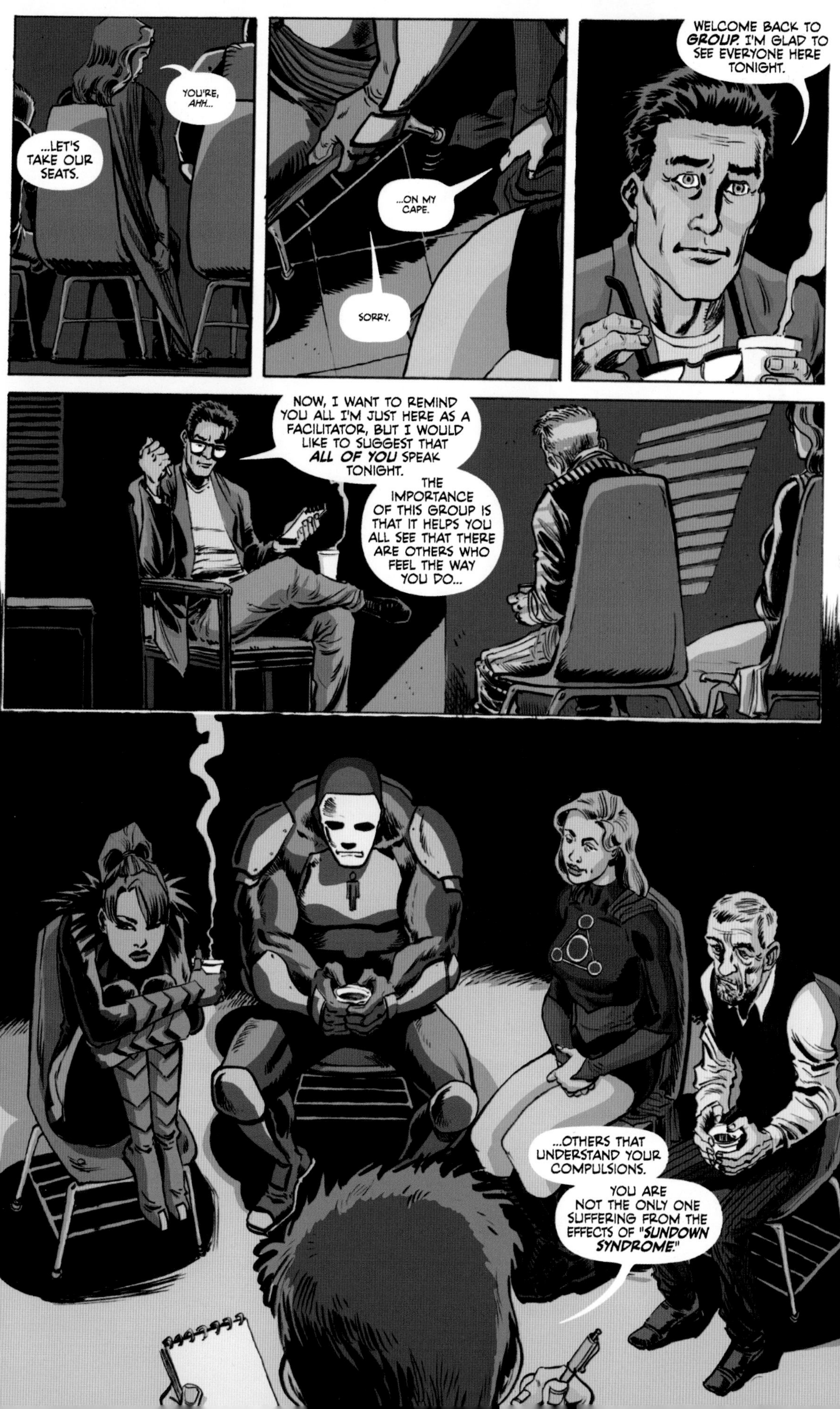
YOU'RE, AHH...
...LET'S TAKE OUR SEATS.
...ON MY CAPE.
SORRY.
WELCOME BACK TO GROUP. I'M GLAD TO SEE EVERYONE HERE TONIGHT.
NOW, I WANT TO REMIND YOU ALL I'M JUST HERE AS A FACILITATOR, BUT I WOULD LIKE TO SUGGEST THAT ALL OF YOU SPEAK TONIGHT.
THE IMPORTANCE OF THIS GROUP IS THAT IT HELPS YOU ALL SEE THAT THERE ARE OTHERS WHO FEEL THE WAY YOU DO...
...OTHERS THAT UNDERSTAND YOUR COMPULSIONS.
YOU ARE NOT THE ONLY ONE SUFFERING FROM THE EFFECTS OF "SUNDOWN SYNDROME."

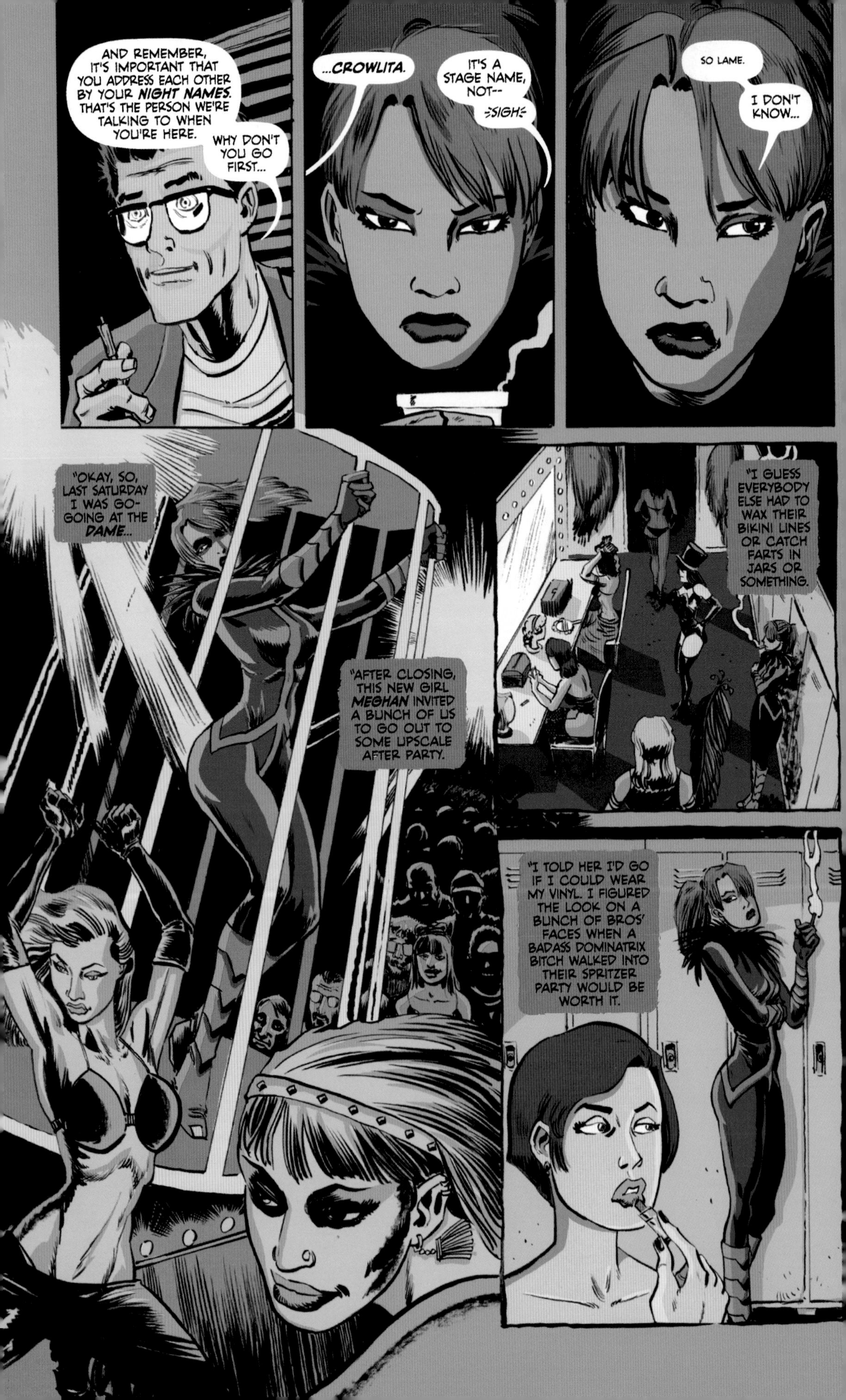
AND REMEMBER, IT'S IMPORTANT THAT YOU ADDRESS EACH OTHER BY YOUR NIGHT NAMES. THAT'S THE PERSON WE'RE TALKING TO WHEN YOU'RE HERE.
WHY DON'T YOU GO FIRST...
...CROWLITA.
IT'S A STAGE NAME, NOT--
SIGH
SO LAME.
I DON'T KNOW...
"OKAY, SO, LAST SATURDAY I WAS GO-GOING AT THE DAME...
"AFTER CLOSING, THIS NEW GIRL MEGHAN INVITED A BUNCH OF US TO GO OUT TO SOME UPSCALE AFTER PARTY.
"I GUESS EVERYBODY ELSE HAD TO WAX THEIR BIKINI LINES OR CATCH FARTS IN JARS OR SOMETHING.
"I TOLD HER I'D GO IF I COULD WEAR MY VINYL. I FIGURED THE LOOK ON A BUNCH OF BROS' FACES WHEN A BADASS DOMINATRIX BITCH WALKED INTO THEIR SPRITZER PARTY WOULD BE WORTH IT.

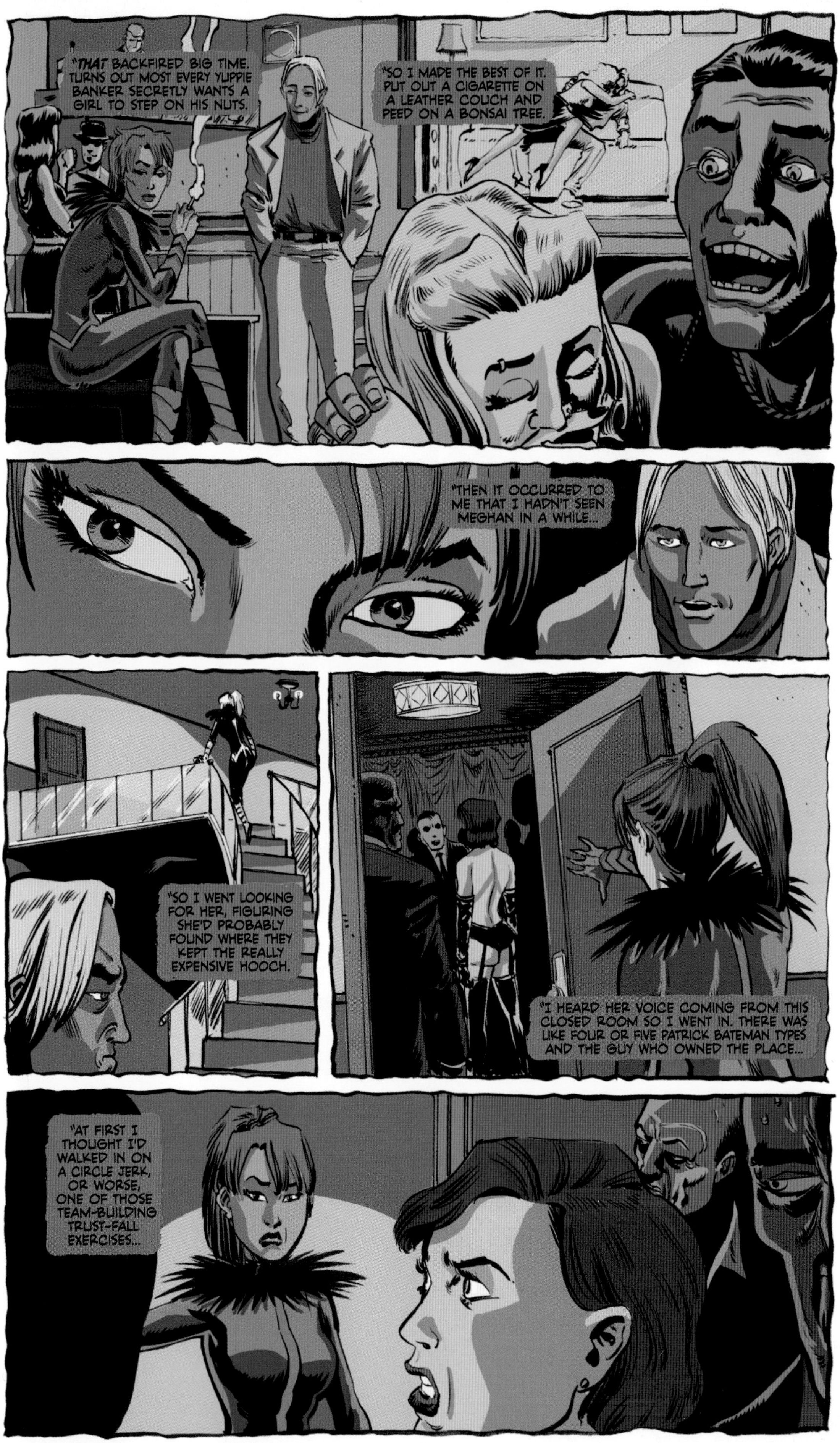
"THAT BACKFIRED BIG TIME. TURNS OUT MOST EVERY YUPPIE BANKER SECRETLY WANTS A GIRL TO STEP ON HIS NUTS.
"SO I MADE THE BEST OF IT. PUT OUT A CIGARETTE ON A LEATHER COUCH AND PEED ON A BONSAI TREE.
"THEN IT OCCURRED TO ME THAT I HADN'T SEEN MEGHAN IN A WHILE...
"SO I WENT LOOKING FOR HER, FIGURING SHE'D PROBABLY FOUND WHERE THEY KEPT THE REALLY EXPENSIVE HOOCH.
"I HEARD HER VOICE COMING FROM THIS CLOSED ROOM SO I WENT IN. THERE WAS LIKE FOUR OR FIVE PATRICK BATEMAN TYPES AND THE GUY WHO OWNED THE PLACE...
"AT FIRST I THOUGHT I'D WALKED IN ON A CIRCLE JERK, OR WORSE, ONE OF THOSE TEAM-BUILDING TRUST-FALL EXERCISES...

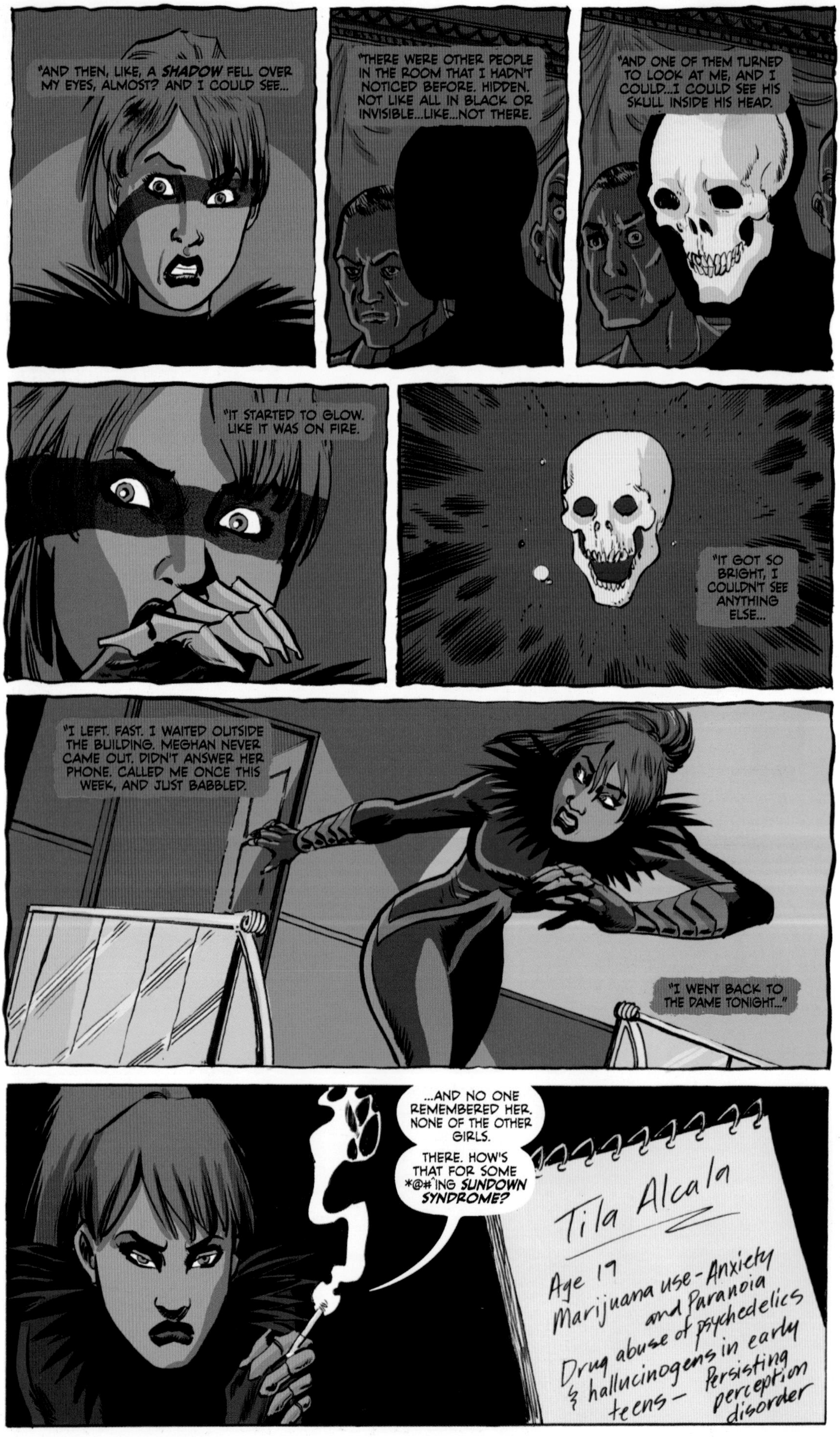
"AND THEN, LIKE, A SHADOW FELL OVER MY EYES, ALMOST? AND I COULD SEE...
"THERE WERE OTHER PEOPLE IN THE ROOM THAT I HADN'T NOTICED BEFORE. HIDDEN. NOT LIKE ALL IN BLACK OR INVISIBLE...LIKE...NOT THERE.
"AND ONE OF THEM TURNED TO LOOK AT ME, AND I COULD...I COULD SEE HIS SKULL INSIDE HIS HEAD.
"IT STARTED TO GLOW. LIKE IT WAS ON FIRE.
"IT GOT SO BRIGHT, I COULDN'T SEE ANYTHING ELSE...
"I LEFT. FAST. I WAITED OUTSIDE THE BUILDING. MEGHAN NEVER CAME OUT. DIDN'T ANSWER HER PHONE. CALLED ME ONCE THIS WEEK, AND JUST BABBLED.
"I WENT BACK TO THE DAME TONIGHT..."
...AND NO ONE REMEMBERED HER. NONE OF THE OTHER GIRLS.
THERE. HOW'S THAT FOR SOME *@#^ING SUNDOWN SYNDROME?
Tila Alcala
Age 17
Marijuana use - Anxiety and Paranoia
Drug abuse of psychedelics & hallucinogens in early teens - Persisting perception disorder

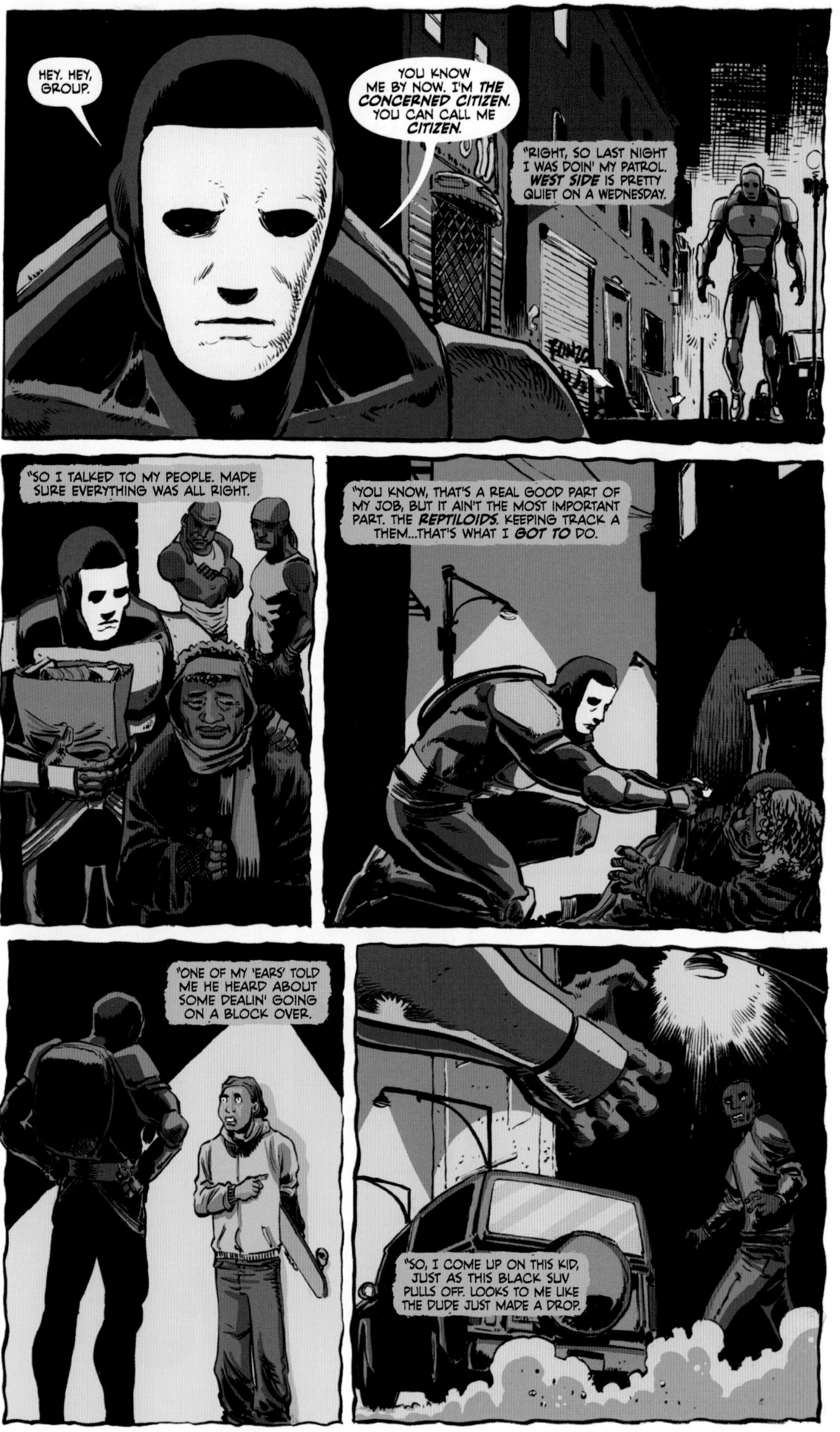
HEY. HEY, GROUP.
YOU KNOW ME BY NOW. I'M THE CONCERNED CITIZEN. YOU CAN CALL ME CITIZEN.
"RIGHT, SO LAST NIGHT I WAS DOIN' MY PATROL. WEST SIDE IS PRETTY QUIET ON A WEDNESDAY.
"SO I TALKED TO MY PEOPLE. MADE SURE EVERYTHING WAS ALL RIGHT.
"YOU KNOW, THAT'S A REAL GOOD PART OF MY JOB, BUT IT AIN'T THE MOST IMPORTANT PART. THE REPTILOIDS. KEEPING TRACK A THEM...THAT'S WHAT I GOT TO DO.
"ONE OF MY 'EARS' TOLD ME HE HEARD ABOUT SOME DEALIN' GOING ON A BLOCK OVER.
"SO, I COME UP ON THIS KID, JUST AS THIS BLACK SUV PULLS OFF. LOOKS TO ME LIKE THE DUDE JUST MADE A DROP.

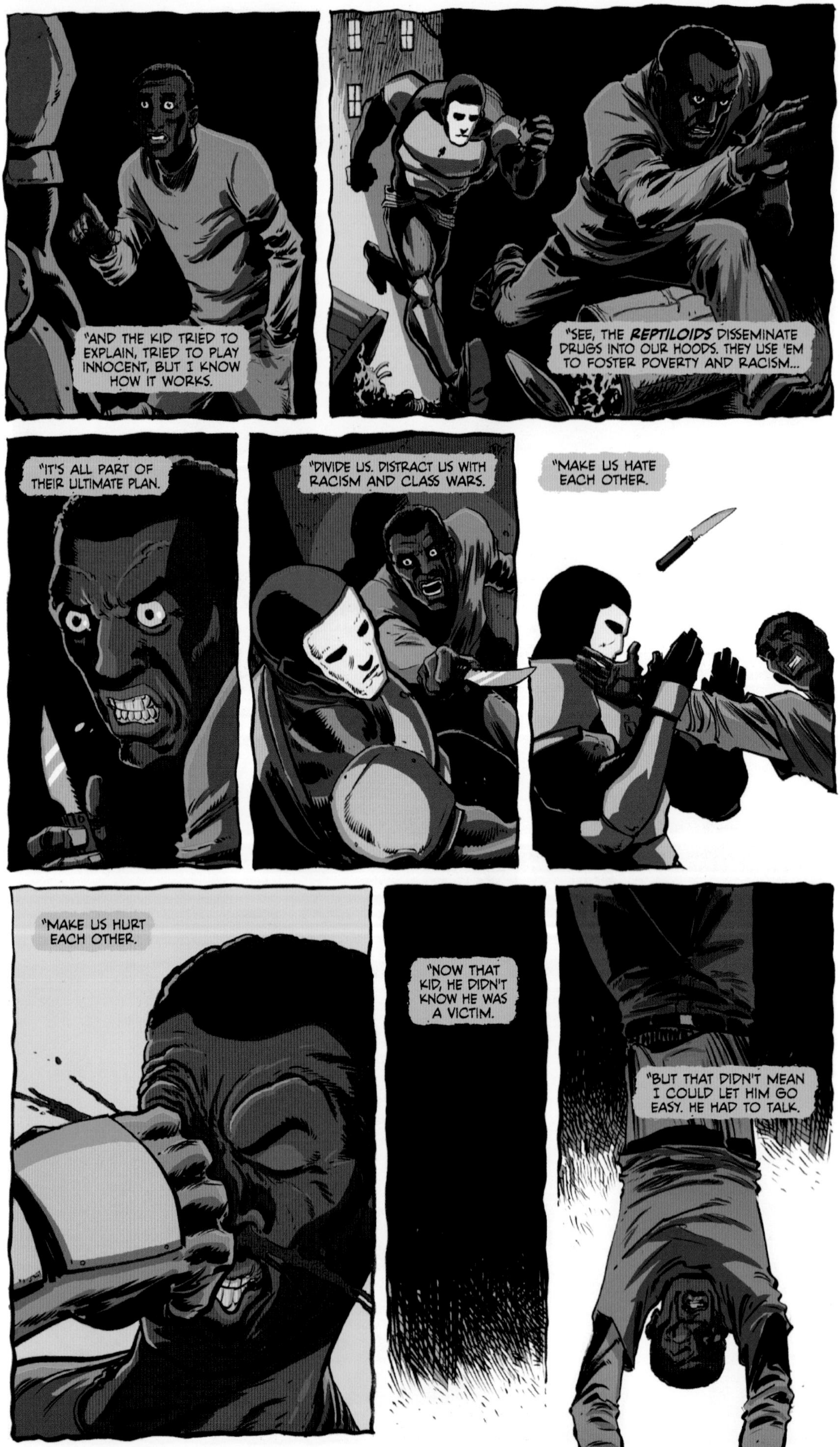
"AND THE KID TRIED TO EXPLAIN, TRIED TO PLAY INNOCENT, BUT I KNOW HOW IT WORKS.
"SEE, THE REPTILOIDS DISSEMINATE DRUGS INTO OUR HOODS. THEY USE 'EM TO FOSTER POVERTY AND RACISM...
"IT'S ALL PART OF THEIR ULTIMATE PLAN.
"DIVIDE US. DISTRACT US WITH RACISM AND CLASS WARS.
"MAKE US HATE EACH OTHER.
"MAKE US HURT EACH OTHER.
"NOW THAT KID, HE DIDN'T KNOW HE WAS A VICTIM.
"BUT THAT DIDN'T MEAN I COULD LET HIM GO EASY. HE HAD TO TALK.

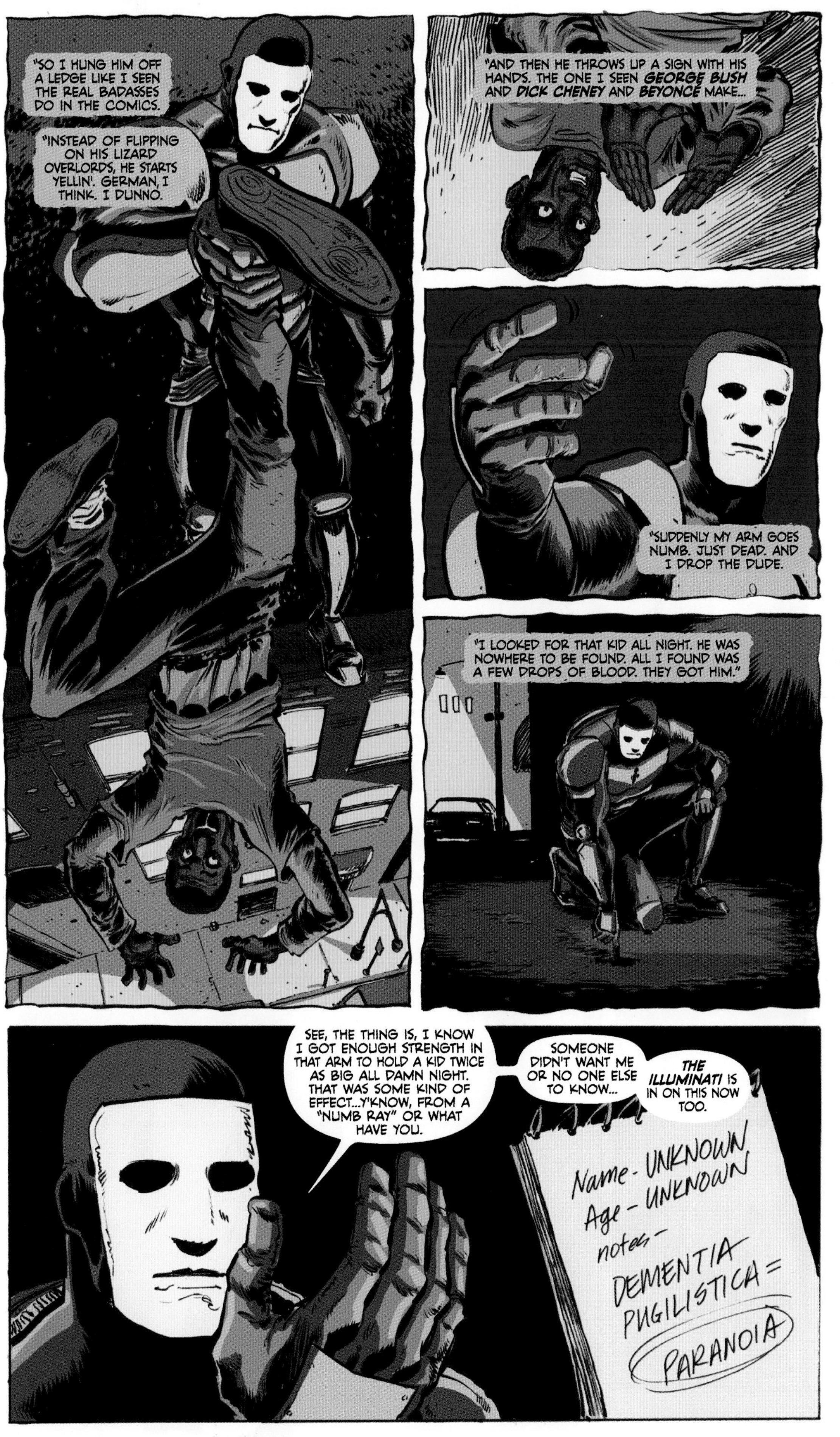

"SO I HUNG HIM OFF A LEDGE LIKE I SEEN THE REAL BADASSES DO IN THE COMICS.
"INSTEAD OF FLIPPING ON HIS LIZARD OVERLORDS, HE STARTS YELLIN'. GERMAN, I THINK. I DUNNO.
"AND THEN HE THROWS UP A SIGN WITH HIS HANDS. THE ONE I SEEN *GEORGE BUSH* AND *DICK CHENEY* AND *BEYONCE* MAKE...
"SUDDENLY MY ARM GOES NUMB. JUST DEAD. AND I DROP THE DUDE.
"I LOOKED FOR THAT KID ALL NIGHT. HE WAS NOWHERE TO BE FOUND. ALL I FOUND WAS A FEW DROPS OF BLOOD. THEY GOT HIM."
SEE, THE THING IS, I KNOW I GOT ENOUGH STRENGTH IN THAT ARM TO HOLD A KID TWICE AS BIG ALL DAMN NIGHT. THAT WAS SOME KIND OF EFFECT...Y'KNOW, FROM A "NUMB RAY" OR WHAT HAVE YOU.
SOMEONE DIDN'T WANT ME OR NO ONE ELSE TO KNOW...
THE ILLUMINATI IS IN ON THIS NOW TOO.
Name - UNKNOWN
Age - UNKNOWN
notes -
DEMENTIA PUGILISTICA =
PARANOIA

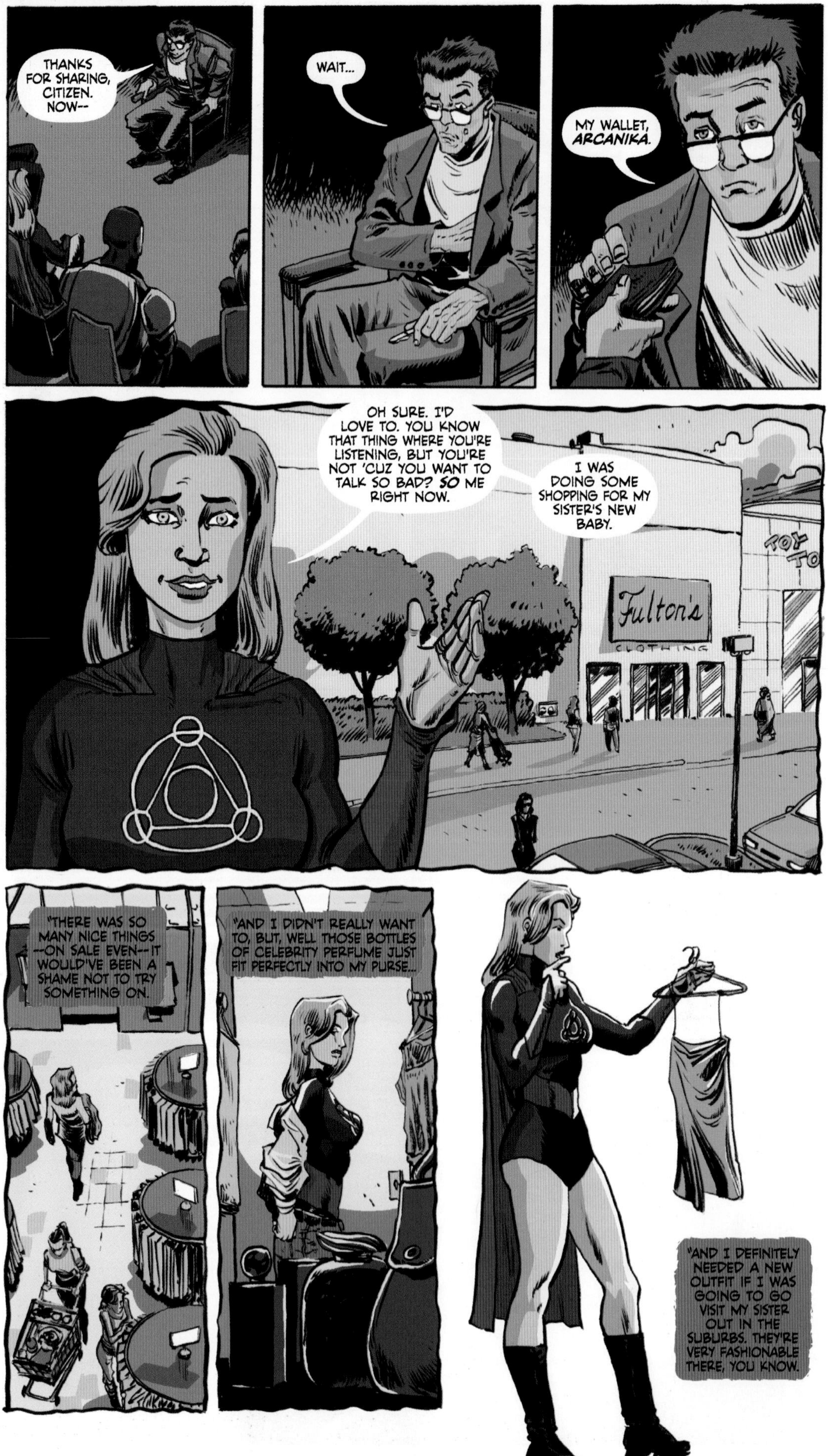

THANKS FOR SHARING, CITIZEN. NOW--
WAIT...
MY WALLET, ARCANIKA.
OH SURE. I'D LOVE TO. YOU KNOW THAT THING WHERE YOU'RE LISTENING, BUT YOU'RE NOT 'CUZ YOU WANT TO TALK SO BAD? SO ME RIGHT NOW.
I WAS DOING SOME SHOPPING FOR MY SISTER'S NEW BABY.
Fulton's
CLOTHING
TOY
"THERE WAS SO MANY NICE THINGS --ON SALE EVEN--IT WOULD'VE BEEN A SHAME NOT TO TRY SOMETHING ON.
"AND I DIDN'T REALLY WANT TO, BUT, WELL THOSE BOTTLES OF CELEBRITY PERFUME JUST FIT PERFECTLY INTO MY PURSE...
"AND I DEFINITELY NEEDED A NEW OUTFIT IF I WAS GOING TO GO VISIT MY SISTER OUT IN THE SUBURBS. THEY'RE VERY FASHIONABLE THERE, YOU KNOW.

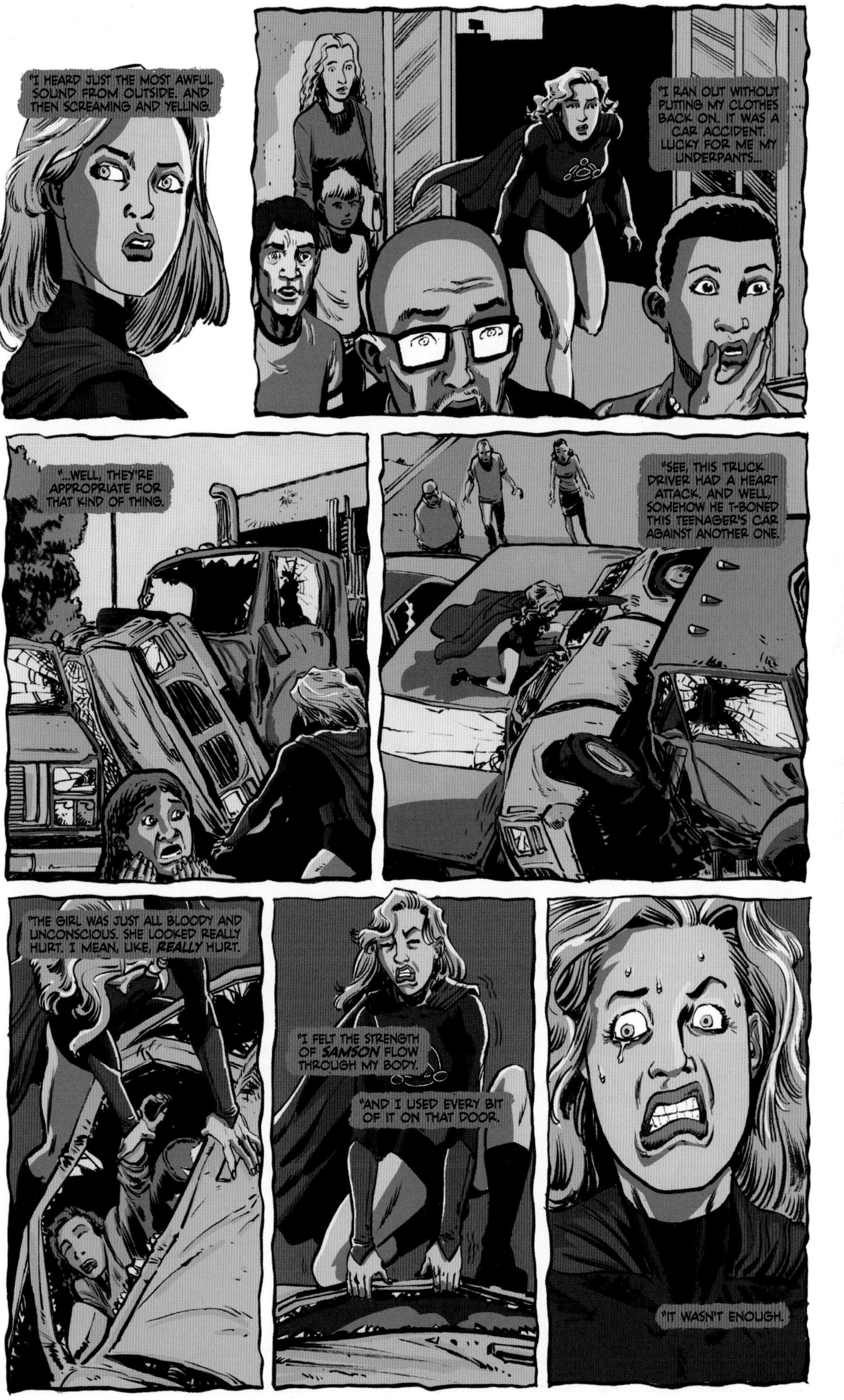
"I HEARD JUST THE MOST AWFUL SOUND FROM OUTSIDE. AND THEN SCREAMING AND YELLING.
"I RAN OUT WITHOUT PUTTING MY CLOTHES BACK ON. IT WAS A CAR ACCIDENT. LUCKY FOR ME MY UNDERPANTS...
"...WELL, THEY'RE APPROPRIATE FOR THAT KIND OF THING.
"SEE, THIS TRUCK DRIVER HAD A HEART ATTACK. AND WELL, SOMEHOW HE T-BONED THIS TEENAGER'S CAR AGAINST ANOTHER ONE.
"THE GIRL WAS JUST ALL BLOODY AND UNCONSCIOUS. SHE LOOKED REALLY HURT. I MEAN, LIKE, *REALLY* HURT.
"I FELT THE STRENGTH OF *SAMSON* FLOW THROUGH MY BODY.
"AND I USED EVERY BIT OF IT ON THAT DOOR.
"IT WASN'T ENOUGH.

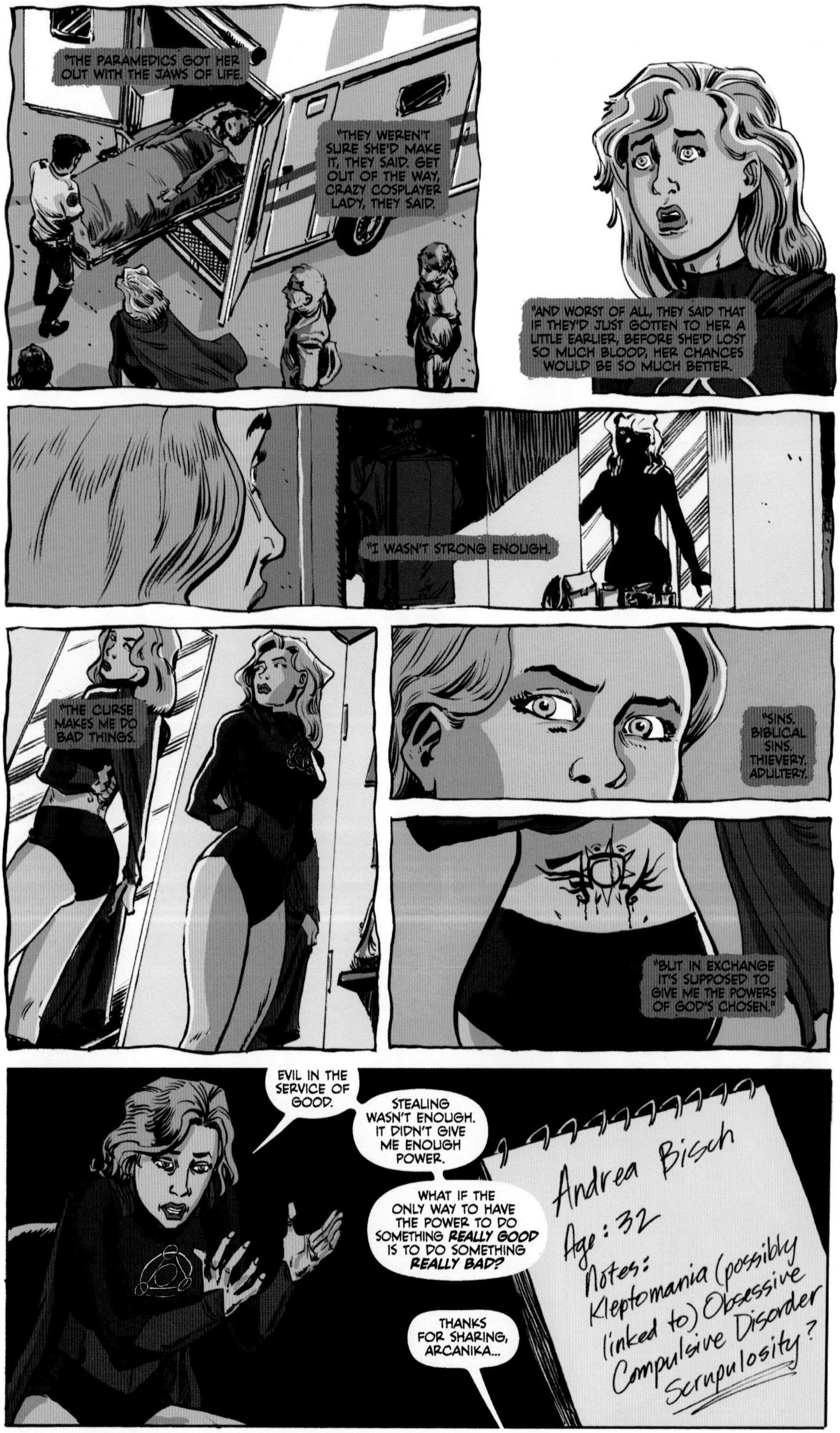
"THE PARAMEDICS GOT HER OUT WITH THE JAWS OF LIFE.
"THEY WEREN'T SURE SHE'D MAKE IT, THEY SAID. GET OUT OF THE WAY, CRAZY COSPLAYER LADY, THEY SAID.
"AND WORST OF ALL, THEY SAID THAT IF THEY'D JUST GOTTEN TO HER A LITTLE EARLIER, BEFORE SHE'D LOST SO MUCH BLOOD, HER CHANCES WOULD BE SO MUCH BETTER.
"I WASN'T STRONG ENOUGH.
"THE CURSE MAKES ME DO BAD THINGS.
"SINS. BIBLICAL SINS. THIEVERY. ADULTERY.
"BUT IN EXCHANGE IT'S SUPPOSED TO GIVE ME THE POWERS OF GOD'S CHOSEN."
EVIL IN THE SERVICE OF GOOD.
STEALING WASN'T ENOUGH. IT DIDN'T GIVE ME ENOUGH POWER.
WHAT IF THE ONLY WAY TO HAVE THE POWER TO DO SOMETHING REALLY GOOD IS TO DO SOMETHING REALLY BAD?
THANKS FOR SHARING, ARCANIKA...
Andrea Bisch
Age: 32
Notes:
Kleptomania (possibly linked to) Obsessive Compulsive Disorder
Scrupulosity?

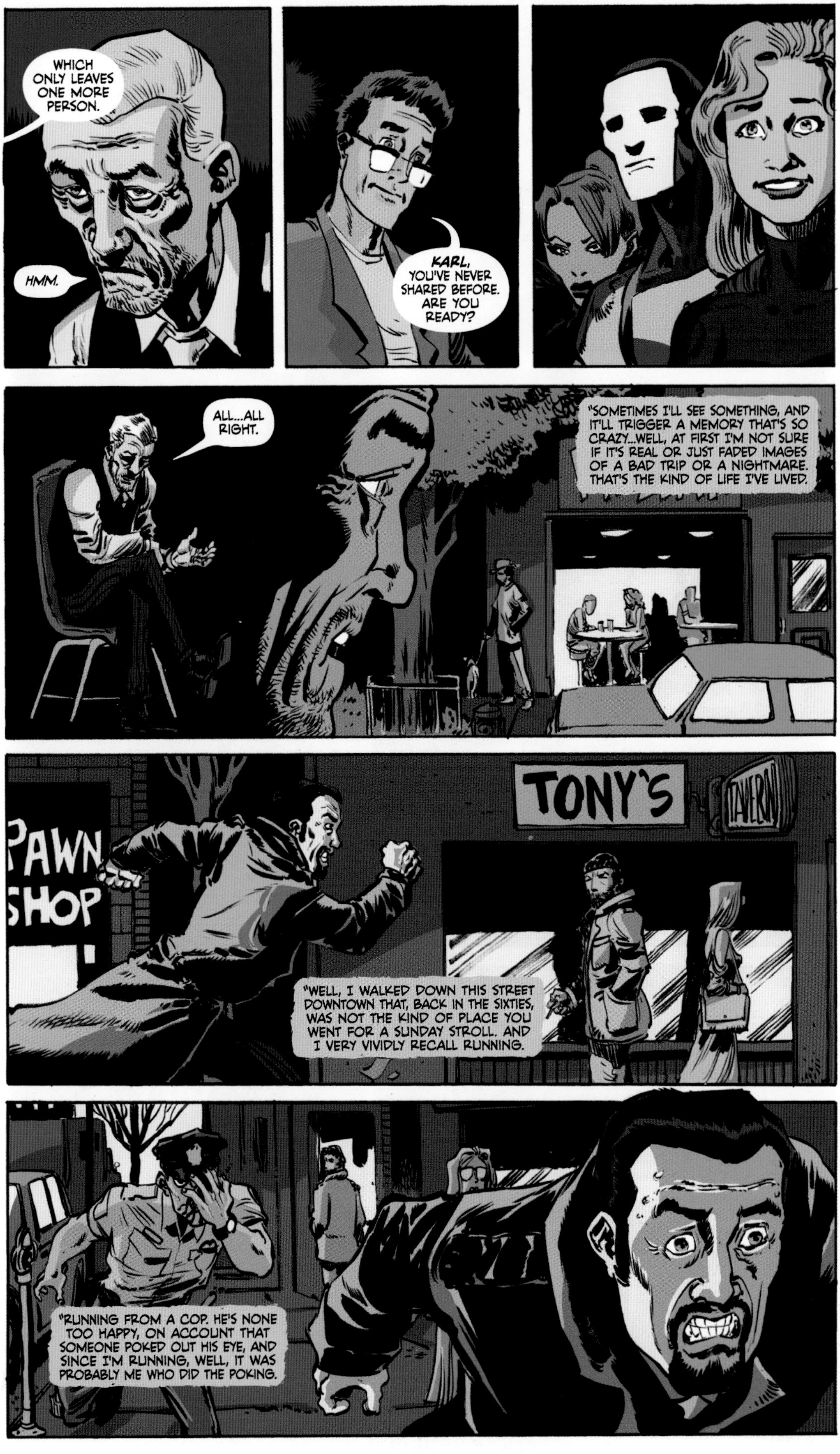
WHICH ONLY LEAVES ONE MORE PERSON.
HMM.
KARL, YOU'VE NEVER SHARED BEFORE. ARE YOU READY?
ALL...ALL RIGHT.
"SOMETIMES I'LL SEE SOMETHING, AND IT'LL TRIGGER A MEMORY THAT'S SO CRAZY...WELL, AT FIRST I'M NOT SURE IF IT'S REAL OR JUST FADED IMAGES OF A BAD TRIP OR A NIGHTMARE. THAT'S THE KIND OF LIFE I'VE LIVED.
PAWN SHOP
TONY'S
TAVERN
"WELL, I WALKED DOWN THIS STREET DOWNTOWN THAT, BACK IN THE SIXTIES, WAS NOT THE KIND OF PLACE YOU WENT FOR A SUNDAY STROLL. AND I VERY VIVIDLY RECALL RUNNING.
"RUNNING FROM A COP. HE'S NONE TOO HAPPY, ON ACCOUNT THAT SOMEONE POKED OUT HIS EYE, AND SINCE I'M RUNNING, WELL, IT WAS PROBABLY ME WHO DID THE POKING.

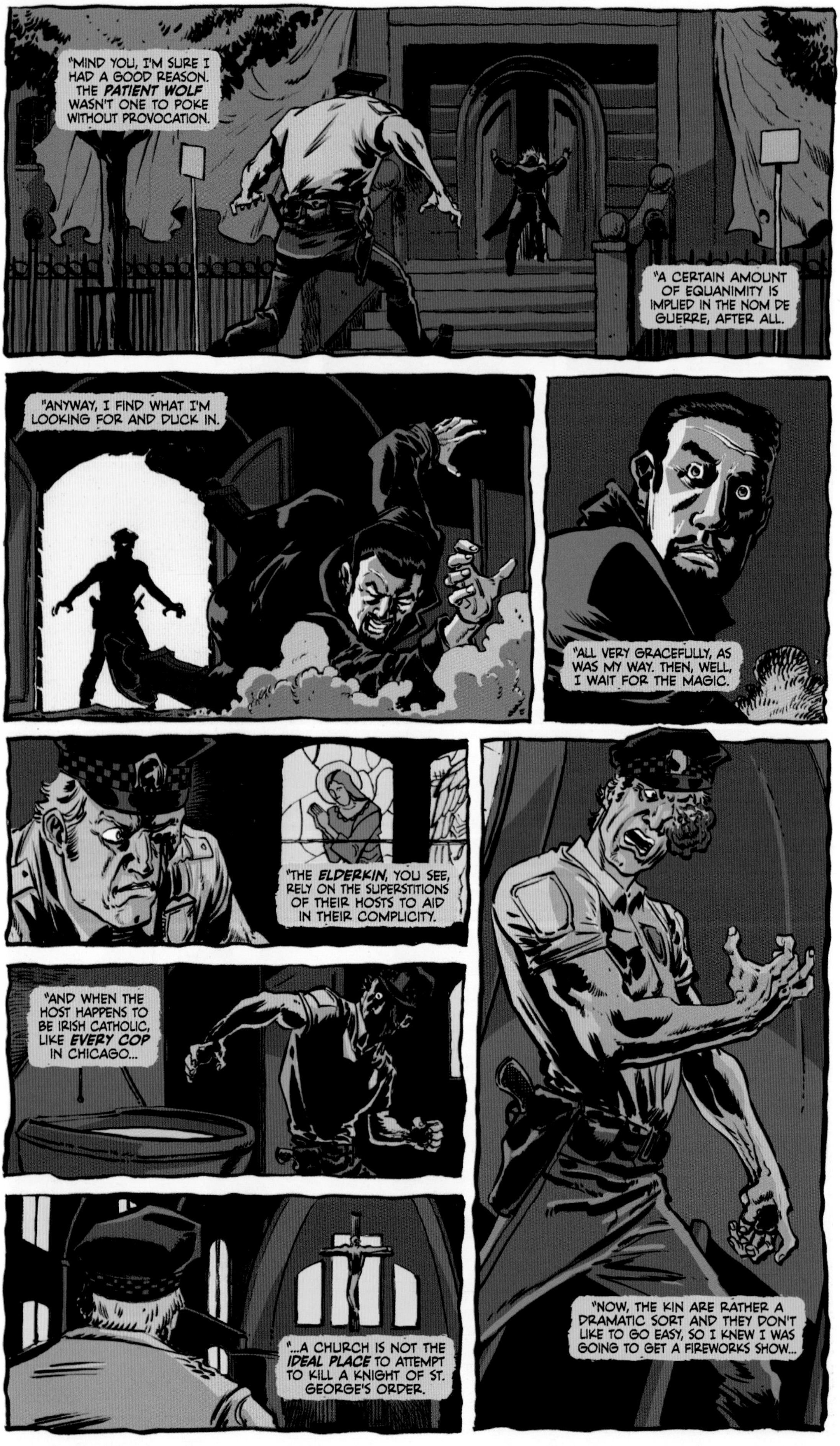
"MIND YOU, I'M SURE I HAD A GOOD REASON. THE PATIENT WOLF WASN'T ONE TO POKE WITHOUT PROVOCATION.
"A CERTAIN AMOUNT OF EQUANIMITY IS IMPLIED IN THE NOM DE GUERRE, AFTER ALL.
"ANYWAY, I FIND WHAT I'M LOOKING FOR AND DUCK IN.
"ALL VERY GRACEFULLY, AS WAS MY WAY. THEN, WELL, I WAIT FOR THE MAGIC.
"THE ELDERKIN, YOU SEE, RELY ON THE SUPERSTITIONS OF THEIR HOSTS TO AID IN THEIR COMPLICITY.
"AND WHEN THE HOST HAPPENS TO BE IRISH CATHOLIC, LIKE EVERY COP IN CHICAGO...
"...A CHURCH IS NOT THE IDEAL PLACE TO ATTEMPT TO KILL A KNIGHT OF ST. GEORGE'S ORDER.
"NOW, THE KIN ARE RATHER A DRAMATIC SORT AND THEY DON'T LIKE TO GO EASY, SO I KNEW I WAS GOING TO GET A FIREWORKS SHOW...

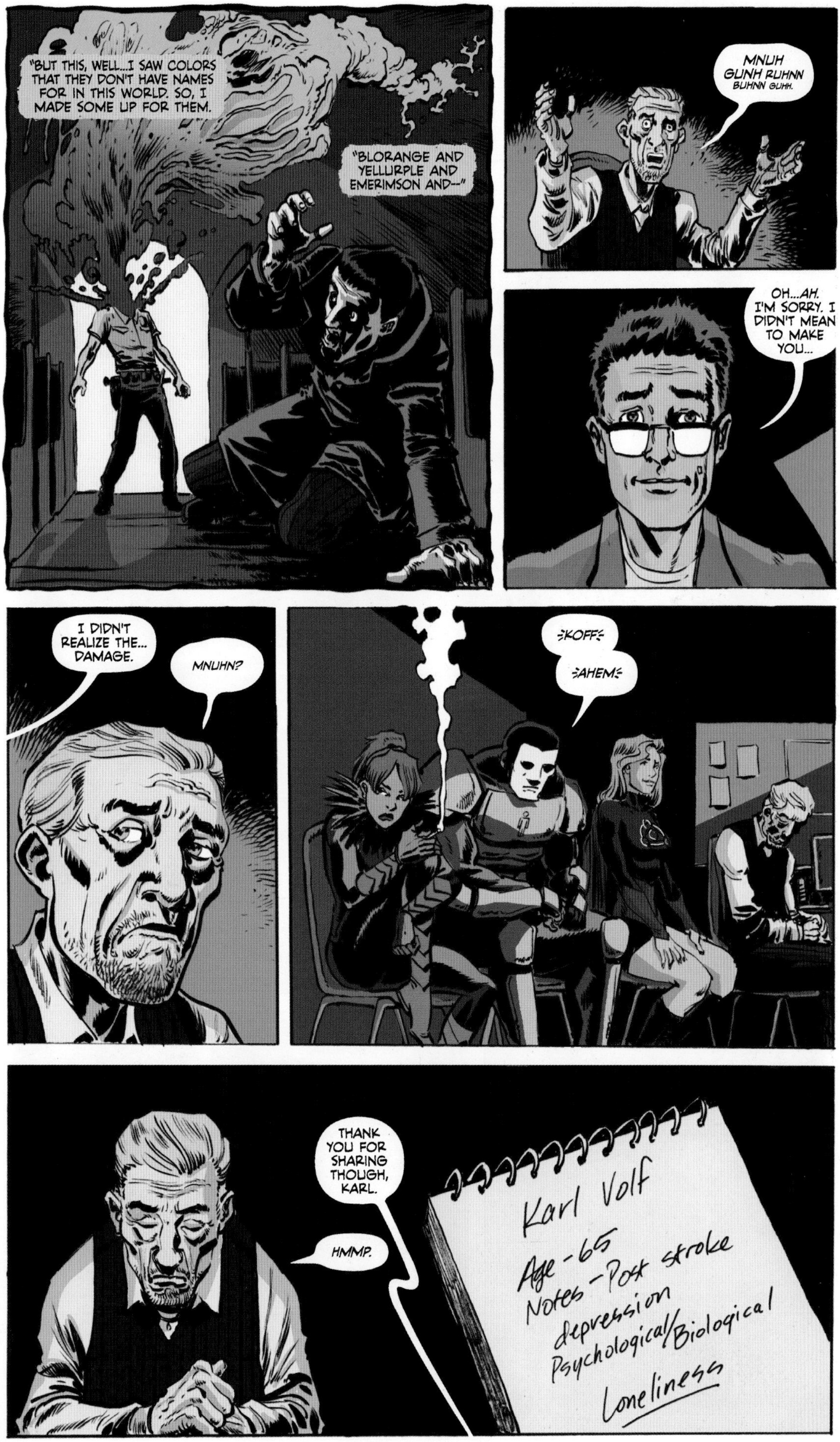
"BUT THIS, WELL...I SAW COLORS THAT THEY DON'T HAVE NAMES FOR IN THIS WORLD. SO, I MADE SOME UP FOR THEM.
"BLORANGE AND YELLURPLE AND EMERIMSON AND--"
MNUH GUNH RUHNN BUHNN GUHH.
OH...AH. I'M SORRY. I DIDN'T MEAN TO MAKE YOU...
I DIDN'T REALIZE THE... DAMAGE.
MNUHN?
KOFF
AHEM
THANK YOU FOR SHARING THOUGH, KARL.
HMMP.
Karl Volf
Age - 65
Notes - Post stroke depression
Psychological/Biological
Loneliness

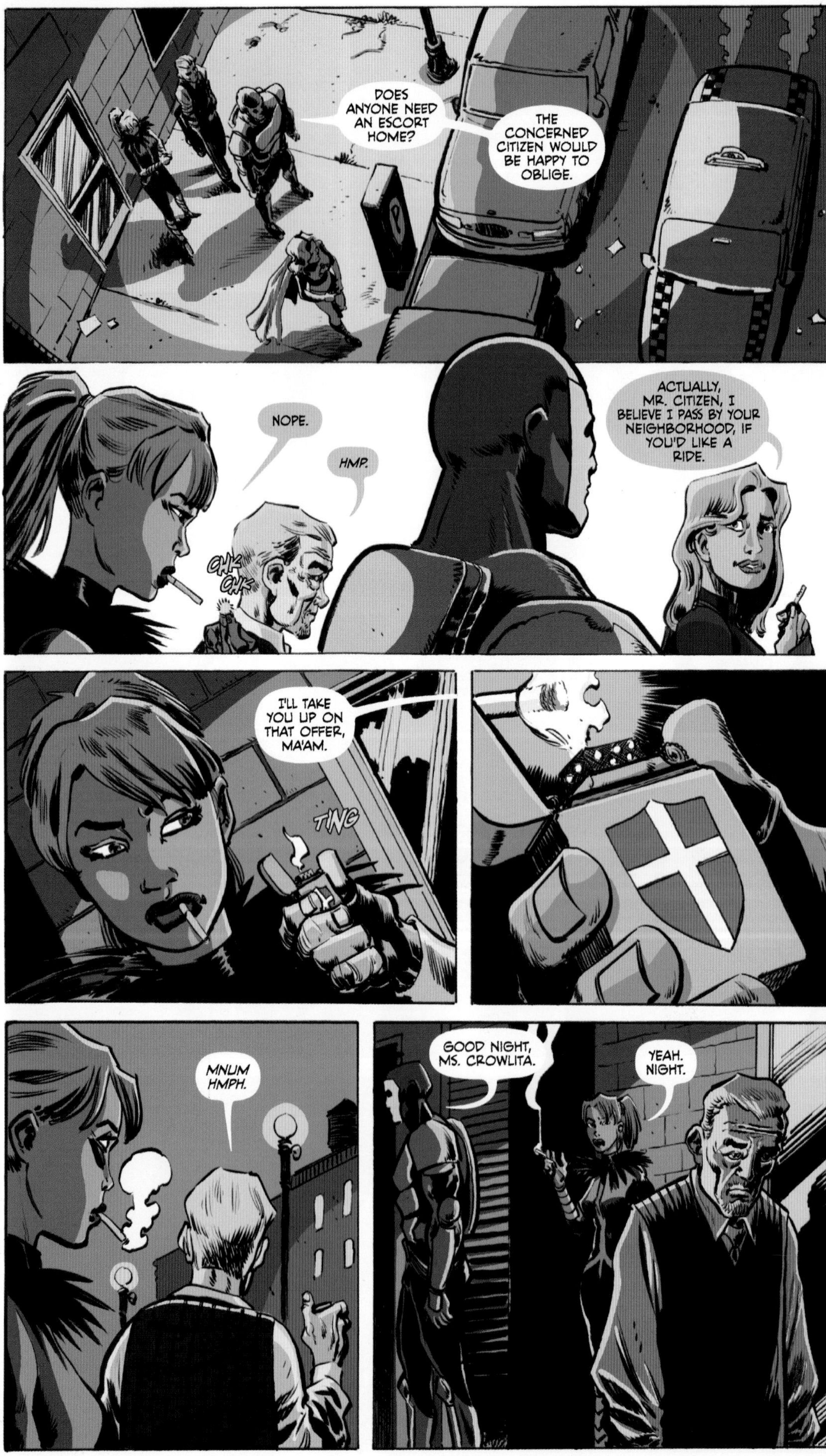
DOES ANYONE NEED AN ESCORT HOME?
THE CONCERNED CITIZEN WOULD BE HAPPY TO OBLIGE.
NOPE.
HMP.
CHK CHK
ACTUALLY, MR. CITIZEN, I BELIEVE I PASS BY YOUR NEIGHBORHOOD, IF YOU'D LIKE A RIDE.
I'LL TAKE YOU UP ON THAT OFFER, MA'AM.
TING
MNUM HMPH.
GOOD NIGHT, MS. CROWLITA.
YEAH. NIGHT.

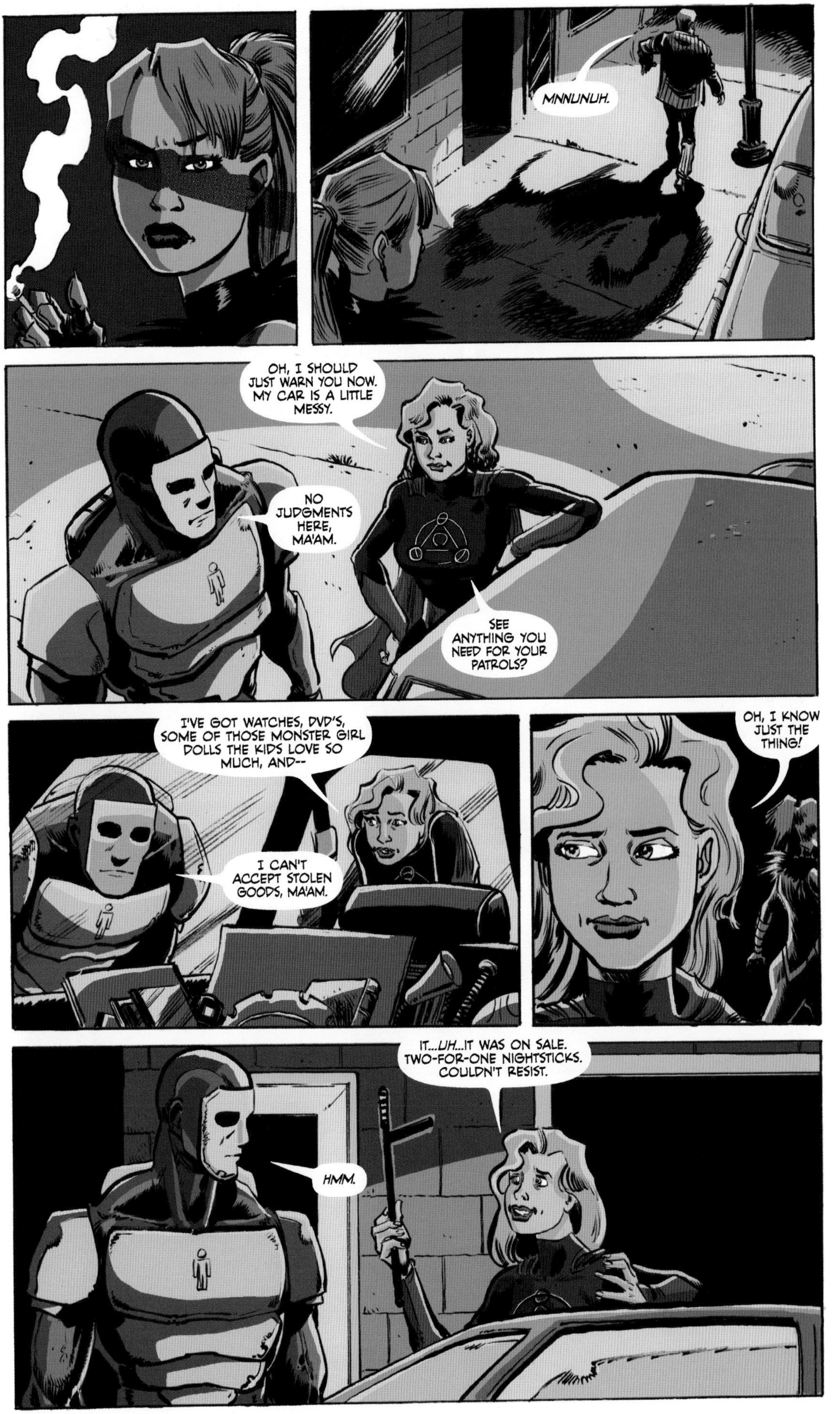
MNNUNUH.
OH, I SHOULD JUST WARN YOU NOW. MY CAR IS A LITTLE MESSY.
NO JUDGMENTS HERE, MA'AM.
SEE ANYTHING YOU NEED FOR YOUR PATROLS?
I'VE GOT WATCHES, DVD'S, SOME OF THOSE MONSTER GIRL DOLLS THE KIDS LOVE SO MUCH, AND--
I CAN'T ACCEPT STOLEN GOODS, MA'AM.
OH, I KNOW JUST THE THING!
IT...UH...IT WAS ON SALE. TWO-FOR-ONE NIGHTSTICKS. COULDN'T RESIST.
HMM.

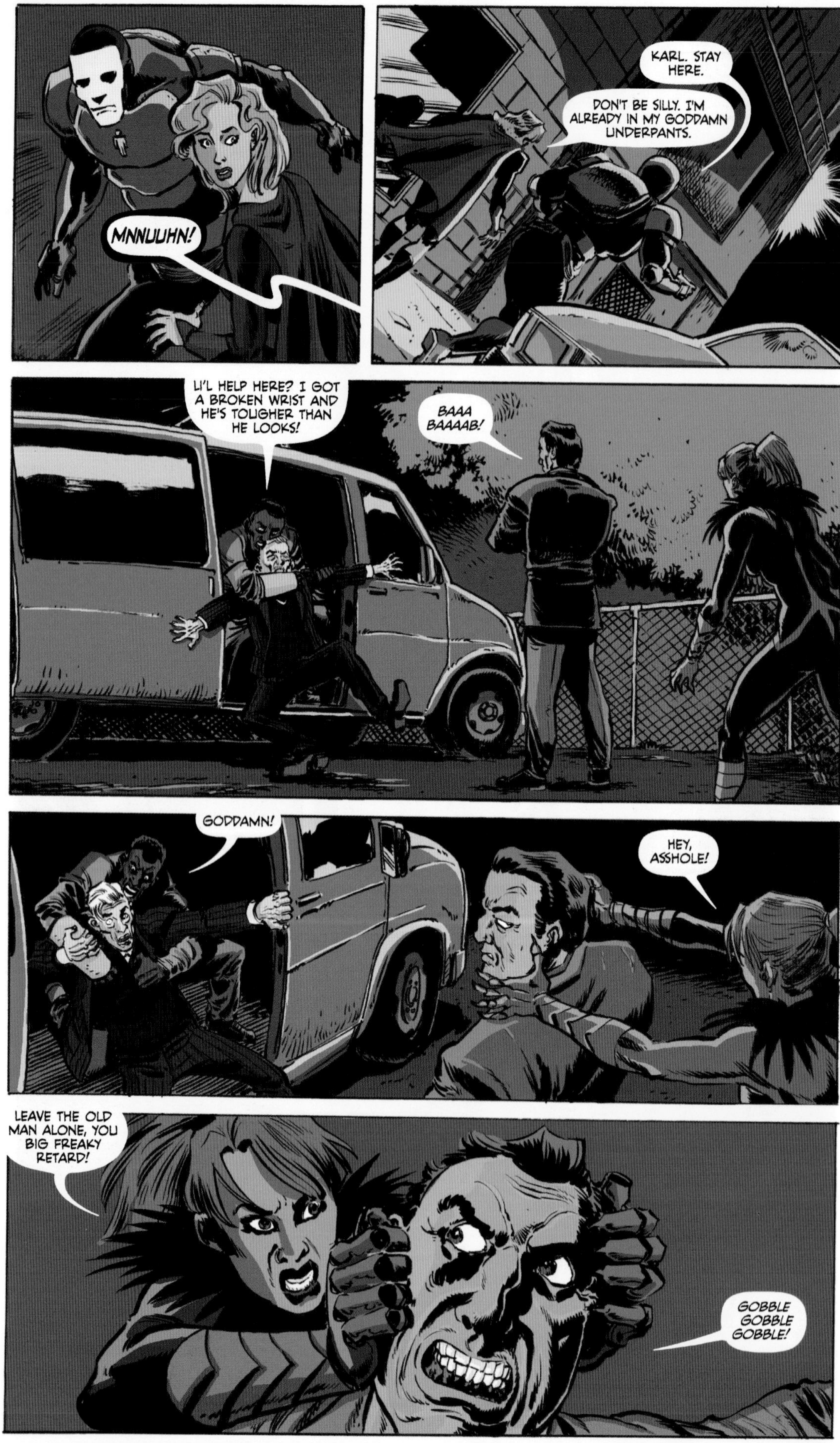
MNNUUHN!
KARL. STAY HERE.
DON'T BE SILLY. I'M ALREADY IN MY GODDAMN UNDERPANTS.
LI'L HELP HERE? I GOT A BROKEN WRIST AND HE'S TOUGHER THAN HE LOOKS!
BAAA BAAAAB!
GODDAMN!
HEY, ASSHOLE!
LEAVE THE OLD MAN ALONE, YOU BIG FREAKY RETARD!
GOBBLE GOBBLE GOBBLE!

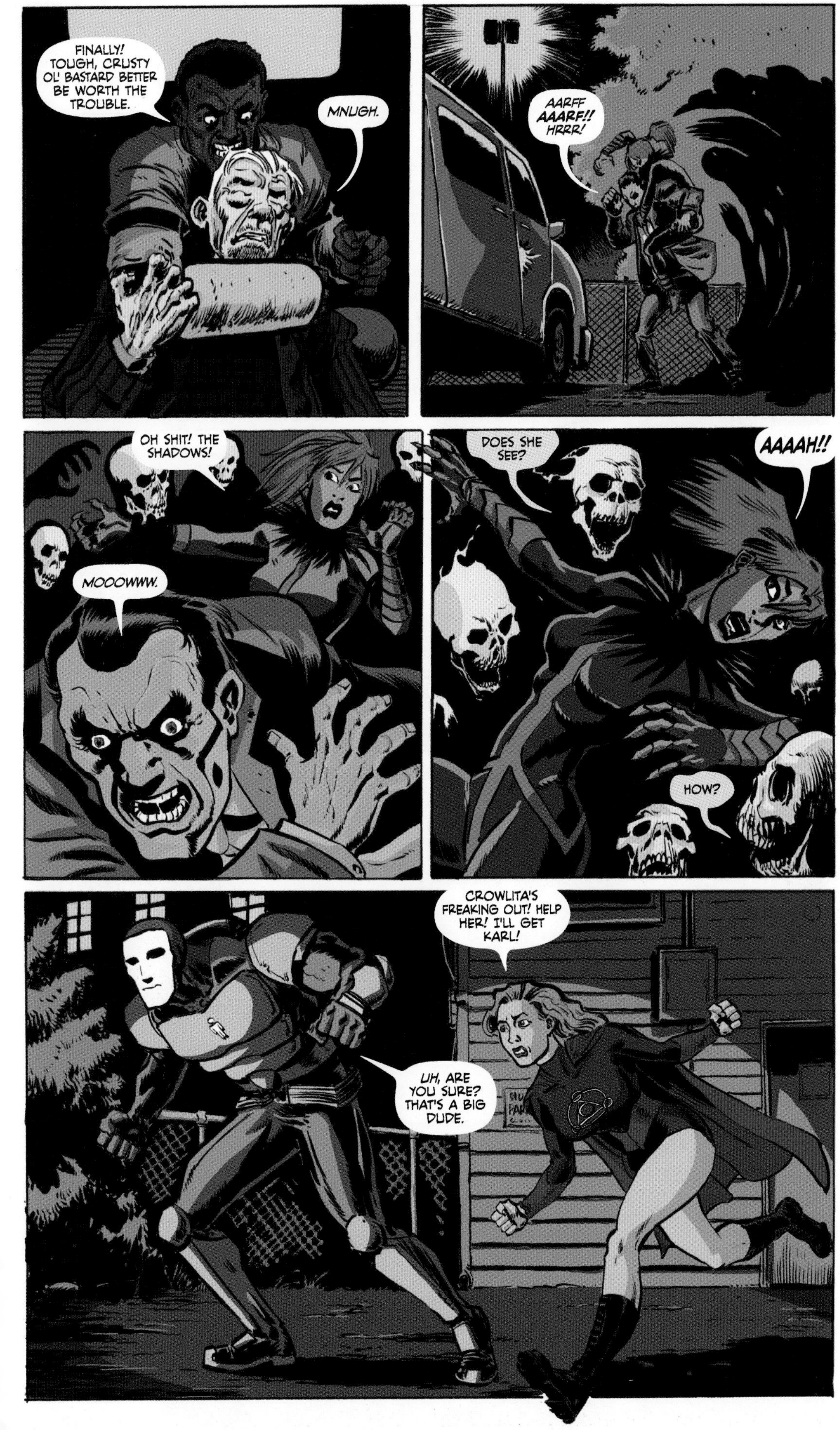
FINALLY! TOUGH, CRUSTY OL' BASTARD BETTER BE WORTH THE TROUBLE.
MNUGH.
AARFF AAARF!! HRRR!
OH SHIT! THE SHADOWS!
MOOOWWW.
DOES SHE SEE?
AAAAH!!
HOW?
CROWLITA'S FREAKING OUT! HELP HER! I'LL GET KARL!
UH, ARE YOU SURE? THAT'S A BIG DUDE.

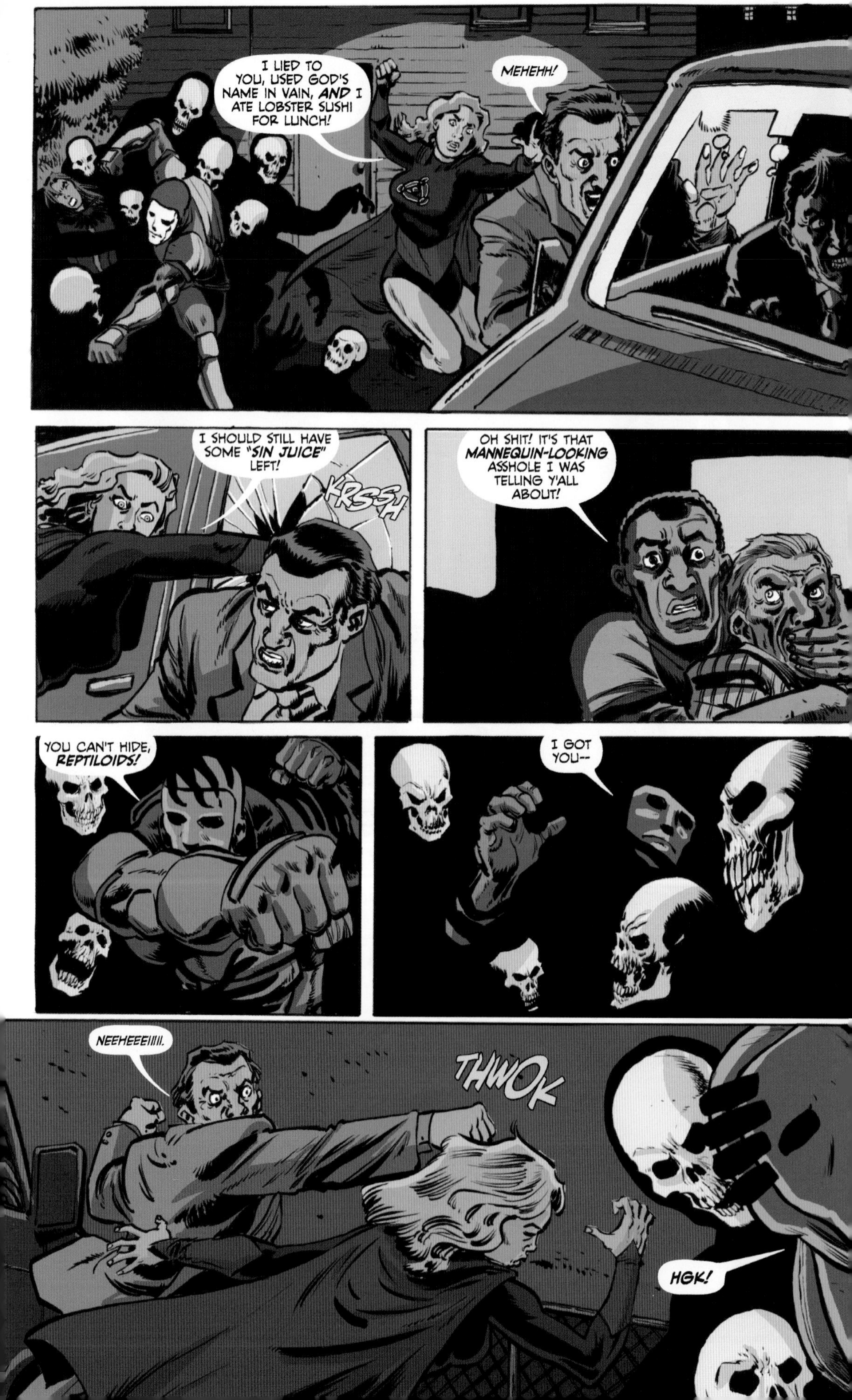
I LIED TO YOU, USED GOD'S NAME IN VAIN, AND I ATE LOBSTER SUSHI FOR LUNCH!
MEHEHH!
I SHOULD STILL HAVE SOME "SIN JUICE" LEFT!
KRSSH
OH SHIT! IT'S THAT MANNEQUIN-LOOKING ASSHOLE I WAS TELLING Y'ALL ABOUT!
YOU CAN'T HIDE, REPTILOIDS!
I GOT YOU--
NEEHEEEIIIII.
THWOK
HGK!

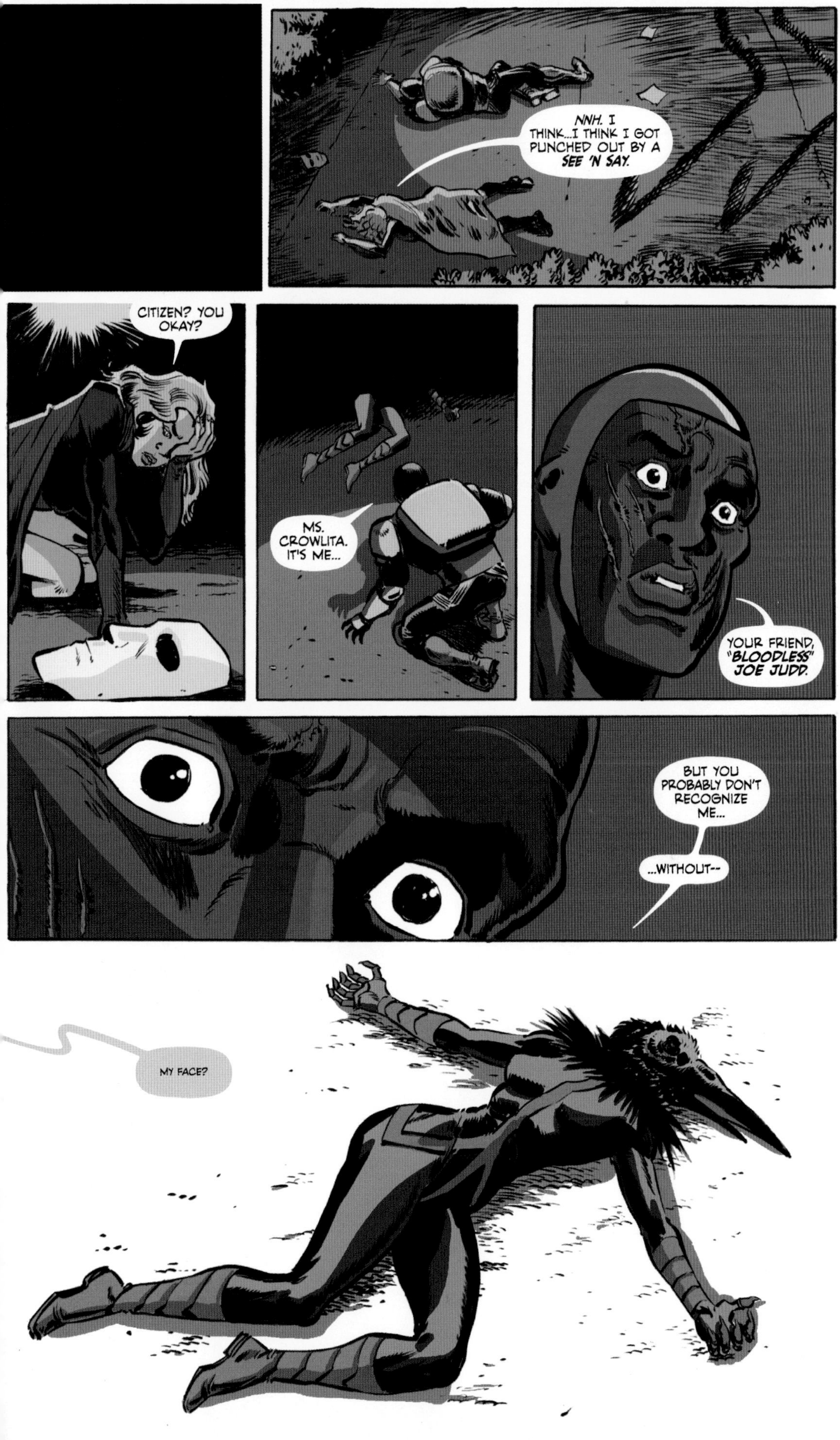
NNH. I THINK...I THINK I GOT PUNCHED OUT BY A SEE 'N SAY.
CITIZEN? YOU OKAY?
MS. CROWLITA. IT'S ME...
YOUR FRIEND, "BLOODLESS" JOE JUDD.
BUT YOU PROBABLY DON'T RECOGNIZE ME...
...WITHOUT--
MY FACE?

SUNDOWNERS™

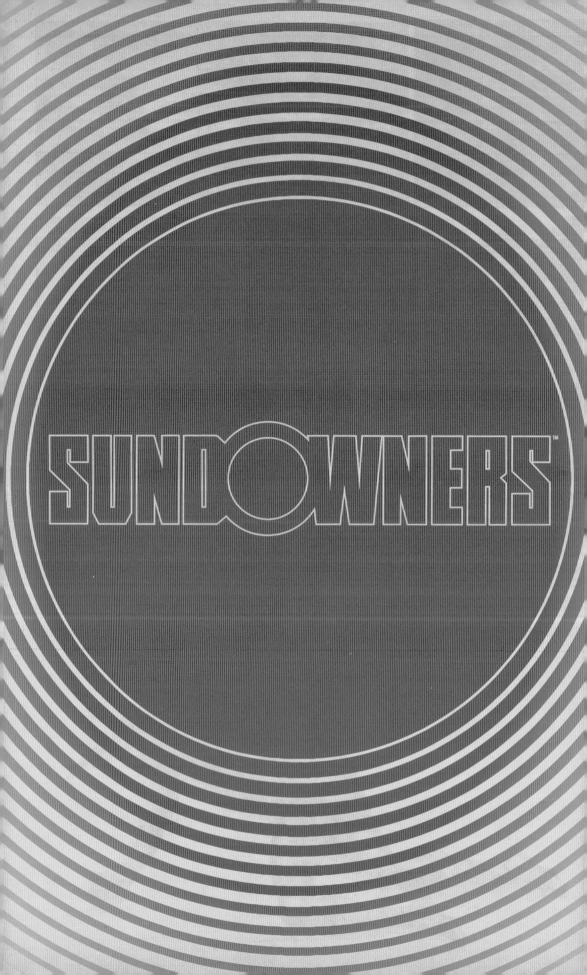

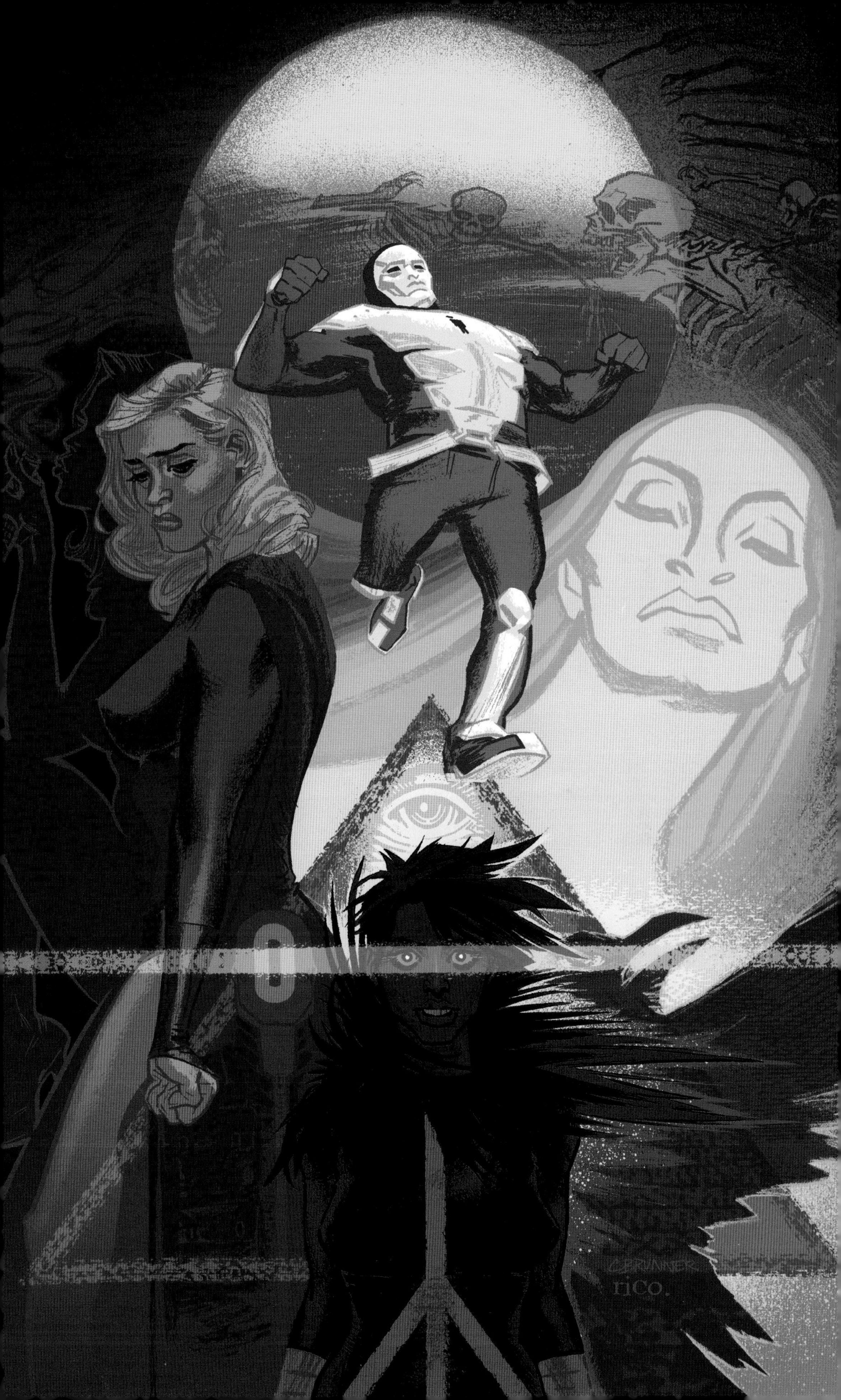

C.BRUNNER
rico.

SUNDOWNERS™ 2

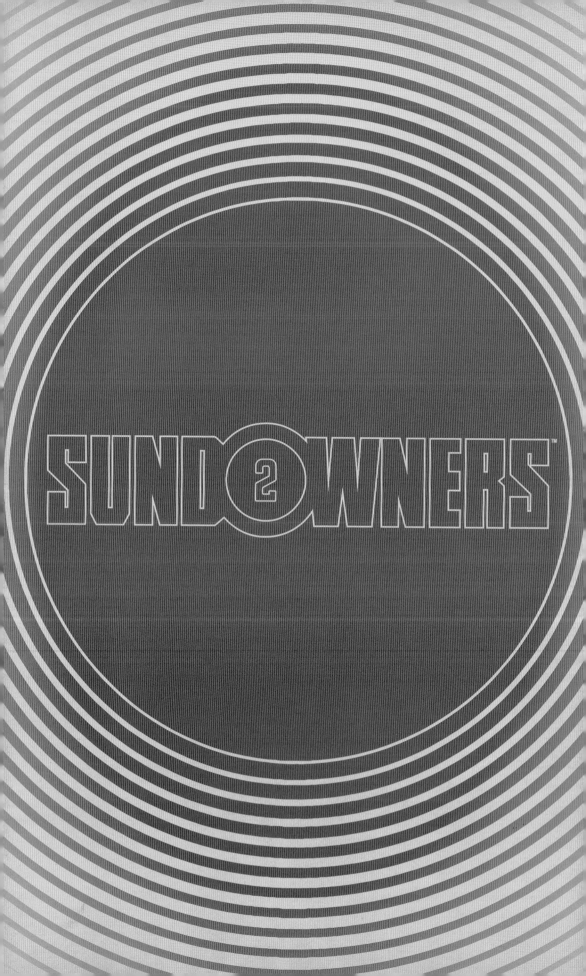

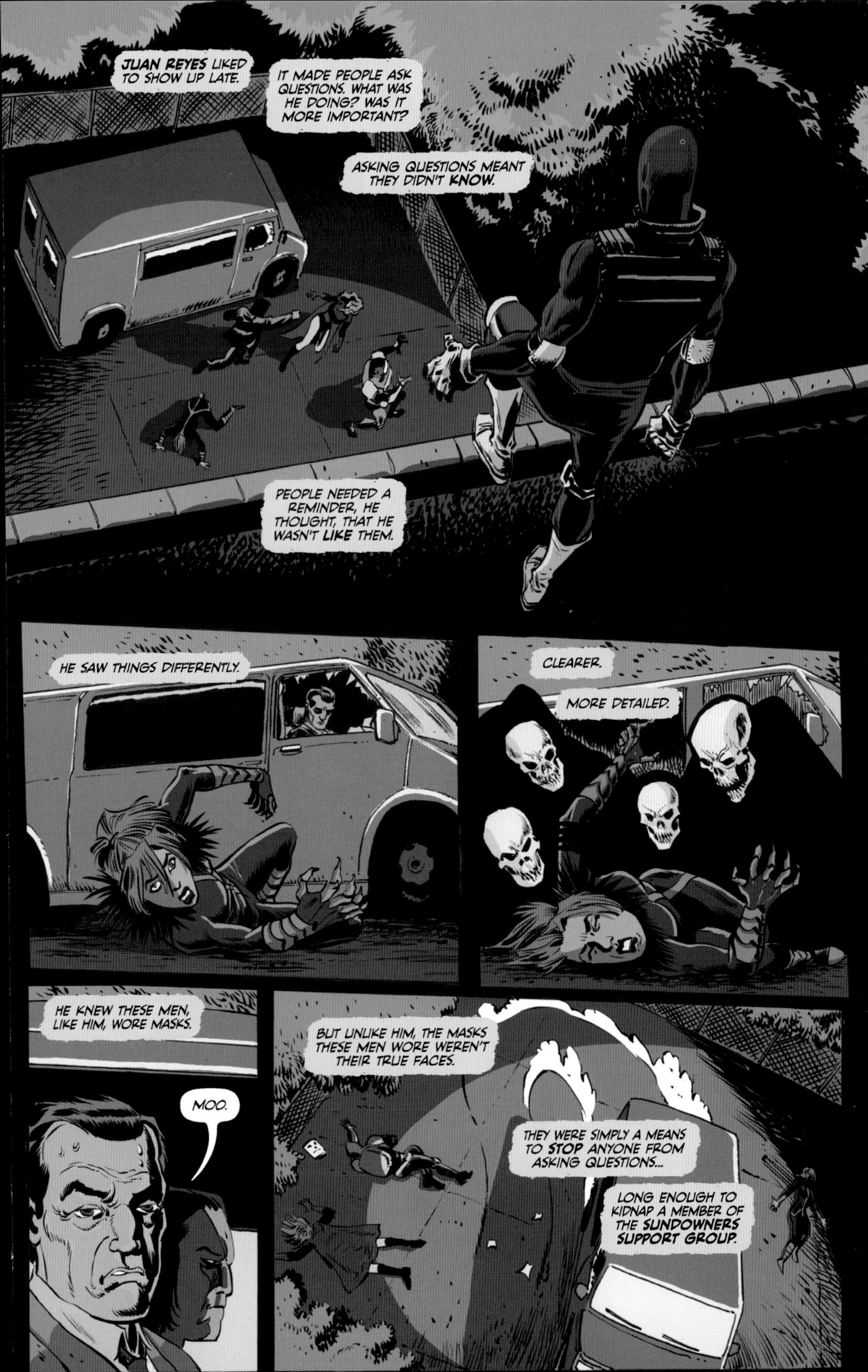
JUAN REYES LIKED TO SHOW UP LATE.
IT MADE PEOPLE ASK QUESTIONS. WHAT WAS HE DOING? WAS IT MORE IMPORTANT?
ASKING QUESTIONS MEANT THEY DIDN'T KNOW.
PEOPLE NEEDED A REMINDER, HE THOUGHT, THAT HE WASN'T LIKE THEM.
HE SAW THINGS DIFFERENTLY.
CLEARER.
MORE DETAILED.
HE KNEW THESE MEN, LIKE HIM, WORE MASKS.
MOO.
BUT UNLIKE HIM, THE MASKS THESE MEN WORE WEREN'T THEIR TRUE FACES.
THEY WERE SIMPLY A MEANS TO STOP ANYONE FROM ASKING QUESTIONS...
LONG ENOUGH TO KIDNAP A MEMBER OF THE SUNDOWNERS SUPPORT GROUP.

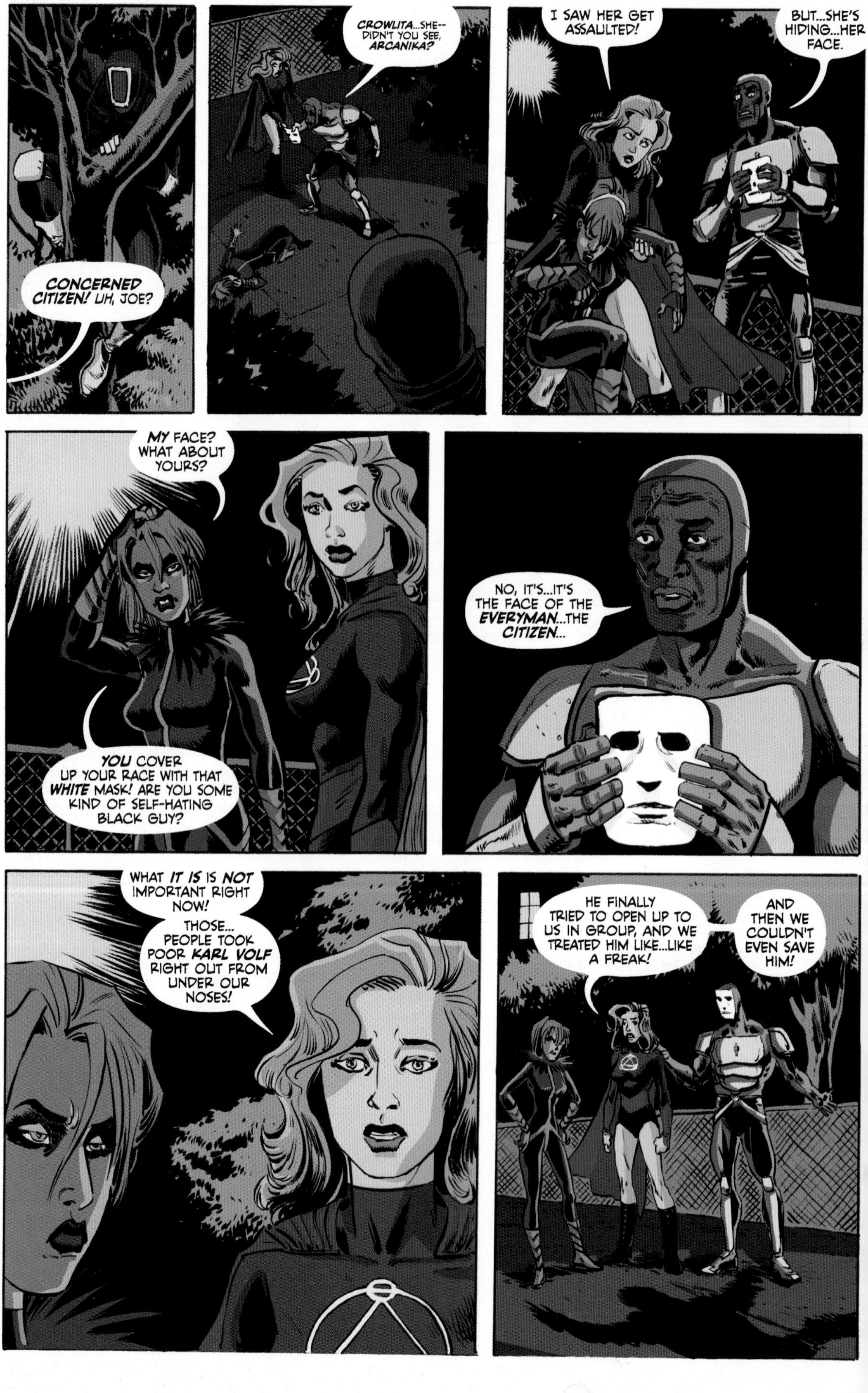
CONCERNED CITIZEN! UH, JOE?
CROWLITA...SHE-- DIDN'T YOU SEE, ARCANIKA?
I SAW HER GET ASSAULTED!
BUT...SHE'S HIDING...HER FACE.
MY FACE? WHAT ABOUT YOURS?
YOU COVER UP YOUR RACE WITH THAT WHITE MASK! ARE YOU SOME KIND OF SELF-HATING BLACK GUY?
NO, IT'S...IT'S THE FACE OF THE EVERYMAN...THE CITIZEN...
WHAT IT IS IS NOT IMPORTANT RIGHT NOW!
THOSE... PEOPLE TOOK POOR KARL VOLF RIGHT OUT FROM UNDER OUR NOSES!
HE FINALLY TRIED TO OPEN UP TO US IN GROUP, AND WE TREATED HIM LIKE...LIKE A FREAK!
AND THEN WE COULDN'T EVEN SAVE HIM!

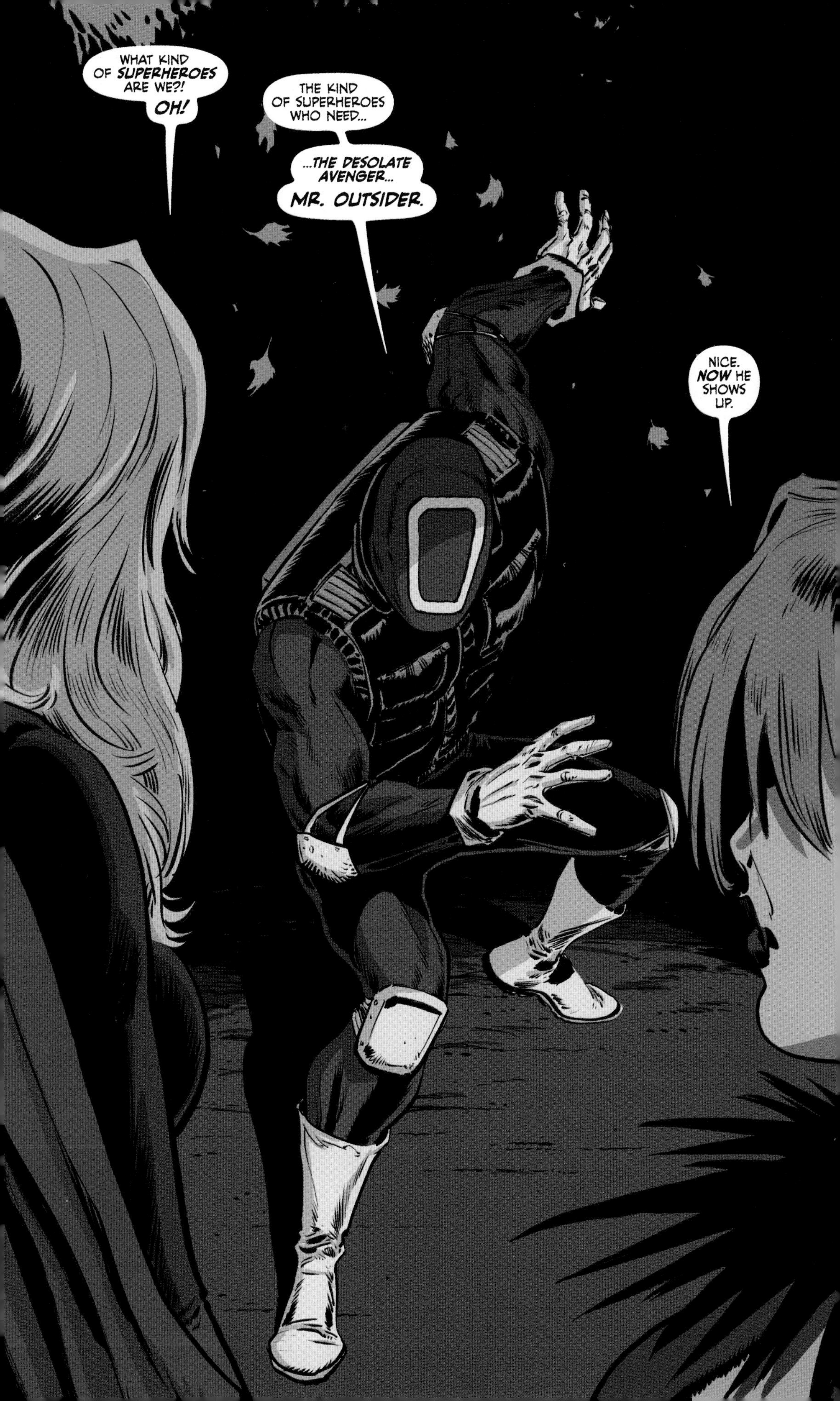
WHAT KIND OF SUPERHEROES ARE WE?! OH!
THE KIND OF SUPERHEROES WHO NEED...
...THE DESOLATE AVENGER...
MR. OUTSIDER.
NICE. NOW HE SHOWS UP.

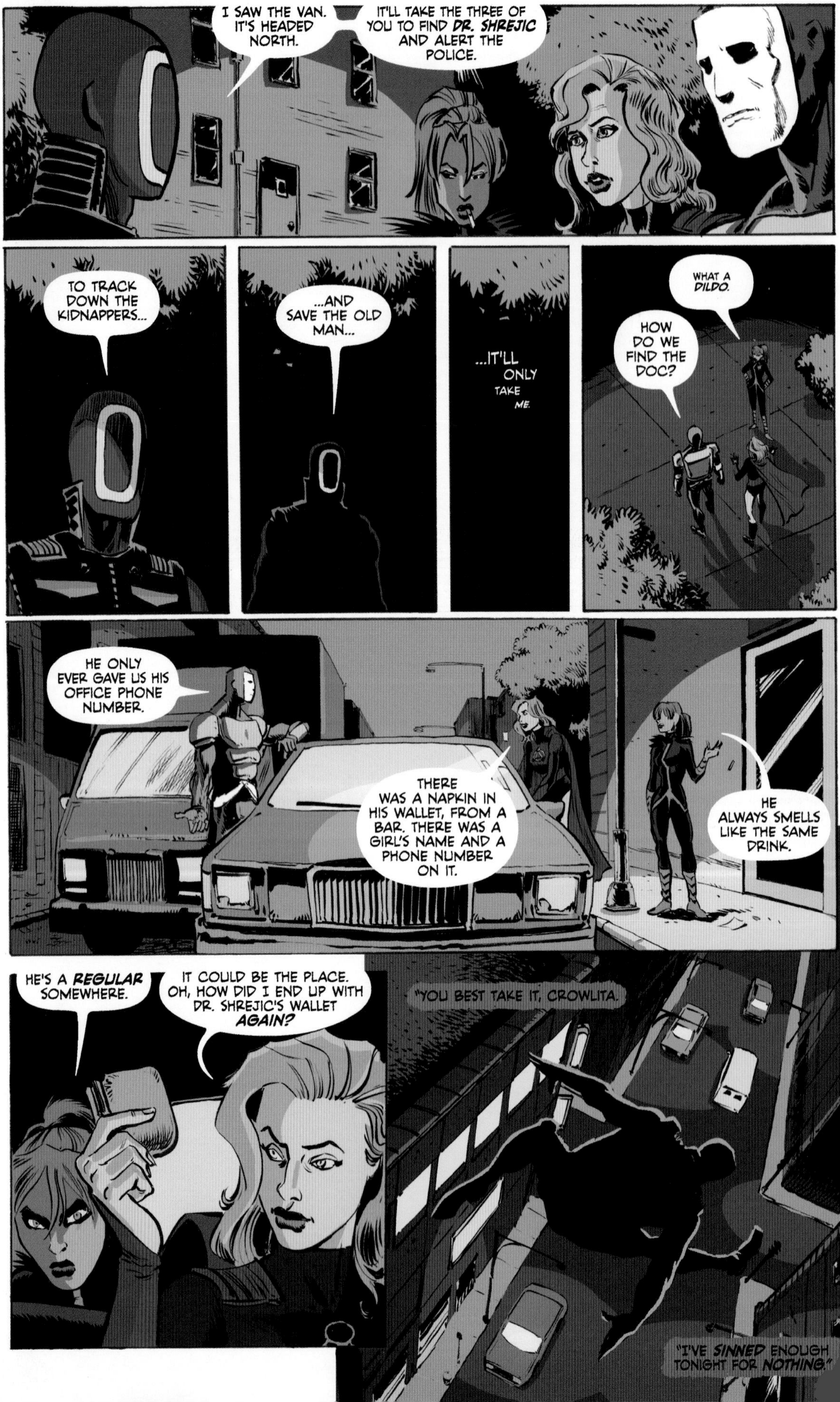
I SAW THE VAN. IT'S HEADED NORTH.
IT'LL TAKE THE THREE OF YOU TO FIND DR. SHREJIC AND ALERT THE POLICE.
TO TRACK DOWN THE KIDNAPPERS...
...AND SAVE THE OLD MAN...
...IT'LL ONLY TAKE ME.
WHAT A DILDO.
HOW DO WE FIND THE DOC?
HE ONLY EVER GAVE US HIS OFFICE PHONE NUMBER.
THERE WAS A NAPKIN IN HIS WALLET, FROM A BAR. THERE WAS A GIRL'S NAME AND A PHONE NUMBER ON IT.
HE ALWAYS SMELLS LIKE THE SAME DRINK.
HE'S A REGULAR SOMEWHERE.
IT COULD BE THE PLACE. OH, HOW DID I END UP WITH DR. SHREJIC'S WALLET AGAIN?
"YOU BEST TAKE IT, CROWLITA.
"I'VE SINNED ENOUGH TONIGHT FOR NOTHING."

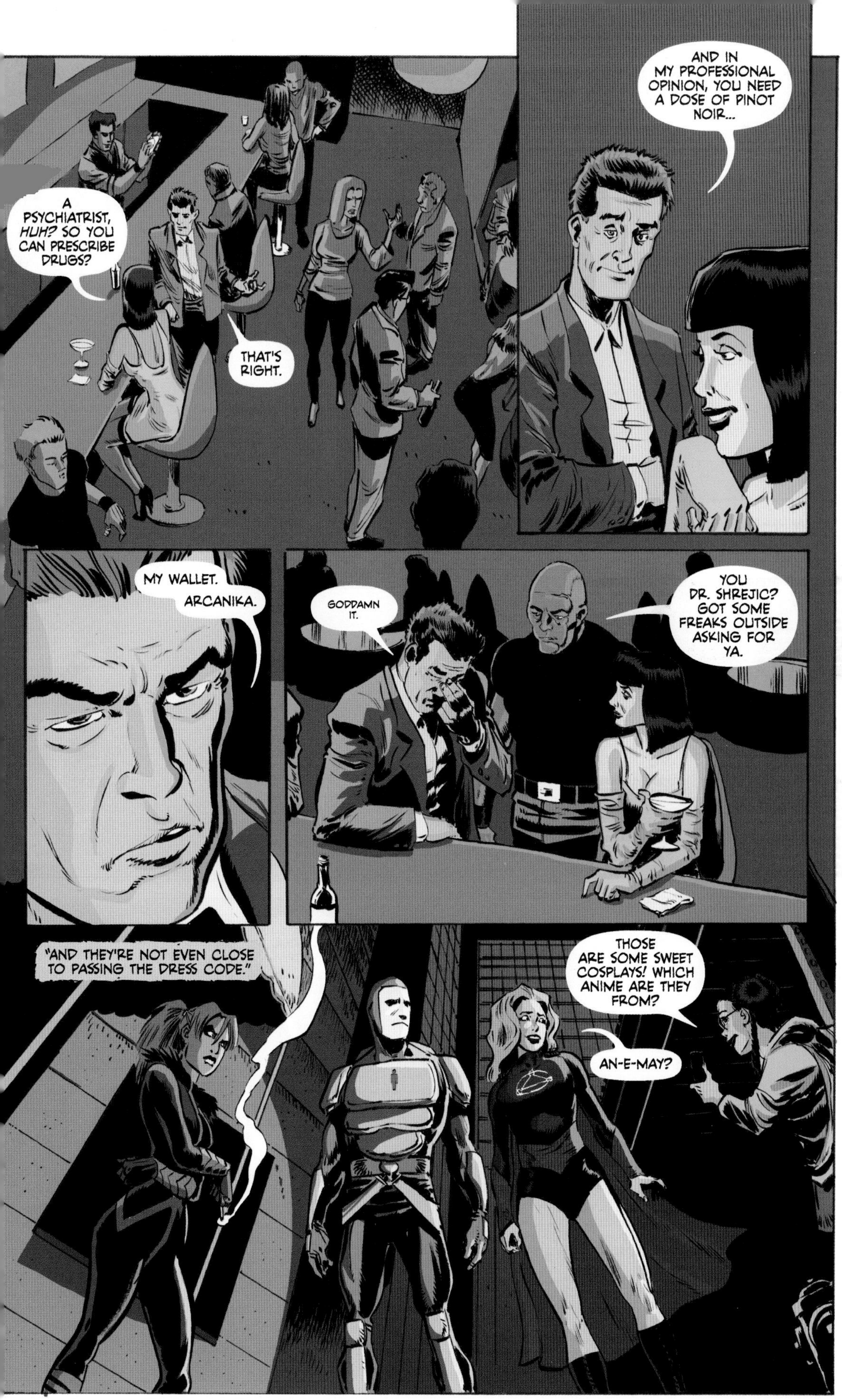
A PSYCHIATRIST, HUH? SO YOU CAN PRESCRIBE DRUGS?
THAT'S RIGHT.
AND IN MY PROFESSIONAL OPINION, YOU NEED A DOSE OF PINOT NOIR...
MY WALLET.
ARCANIKA.
GODDAMN IT.
YOU DR. SHREJIC? GOT SOME FREAKS OUTSIDE ASKING FOR YA.
"AND THEY'RE NOT EVEN CLOSE TO PASSING THE DRESS CODE."
THOSE ARE SOME SWEET COSPLAYS! WHICH ANIME ARE THEY FROM?
AN-E-MAY?

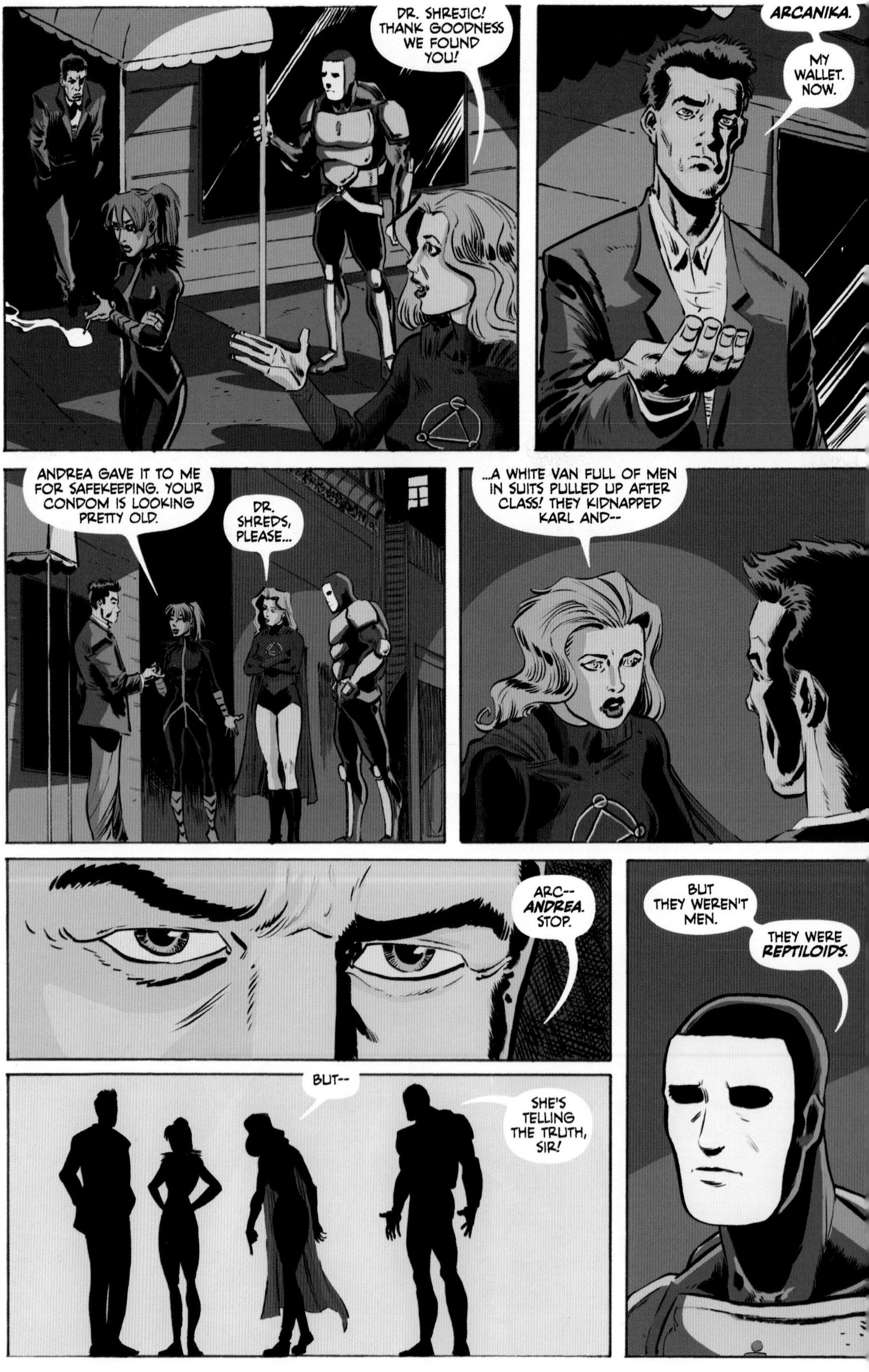
DR. SHREJIC! THANK GOODNESS WE FOUND YOU!
ARCANIKA.
MY WALLET. NOW.
ANDREA GAVE IT TO ME FOR SAFEKEEPING. YOUR CONDOM IS LOOKING PRETTY OLD.
DR. SHREDS, PLEASE...
...A WHITE VAN FULL OF MEN IN SUITS PULLED UP AFTER CLASS! THEY KIDNAPPED KARL AND--
ARC-- ANDREA. STOP.
BUT THEY WEREN'T MEN.
THEY WERE REPTILOIDS.
BUT--
SHE'S TELLING THE TRUTH, SIR!

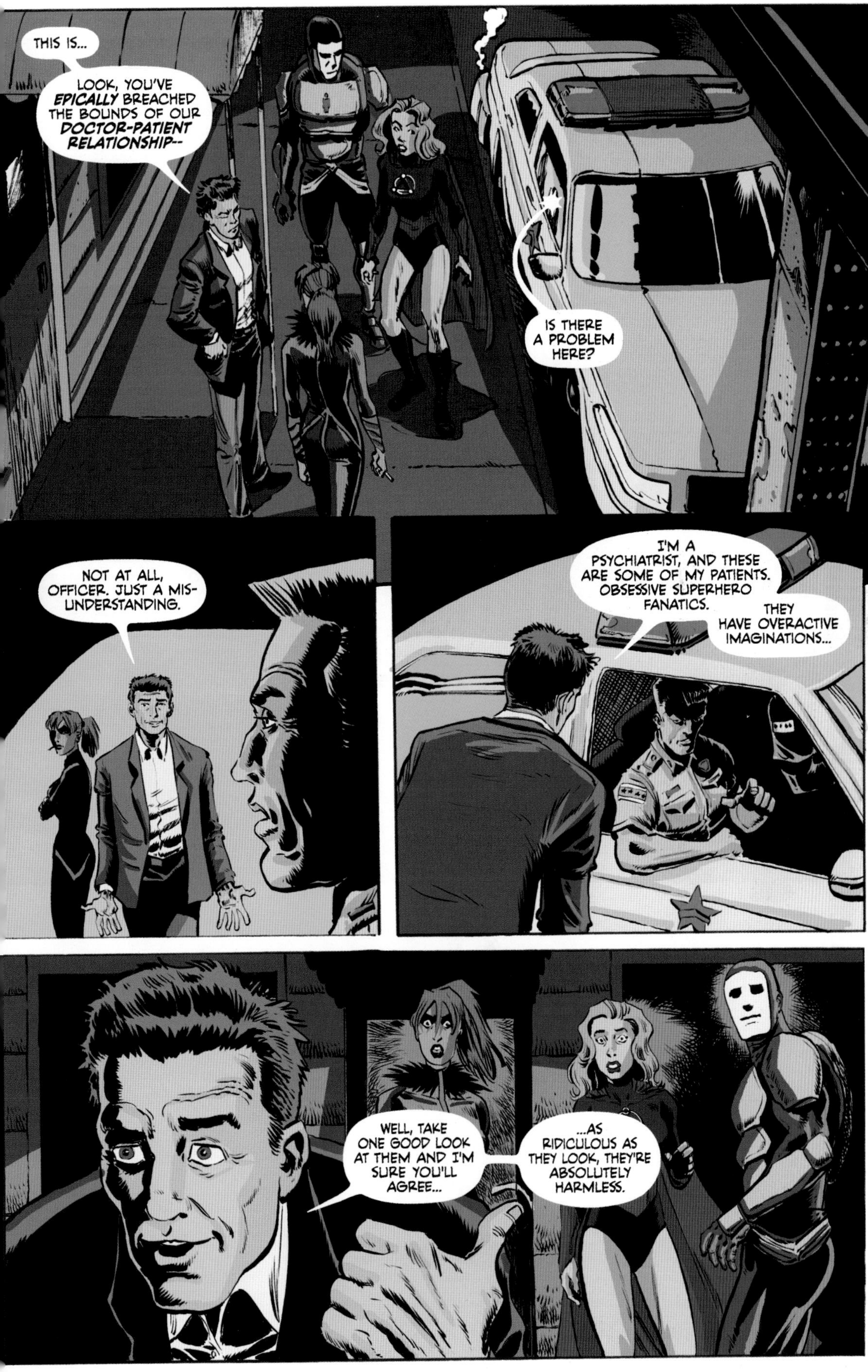

THIS IS...
LOOK, YOU'VE *EPICALLY* BREACHED THE BOUNDS OF OUR *DOCTOR-PATIENT RELATIONSHIP*--
IS THERE A PROBLEM HERE?
NOT AT ALL, OFFICER. JUST A MIS-UNDERSTANDING.
I'M A PSYCHIATRIST, AND THESE ARE SOME OF MY PATIENTS. OBSESSIVE SUPERHERO FANATICS.
THEY HAVE OVERACTIVE IMAGINATIONS...
WELL, TAKE ONE GOOD LOOK AT THEM AND I'M SURE YOU'LL AGREE...
...AS RIDICULOUS AS THEY LOOK, THEY'RE ABSOLUTELY HARMLESS.

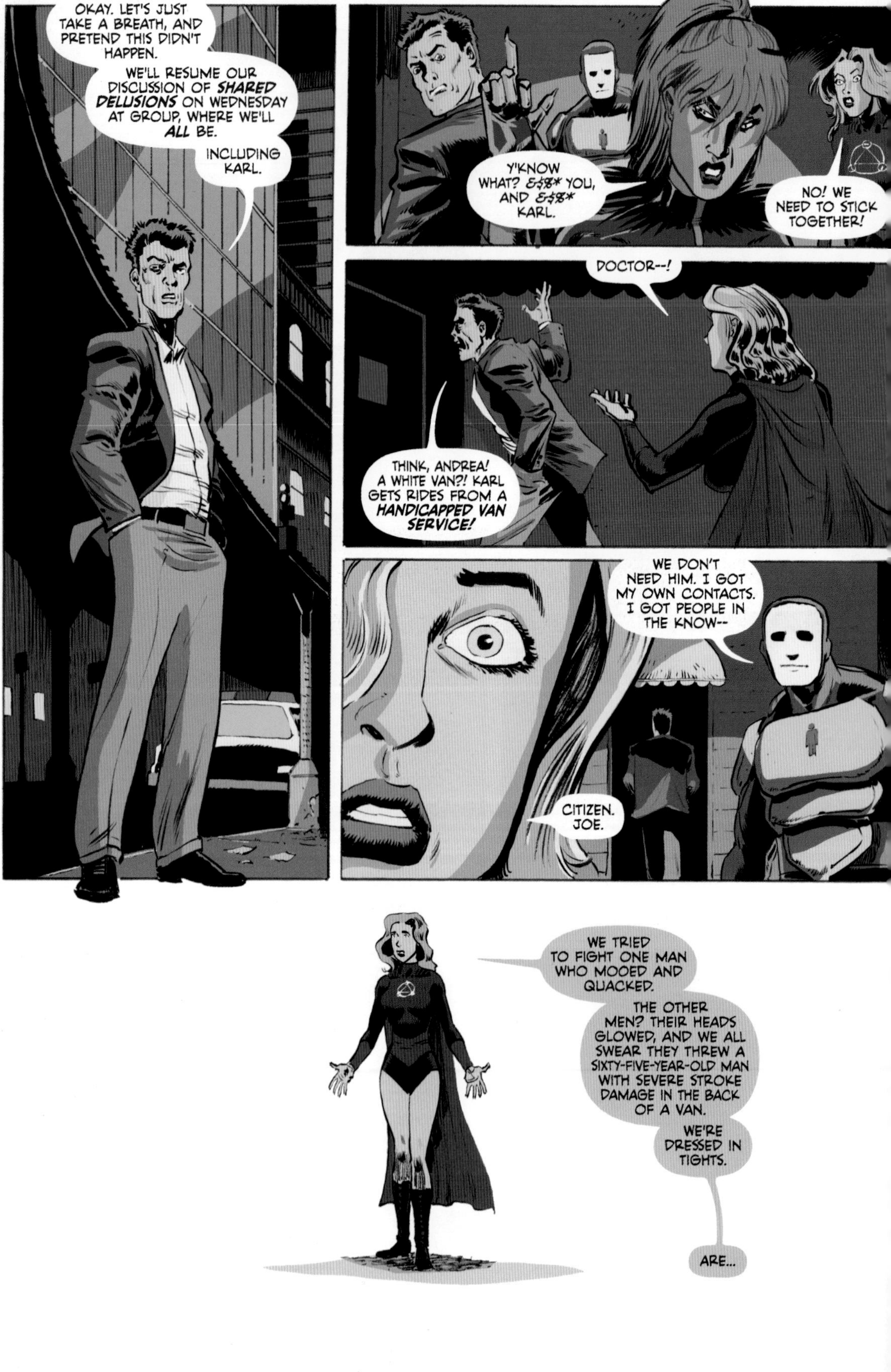

OKAY. LET'S JUST TAKE A BREATH, AND PRETEND THIS DIDN'T HAPPEN.
WE'LL RESUME OUR DISCUSSION OF SHARED DELUSIONS ON WEDNESDAY AT GROUP, WHERE WE'LL ALL BE.
INCLUDING KARL.
Y'KNOW WHAT? &$%* YOU, AND &$%* KARL.
NO! WE NEED TO STICK TOGETHER!
DOCTOR--!
THINK, ANDREA! A WHITE VAN?! KARL GETS RIDES FROM A HANDICAPPED VAN SERVICE!
WE DON'T NEED HIM. I GOT MY OWN CONTACTS. I GOT PEOPLE IN THE KNOW--
CITIZEN. JOE.
WE TRIED TO FIGHT ONE MAN WHO MOOED AND QUACKED.
THE OTHER MEN? THEIR HEADS GLOWED, AND WE ALL SWEAR THEY THREW A SIXTY-FIVE-YEAR-OLD MAN WITH SEVERE STROKE DAMAGE IN THE BACK OF A VAN.
WE'RE DRESSED IN TIGHTS.
ARE...

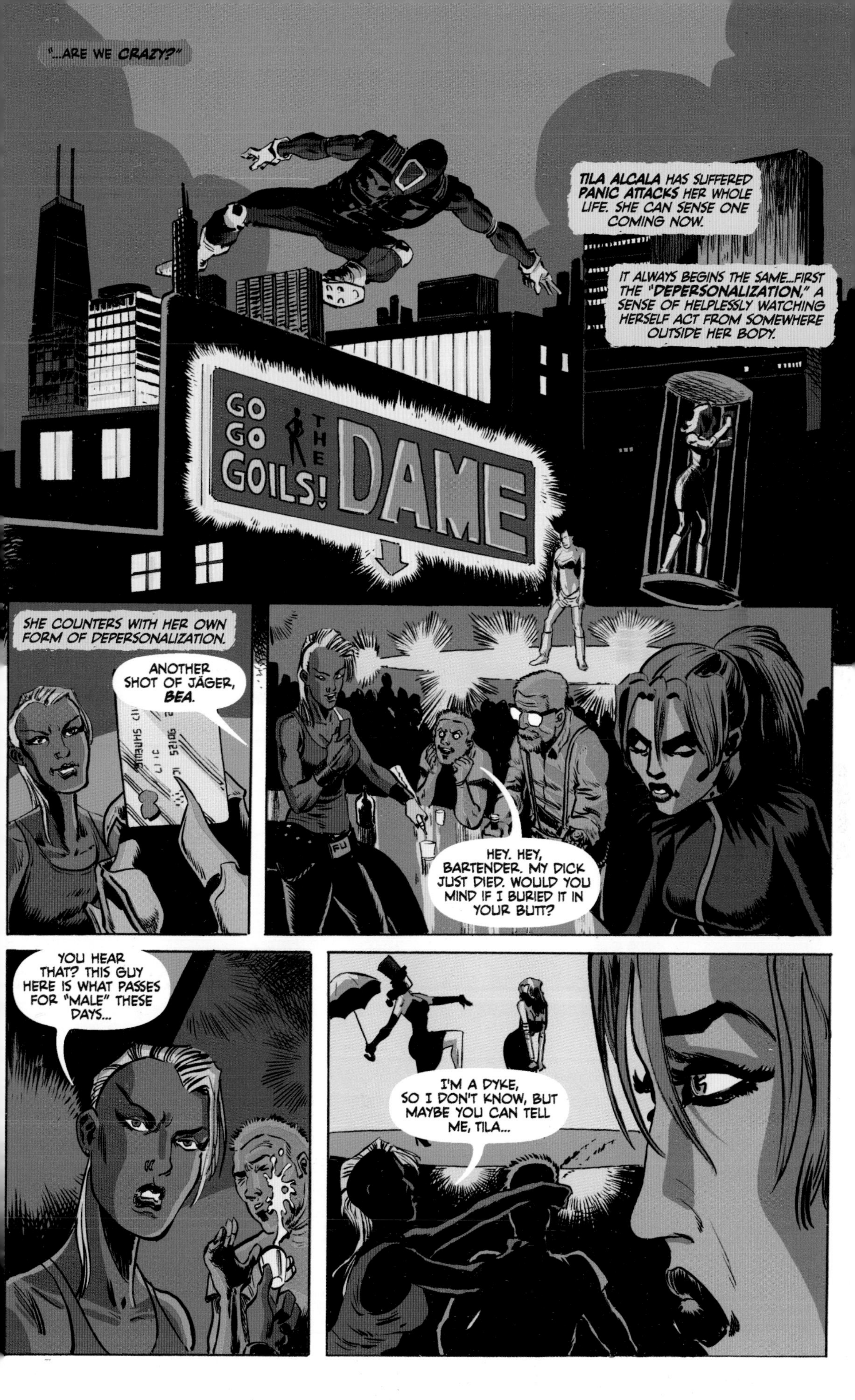
"...ARE WE CRAZY?"
TILA ALCALA HAS SUFFERED PANIC ATTACKS HER WHOLE LIFE. SHE CAN SENSE ONE COMING NOW.
IT ALWAYS BEGINS THE SAME...FIRST THE "DEPERSONALIZATION," A SENSE OF HELPLESSLY WATCHING HERSELF ACT FROM SOMEWHERE OUTSIDE HER BODY.
GO GO GOILS!
THE DAME
SHE COUNTERS WITH HER OWN FORM OF DEPERSONALIZATION.
ANOTHER SHOT OF JÄGER, BEA.
HEY. HEY, BARTENDER. MY DICK JUST DIED. WOULD YOU MIND IF I BURIED IT IN YOUR BUTT?
YOU HEAR THAT? THIS GUY HERE IS WHAT PASSES FOR "MALE" THESE DAYS...
I'M A DYKE, SO I DON'T KNOW, BUT MAYBE YOU CAN TELL ME, TILA...

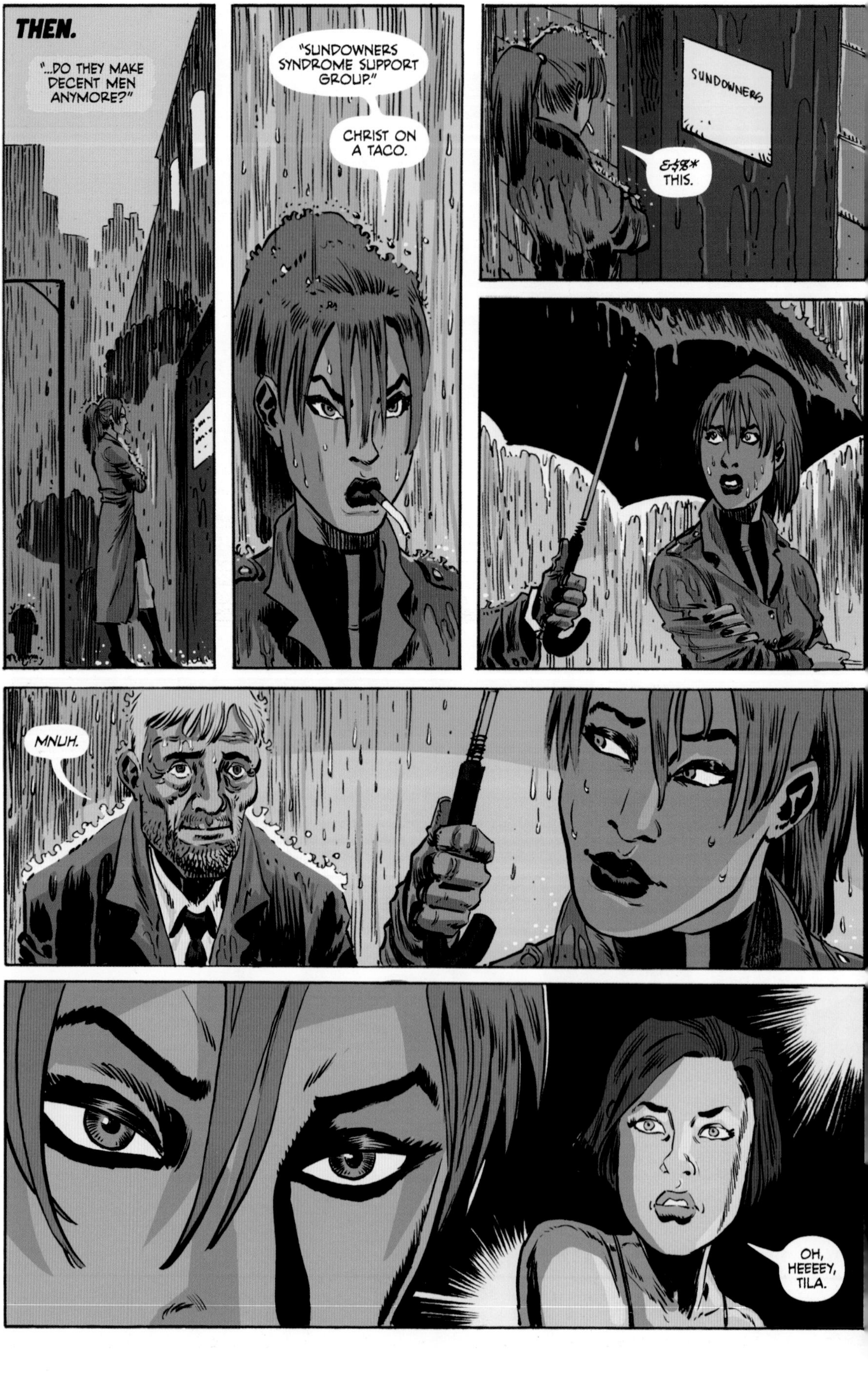
THEN.
"...DO THEY MAKE DECENT MEN ANYMORE?"
"SUNDOWNERS SYNDROME SUPPORT GROUP."
CHRIST ON A TACO.
SUNDOWNERS
&$%* THIS.
MNUH.
OH, HEEEEY, TILA.

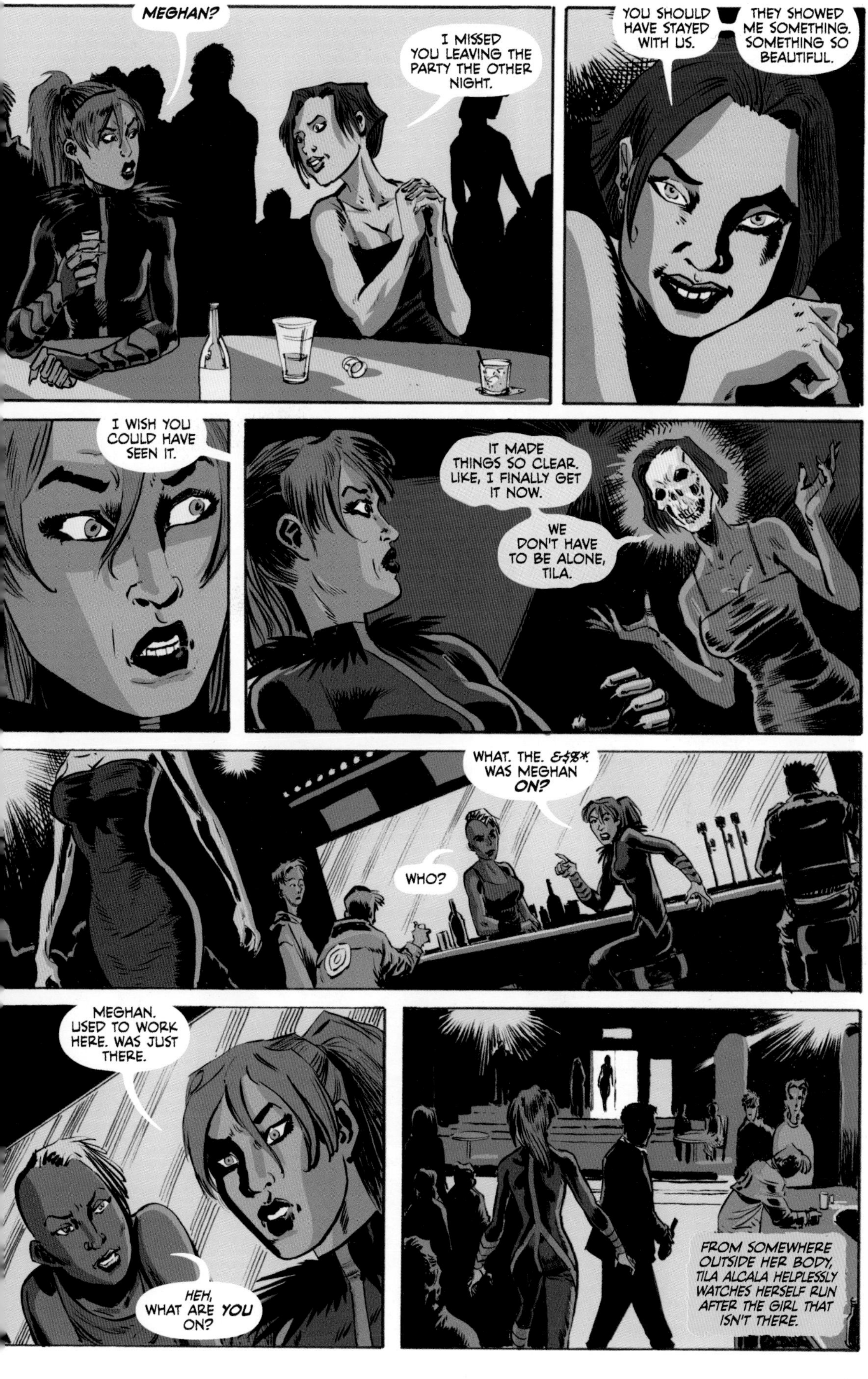

MEGHAN?
I MISSED YOU LEAVING THE PARTY THE OTHER NIGHT.
YOU SHOULD HAVE STAYED WITH US.
THEY SHOWED ME SOMETHING. SOMETHING SO BEAUTIFUL.
I WISH YOU COULD HAVE SEEN IT.
IT MADE THINGS SO CLEAR. LIKE, I FINALLY GET IT NOW.
WE DON'T HAVE TO BE ALONE, TILA.
WHAT. THE. &$%*. WAS MEGHAN ON?
WHO?
MEGHAN. USED TO WORK HERE. WAS JUST THERE.
HEH, WHAT ARE YOU ON?
FROM SOMEWHERE OUTSIDE HER BODY, TILA ALCALA HELPLESSLY WATCHES HERSELF RUN AFTER THE GIRL THAT ISN'T THERE.

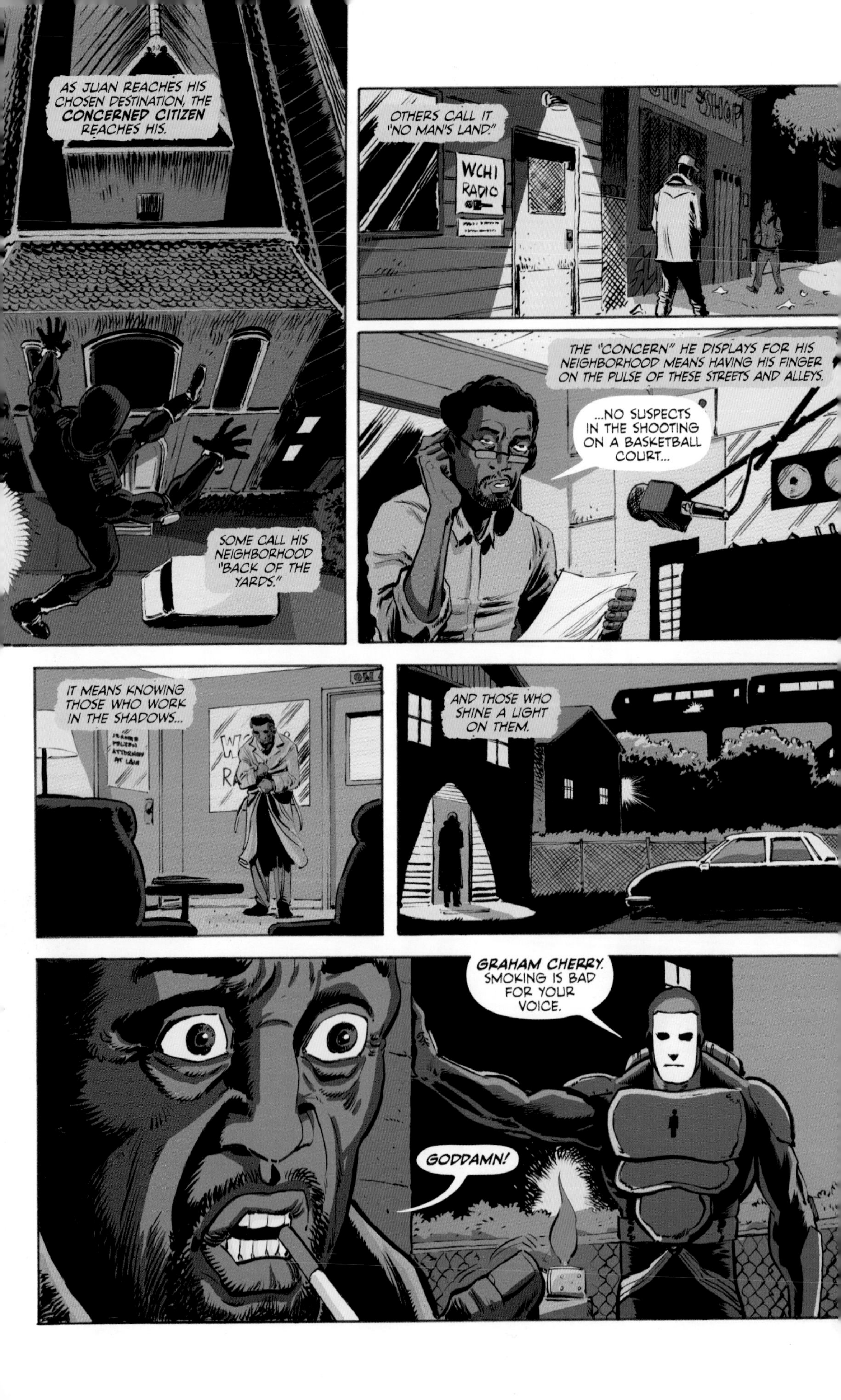
AS JUAN REACHES HIS CHOSEN DESTINATION, THE CONCERNED CITIZEN REACHES HIS.
SOME CALL HIS NEIGHBORHOOD "BACK OF THE YARDS."
OTHERS CALL IT "NO MAN'S LAND."
WCHI RADIO
THE "CONCERN" HE DISPLAYS FOR HIS NEIGHBORHOOD MEANS HAVING HIS FINGER ON THE PULSE OF THESE STREETS AND ALLEYS.
...NO SUSPECTS IN THE SHOOTING ON A BASKETBALL COURT...
IT MEANS KNOWING THOSE WHO WORK IN THE SHADOWS...
AND THOSE WHO SHINE A LIGHT ON THEM.
GRAHAM CHERRY. SMOKING IS BAD FOR YOUR VOICE.
GODDAMN!

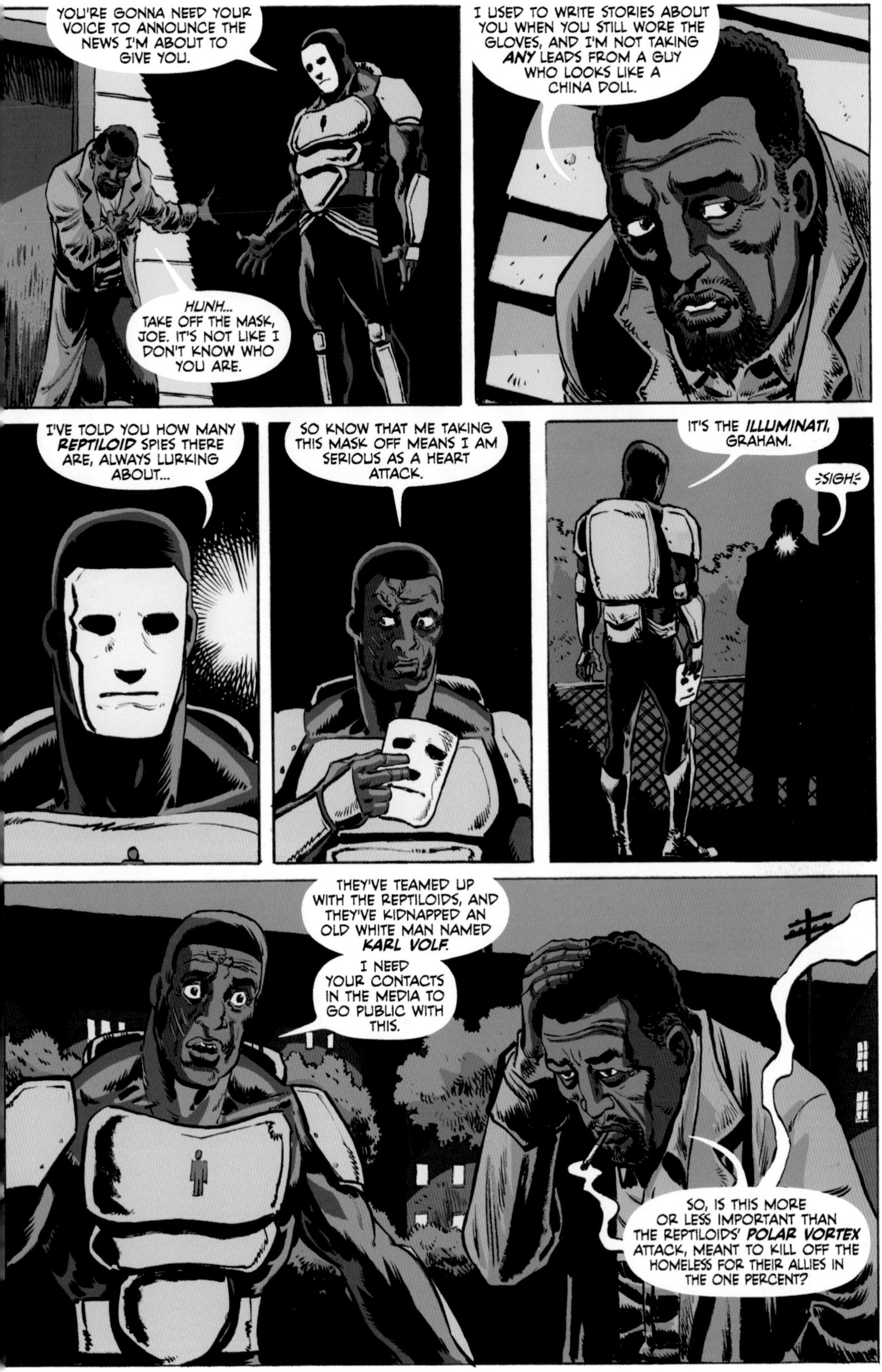
YOU'RE GONNA NEED YOUR VOICE TO ANNOUNCE THE NEWS I'M ABOUT TO GIVE YOU.
HUNH... TAKE OFF THE MASK, JOE. IT'S NOT LIKE I DON'T KNOW WHO YOU ARE.
I USED TO WRITE STORIES ABOUT YOU WHEN YOU STILL WORE THE GLOVES, AND I'M NOT TAKING ANY LEADS FROM A GUY WHO LOOKS LIKE A CHINA DOLL.
I'VE TOLD YOU HOW MANY REPTILOID SPIES THERE ARE, ALWAYS LURKING ABOUT...
SO KNOW THAT ME TAKING THIS MASK OFF MEANS I AM SERIOUS AS A HEART ATTACK.
IT'S THE ILLUMINATI, GRAHAM.
SIGH
THEY'VE TEAMED UP WITH THE REPTILOIDS, AND THEY'VE KIDNAPPED AN OLD WHITE MAN NAMED KARL VOLF.
I NEED YOUR CONTACTS IN THE MEDIA TO GO PUBLIC WITH THIS.
SO, IS THIS MORE OR LESS IMPORTANT THAN THE REPTILOIDS' POLAR VORTEX ATTACK, MEANT TO KILL OFF THE HOMELESS FOR THEIR ALLIES IN THE ONE PERCENT?

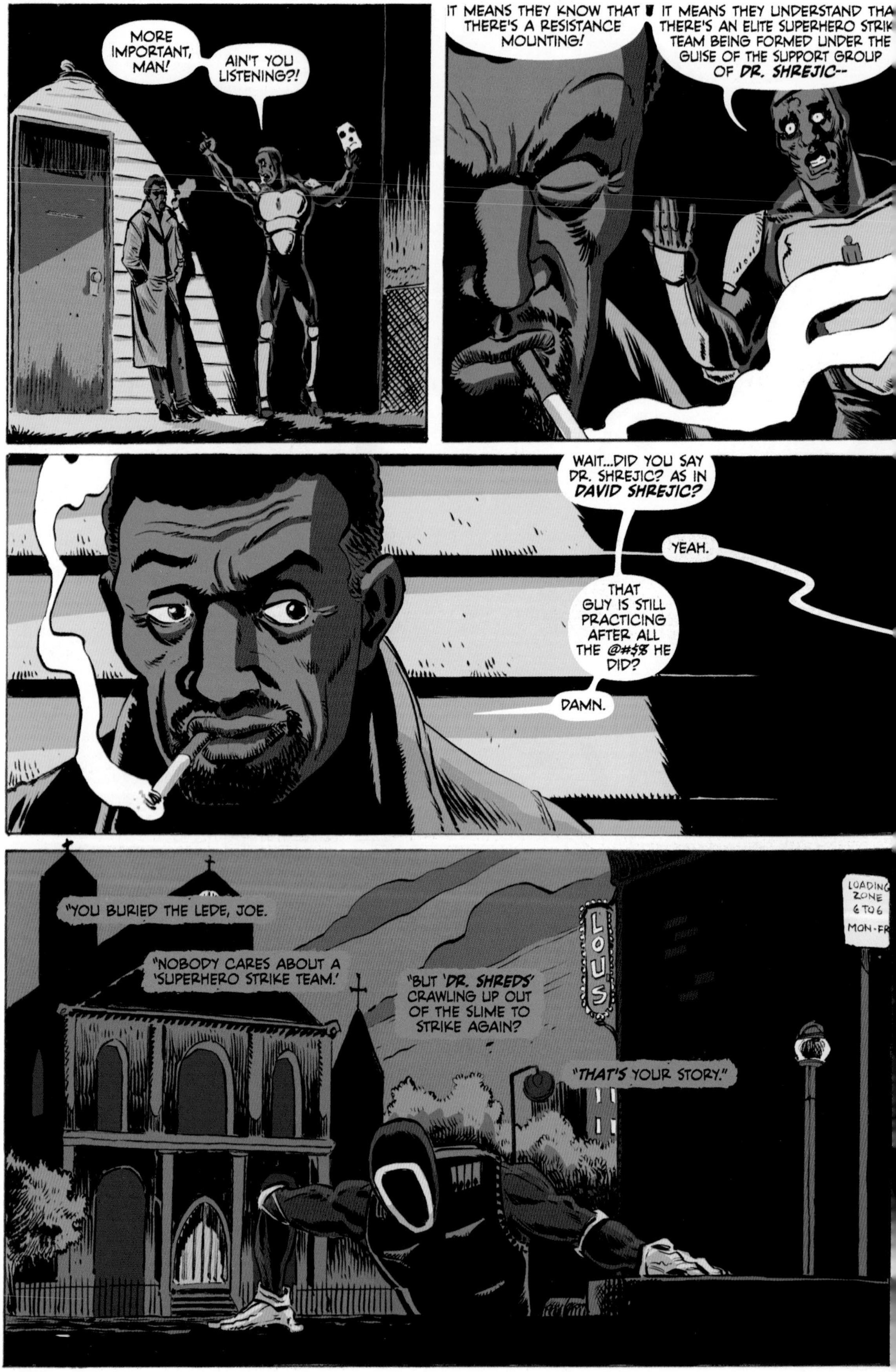
MORE IMPORTANT, MAN!
AIN'T YOU LISTENING?!
IT MEANS THEY KNOW THAT THERE'S A RESISTANCE MOUNTING!
IT MEANS THEY UNDERSTAND THA THERE'S AN ELITE SUPERHERO STRIK TEAM BEING FORMED UNDER THE GUISE OF THE SUPPORT GROUP OF DR. SHREJIC--
WAIT...DID YOU SAY DR. SHREJIC? AS IN DAVID SHREJIC?
YEAH.
THAT GUY IS STILL PRACTICING AFTER ALL THE @#$8 HE DID?
DAMN.
"YOU BURIED THE LEDE, JOE.
"NOBODY CARES ABOUT A 'SUPERHERO STRIKE TEAM.'
"BUT 'DR. SHREDS' CRAWLING UP OUT OF THE SLIME TO STRIKE AGAIN?
"THAT'S YOUR STORY."
LOUS
LOADING ZONE 6 TO 6 MON-FR

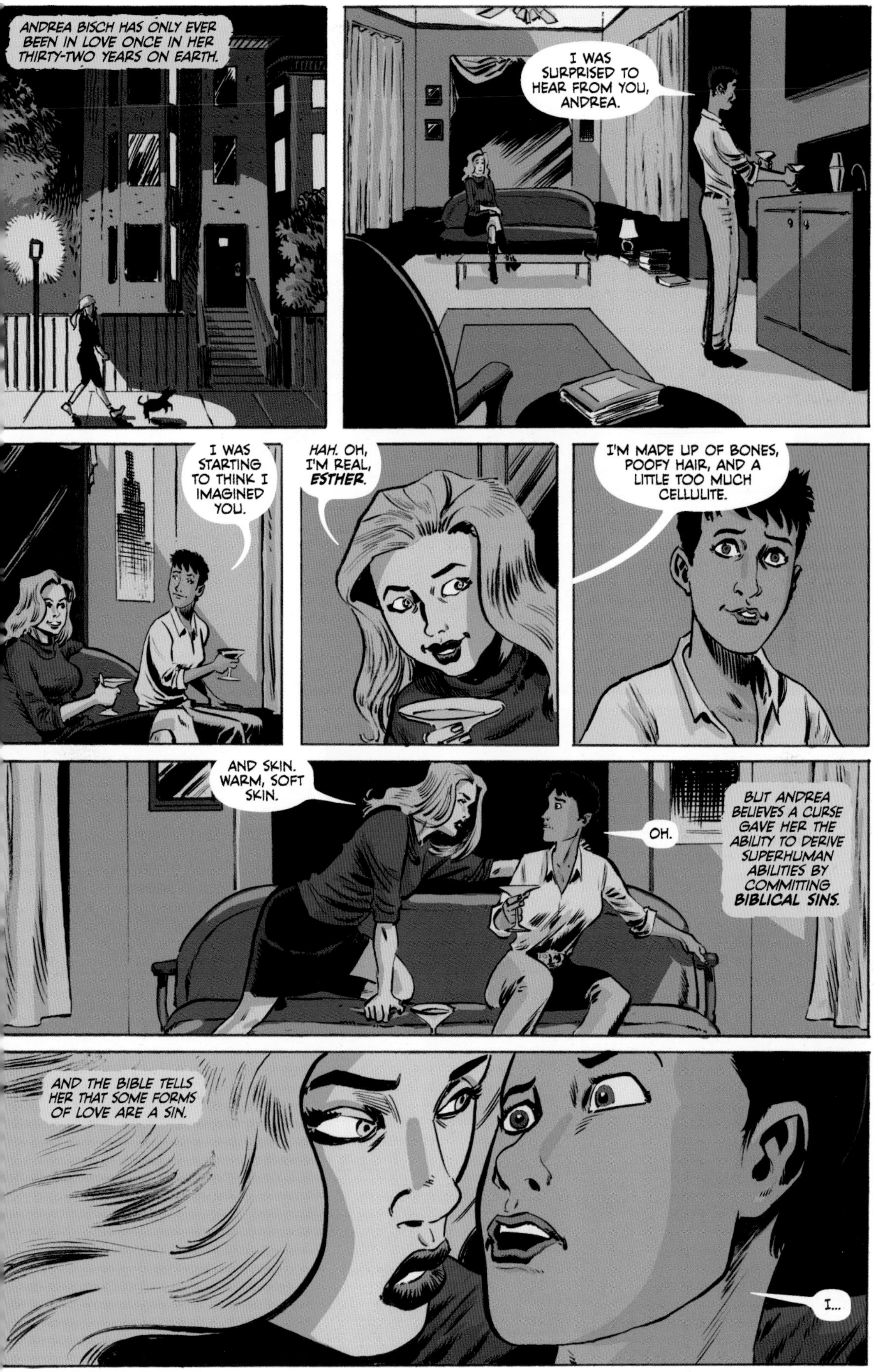
ANDREA BISCH HAS ONLY EVER BEEN IN LOVE ONCE IN HER THIRTY-TWO YEARS ON EARTH.
I WAS SURPRISED TO HEAR FROM YOU, ANDREA.
I WAS STARTING TO THINK I IMAGINED YOU.
HAH. OH, I'M REAL, ESTHER.
I'M MADE UP OF BONES, POOFY HAIR, AND A LITTLE TOO MUCH CELLULITE.
AND SKIN. WARM, SOFT SKIN.
OH.
BUT ANDREA BELIEVES A CURSE GAVE HER THE ABILITY TO DERIVE SUPERHUMAN ABILITIES BY COMMITTING BIBLICAL SINS.
AND THE BIBLE TELLS HER THAT SOME FORMS OF LOVE ARE A SIN.
I...

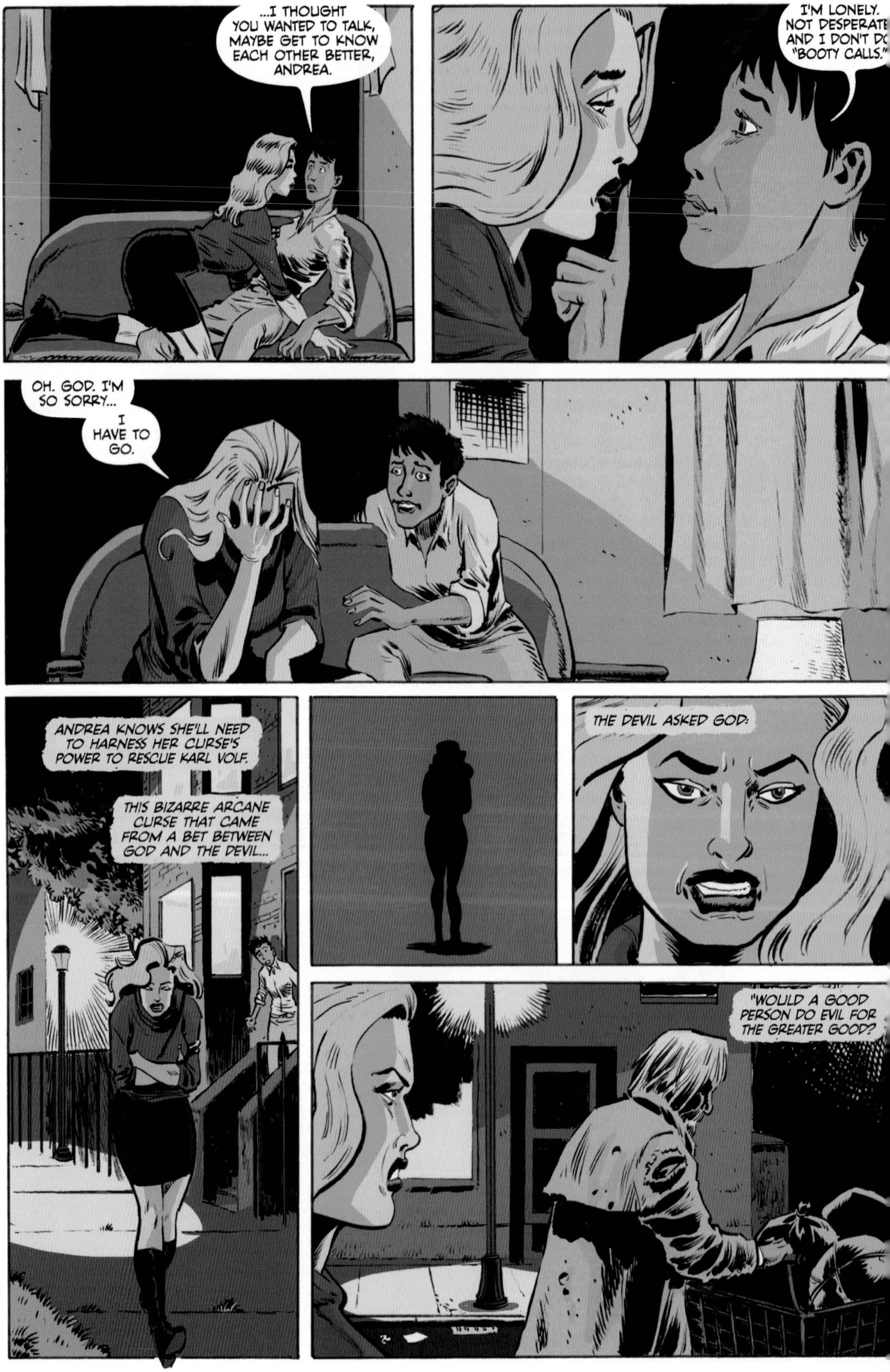

...I THOUGHT YOU WANTED TO TALK, MAYBE GET TO KNOW EACH OTHER BETTER, ANDREA.
I'M LONELY. NOT DESPERATE AND I DON'T DO "BOOTY CALLS."
OH. GOD. I'M SO SORRY...
I HAVE TO GO.
ANDREA KNOWS SHE'LL NEED TO HARNESS HER CURSE'S POWER TO RESCUE KARL VOLF.
THIS BIZARRE ARCANE CURSE THAT CAME FROM A BET BETWEEN GOD AND THE DEVIL...
THE DEVIL ASKED GOD:
"WOULD A GOOD PERSON DO EVIL FOR THE GREATER GOOD?

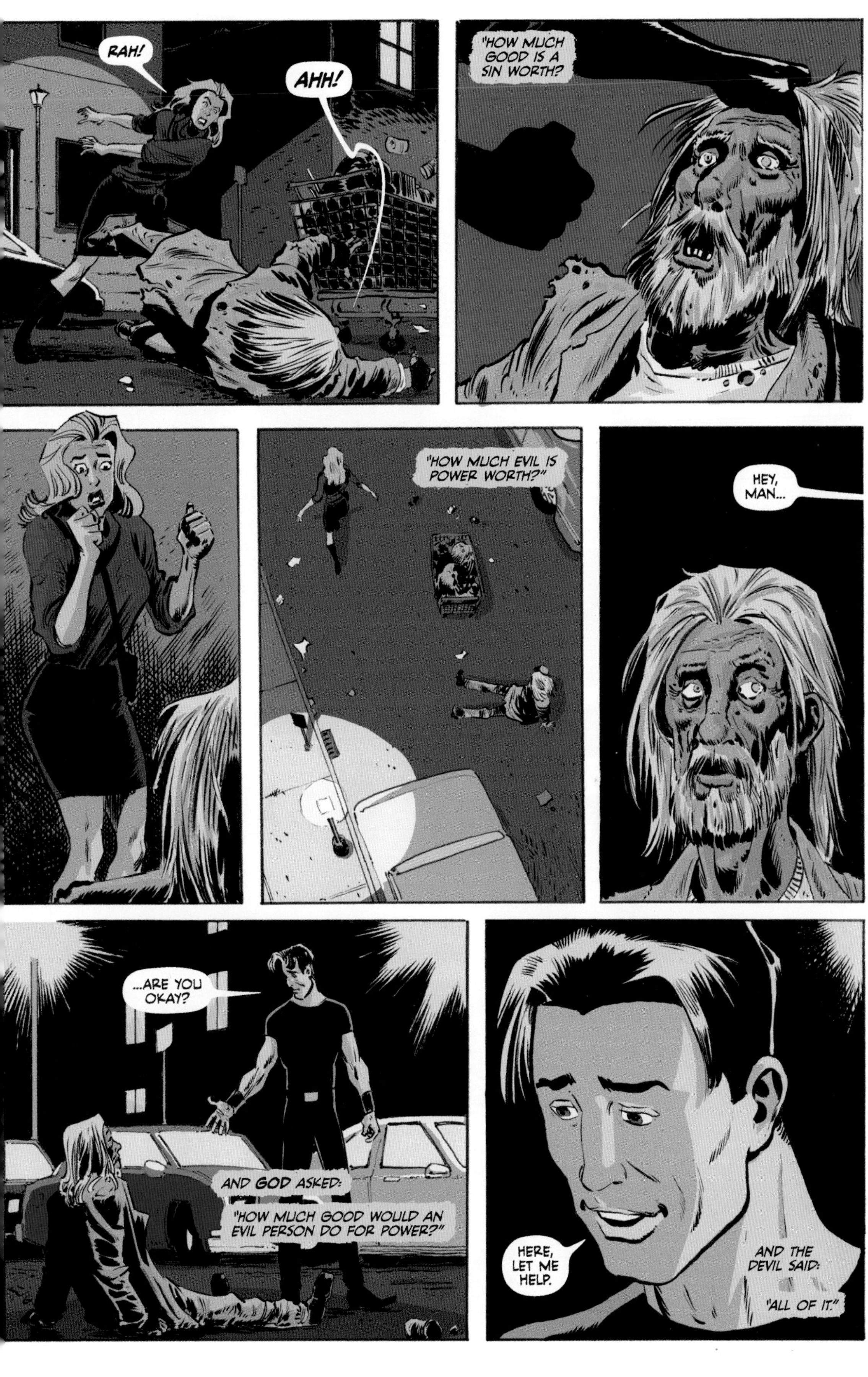
RAH!
AHH!
"HOW MUCH GOOD IS A SIN WORTH?
"HOW MUCH EVIL IS POWER WORTH?"
HEY, MAN...
...ARE YOU OKAY?
AND GOD ASKED:
"HOW MUCH GOOD WOULD AN EVIL PERSON DO FOR POWER?"
HERE, LET ME HELP.
AND THE DEVIL SAID:
"ALL OF IT."

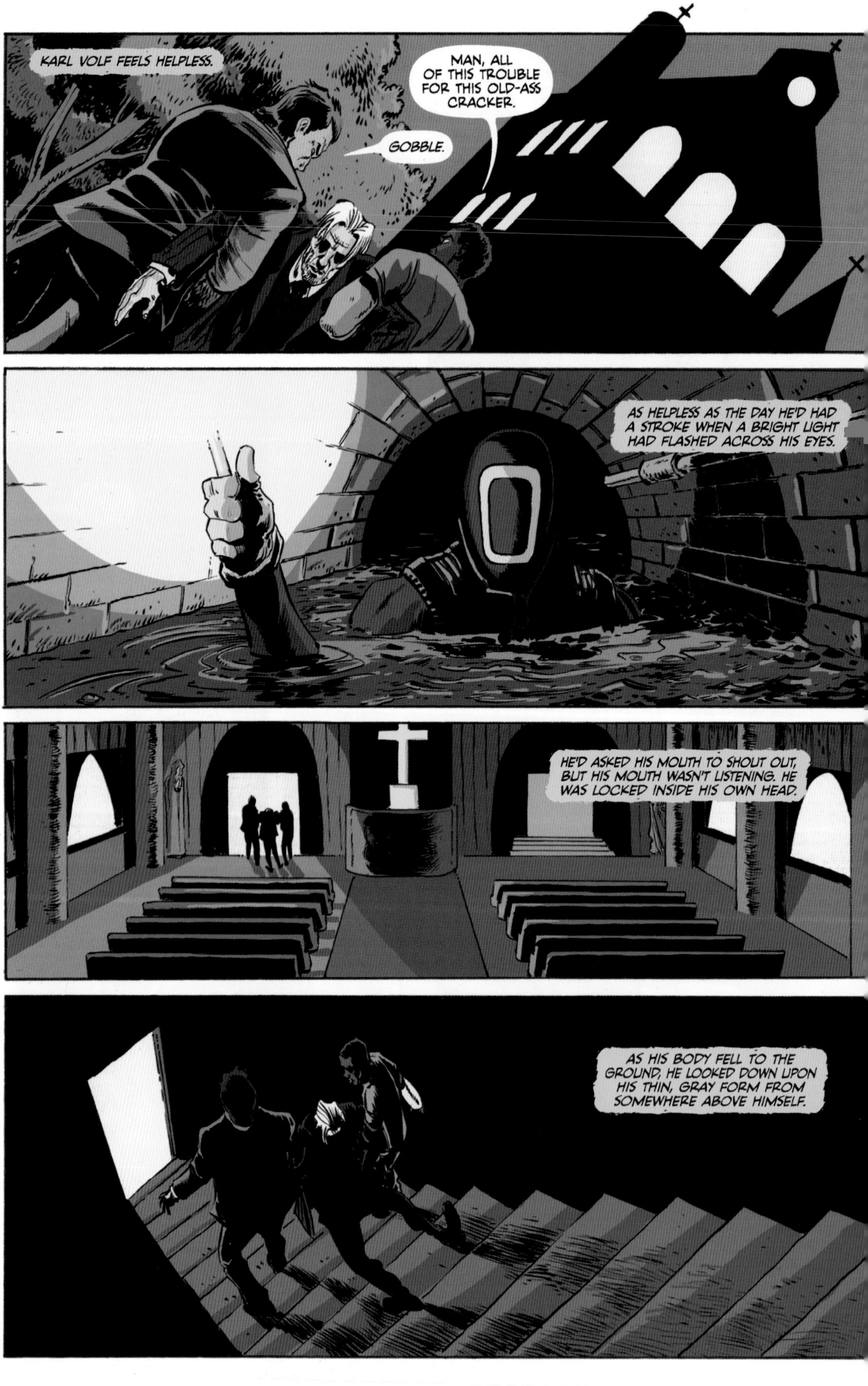
KARL VOLF FEELS HELPLESS.
MAN, ALL OF THIS TROUBLE FOR THIS OLD-ASS CRACKER.
GOBBLE.
AS HELPLESS AS THE DAY HE'D HAD A STROKE WHEN A BRIGHT LIGHT HAD FLASHED ACROSS HIS EYES.
HE'D ASKED HIS MOUTH TO SHOUT OUT, BUT HIS MOUTH WASN'T LISTENING. HE WAS LOCKED INSIDE HIS OWN HEAD.
AS HIS BODY FELL TO THE GROUND, HE LOOKED DOWN UPON HIS THIN, GRAY FORM FROM SOMEWHERE ABOVE HIMSELF.

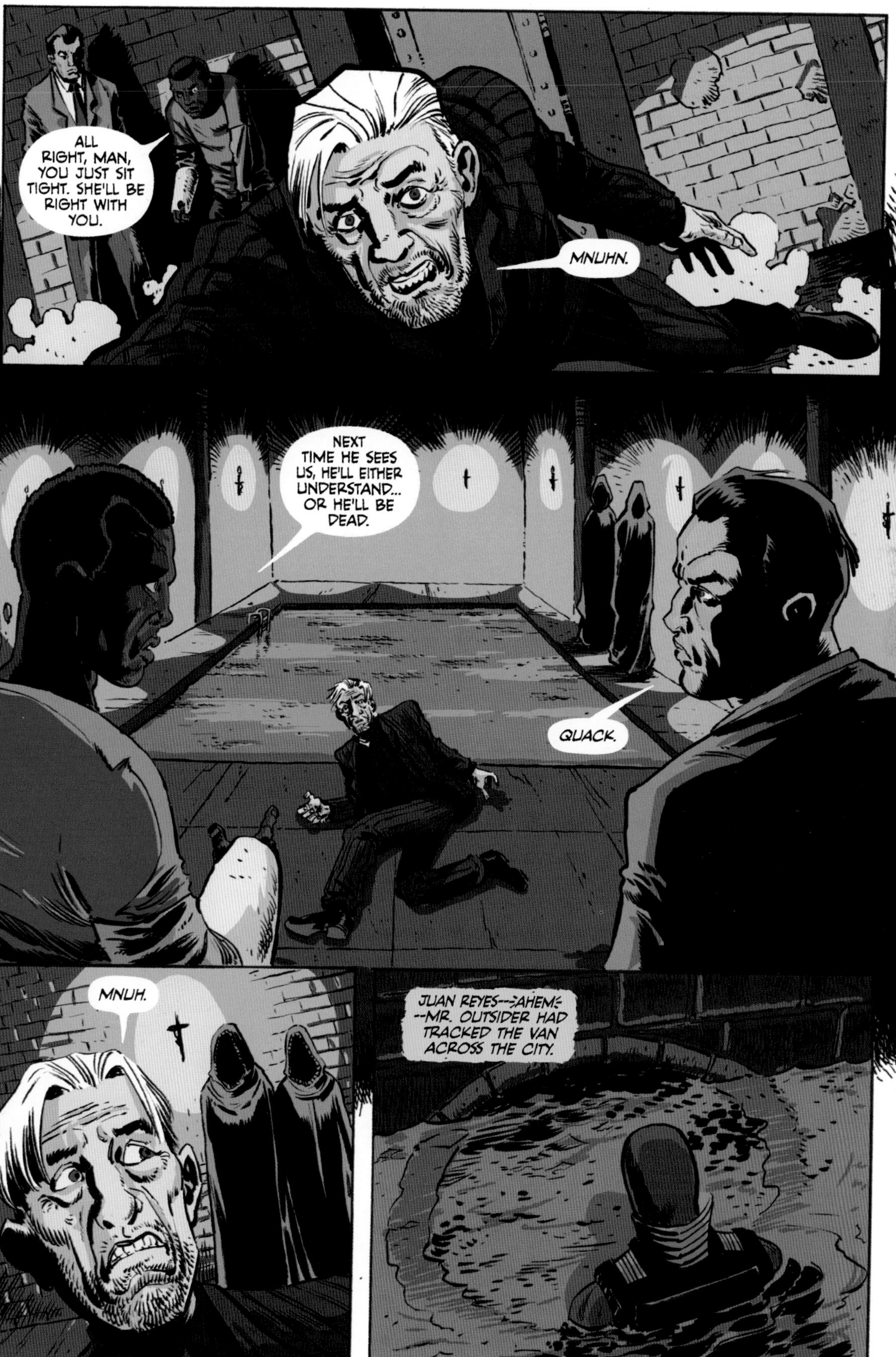
ALL RIGHT, MAN, YOU JUST SIT TIGHT. SHE'LL BE RIGHT WITH YOU.
MNUHN.
NEXT TIME HE SEES US, HE'LL EITHER UNDERSTAND... OR HE'LL BE DEAD.
QUACK.
MNUH.
JUAN REYES---AHEM--- --MR. OUTSIDER HAD TRACKED THE VAN ACROSS THE CITY.

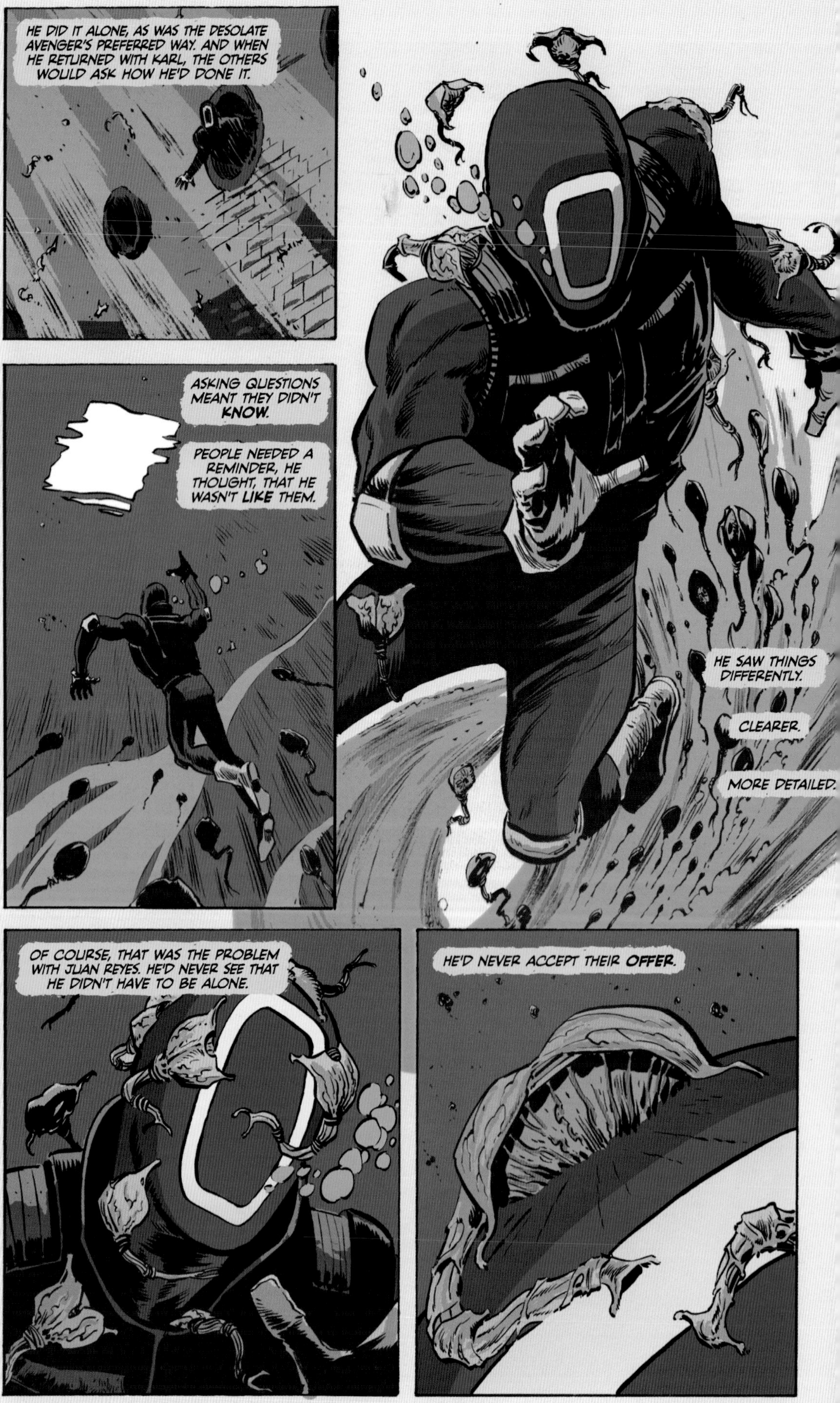

HE DID IT ALONE, AS WAS THE DESOLATE AVENGER'S PREFERRED WAY. AND WHEN HE RETURNED WITH KARL, THE OTHERS WOULD ASK HOW HE'D DONE IT.
ASKING QUESTIONS MEANT THEY DIDN'T **KNOW**.
PEOPLE NEEDED A REMINDER, HE THOUGHT, THAT HE WASN'T **LIKE** THEM.
HE SAW THINGS DIFFERENTLY.
CLEARER.
MORE DETAILED.
OF COURSE, THAT WAS THE PROBLEM WITH JUAN REYES. HE'D NEVER SEE THAT HE DIDN'T HAVE TO BE ALONE.
HE'D NEVER ACCEPT THEIR **OFFER**.

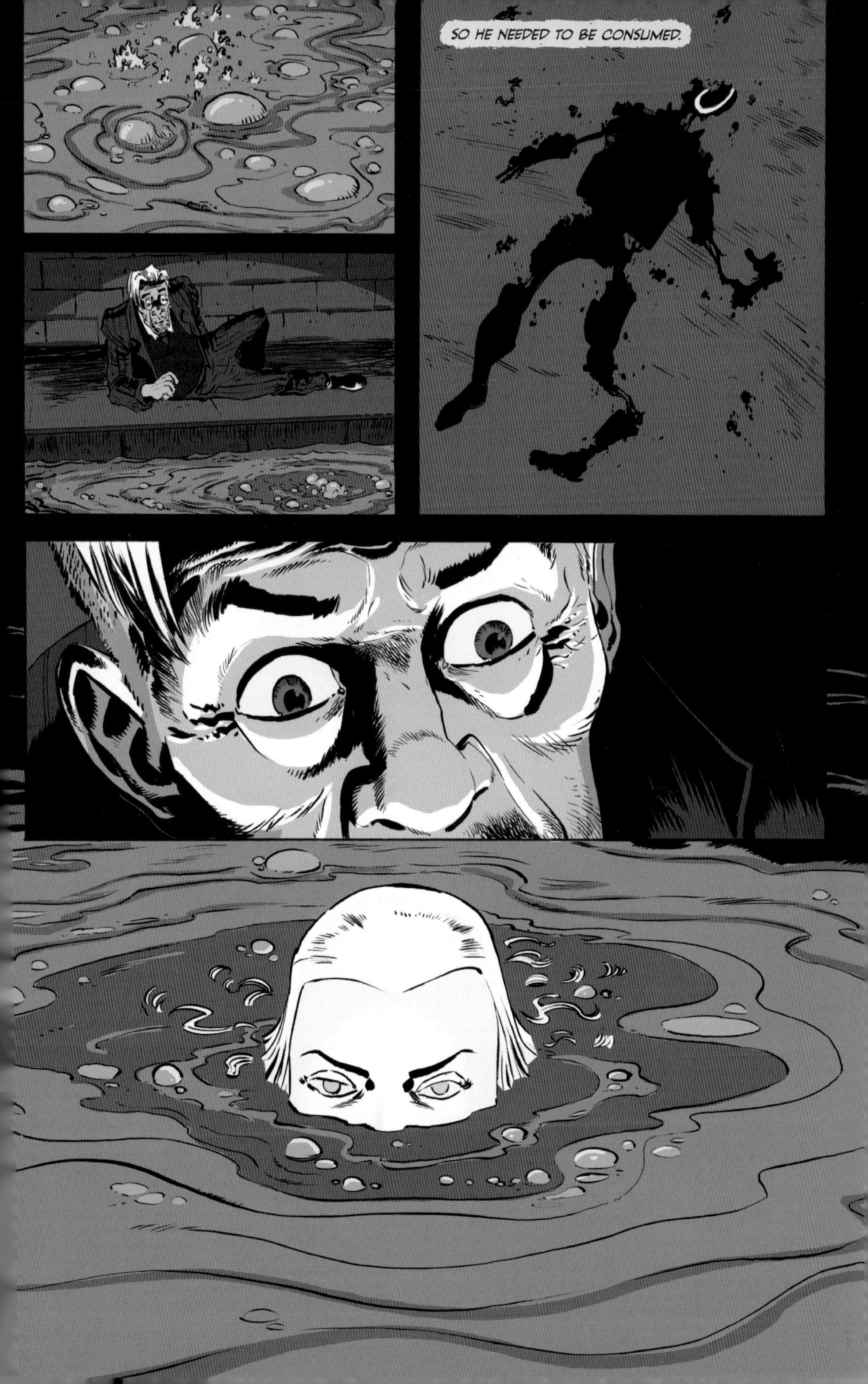
SO HE NEEDED TO BE CONSUMED.

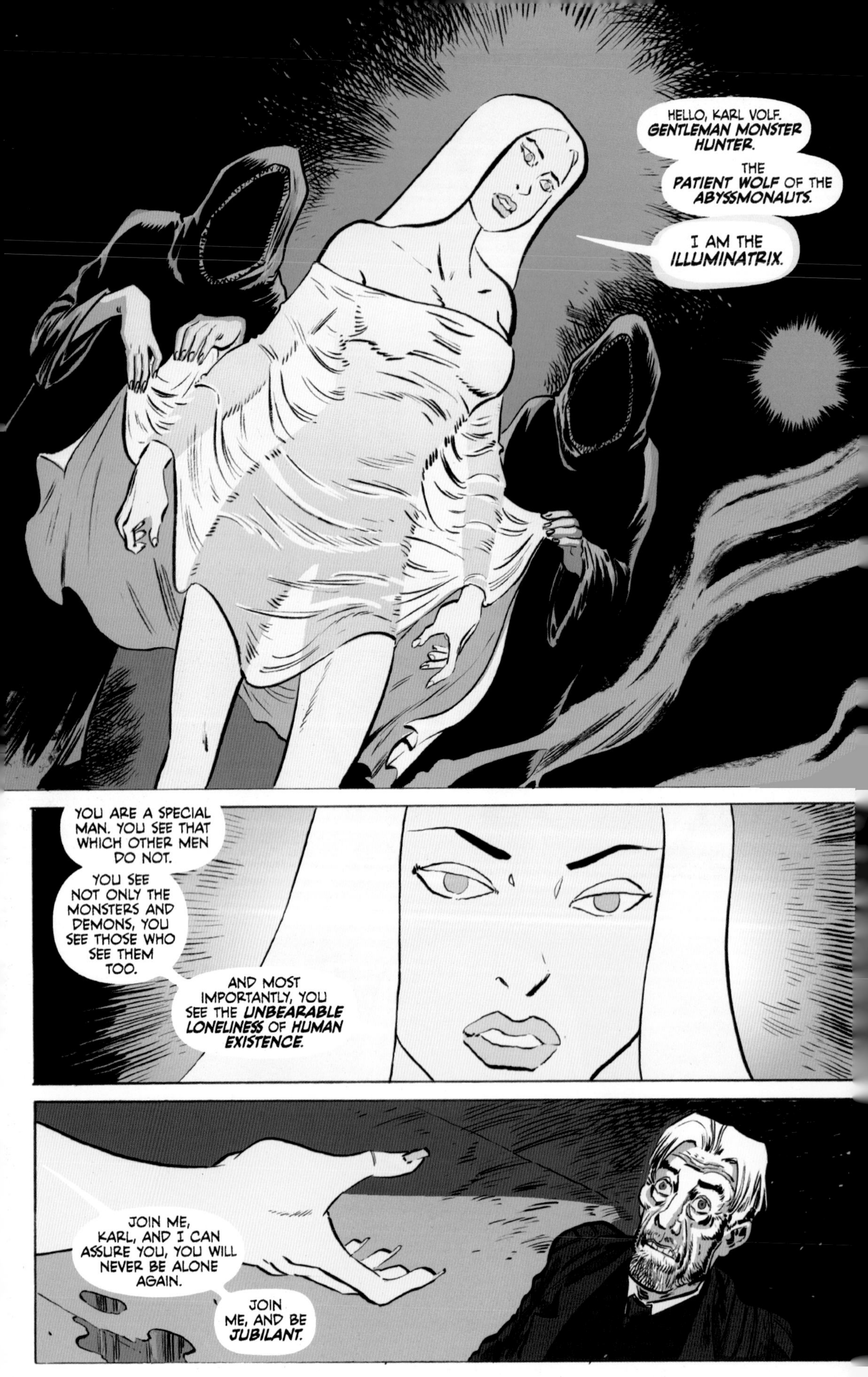
HELLO, KARL VOLF. GENTLEMAN MONSTER HUNTER.
THE PATIENT WOLF OF THE ABYSSMONAUTS.
I AM THE ILLUMINATRIX.
YOU ARE A SPECIAL MAN. YOU SEE THAT WHICH OTHER MEN DO NOT.
YOU SEE NOT ONLY THE MONSTERS AND DEMONS, YOU SEE THOSE WHO SEE THEM TOO.
AND MOST IMPORTANTLY, YOU SEE THE UNBEARABLE LONELINESS OF HUMAN EXISTENCE.
JOIN ME, KARL, AND I CAN ASSURE YOU, YOU WILL NEVER BE ALONE AGAIN.
JOIN ME, AND BE JUBILANT.

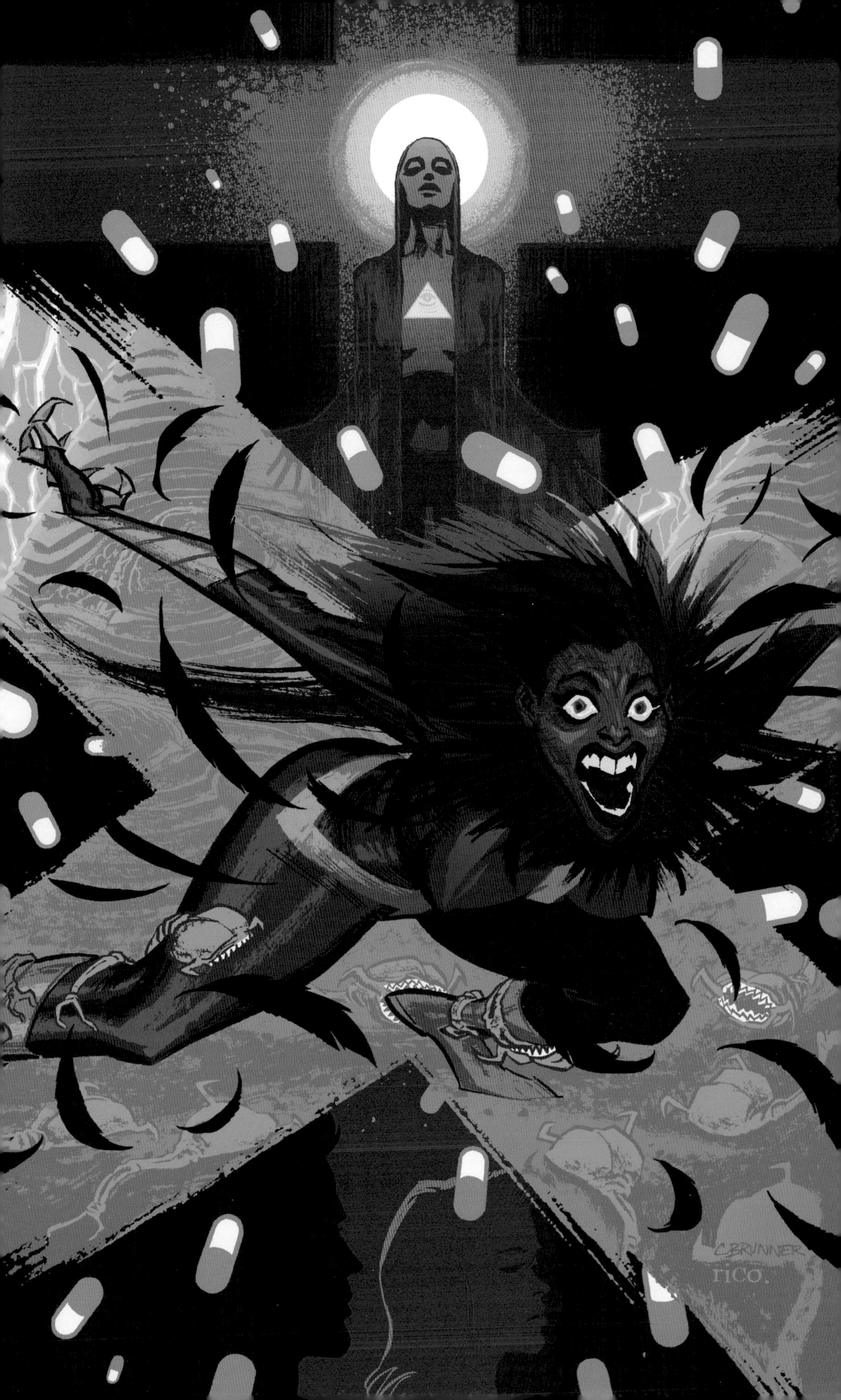
C.BRUNNER
rico.

SUNDOWNERS™ 3

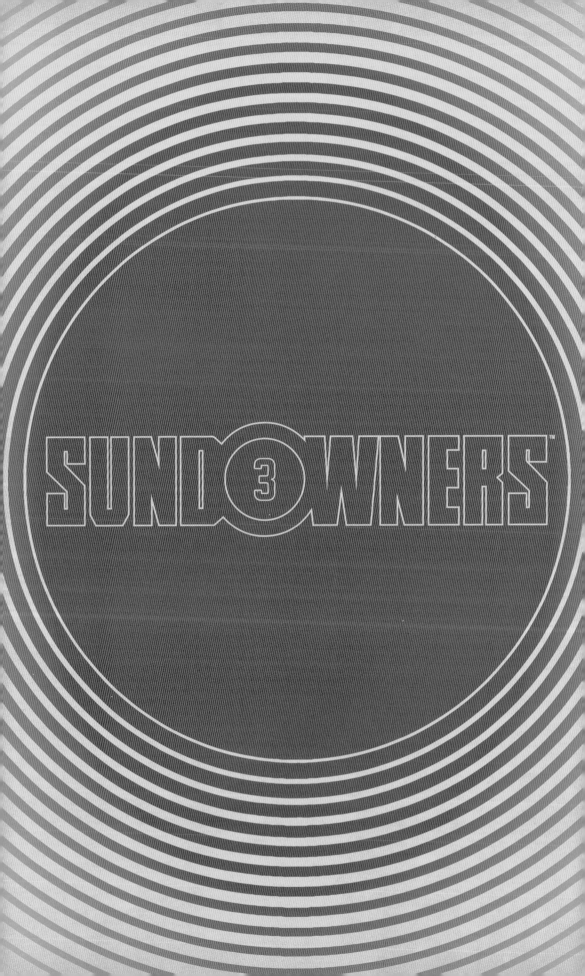

ALBANY PARK.
CHICAGO.

BRRRING

THE APARTMENT
OF KARL VOLF.

BRRRING
BRRRING

BRRRING

BRRRING
BRRRING

BRRRING

THE BLUE
ROSE MOTEL.
DOWNTOWN.

COME
ON, KARL.
PICK UP.

ARE
WE DOING
THIS?

JUST A SEC.
CHECKING ON A...
FRIEND.

HE'S
SLEEPING. HE
CAN'T HEAR
THE PHONE.
YEAH.

I'M
STARTING TO
SOBER UP
HERE...

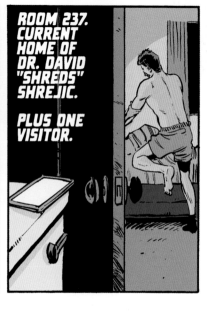

ROOM 237.
CURRENT
HOME OF
DR. DAVID
"SHREDS"
SHREJIC.

PLUS ONE
VISITOR.

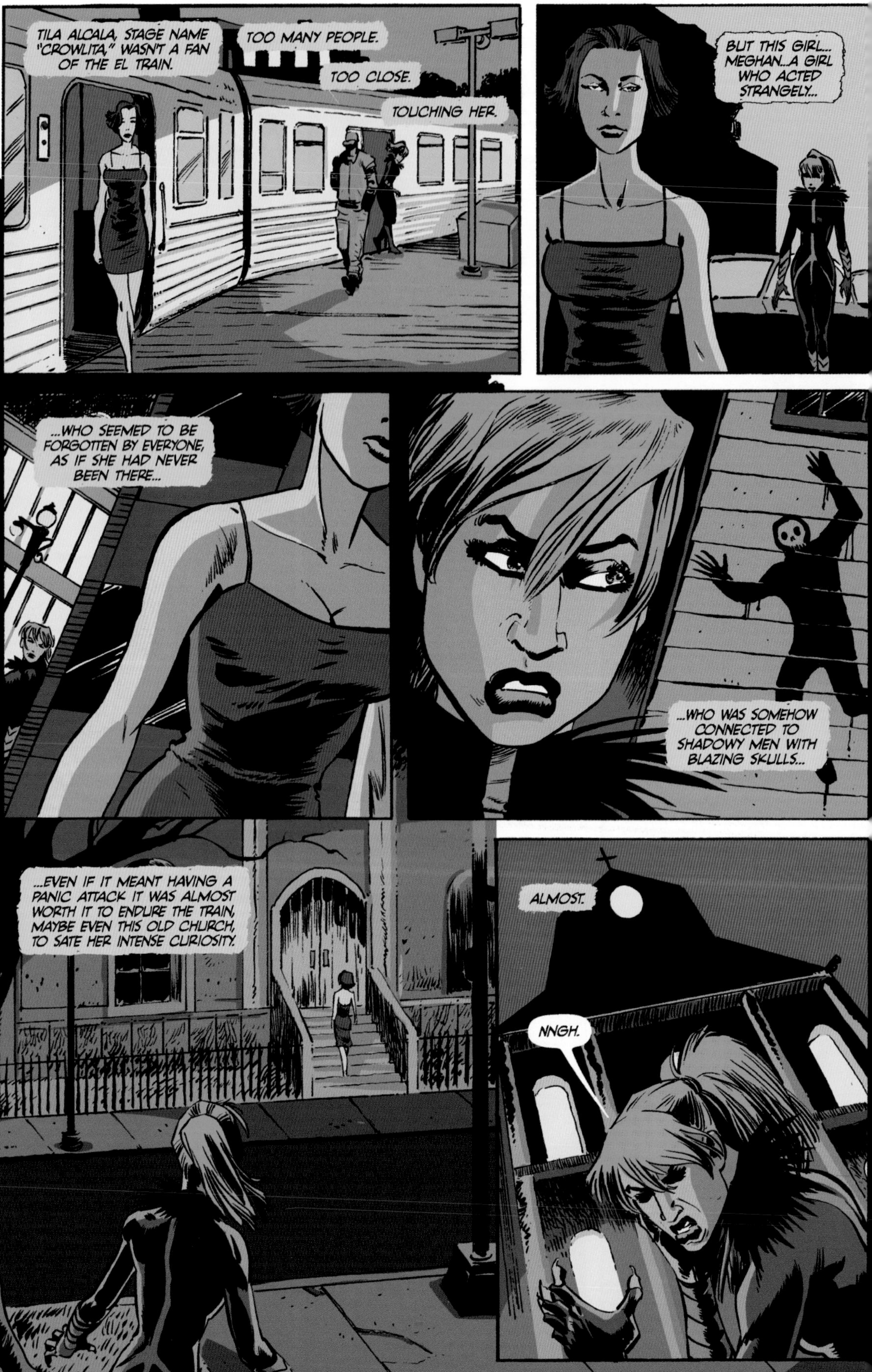
TILA ALCALA, STAGE NAME "CROWLITA," WASN'T A FAN OF THE EL TRAIN.
TOO MANY PEOPLE.
TOO CLOSE.
TOUCHING HER.
BUT THIS GIRL... MEGHAN...A GIRL WHO ACTED STRANGELY...
...WHO SEEMED TO BE FORGOTTEN BY EVERYONE, AS IF SHE HAD NEVER BEEN THERE...
...WHO WAS SOMEHOW CONNECTED TO SHADOWY MEN WITH BLAZING SKULLS...
...EVEN IF IT MEANT HAVING A PANIC ATTACK IT WAS ALMOST WORTH IT TO ENDURE THE TRAIN, MAYBE EVEN THIS OLD CHURCH, TO SATE HER INTENSE CURIOSITY.
ALMOST.
NNGH.

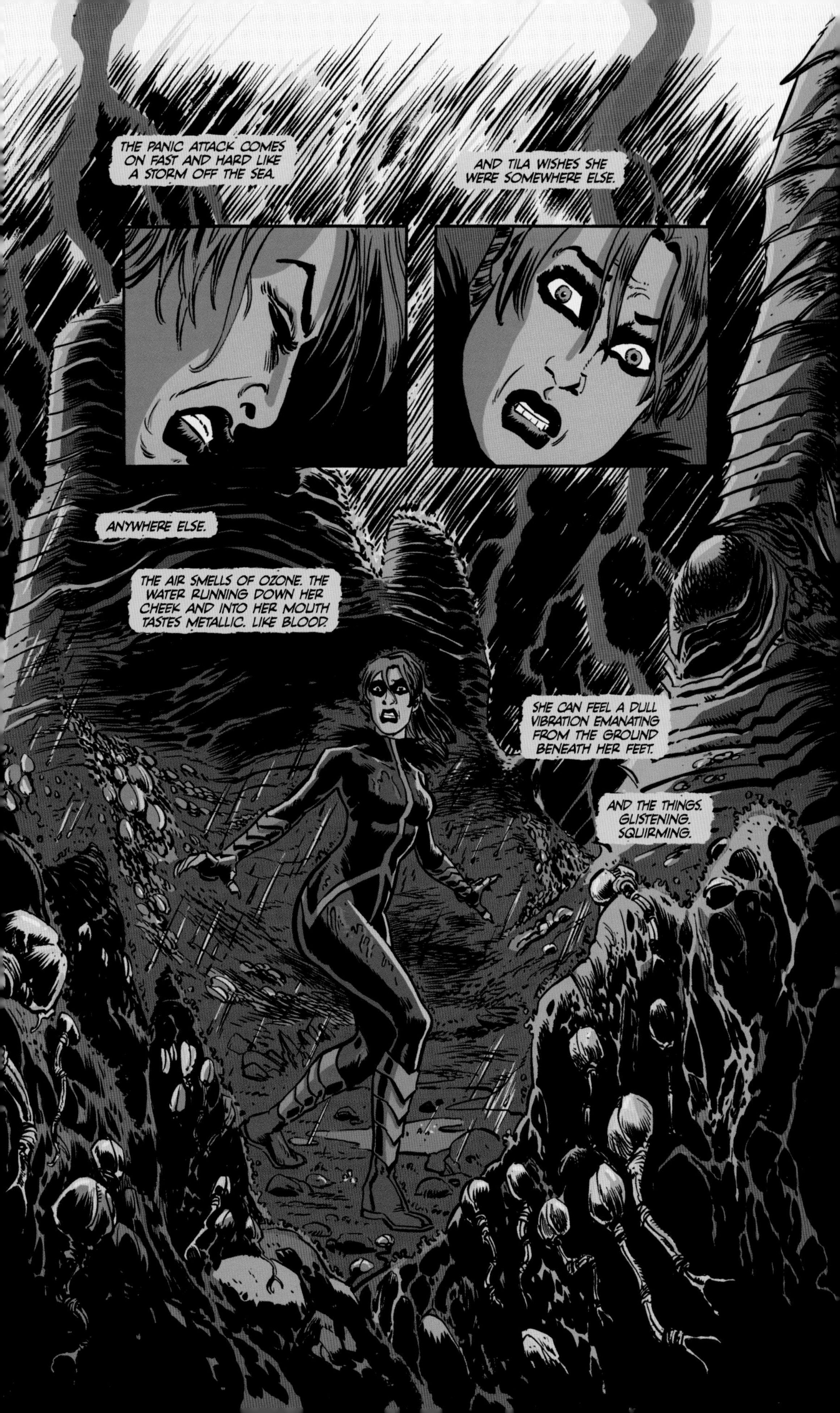
THE PANIC ATTACK COMES ON FAST AND HARD LIKE A STORM OFF THE SEA.
AND TILA WISHES SHE WERE SOMEWHERE ELSE.
ANYWHERE ELSE.
THE AIR SMELLS OF OZONE. THE WATER RUNNING DOWN HER CHEEK AND INTO HER MOUTH TASTES METALLIC. LIKE BLOOD.
SHE CAN FEEL A DULL VIBRATION EMANATING FROM THE GROUND BENEATH HER FEET.
AND THE THINGS. GLISTENING. SQUIRMING.

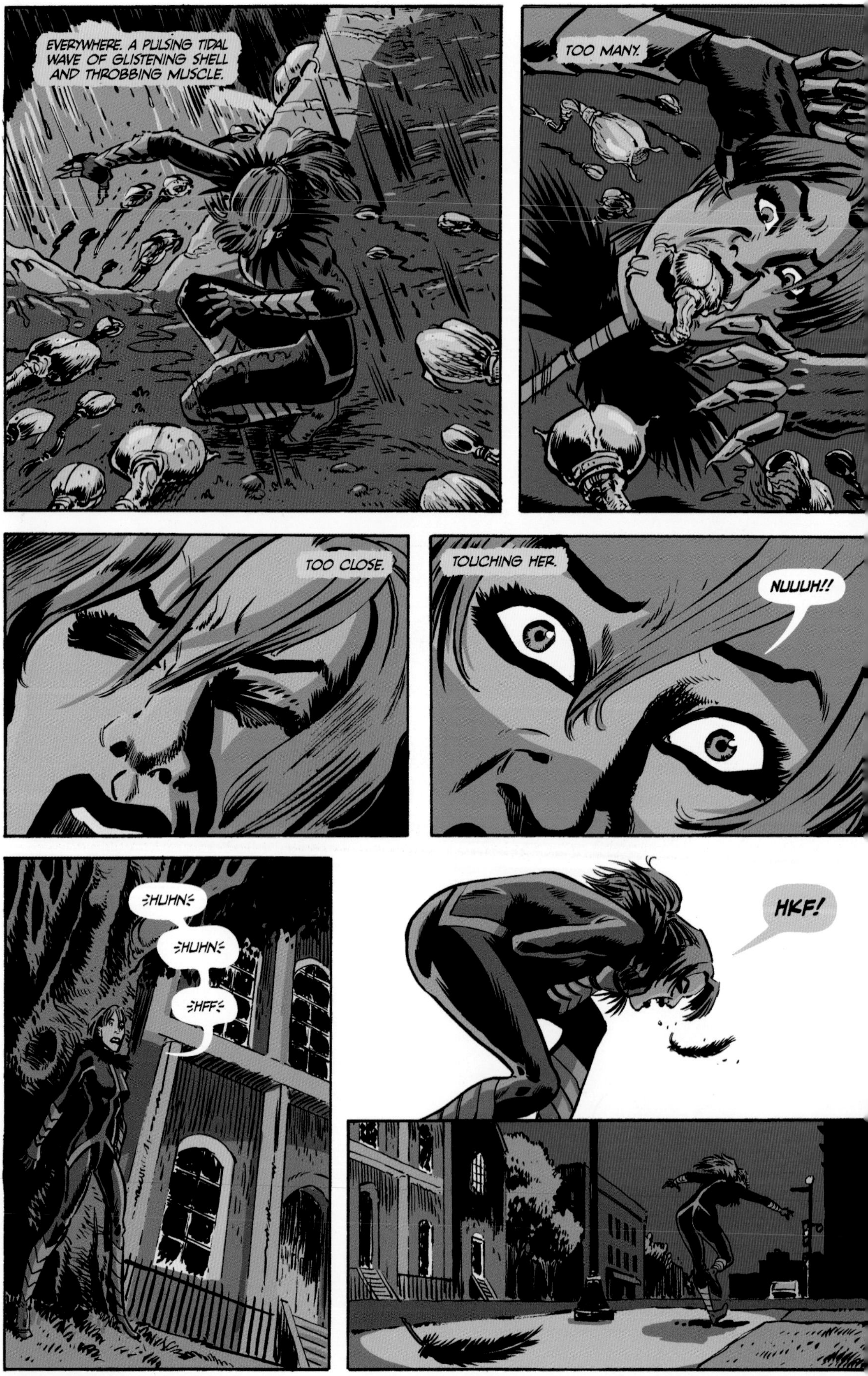
EVERYWHERE. A PULSING TIDAL WAVE OF GLISTENING SHELL AND THROBBING MUSCLE.
TOO MANY.
TOO CLOSE.
TOUCHING HER.
NUUUH!!
HUHN
HUHN
HFF
HKF!

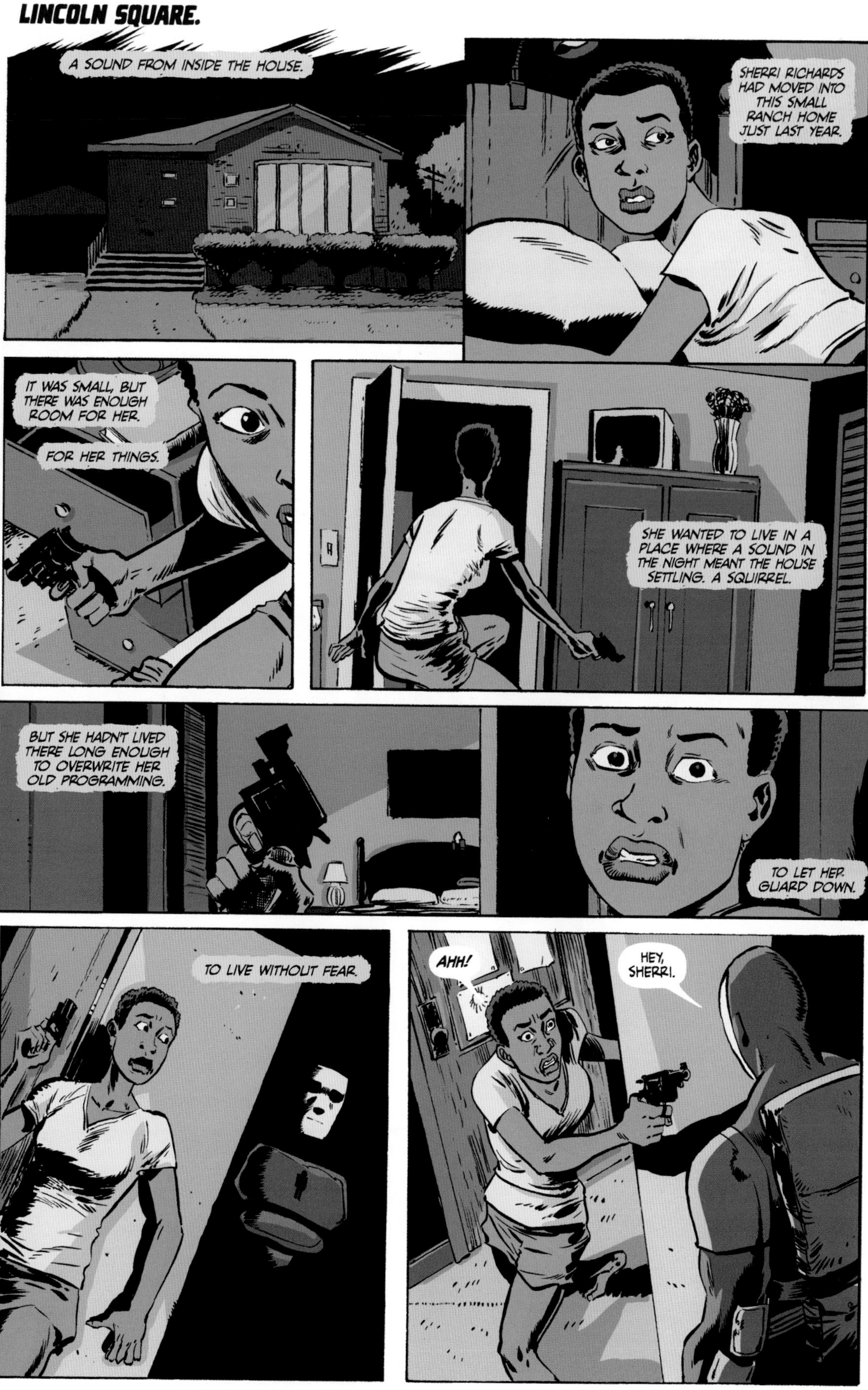
LINCOLN SQUARE.
A SOUND FROM INSIDE THE HOUSE.
SHERRI RICHARDS HAD MOVED INTO THIS SMALL RANCH HOME JUST LAST YEAR.
IT WAS SMALL, BUT THERE WAS ENOUGH ROOM FOR HER.
FOR HER THINGS.
SHE WANTED TO LIVE IN A PLACE WHERE A SOUND IN THE NIGHT MEANT THE HOUSE SETTLING. A SQUIRREL.
BUT SHE HADN'T LIVED THERE LONG ENOUGH TO OVERWRITE HER OLD PROGRAMMING.
TO LET HER GUARD DOWN.
TO LIVE WITHOUT FEAR.
AHH!
HEY, SHERRI.

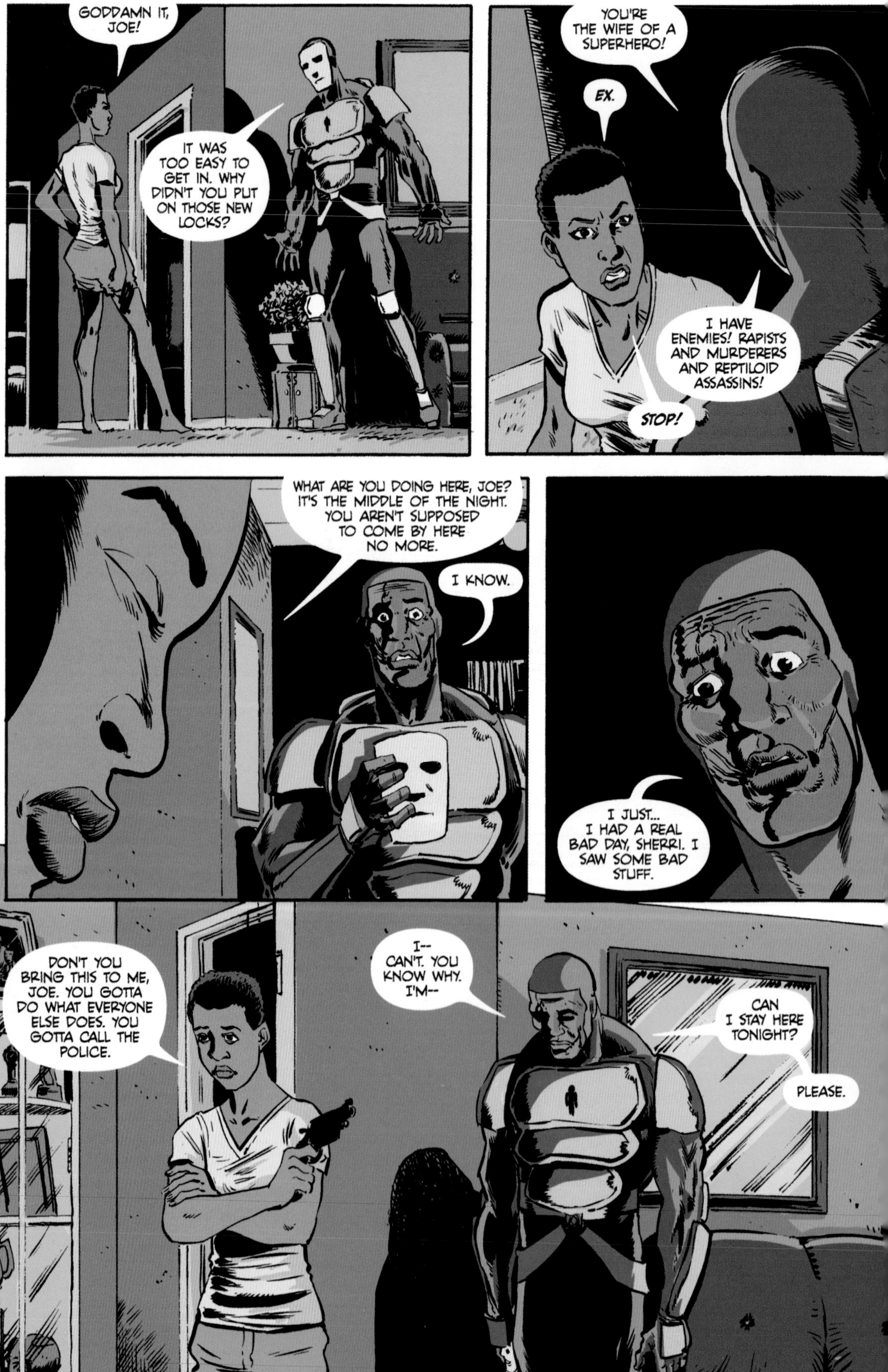
GODDAMN IT, JOE!
IT WAS TOO EASY TO GET IN. WHY DIDN'T YOU PUT ON THOSE NEW LOCKS?
YOU'RE THE WIFE OF A SUPERHERO!
EX.
I HAVE ENEMIES! RAPISTS AND MURDERERS AND REPTILOID ASSASSINS!
STOP!
WHAT ARE YOU DOING HERE, JOE? IT'S THE MIDDLE OF THE NIGHT. YOU AREN'T SUPPOSED TO COME BY HERE NO MORE.
I KNOW.
I JUST... I HAD A REAL BAD DAY, SHERRI. I SAW SOME BAD STUFF.
DON'T YOU BRING THIS TO ME, JOE. YOU GOTTA DO WHAT EVERYONE ELSE DOES. YOU GOTTA CALL THE POLICE.
I-- CAN'T. YOU KNOW WHY. I'M--
CAN I STAY HERE TONIGHT?
PLEASE.

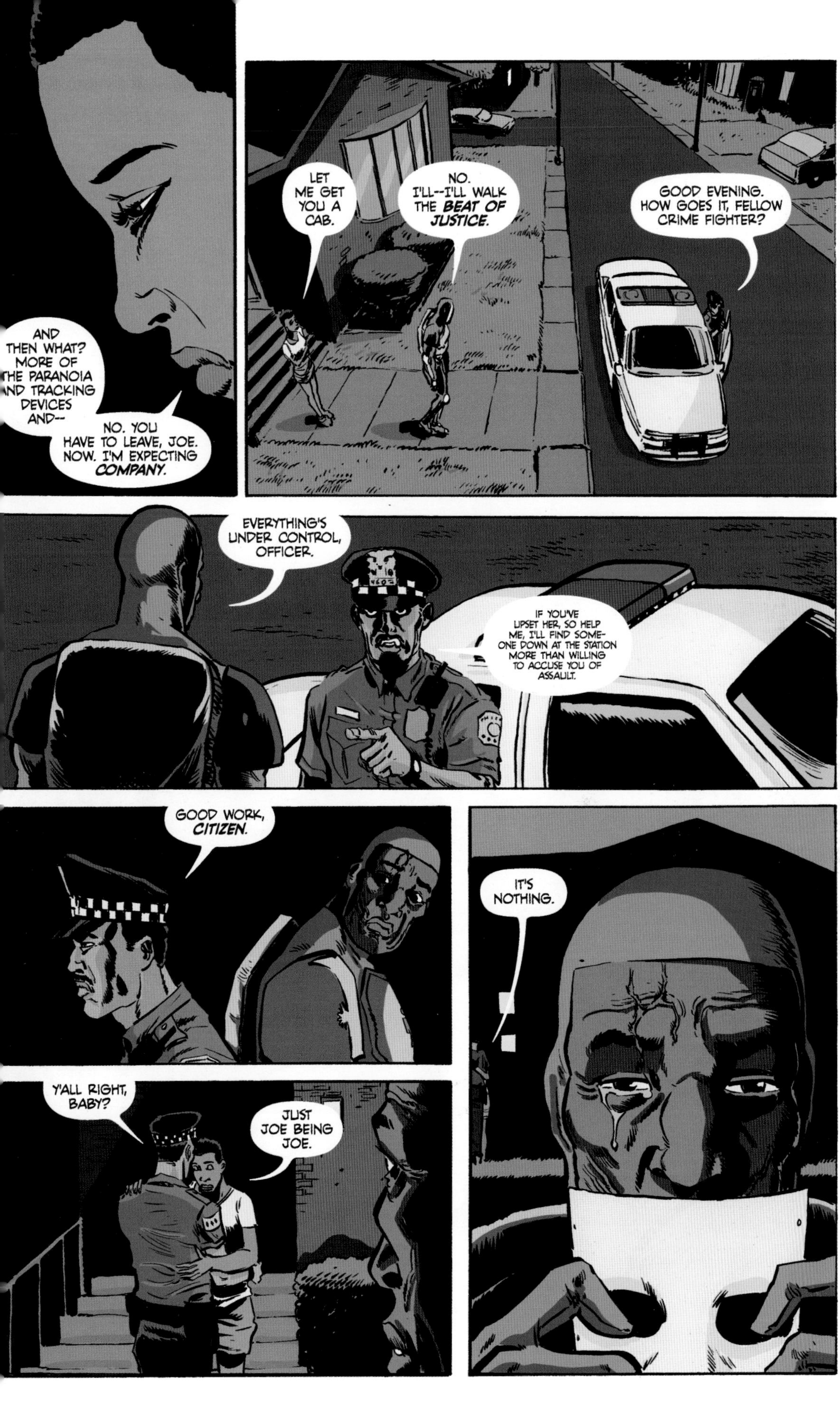
AND THEN WHAT? MORE OF THE PARANOIA AND TRACKING DEVICES AND--
NO. YOU HAVE TO LEAVE, JOE. NOW. I'M EXPECTING *COMPANY*.
LET ME GET YOU A CAB.
NO. I'LL--I'LL WALK THE *BEAT OF JUSTICE*.
GOOD EVENING. HOW GOES IT, FELLOW CRIME FIGHTER?
EVERYTHING'S UNDER CONTROL, OFFICER.
IF YOU'VE UPSET HER, SO HELP ME, I'LL FIND SOME-ONE DOWN AT THE STATION MORE THAN WILLING TO ACCUSE YOU OF ASSAULT.
GOOD WORK, *CITIZEN*.
Y'ALL RIGHT, BABY?
JUST JOE BEING JOE.
IT'S NOTHING.

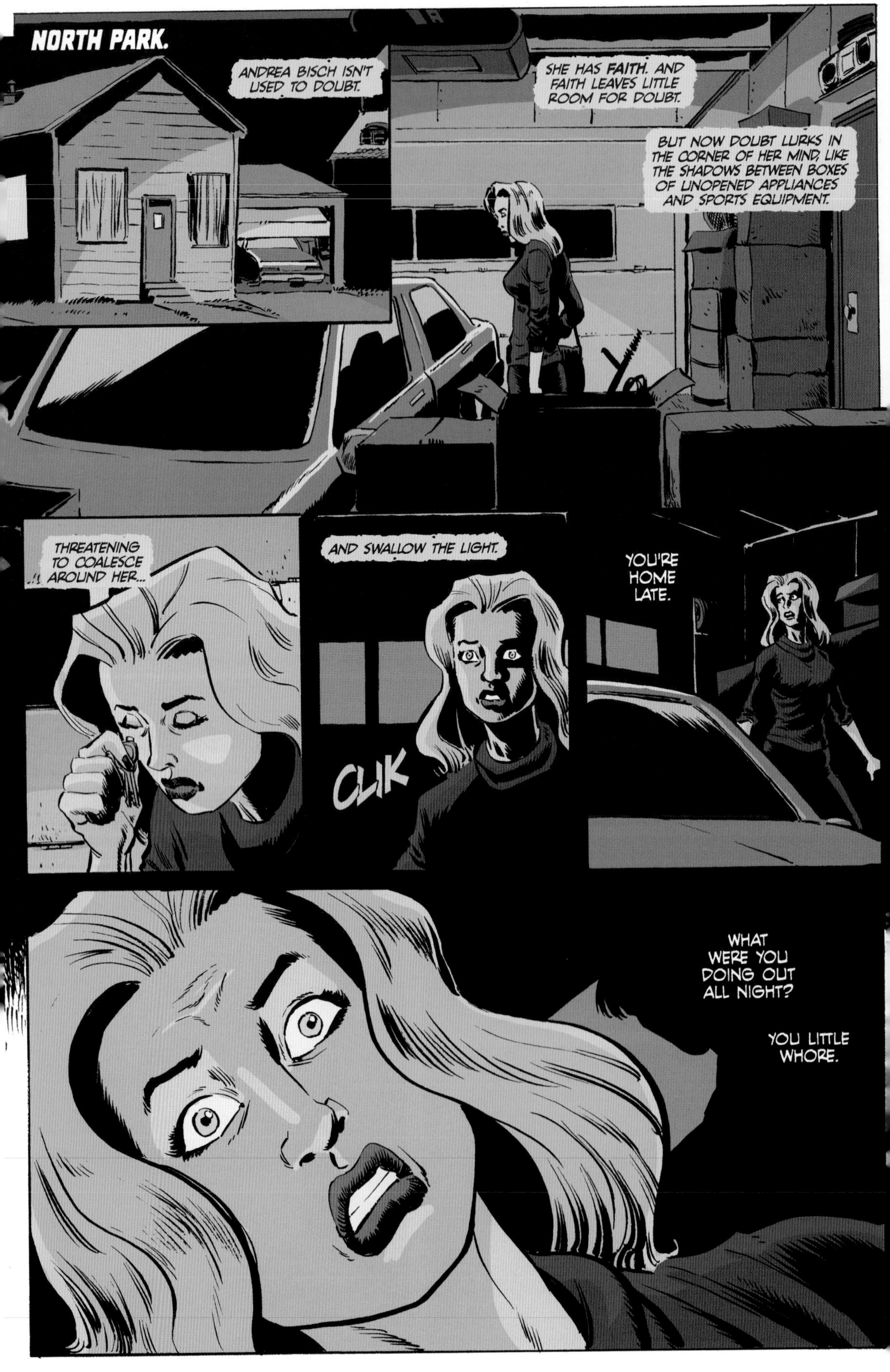
NORTH PARK.
ANDREA BISCH ISN'T USED TO DOUBT.
SHE HAS FAITH. AND FAITH LEAVES LITTLE ROOM FOR DOUBT.
BUT NOW DOUBT LURKS IN THE CORNER OF HER MIND, LIKE THE SHADOWS BETWEEN BOXES OF UNOPENED APPLIANCES AND SPORTS EQUIPMENT.
THREATENING TO COALESCE AROUND HER...
AND SWALLOW THE LIGHT.
CLIK
YOU'RE HOME LATE.
WHAT WERE YOU DOING OUT ALL NIGHT?
YOU LITTLE WHORE.

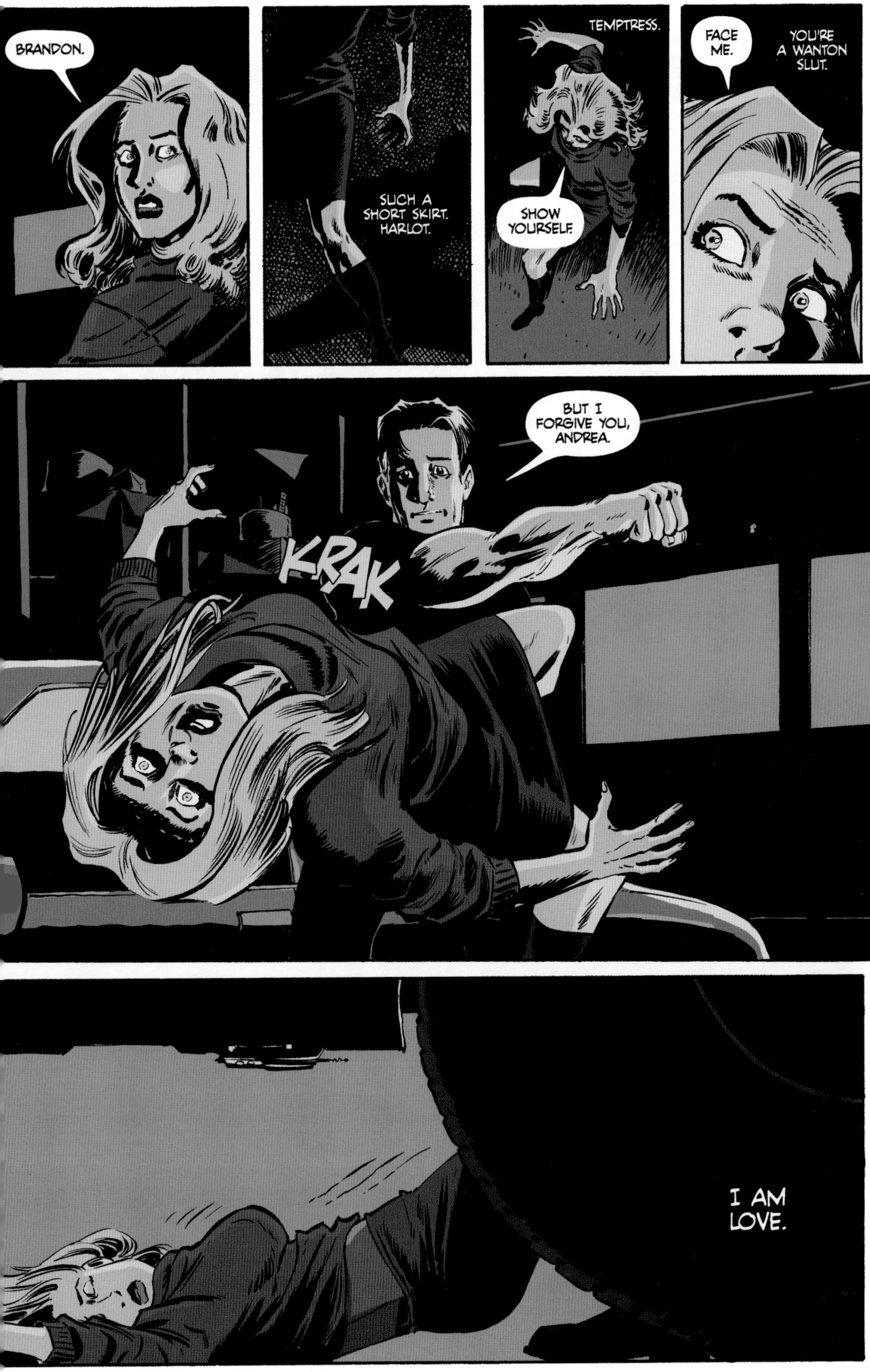

BRANDON.
SUCH A SHORT SKIRT. HARLOT.
TEMPTRESS.
SHOW YOURSELF.
FACE ME.
YOU'RE A WANTON SLUT.
BUT I FORGIVE YOU, ANDREA.
KRAK
I AM LOVE.

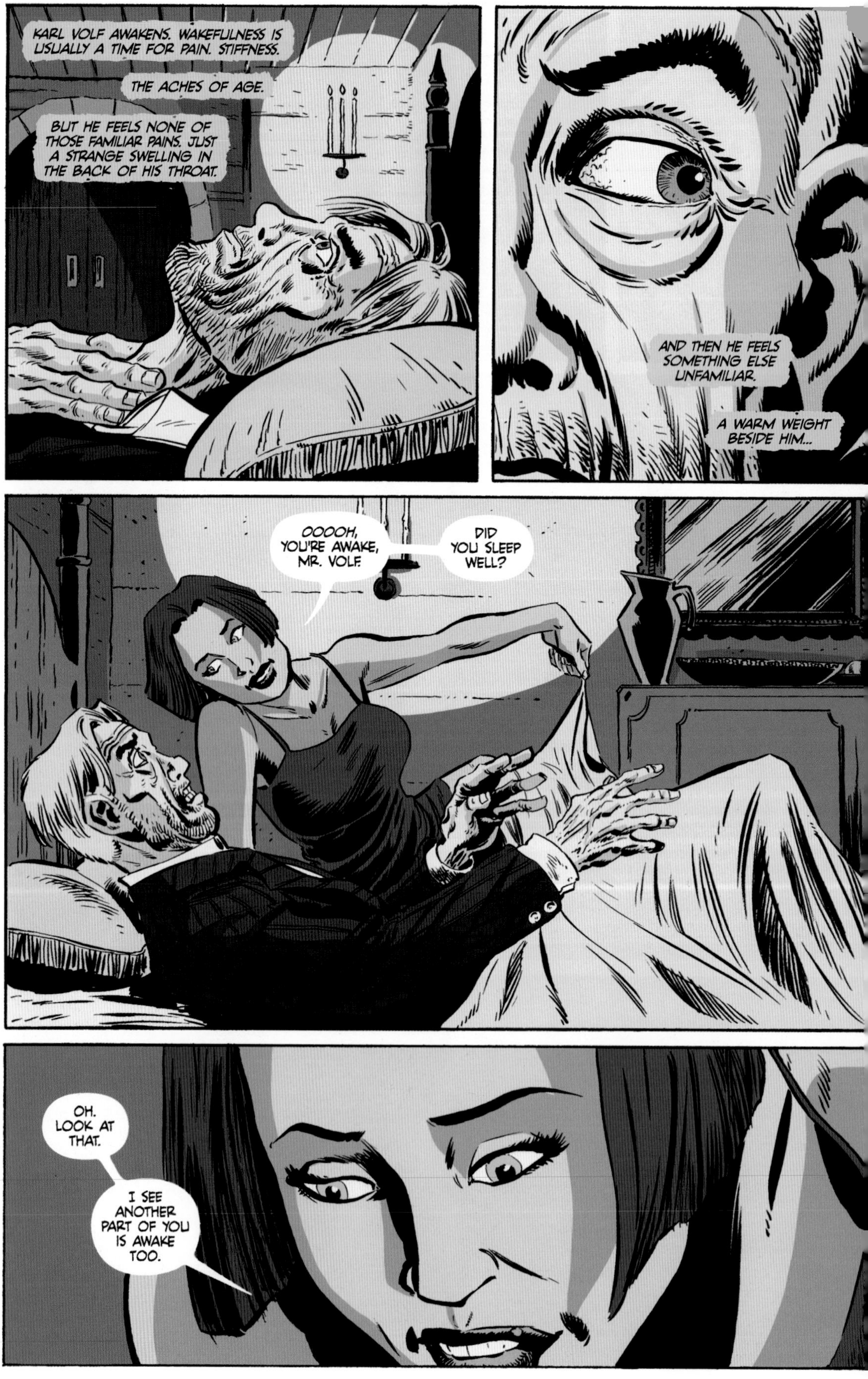

KARL VOLF AWAKENS. WAKEFULNESS IS USUALLY A TIME FOR PAIN. STIFFNESS.
THE ACHES OF AGE.
BUT HE FEELS NONE OF THOSE FAMILIAR PAINS. JUST A STRANGE SWELLING IN THE BACK OF HIS THROAT.
AND THEN HE FEELS SOMETHING ELSE UNFAMILIAR.
A WARM WEIGHT BESIDE HIM...
OOOOH, YOU'RE AWAKE, MR. VOLF.
DID YOU SLEEP WELL?
OH. LOOK AT THAT.
I SEE ANOTHER PART OF YOU IS AWAKE TOO.

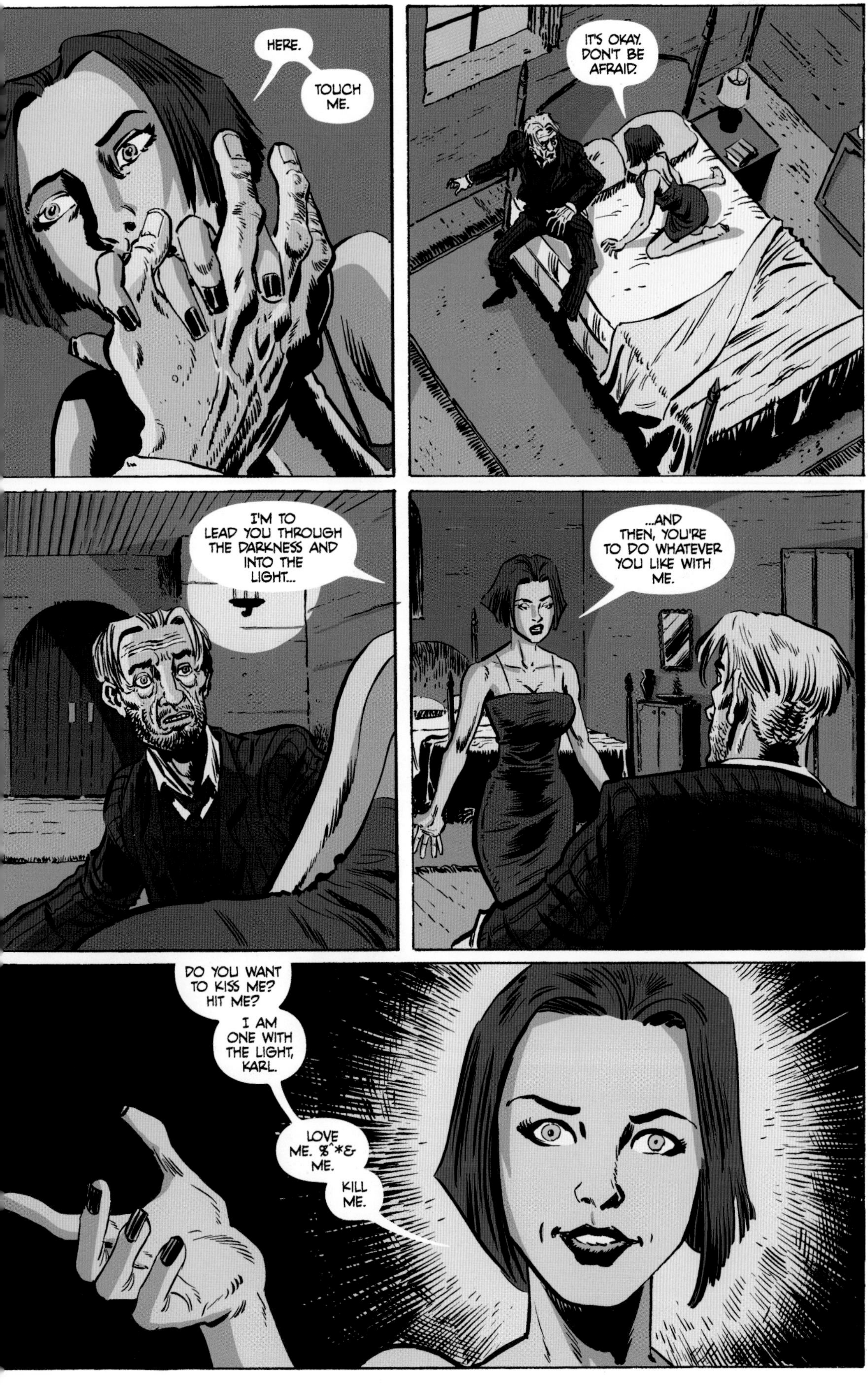
HERE.
TOUCH ME.
IT'S OKAY. DON'T BE AFRAID.
I'M TO LEAD YOU THROUGH THE DARKNESS AND INTO THE LIGHT...
...AND THEN, YOU'RE TO DO WHATEVER YOU LIKE WITH ME.
DO YOU WANT TO KISS ME? HIT ME?
I AM ONE WITH THE LIGHT, KARL.
LOVE ME. %^*& ME.
KILL ME.

I'M A GIFT. A PRESENT TO REMIND YOU THAT LONELINESS IS UNNECESSARY.

TOGETHERNESS IS TRUE BEAUTY.

KARL VOLF IS USED TO DOUBT.

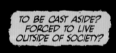

HE SPENT HIS ADULT LIFE FIGHTING FOR THE GOOD OF HUMANITY.

BATTLING BACK AGAINST THE THINGS IN THE SHADOWS.

AND FOR WHAT?

TO BE CAST ASIDE? FORCED TO LIVE OUTSIDE OF SOCIETY?

TO BE DEEMED UNTOUCHABLE?

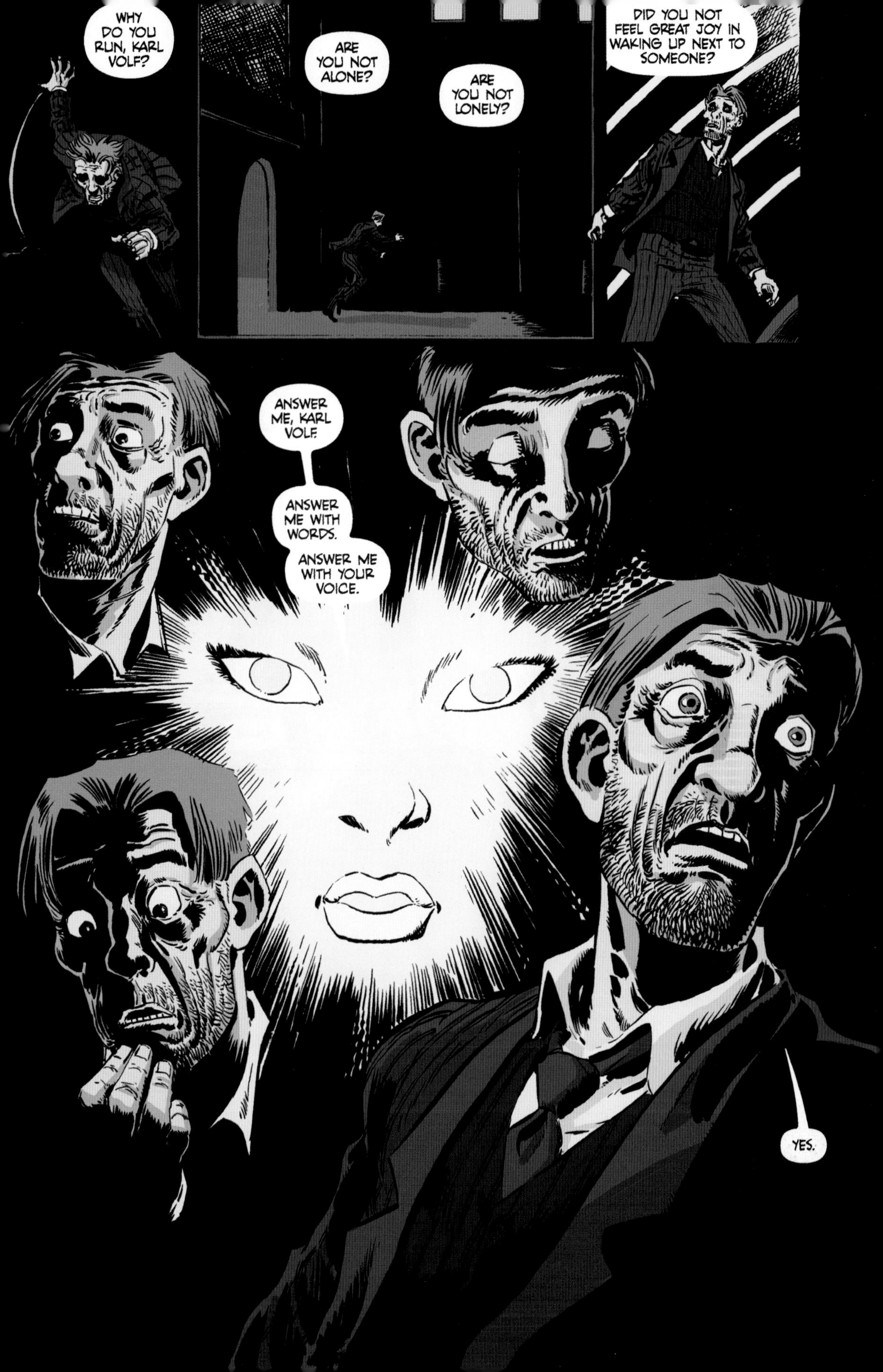
WHY DO YOU RUN, KARL VOLF?
ARE YOU NOT ALONE?
ARE YOU NOT LONELY?
DID YOU NOT FEEL GREAT JOY IN WAKING UP NEXT TO SOMEONE?
ANSWER ME, KARL VOLF.
ANSWER ME WITH WORDS.
ANSWER ME WITH YOUR VOICE.
YES.

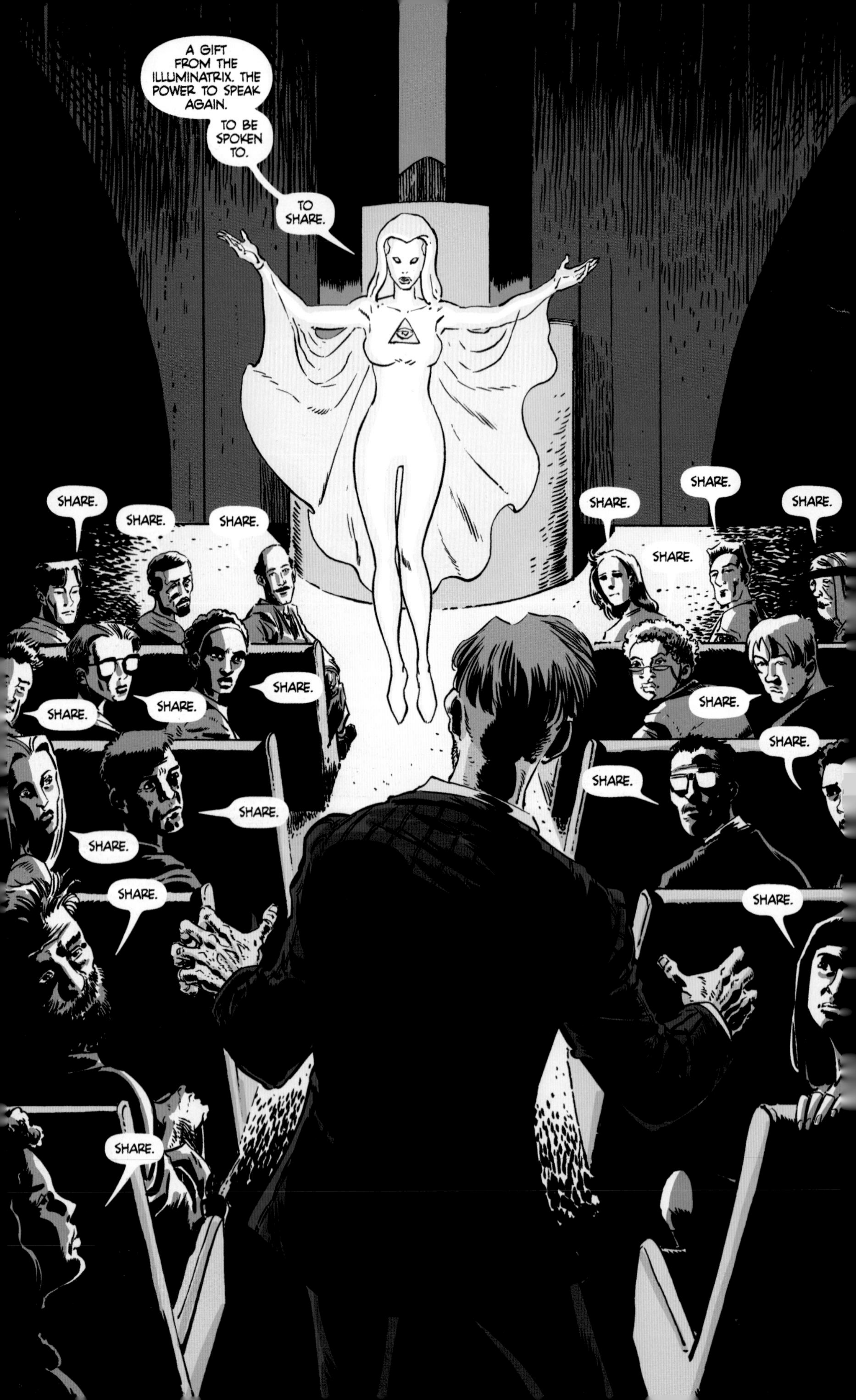
A GIFT FROM THE ILLUMINATRIX. THE POWER TO SPEAK AGAIN.
TO BE SPOKEN TO.
TO SHARE.
SHARE.
SHARE.
SHARE.
SHARE.
SHARE.
SHARE.
SHARE.
SHARE.
SHARE.
SHARE.
SHARE.
SHARE.
SHARE.
SHARE.
SHARE.
SHARE.
SHARE.
SHARE.

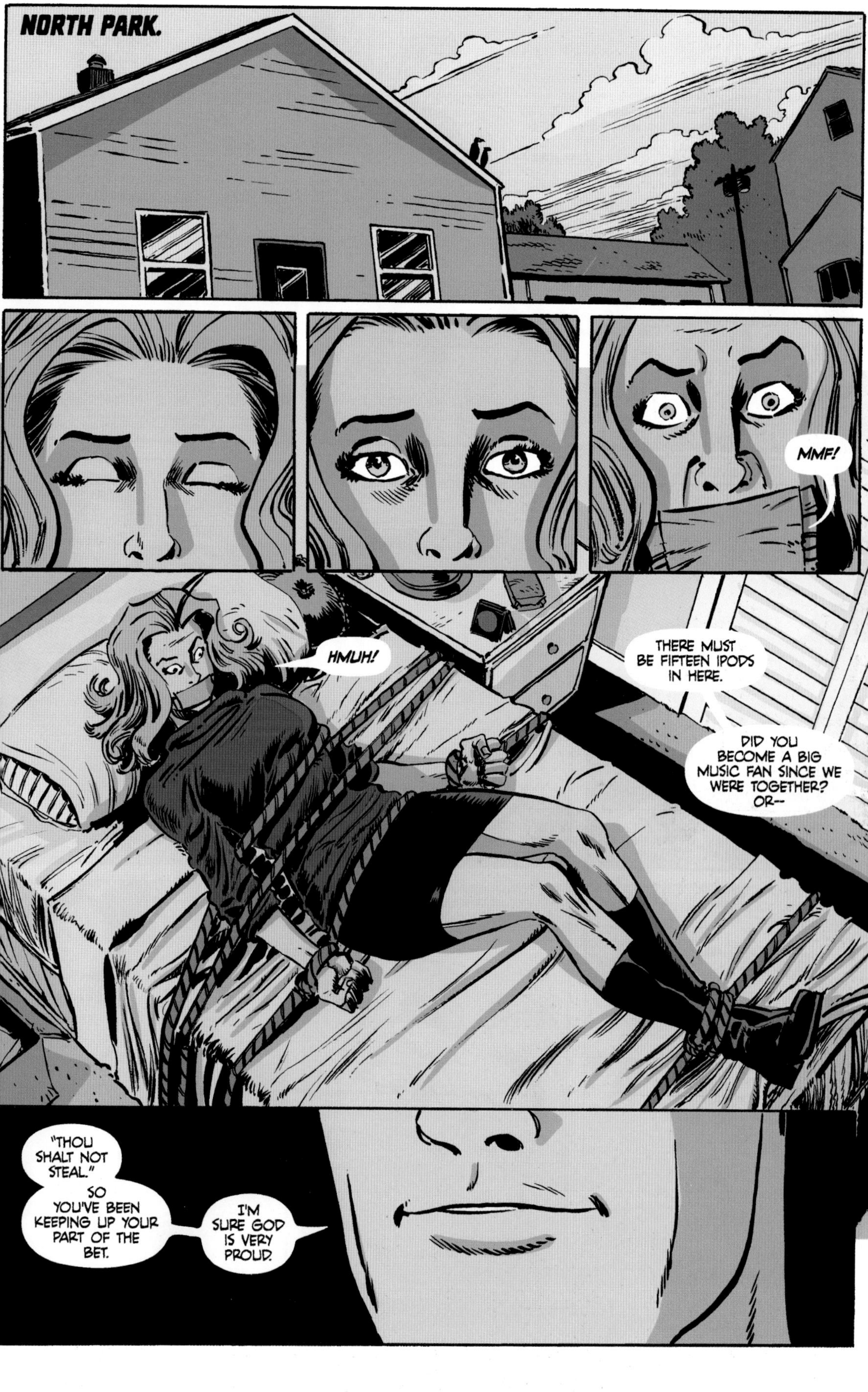
NORTH PARK.
MMF!
HMUH!
THERE MUST BE FIFTEEN IPODS IN HERE.
DID YOU BECOME A BIG MUSIC FAN SINCE WE WERE TOGETHER? OR--
"THOU SHALT NOT STEAL."
SO YOU'VE BEEN KEEPING UP YOUR PART OF THE BET.
I'M SURE GOD IS VERY PROUD.

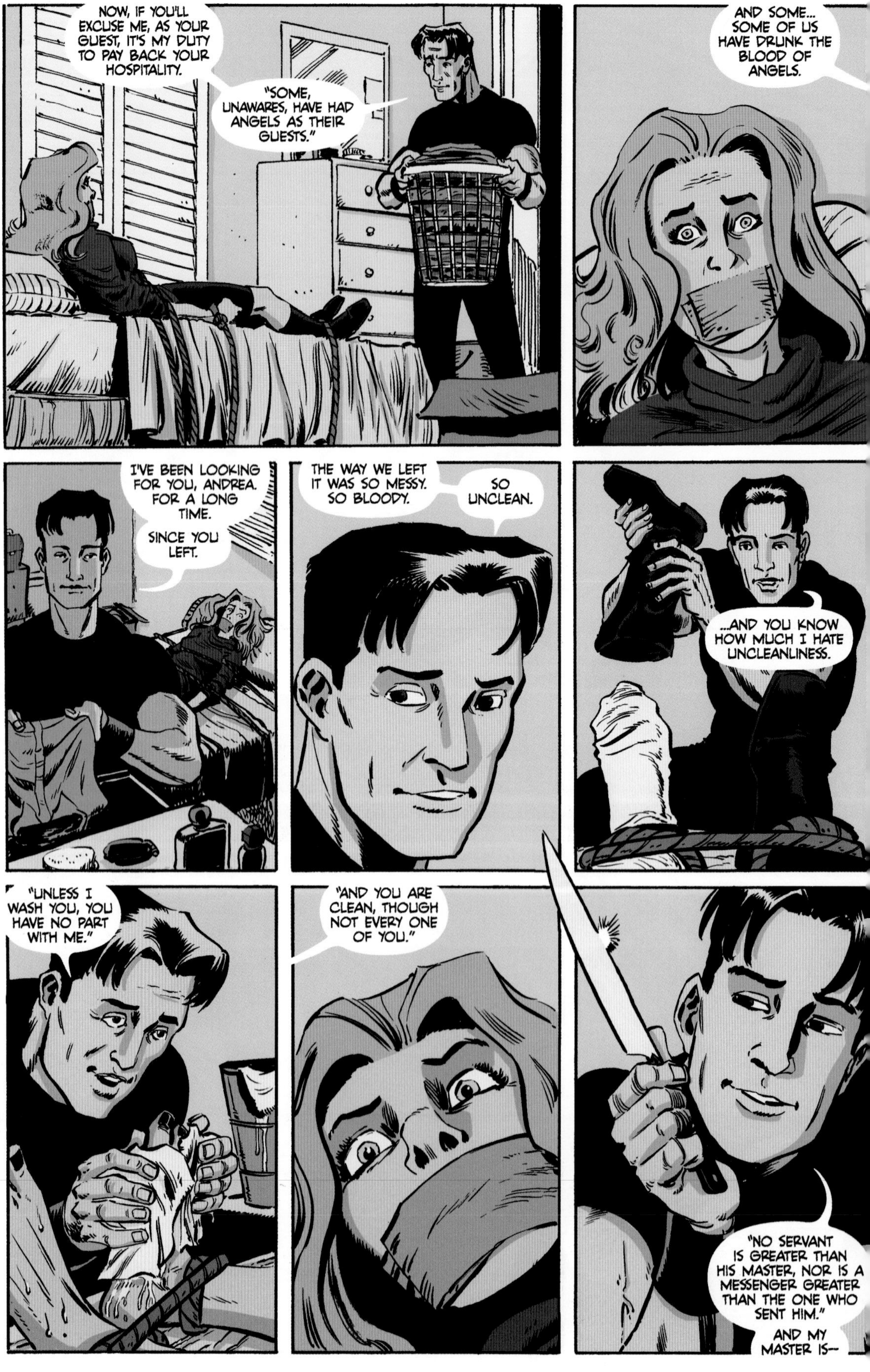
NOW, IF YOU'LL EXCUSE ME, AS YOUR GUEST, IT'S MY DUTY TO PAY BACK YOUR HOSPITALITY.
"SOME, UNAWARES, HAVE HAD ANGELS AS THEIR GUESTS."
AND SOME... SOME OF US HAVE DRUNK THE BLOOD OF ANGELS.
I'VE BEEN LOOKING FOR YOU, ANDREA. FOR A LONG TIME.
SINCE YOU LEFT.
THE WAY WE LEFT IT WAS SO MESSY. SO BLOODY.
SO UNCLEAN.
...AND YOU KNOW HOW MUCH I HATE UNCLEANLINESS.
"UNLESS I WASH YOU, YOU HAVE NO PART WITH ME."
"AND YOU ARE CLEAN, THOUGH NOT EVERY ONE OF YOU."
"NO SERVANT IS GREATER THAN HIS MASTER, NOR IS A MESSENGER GREATER THAN THE ONE WHO SENT HIM."
AND MY MASTER IS--

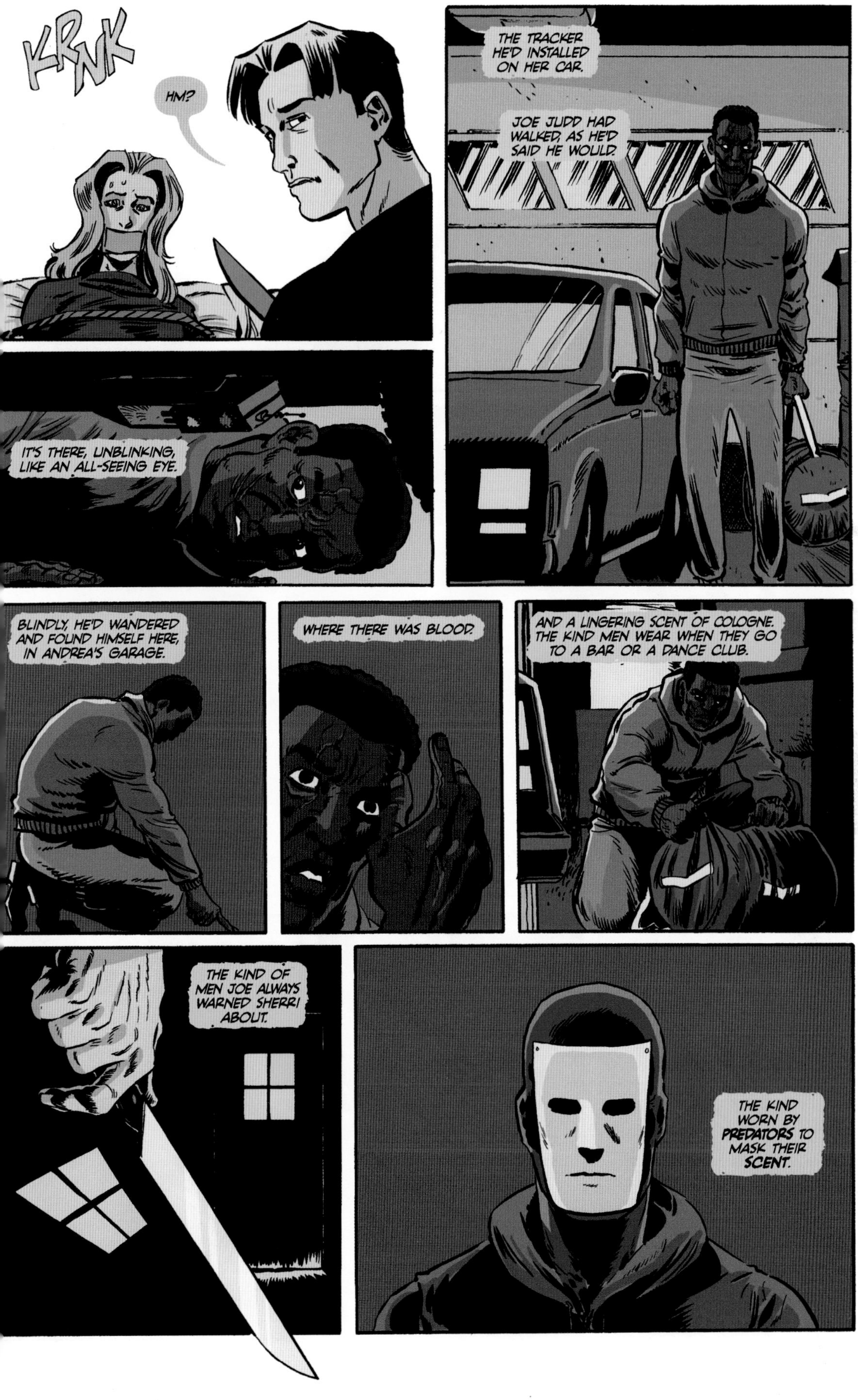
KRNK
HM?
THE TRACKER HE'D INSTALLED ON HER CAR.
JOE JUDD HAD WALKED, AS HE'D SAID HE WOULD.
IT'S THERE, UNBLINKING, LIKE AN ALL-SEEING EYE.
BLINDLY, HE'D WANDERED AND FOUND HIMSELF HERE, IN ANDREA'S GARAGE.
WHERE THERE WAS BLOOD.
AND A LINGERING SCENT OF COLOGNE. THE KIND MEN WEAR WHEN THEY GO TO A BAR OR A DANCE CLUB.
THE KIND OF MEN JOE ALWAYS WARNED SHERRI ABOUT.
THE KIND WORN BY PREDATORS TO MASK THEIR SCENT.

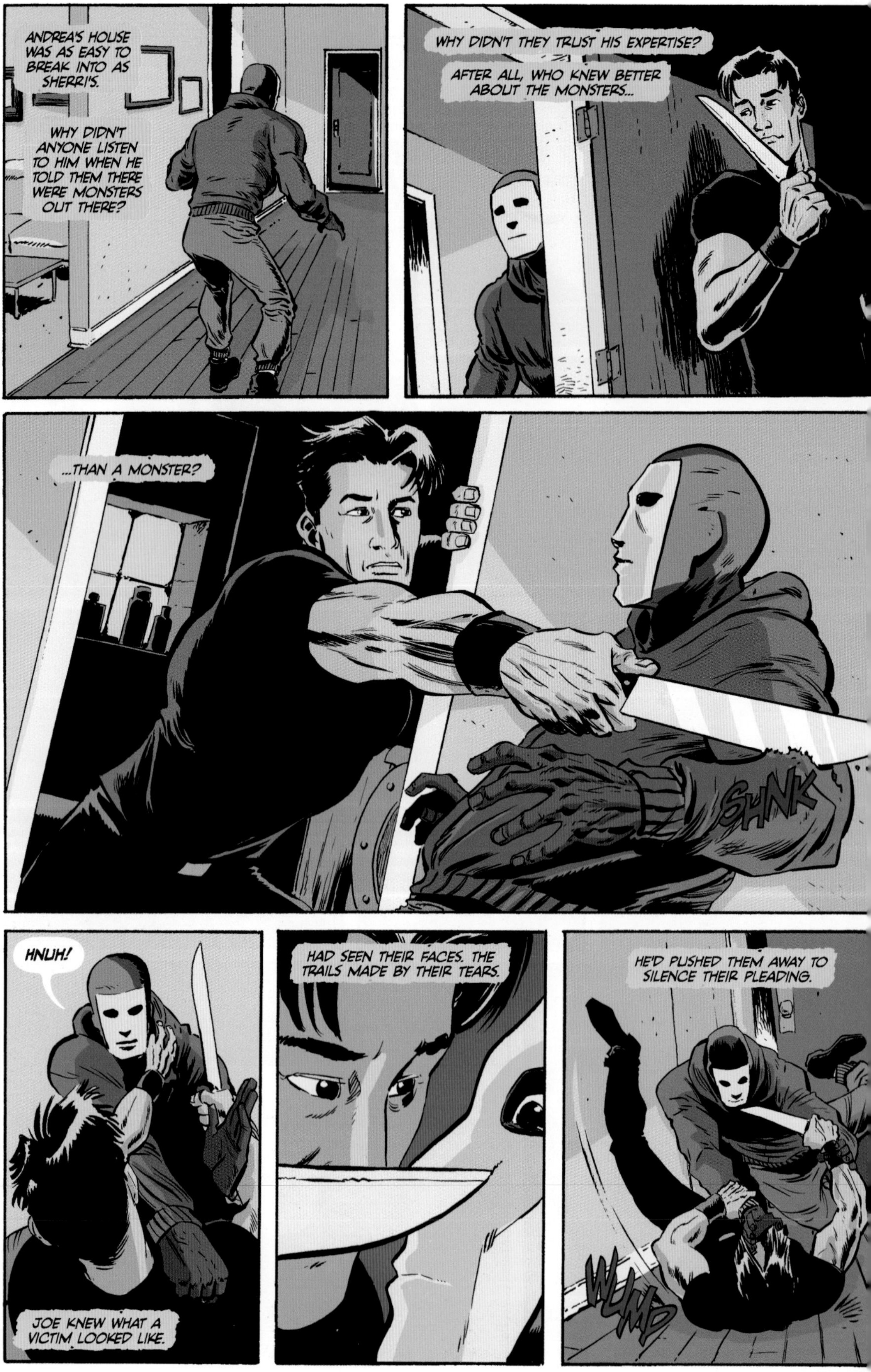
ANDREA'S HOUSE WAS AS EASY TO BREAK INTO AS SHERRI'S.
WHY DIDN'T ANYONE LISTEN TO HIM WHEN HE TOLD THEM THERE WERE MONSTERS OUT THERE?
WHY DIDN'T THEY TRUST HIS EXPERTISE?
AFTER ALL, WHO KNEW BETTER ABOUT THE MONSTERS...
...THAN A MONSTER?
SHNK
HNUH!
JOE KNEW WHAT A VICTIM LOOKED LIKE.
HAD SEEN THEIR FACES. THE TRAILS MADE BY THEIR TEARS.
HE'D PUSHED THEM AWAY TO SILENCE THEIR PLEADING.
WUMP

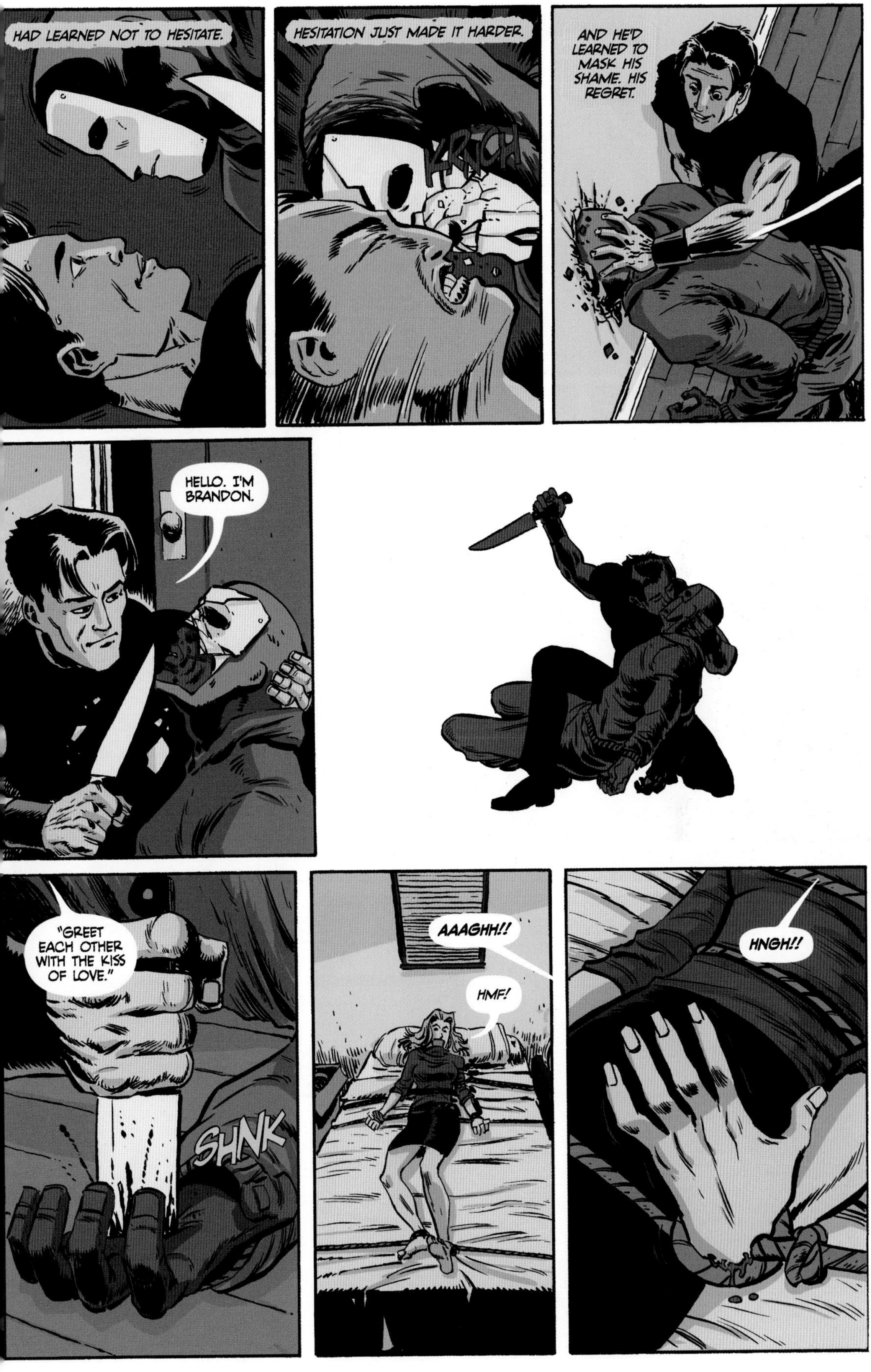
HAD LEARNED NOT TO HESITATE.
HESITATION JUST MADE IT HARDER.
KRICH
AND HE'D LEARNED TO MASK HIS SHAME. HIS REGRET.
HELLO. I'M BRANDON.
"GREET EACH OTHER WITH THE KISS OF LOVE."
SHNK
AAAGHH!!
HMF!
HNGH!!

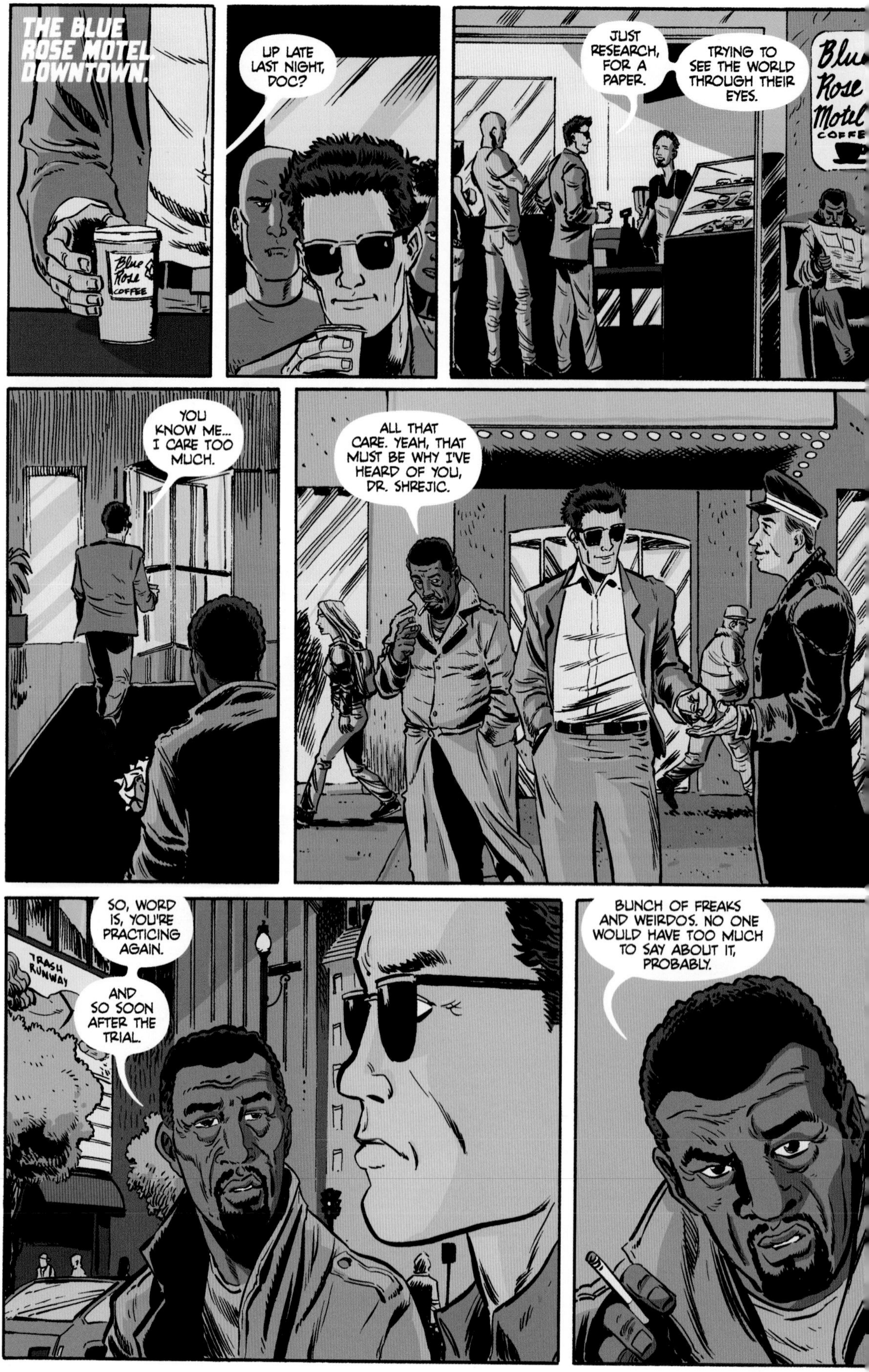

THE BLUE ROSE MOTEL DOWNTOWN.
Blue Rose COFFEE
UP LATE LAST NIGHT, DOC?
JUST RESEARCH, FOR A PAPER.
TRYING TO SEE THE WORLD THROUGH THEIR EYES.
Blue Rose Motel COFFEE
YOU KNOW ME... I CARE TOO MUCH.
ALL THAT CARE. YEAH, THAT MUST BE WHY I'VE HEARD OF YOU, DR. SHREJIC.
SO, WORD IS, YOU'RE PRACTICING AGAIN.
AND SO SOON AFTER THE TRIAL.
TRASH RUNWAY
BUNCH OF FREAKS AND WEIRDOS. NO ONE WOULD HAVE TOO MUCH TO SAY ABOUT IT, PROBABLY.

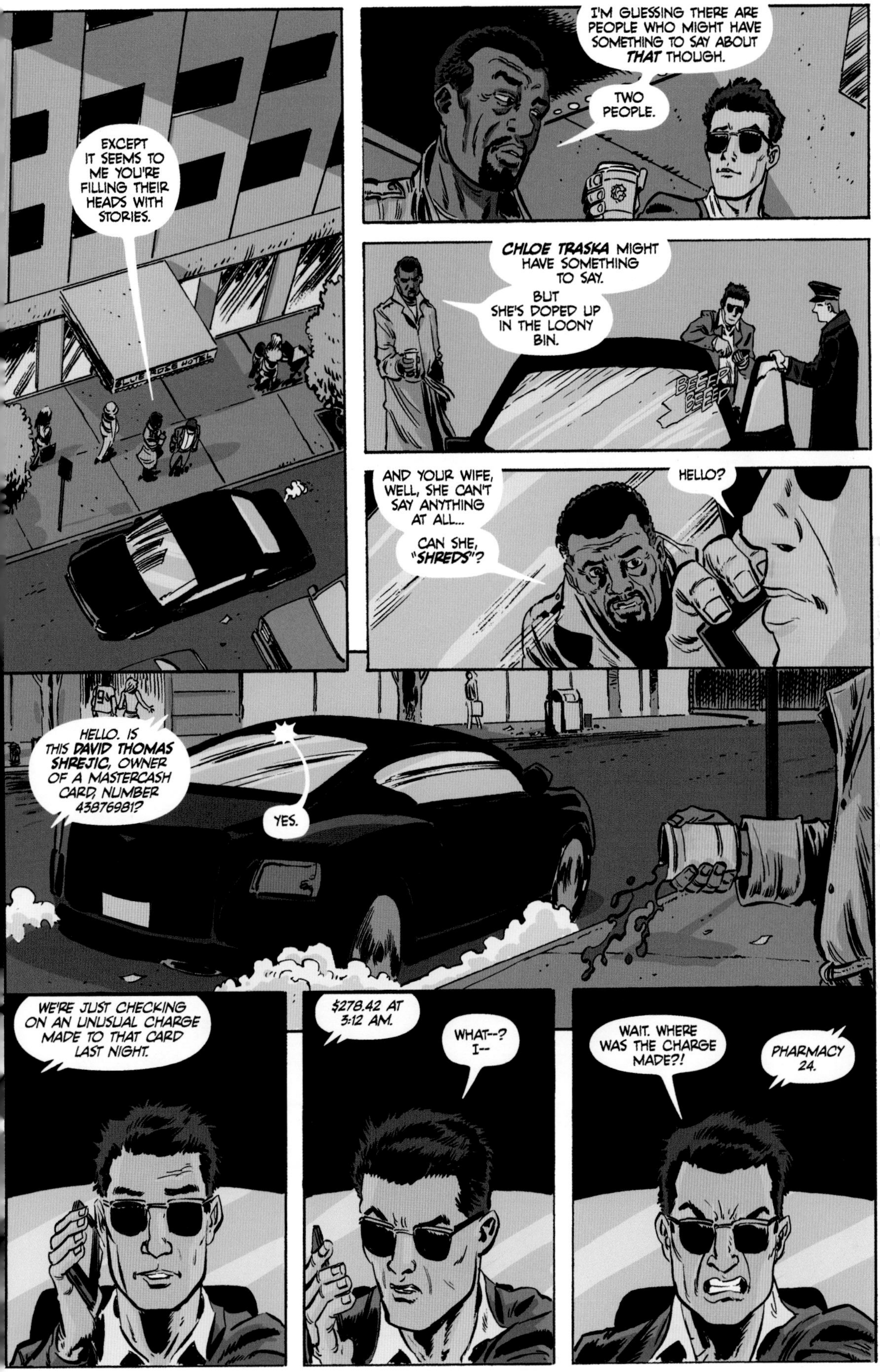

EXCEPT IT SEEMS TO ME YOU'RE FILLING THEIR HEADS WITH STORIES.
I'M GUESSING THERE ARE PEOPLE WHO MIGHT HAVE SOMETHING TO SAY ABOUT THAT THOUGH.
TWO PEOPLE.
CHLOE TRASKA MIGHT HAVE SOMETHING TO SAY.
BUT SHE'S DOPED UP IN THE LOONY BIN.
BEEEP BEEP
AND YOUR WIFE, WELL, SHE CAN'T SAY ANYTHING AT ALL...
CAN SHE, "SHREDS"?
HELLO?
HELLO. IS THIS DAVID THOMAS SHREJIC, OWNER OF A MASTERCASH CARD, NUMBER 43876981?
YES.
WE'RE JUST CHECKING ON AN UNUSUAL CHARGE MADE TO THAT CARD LAST NIGHT.
$278.42 AT 3:12 AM.
WHAT--? I--
WAIT. WHERE WAS THE CHARGE MADE?!
PHARMACY 24.

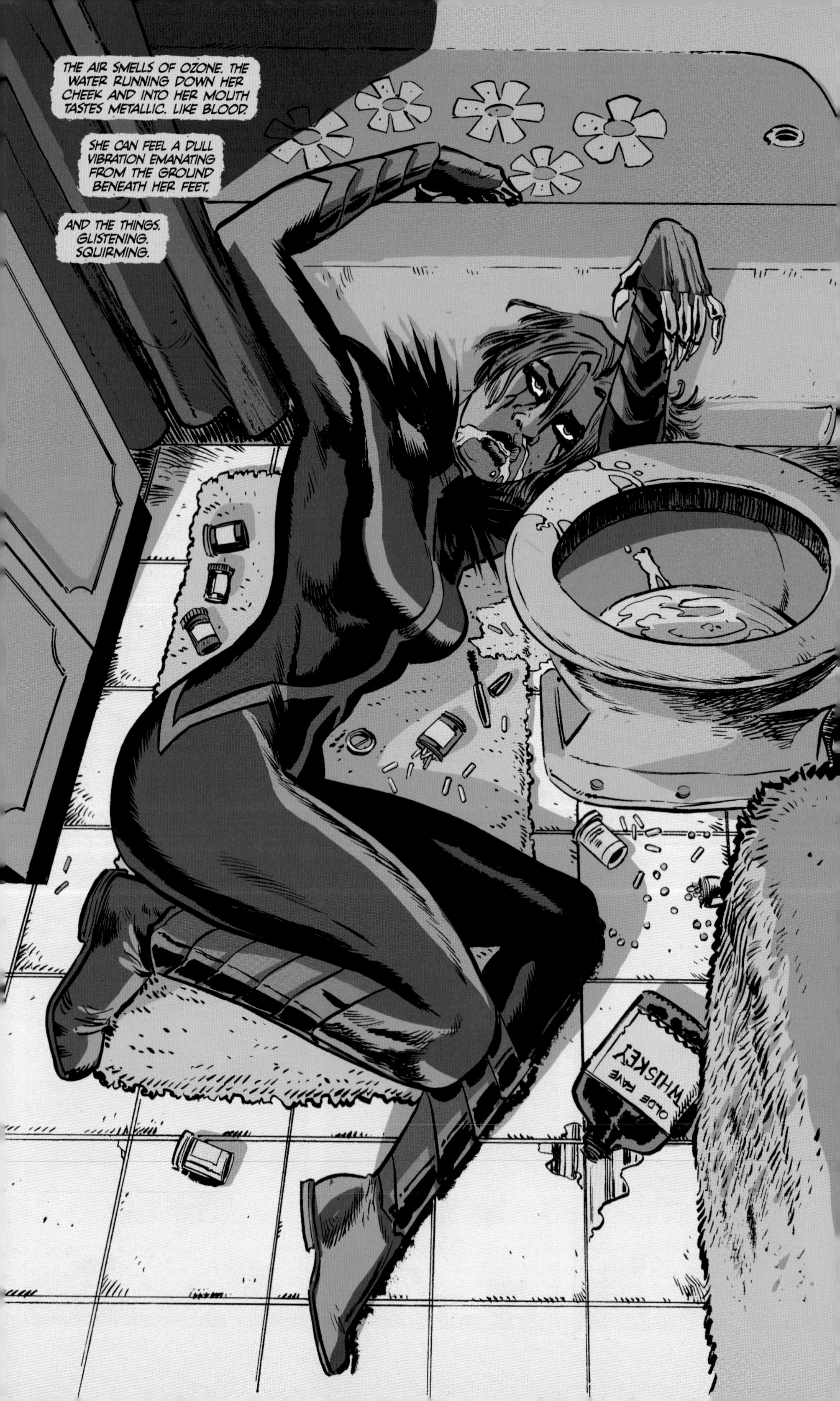
THE AIR SMELLS OF OZONE. THE WATER RUNNING DOWN HER CHEEK AND INTO HER MOUTH TASTES METALLIC. LIKE BLOOD.
SHE CAN FEEL A DULL VIBRATION EMANATING FROM THE GROUND BENEATH HER FEET.
AND THE THINGS. GLISTENING. SQUIRMING.
OLDE FAVE WHISKEY

CITIZEN VS CUTTER

FRIDAY, JUNE 6 AT 8PM CIVIC CENTER BOX OF

C. BRUNNER 'CO

SUND4WNERS™

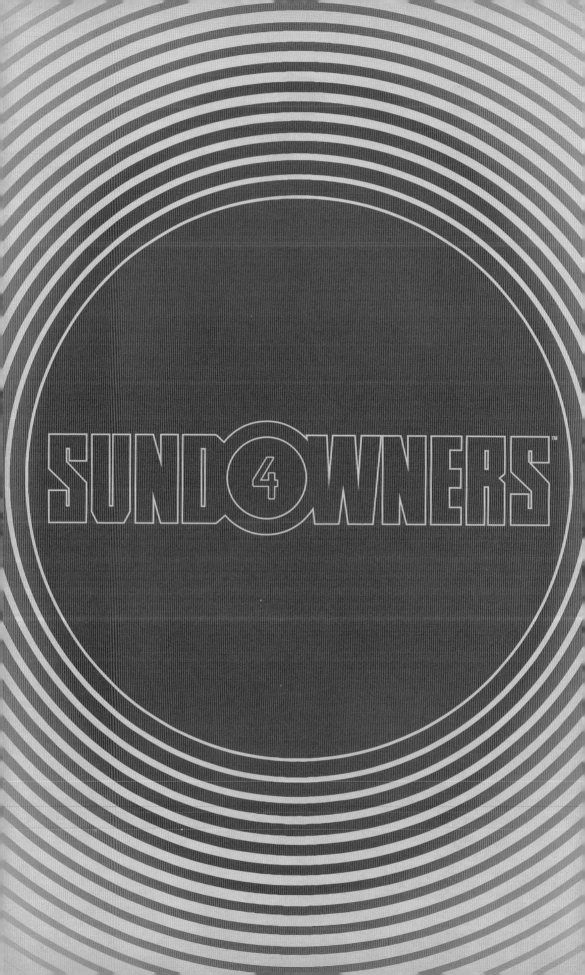

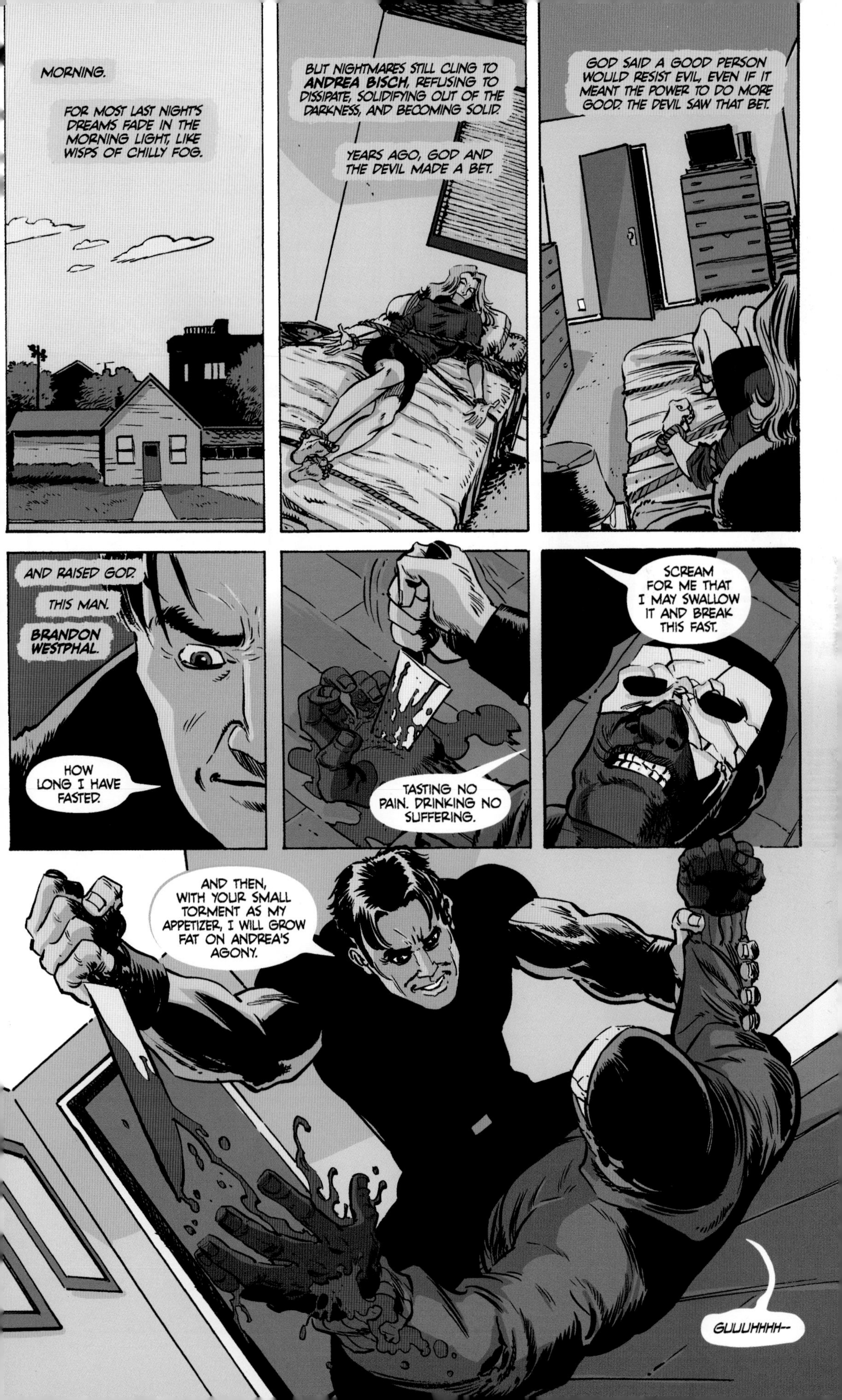
MORNING.
FOR MOST LAST NIGHT'S DREAMS FADE IN THE MORNING LIGHT, LIKE WISPS OF CHILLY FOG.
BUT NIGHTMARES STILL CLING TO ANDREA BISCH, REFUSING TO DISSIPATE, SOLIDIFYING OUT OF THE DARKNESS, AND BECOMING SOLID.
YEARS AGO, GOD AND THE DEVIL MADE A BET.
GOD SAID A GOOD PERSON WOULD RESIST EVIL, EVEN IF IT MEANT THE POWER TO DO MORE GOOD. THE DEVIL SAW THAT BET.
AND RAISED GOD.
THIS MAN.
BRANDON WESTPHAL.
HOW LONG I HAVE FASTED.
TASTING NO PAIN. DRINKING NO SUFFERING.
SCREAM FOR ME THAT I MAY SWALLOW IT AND BREAK THIS FAST.
AND THEN, WITH YOUR SMALL TORMENT AS MY APPETIZER, I WILL GROW FAT ON ANDREA'S AGONY.
GUUUHHHH--

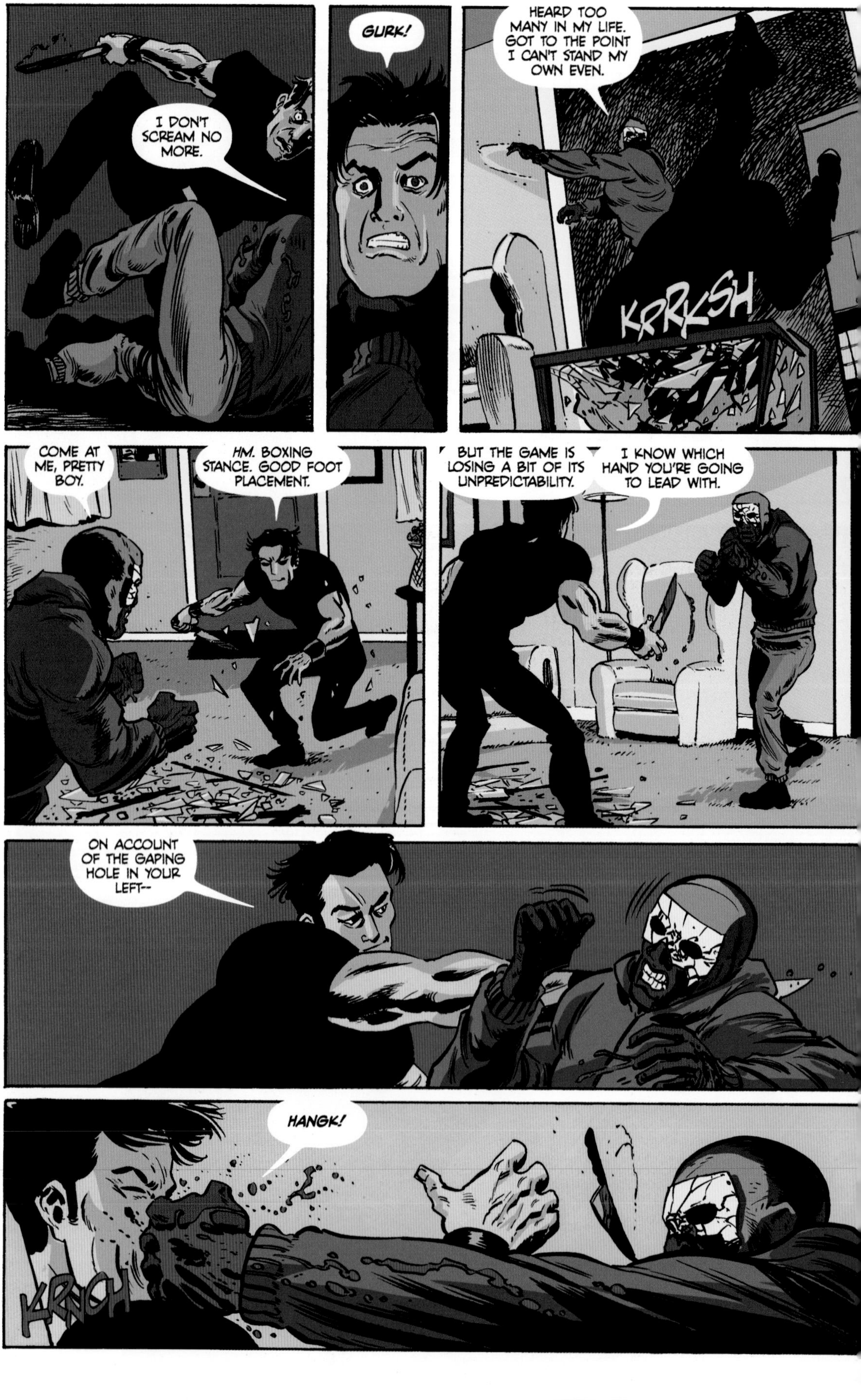
I DON'T SCREAM NO MORE.
GURK!
HEARD TOO MANY IN MY LIFE. GOT TO THE POINT I CAN'T STAND MY OWN EVEN.
KRRKSH
COME AT ME, PRETTY BOY.
HM. BOXING STANCE. GOOD FOOT PLACEMENT.
BUT THE GAME IS LOSING A BIT OF ITS UNPREDICTABILITY.
I KNOW WHICH HAND YOU'RE GOING TO LEAD WITH.
ON ACCOUNT OF THE GAPING HOLE IN YOUR LEFT--
HANGK!
KRNCH

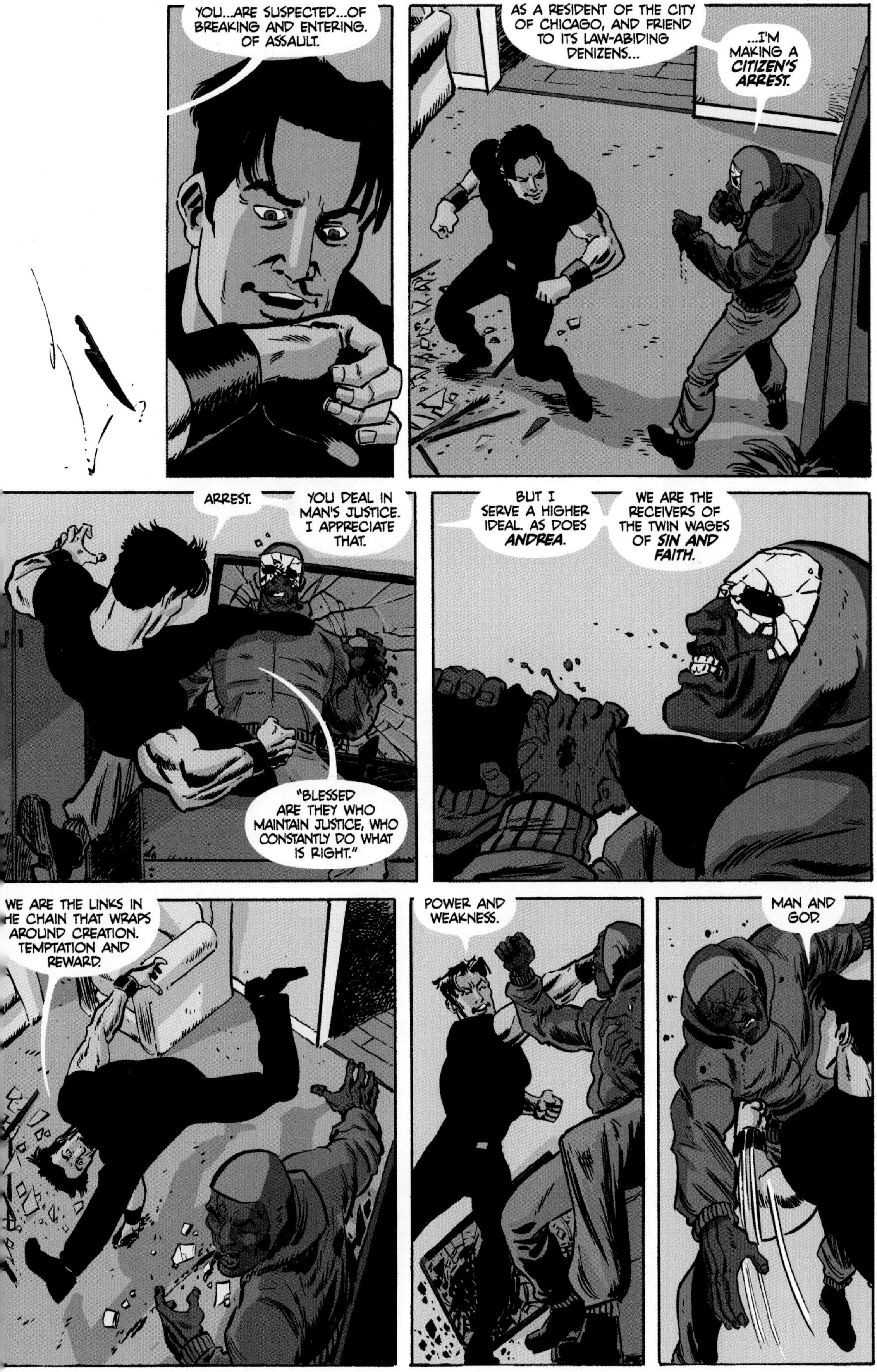
YOU...ARE SUSPECTED...OF BREAKING AND ENTERING. OF ASSAULT.
AS A RESIDENT OF THE CITY OF CHICAGO, AND FRIEND TO ITS LAW-ABIDING DENIZENS...
...I'M MAKING A CITIZEN'S ARREST.
ARREST.
YOU DEAL IN MAN'S JUSTICE. I APPRECIATE THAT.
"BLESSED ARE THEY WHO MAINTAIN JUSTICE, WHO CONSTANTLY DO WHAT IS RIGHT."
BUT I SERVE A HIGHER IDEAL. AS DOES ANDREA.
WE ARE THE RECEIVERS OF THE TWIN WAGES OF SIN AND FAITH.
WE ARE THE LINKS IN HE CHAIN THAT WRAPS AROUND CREATION. TEMPTATION AND REWARD.
POWER AND WEAKNESS.
MAN AND GOD.

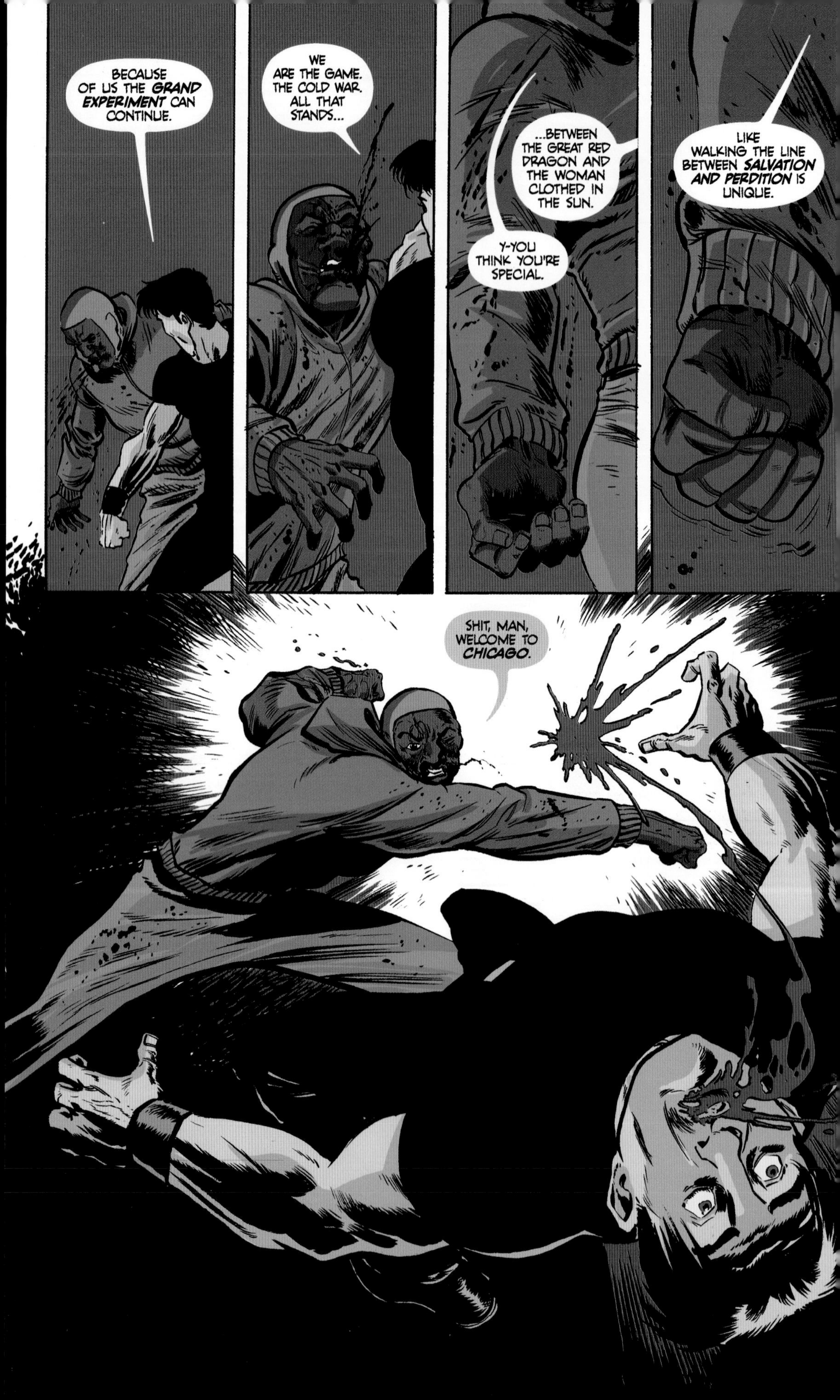
BECAUSE OF US THE GRAND EXPERIMENT CAN CONTINUE.
WE ARE THE GAME. THE COLD WAR. ALL THAT STANDS...
...BETWEEN THE GREAT RED DRAGON AND THE WOMAN CLOTHED IN THE SUN.
Y-YOU THINK YOU'RE SPECIAL.
LIKE WALKING THE LINE BETWEEN SALVATION AND PERDITION IS UNIQUE.
SHIT, MAN, WELCOME TO CHICAGO.

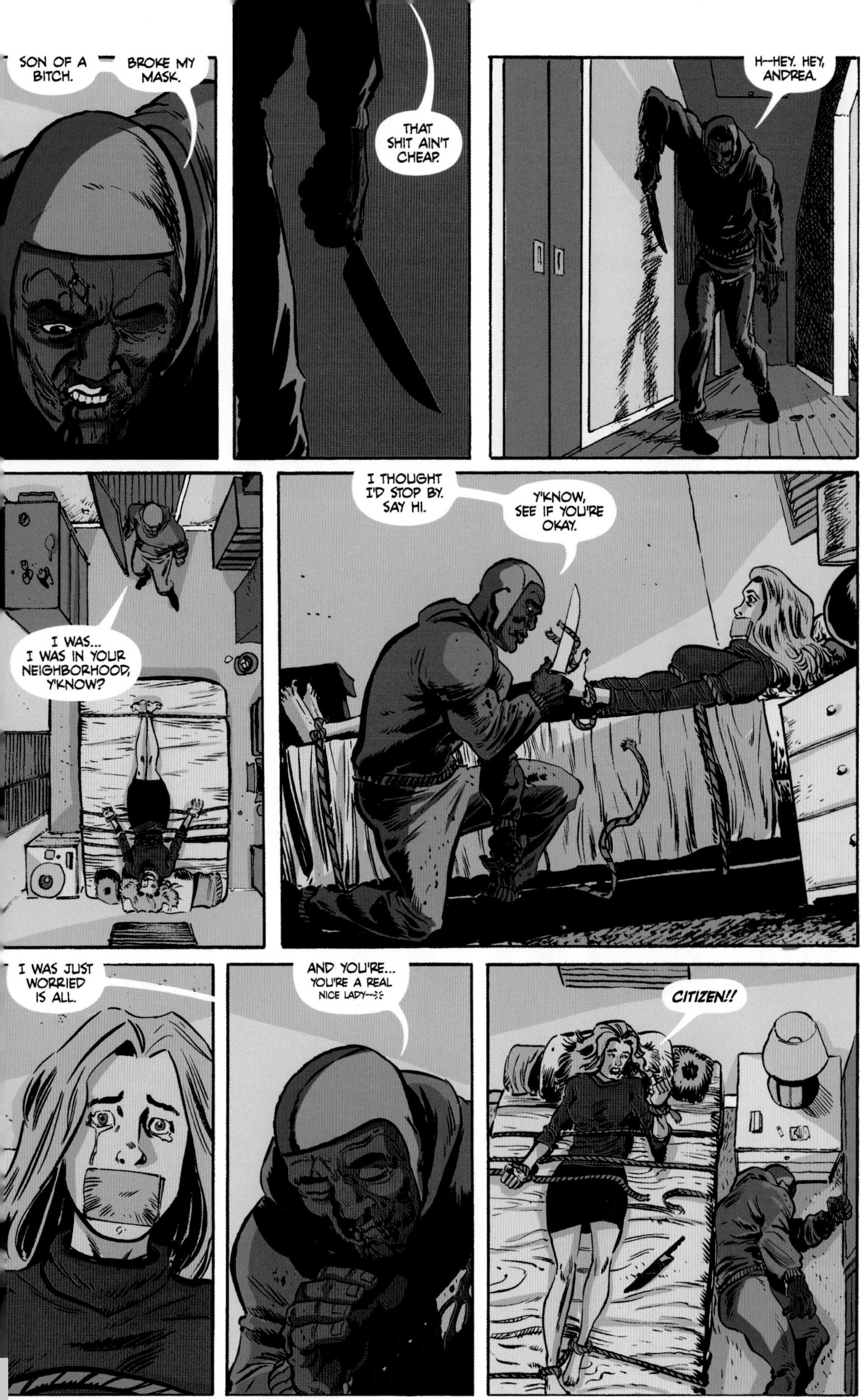
SON OF A BITCH.
BROKE MY MASK.
THAT SHIT AIN'T CHEAP.
H--HEY. HEY, ANDREA.
I WAS... I WAS IN YOUR NEIGHBORHOOD, Y'KNOW?
I THOUGHT I'D STOP BY. SAY HI.
Y'KNOW, SEE IF YOU'RE OKAY.
I WAS JUST WORRIED IS ALL.
AND YOU'RE... YOU'RE A REAL NICE LADY--
CITIZEN!!

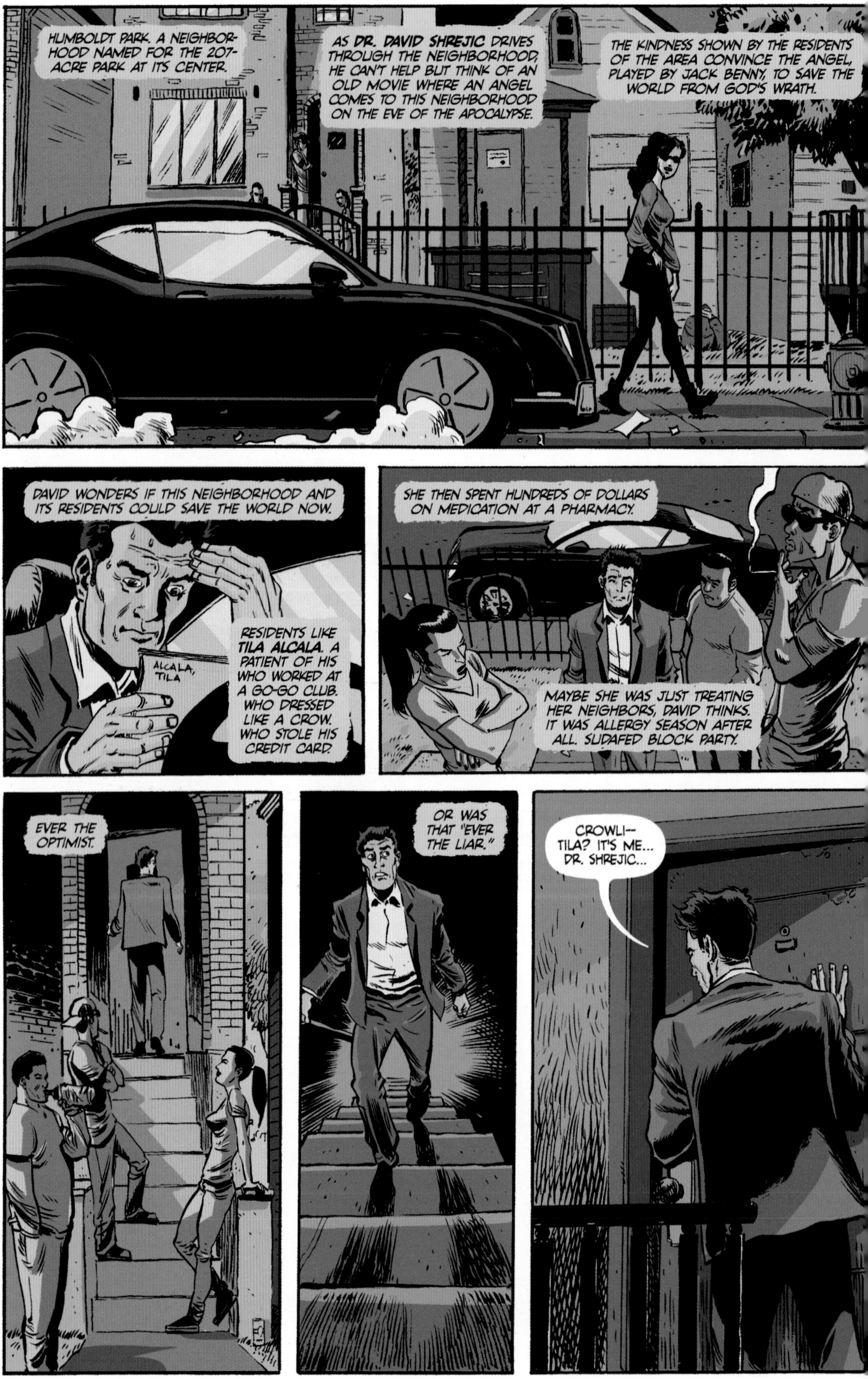
HUMBOLDT PARK. A NEIGHBORHOOD NAMED FOR THE 207-ACRE PARK AT ITS CENTER.
AS DR. DAVID SHREJIC DRIVES THROUGH THE NEIGHBORHOOD, HE CAN'T HELP BUT THINK OF AN OLD MOVIE WHERE AN ANGEL COMES TO THIS NEIGHBORHOOD ON THE EVE OF THE APOCALYPSE.
THE KINDNESS SHOWN BY THE RESIDENTS OF THE AREA CONVINCE THE ANGEL, PLAYED BY JACK BENNY, TO SAVE THE WORLD FROM GOD'S WRATH.
DAVID WONDERS IF THIS NEIGHBORHOOD AND ITS RESIDENTS COULD SAVE THE WORLD NOW.
ALCALA, TILA
RESIDENTS LIKE TILA ALCALA. A PATIENT OF HIS WHO WORKED AT A GO-GO CLUB. WHO DRESSED LIKE A CROW. WHO STOLE HIS CREDIT CARD.
SHE THEN SPENT HUNDREDS OF DOLLARS ON MEDICATION AT A PHARMACY.
MAYBE SHE WAS JUST TREATING HER NEIGHBORS, DAVID THINKS. IT WAS ALLERGY SEASON AFTER ALL. SUDAFED BLOCK PARTY.
EVER THE OPTIMIST.
OR WAS THAT "EVER THE LIAR."
CROWLI-- TILA? IT'S ME... DR. SHREJIC...

DAVID CAN TELL SOMETHING IS WRONG THE SECOND HE OPENS HER UNLOCKED DOOR.

THE AIR SMELLS SICKLY SWEET AND ACRID.

VOMIT.

OVERDOSE.

TILA! WAKE UP!

COME ON, YOU DUMB BITCH. WAKE UP!

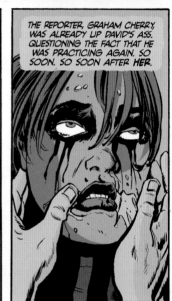

THE REPORTER, GRAHAM CHERRY, WAS ALREADY UP DAVID'S ASS. QUESTIONING THE FACT THAT HE WAS PRACTICING AGAIN. SO SOON. SO SOON AFTER HER.

IF SOMEONE TRACED HIS CALL... IF HE WAS FOUND IN THE APARTMENT OF ANOTHER GIRL—

BEST NOT TO RISK IT. SOMEONE WOULD BE ALONG, HE THOUGHT.

SOMEONE WOULD CALL TILA AN AMBULANCE. TAKE HER TO THE HOSPITAL.

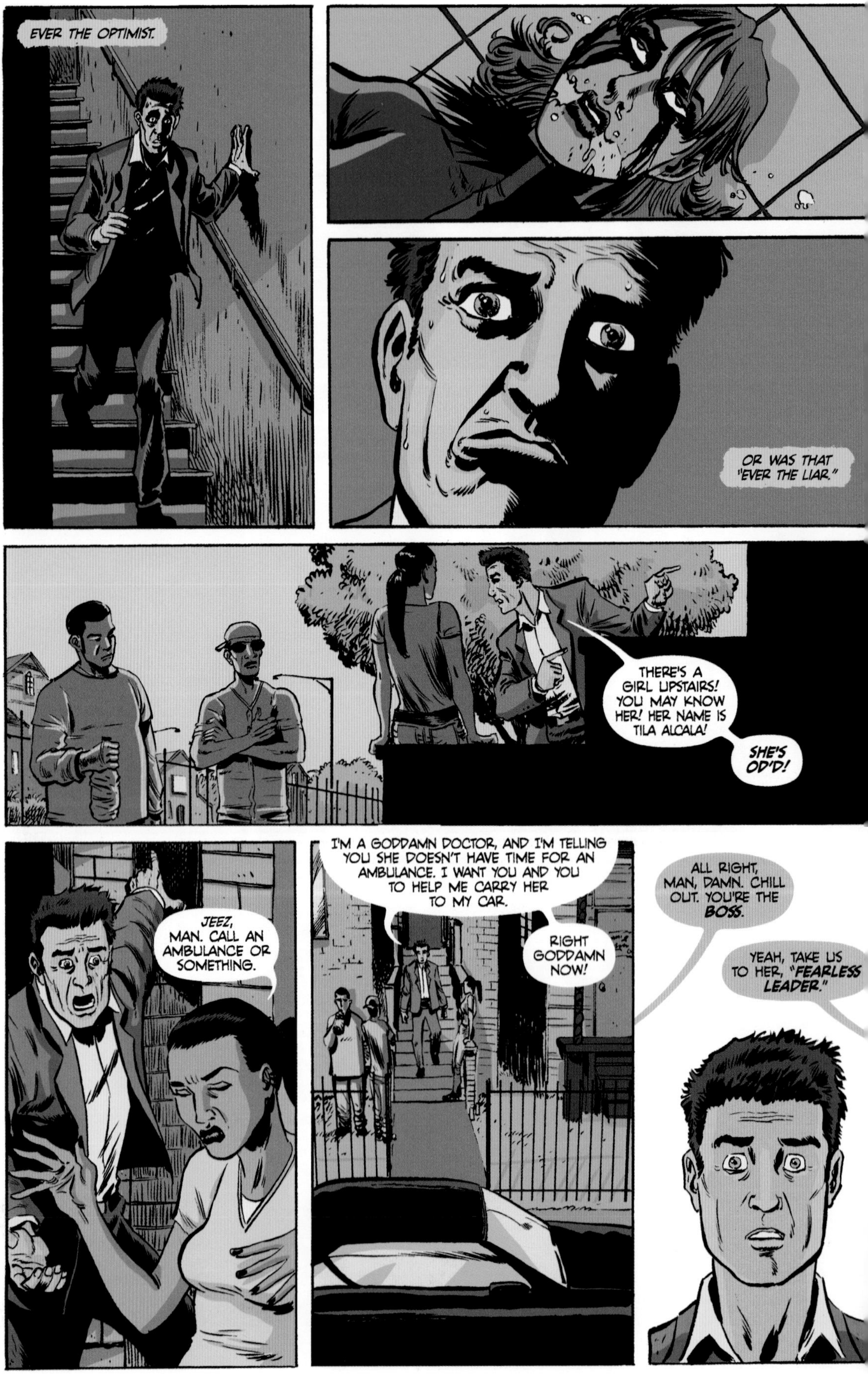
EVER THE OPTIMIST.
OR WAS THAT "EVER THE LIAR."
THERE'S A GIRL UPSTAIRS! YOU MAY KNOW HER! HER NAME IS TILA ALCALA!
SHE'S OD'D!
JEEZ, MAN. CALL AN AMBULANCE OR SOMETHING.
I'M A GODDAMN DOCTOR, AND I'M TELLING YOU SHE DOESN'T HAVE TIME FOR AN AMBULANCE. I WANT YOU AND YOU TO HELP ME CARRY HER TO MY CAR.
RIGHT GODDAMN NOW!
ALL RIGHT, MAN, DAMN. CHILL OUT. YOU'RE THE BOSS.
YEAH, TAKE US TO HER, "FEARLESS LEADER."

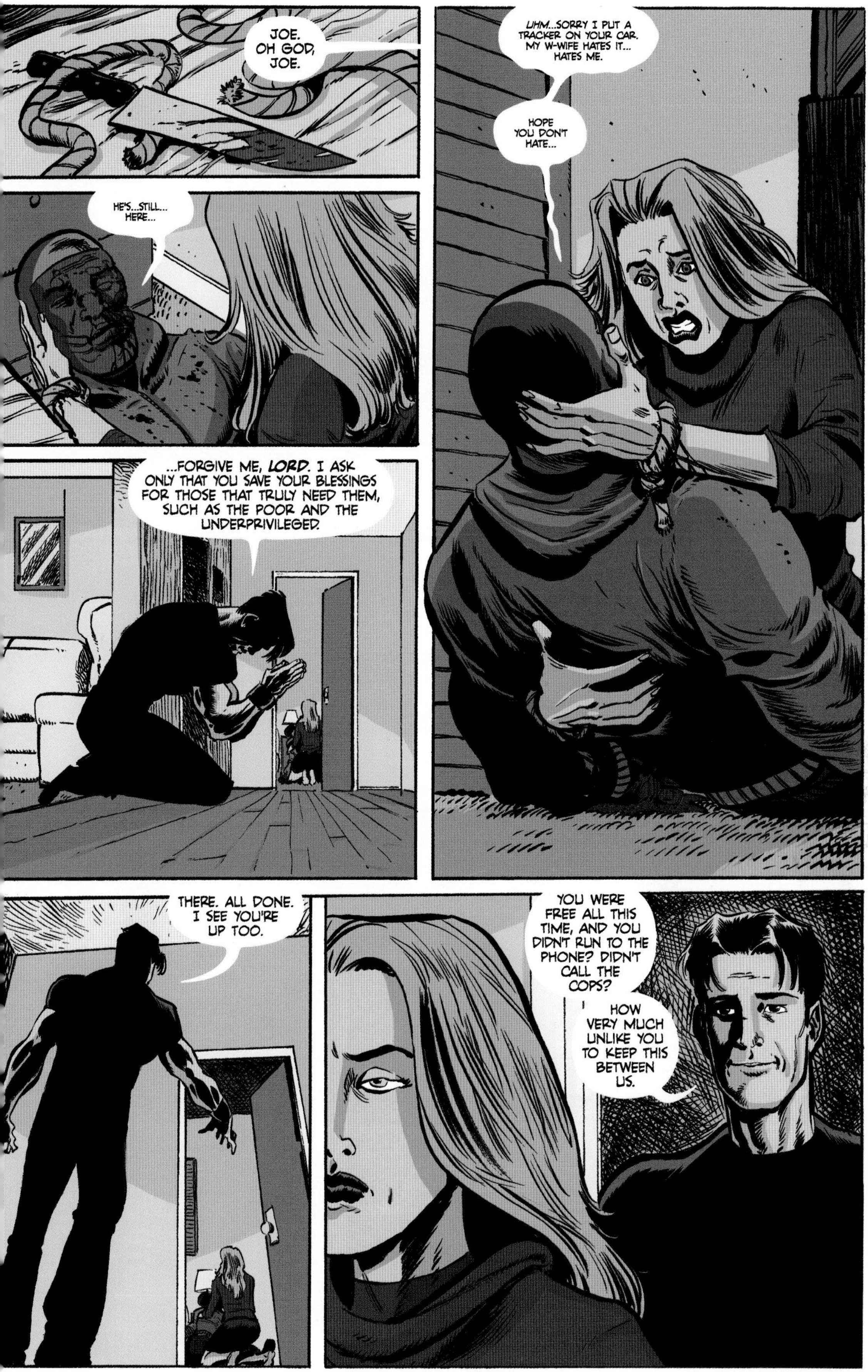
JOE. OH GOD, JOE.
UHM...SORRY I PUT A TRACKER ON YOUR CAR. MY W-WIFE HATES IT... HATES ME.
HOPE YOU DON'T HATE...
HE'S...STILL... HERE...
...FORGIVE ME, LORD. I ASK ONLY THAT YOU SAVE YOUR BLESSINGS FOR THOSE THAT TRULY NEED THEM, SUCH AS THE POOR AND THE UNDERPRIVILEGED.
THERE. ALL DONE. I SEE YOU'RE UP TOO.
YOU WERE FREE ALL THIS TIME, AND YOU DIDN'T RUN TO THE PHONE? DIDN'T CALL THE COPS?
HOW VERY MUCH UNLIKE YOU TO KEEP THIS BETWEEN US.

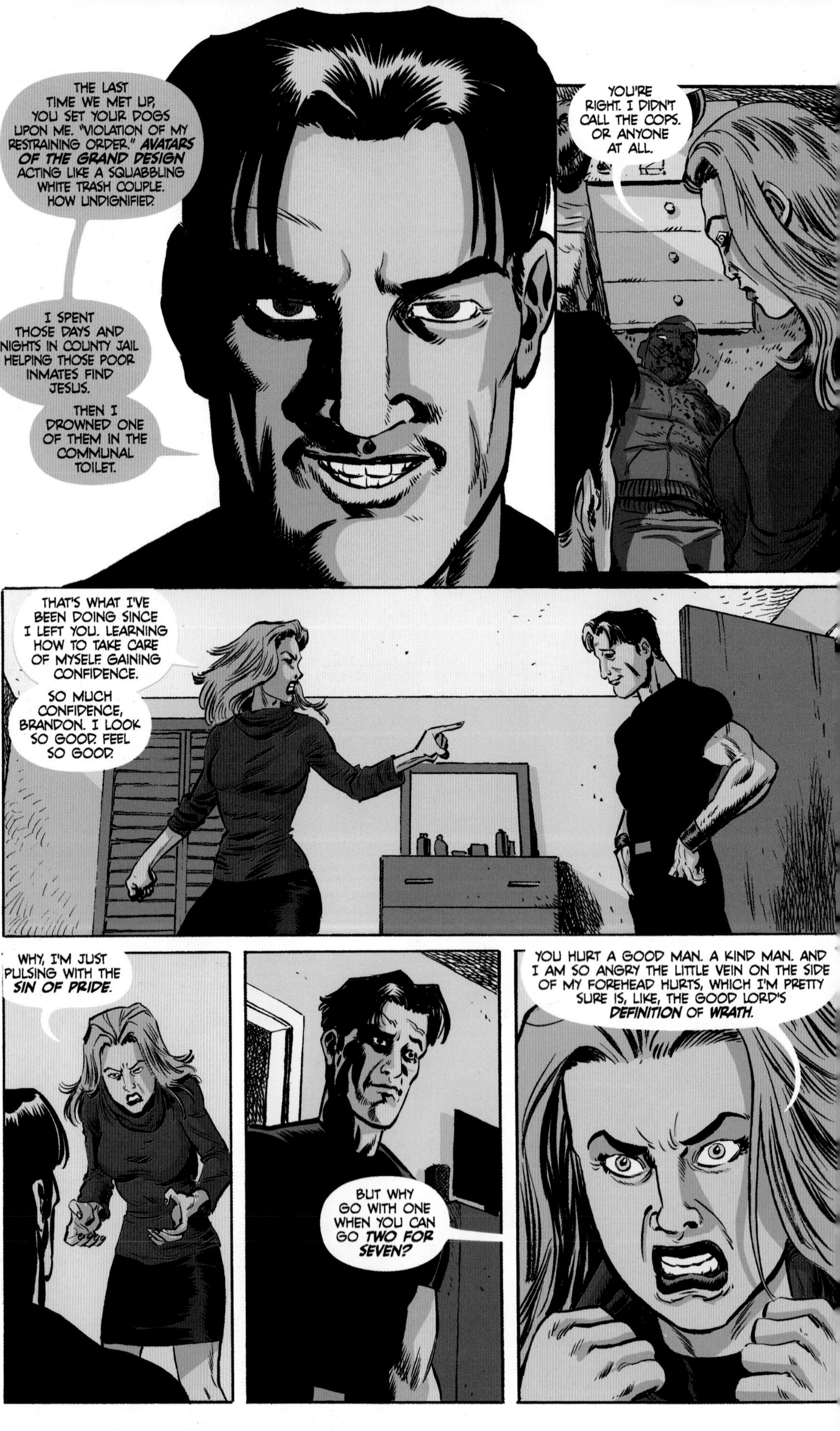

THE LAST TIME WE MET UP, YOU SET YOUR DOGS UPON ME. "VIOLATION OF MY RESTRAINING ORDER." ***AVATARS OF THE GRAND DESIGN*** ACTING LIKE A SQUABBLING WHITE TRASH COUPLE. HOW UNDIGNIFIED.
I SPENT THOSE DAYS AND NIGHTS IN COUNTY JAIL HELPING THOSE POOR INMATES FIND JESUS.
THEN I DROWNED ONE OF THEM IN THE COMMUNAL TOILET.
YOU'RE RIGHT. I DIDN'T CALL THE COPS. OR ANYONE AT ALL.
THAT'S WHAT I'VE BEEN DOING SINCE I LEFT YOU. LEARNING HOW TO TAKE CARE OF MYSELF. GAINING CONFIDENCE.
SO MUCH CONFIDENCE, BRANDON. I LOOK SO GOOD. FEEL SO GOOD.
WHY, I'M JUST PULSING WITH THE ***SIN OF PRIDE.***
BUT WHY GO WITH ONE WHEN YOU CAN GO ***TWO FOR SEVEN?***
YOU HURT A GOOD MAN. A KIND MAN. AND I AM SO ANGRY THE LITTLE VEIN ON THE SIDE OF MY FOREHEAD HURTS, WHICH I'M PRETTY SURE IS, LIKE, THE GOOD LORD'S ***DEFINITION*** OF ***WRATH.***

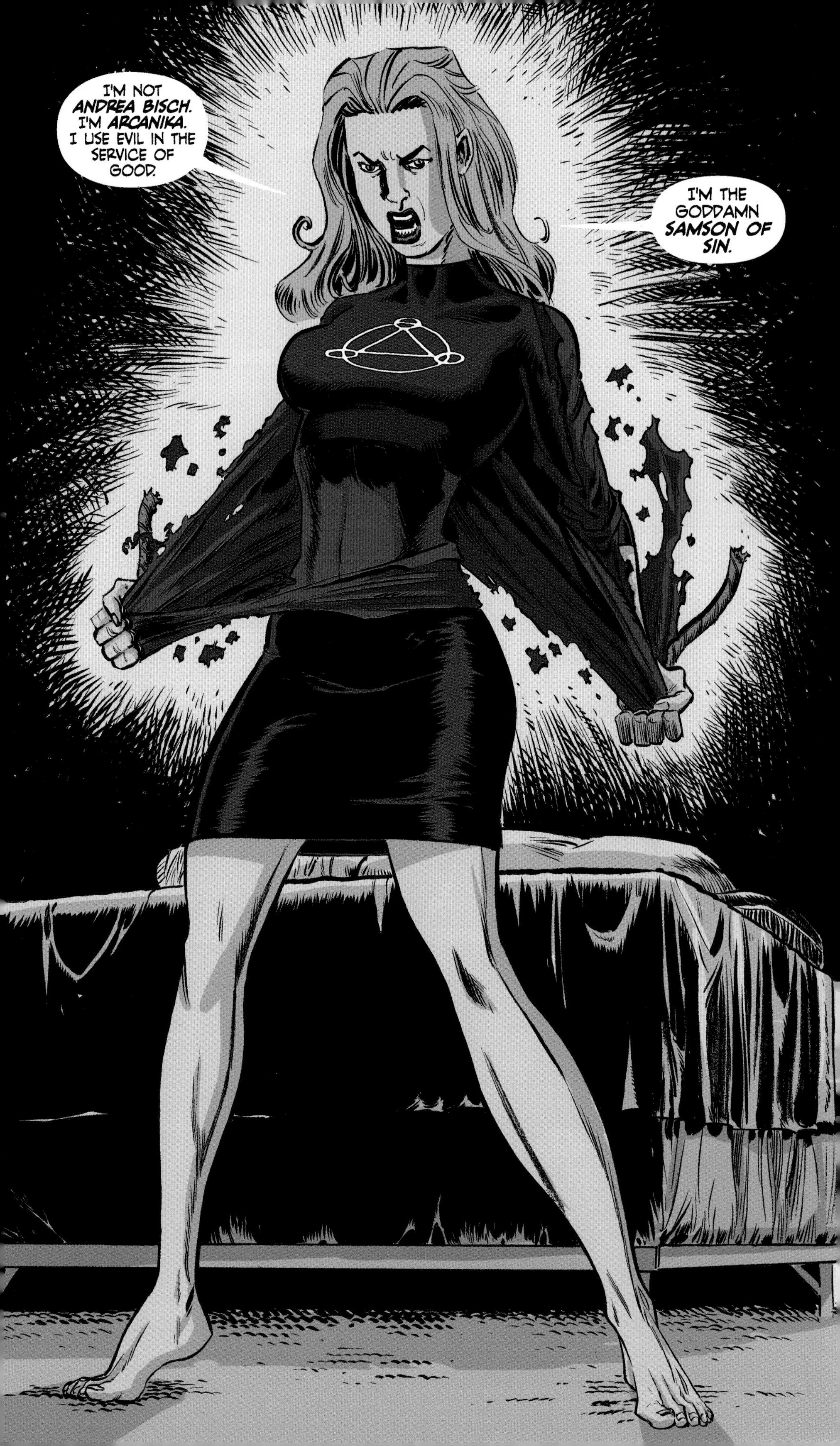
I'M NOT ANDREA BISCH. I'M ARCANIKA. I USE EVIL IN THE SERVICE OF GOOD.
I'M THE GODDAMN SAMSON OF SIN.

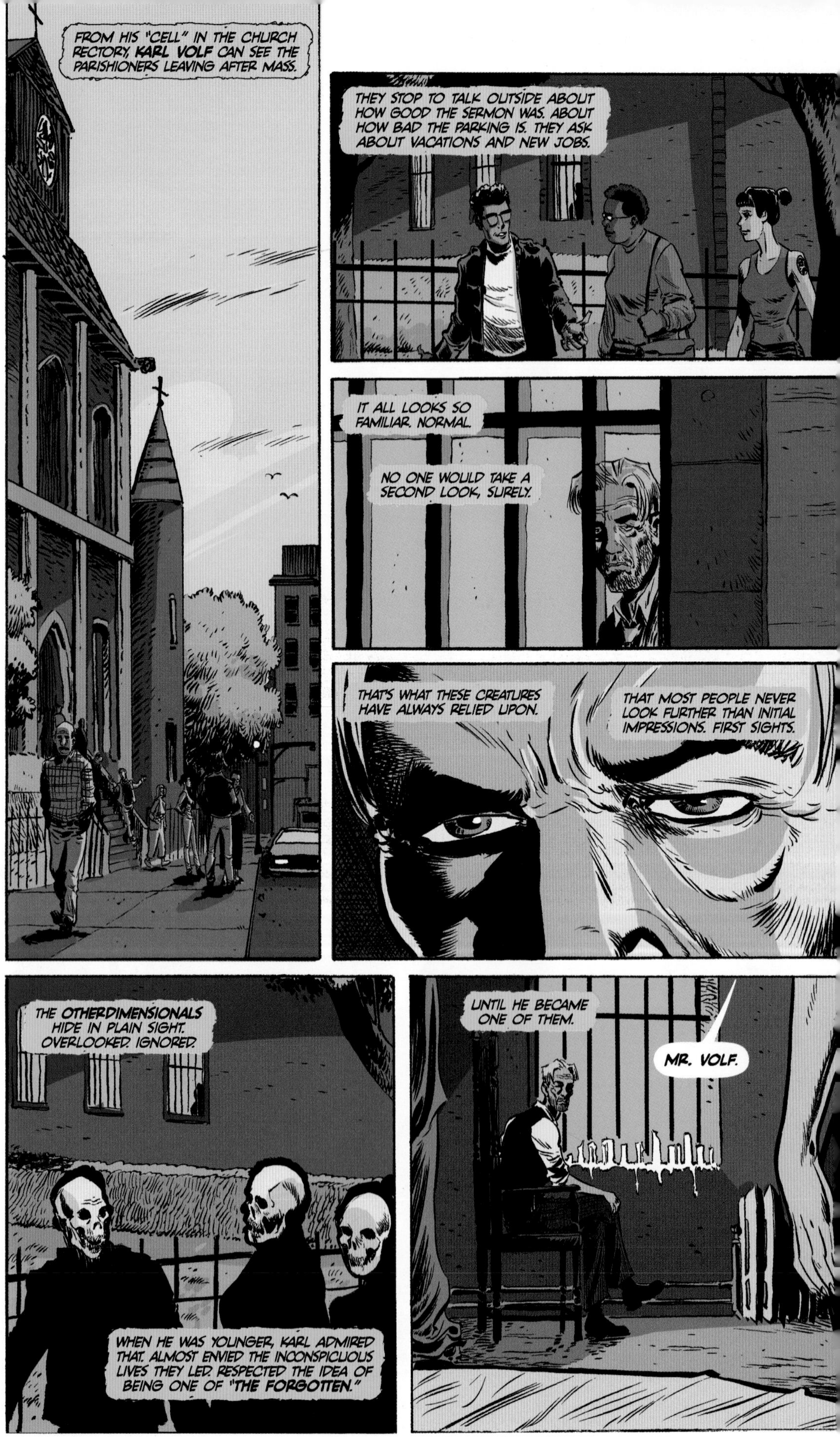
FROM HIS "CELL" IN THE CHURCH RECTORY, KARL VOLF CAN SEE THE PARISHIONERS LEAVING AFTER MASS.
THEY STOP TO TALK OUTSIDE ABOUT HOW GOOD THE SERMON WAS. ABOUT HOW BAD THE PARKING IS. THEY ASK ABOUT VACATIONS AND NEW JOBS.
IT ALL LOOKS SO FAMILIAR. NORMAL.
NO ONE WOULD TAKE A SECOND LOOK, SURELY.
THAT'S WHAT THESE CREATURES HAVE ALWAYS RELIED UPON.
THAT MOST PEOPLE NEVER LOOK FURTHER THAN INITIAL IMPRESSIONS. FIRST SIGHTS.
THE OTHERDIMENSIONALS HIDE IN PLAIN SIGHT. OVERLOOKED. IGNORED.
WHEN HE WAS YOUNGER, KARL ADMIRED THAT. ALMOST ENVIED THE INCONSPICUOUS LIVES THEY LED. RESPECTED THE IDEA OF BEING ONE OF "THE FORGOTTEN."
UNTIL HE BECAME ONE OF THEM.
MR. VOLF.

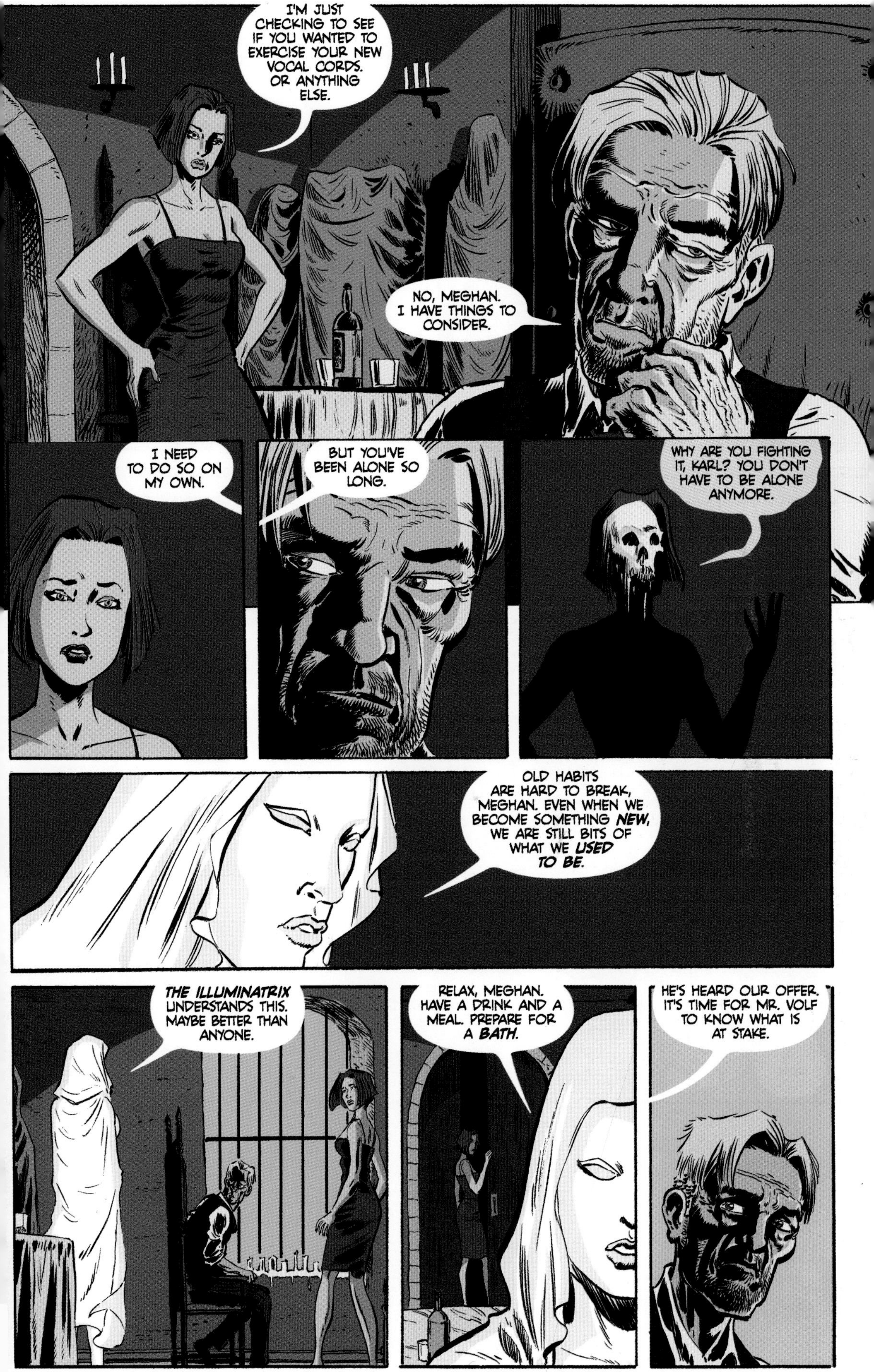
I'M JUST CHECKING TO SEE IF YOU WANTED TO EXERCISE YOUR NEW VOCAL CORDS. OR ANYTHING ELSE.
NO, MEGHAN. I HAVE THINGS TO CONSIDER.
I NEED TO DO SO ON MY OWN.
BUT YOU'VE BEEN ALONE SO LONG.
WHY ARE YOU FIGHTING IT, KARL? YOU DON'T HAVE TO BE ALONE ANYMORE.
OLD HABITS ARE HARD TO BREAK, MEGHAN. EVEN WHEN WE BECOME SOMETHING NEW, WE ARE STILL BITS OF WHAT WE USED TO BE.
THE ILLUMINATRIX UNDERSTANDS THIS. MAYBE BETTER THAN ANYONE.
RELAX, MEGHAN. HAVE A DRINK AND A MEAL. PREPARE FOR A BATH.
HE'S HEARD OUR OFFER. IT'S TIME FOR MR. VOLF TO KNOW WHAT IS AT STAKE.

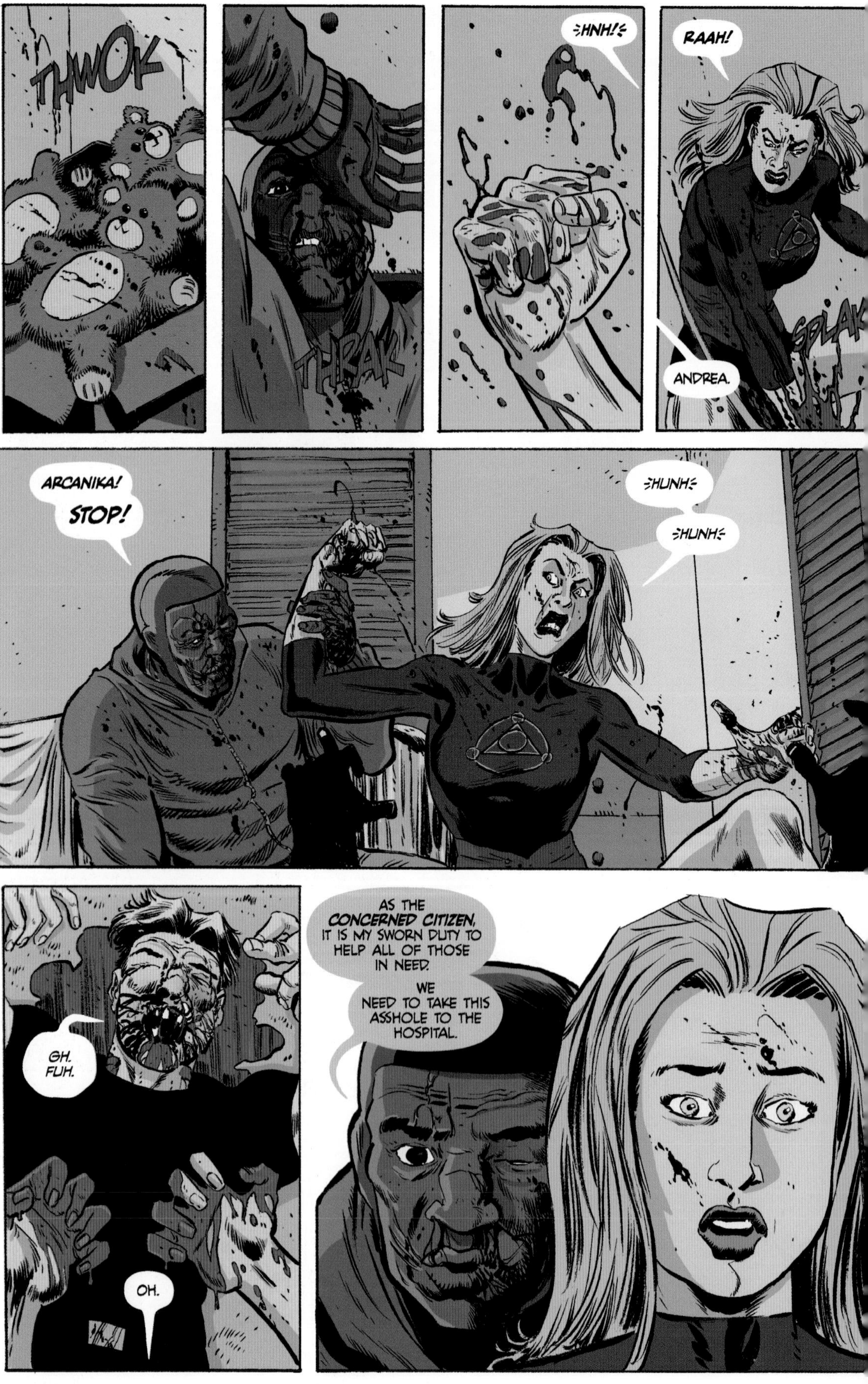

THWOK
THRAK
HNH!
RAAH!
ANDREA.
SPLAK
ARCANIKA! STOP!
HUNH
HUNH
GH. FUH.
OH.
AS THE CONCERNED CITIZEN, IT IS MY SWORN DUTY TO HELP ALL OF THOSE IN NEED. WE NEED TO TAKE THIS ASSHOLE TO THE HOSPITAL.

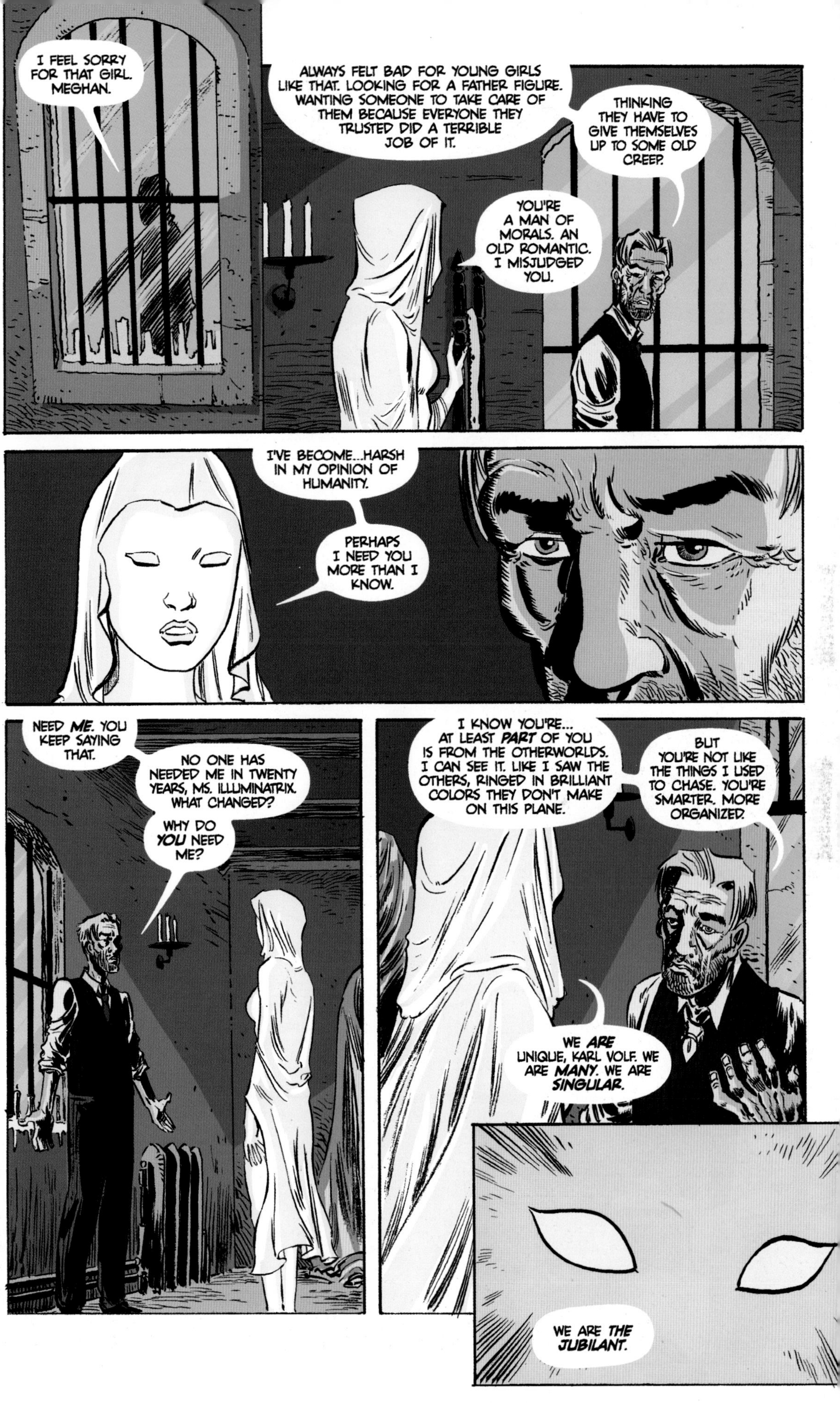
I FEEL SORRY FOR THAT GIRL. MEGHAN.
ALWAYS FELT BAD FOR YOUNG GIRLS LIKE THAT. LOOKING FOR A FATHER FIGURE. WANTING SOMEONE TO TAKE CARE OF THEM BECAUSE EVERYONE THEY TRUSTED DID A TERRIBLE JOB OF IT.
THINKING THEY HAVE TO GIVE THEMSELVES UP TO SOME OLD CREEP.
YOU'RE A MAN OF MORALS. AN OLD ROMANTIC. I MISJUDGED YOU.
I'VE BECOME...HARSH IN MY OPINION OF HUMANITY.
PERHAPS I NEED YOU MORE THAN I KNOW.
NEED *ME*. YOU KEEP SAYING THAT.
NO ONE HAS NEEDED ME IN TWENTY YEARS, MS. ILLUMINATRIX. WHAT CHANGED?
WHY DO *YOU* NEED ME?
I KNOW YOU'RE... AT LEAST *PART* OF YOU IS FROM THE OTHERWORLDS. I CAN SEE IT. LIKE I SAW THE OTHERS, RINGED IN BRILLIANT COLORS THEY DON'T MAKE ON THIS PLANE.
BUT YOU'RE NOT LIKE THE THINGS I USED TO CHASE. YOU'RE SMARTER. MORE ORGANIZED.
WE *ARE* UNIQUE, KARL VOLF. WE ARE *MANY*. WE ARE *SINGULAR*.
WE ARE *THE JUBILANT*.

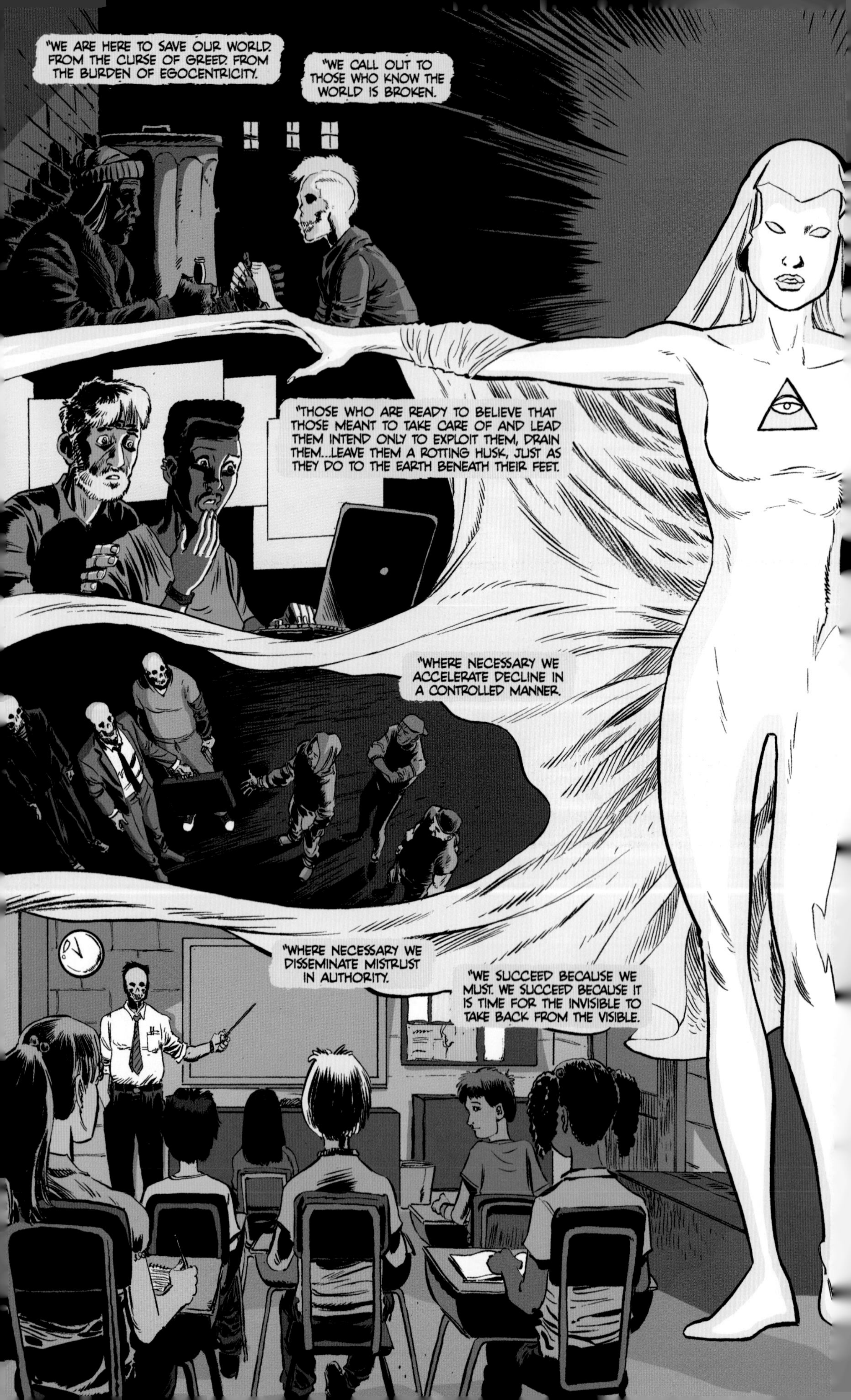
"WE ARE HERE TO SAVE OUR WORLD. FROM THE CURSE OF GREED. FROM THE BURDEN OF EGOCENTRICITY.
"WE CALL OUT TO THOSE WHO KNOW THE WORLD IS BROKEN.
"THOSE WHO ARE READY TO BELIEVE THAT THOSE MEANT TO TAKE CARE OF AND LEAD THEM INTEND ONLY TO EXPLOIT THEM, DRAIN THEM...LEAVE THEM A ROTTING HUSK, JUST AS THEY DO TO THE EARTH BENEATH THEIR FEET.
"WHERE NECESSARY WE ACCELERATE DECLINE IN A CONTROLLED MANNER.
"WHERE NECESSARY WE DISSEMINATE MISTRUST IN AUTHORITY.
"WE SUCCEED BECAUSE WE MUST. WE SUCCEED BECAUSE IT IS TIME FOR THE INVISIBLE TO TAKE BACK FROM THE VISIBLE.

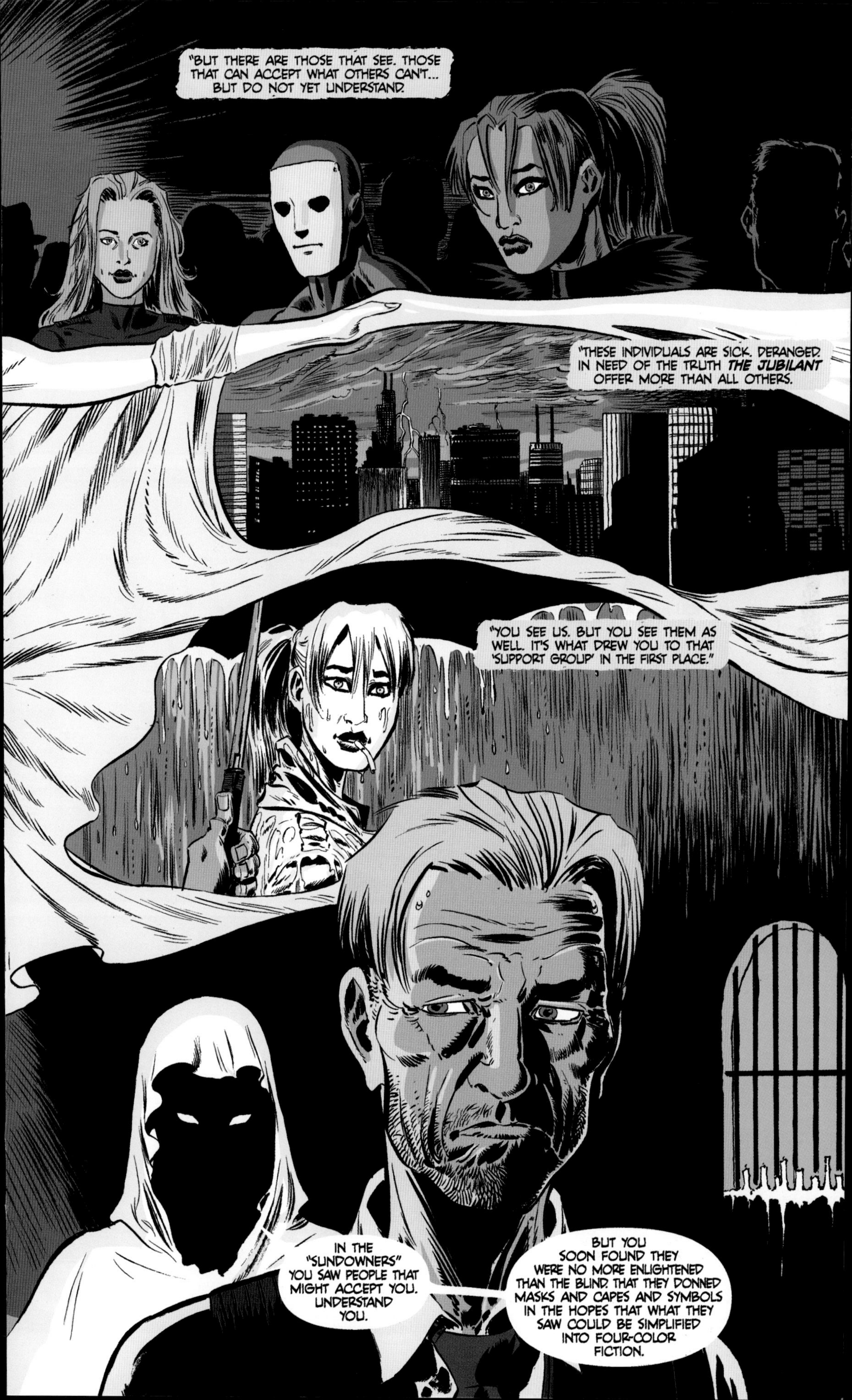
"BUT THERE ARE THOSE THAT SEE. THOSE THAT CAN ACCEPT WHAT OTHERS CAN'T... BUT DO NOT YET UNDERSTAND.
"THESE INDIVIDUALS ARE SICK. DERANGED. IN NEED OF THE TRUTH THE JUBILANT OFFER MORE THAN ALL OTHERS.
"YOU SEE US. BUT YOU SEE THEM AS WELL. IT'S WHAT DREW YOU TO THAT 'SUPPORT GROUP' IN THE FIRST PLACE."
IN THE "SUNDOWNERS" YOU SAW PEOPLE THAT MIGHT ACCEPT YOU. UNDERSTAND YOU.
BUT YOU SOON FOUND THEY WERE NO MORE ENLIGHTENED THAN THE BLIND. THAT THEY DONNED MASKS AND CAPES AND SYMBOLS IN THE HOPES THAT WHAT THEY SAW COULD BE SIMPLIFIED INTO FOUR-COLOR FICTION.

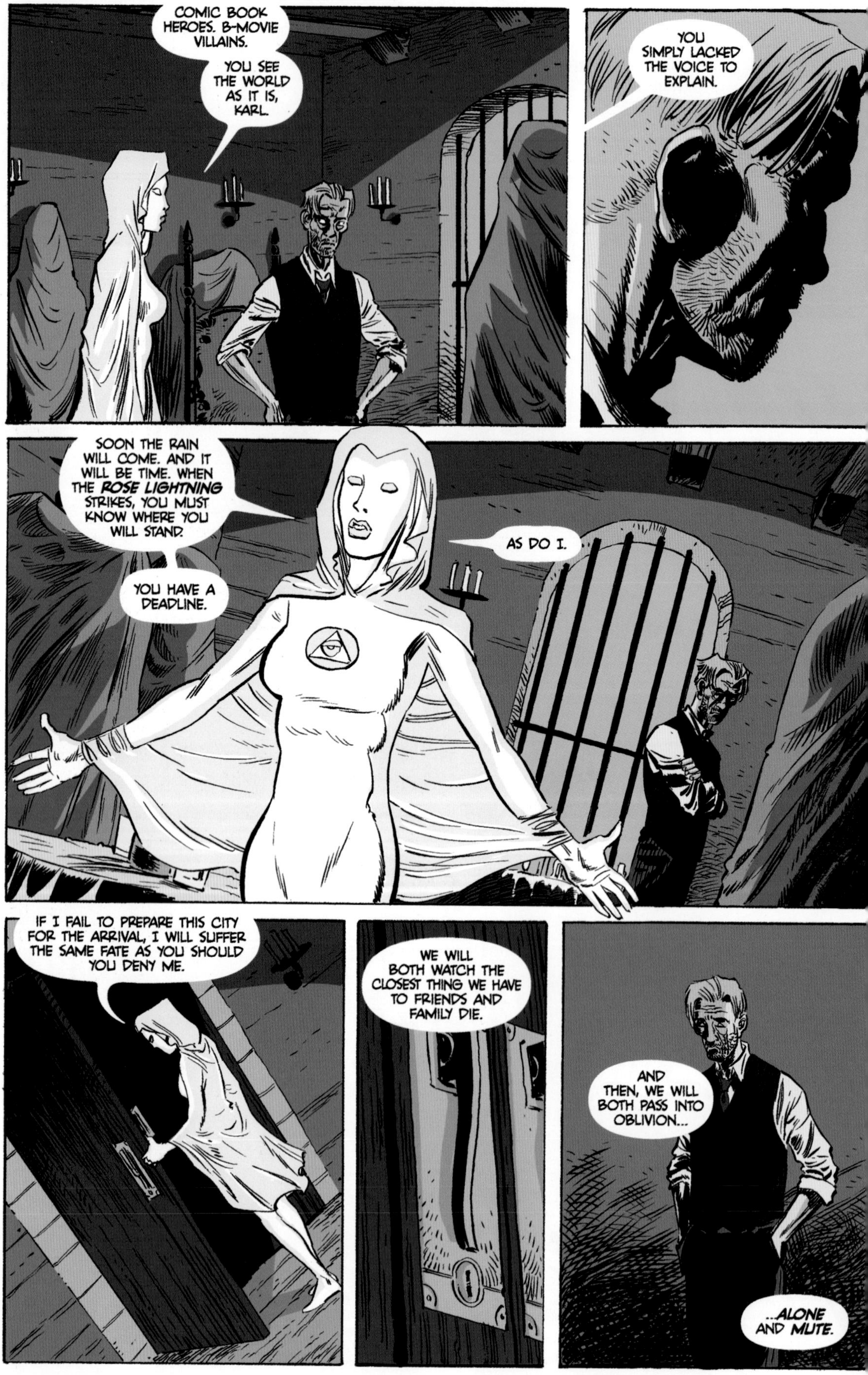
COMIC BOOK HEROES. B-MOVIE VILLAINS.
YOU SEE THE WORLD AS IT IS, KARL.
YOU SIMPLY LACKED THE VOICE TO EXPLAIN.
SOON THE RAIN WILL COME. AND IT WILL BE TIME. WHEN THE *ROSE LIGHTNING* STRIKES, YOU MUST KNOW WHERE YOU WILL STAND.
YOU HAVE A DEADLINE.
AS DO I.
IF I FAIL TO PREPARE THIS CITY FOR THE ARRIVAL, I WILL SUFFER THE SAME FATE AS YOU SHOULD YOU DENY ME.
WE WILL BOTH WATCH THE CLOSEST THING WE HAVE TO FRIENDS AND FAMILY DIE.
AND THEN, WE WILL BOTH PASS INTO OBLIVION...
...*ALONE* AND *MUTE*.

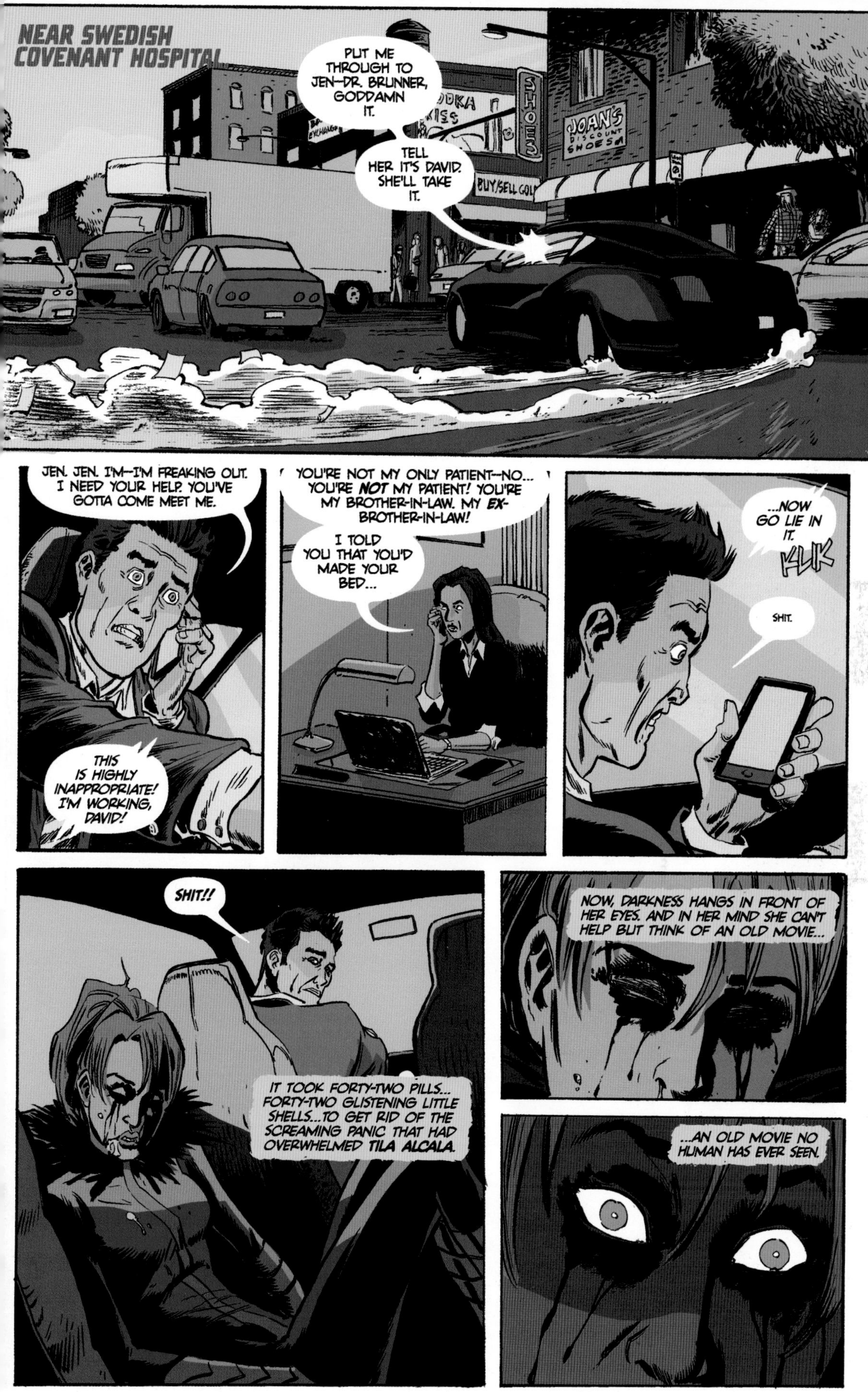
NEAR SWEDISH COVENANT HOSPITAL
PUT ME THROUGH TO JEN--DR. BRUNNER, GODDAMN IT.
TELL HER IT'S DAVID. SHE'LL TAKE IT.
JOAN'S DISCOUNT SHOES
SHOES
BUY/SELL GOL
JEN. JEN. I'M--I'M FREAKING OUT. I NEED YOUR HELP. YOU'VE GOTTA COME MEET ME.
THIS IS HIGHLY INAPPROPRIATE! I'M WORKING, DAVID!
YOU'RE NOT MY ONLY PATIENT--NO... YOU'RE NOT MY PATIENT! YOU'RE MY BROTHER-IN-LAW. MY EX-BROTHER-IN-LAW!
I TOLD YOU THAT YOU'D MADE YOUR BED...
...NOW GO LIE IN IT.
KLIK
SHIT.
SHIT!!
IT TOOK FORTY-TWO PILLS... FORTY-TWO GLISTENING LITTLE SHELLS...TO GET RID OF THE SCREAMING PANIC THAT HAD OVERWHELMED TILA ALCALA.
NOW, DARKNESS HANGS IN FRONT OF HER EYES. AND IN HER MIND SHE CAN'T HELP BUT THINK OF AN OLD MOVIE...
...AN OLD MOVIE NO HUMAN HAS EVER SEEN.

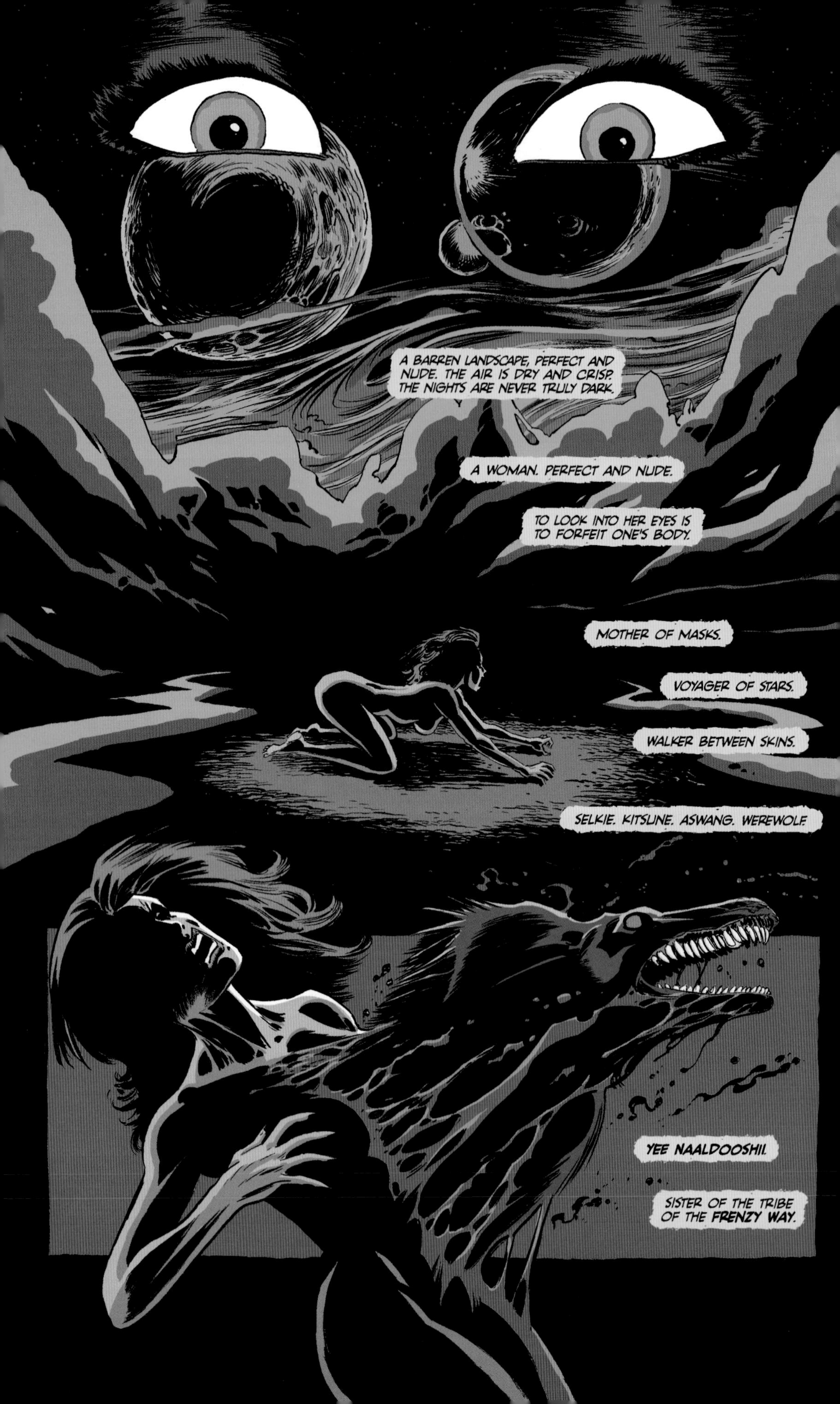
A BARREN LANDSCAPE, PERFECT AND NUDE. THE AIR IS DRY AND CRISP. THE NIGHTS ARE NEVER TRULY DARK.
A WOMAN. PERFECT AND NUDE.
TO LOOK INTO HER EYES IS TO FORFEIT ONE'S BODY.
MOTHER OF MASKS.
VOYAGER OF STARS.
WALKER BETWEEN SKINS.
SELKIE. KITSUNE. ASWANG. WEREWOLF.
YEE NAALDOOSHII.
SISTER OF THE TRIBE OF THE FRENZY WAY.

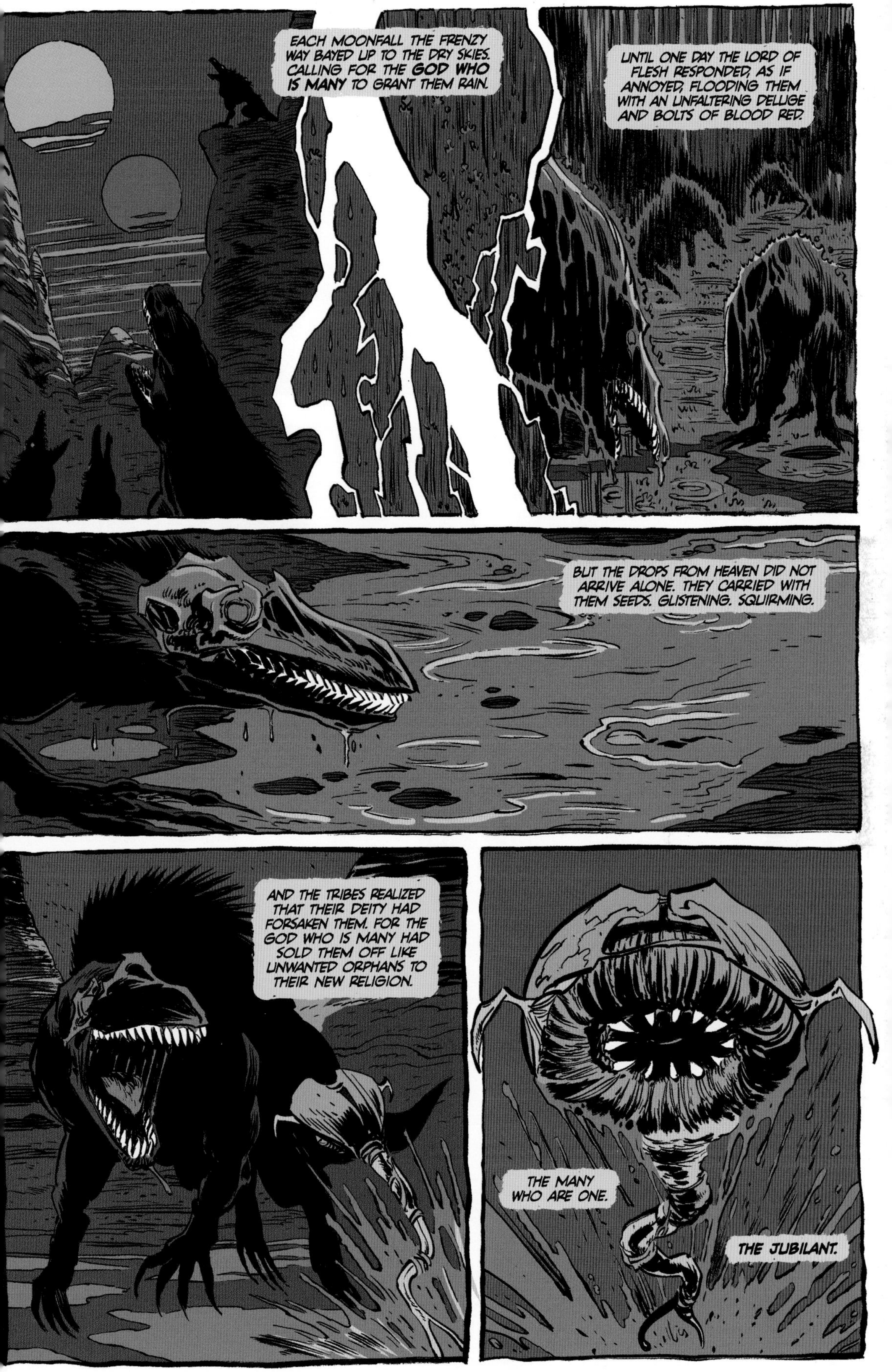
EACH MOONFALL THE FRENZY WAY BAYED UP TO THE DRY SKIES. CALLING FOR THE **GOD WHO IS MANY** TO GRANT THEM RAIN.
UNTIL ONE DAY THE LORD OF FLESH RESPONDED, AS IF ANNOYED, FLOODING THEM WITH AN UNFALTERING DELUGE AND BOLTS OF BLOOD RED.
BUT THE DROPS FROM HEAVEN DID NOT ARRIVE ALONE. THEY CARRIED WITH THEM SEEDS. GLISTENING. SQUIRMING.
AND THE TRIBES REALIZED THAT THEIR DEITY HAD FORSAKEN THEM. FOR THE GOD WHO IS MANY HAD SOLD THEM OFF LIKE UNWANTED ORPHANS TO THEIR NEW RELIGION.
THE MANY WHO ARE ONE.
THE JUBILANT.

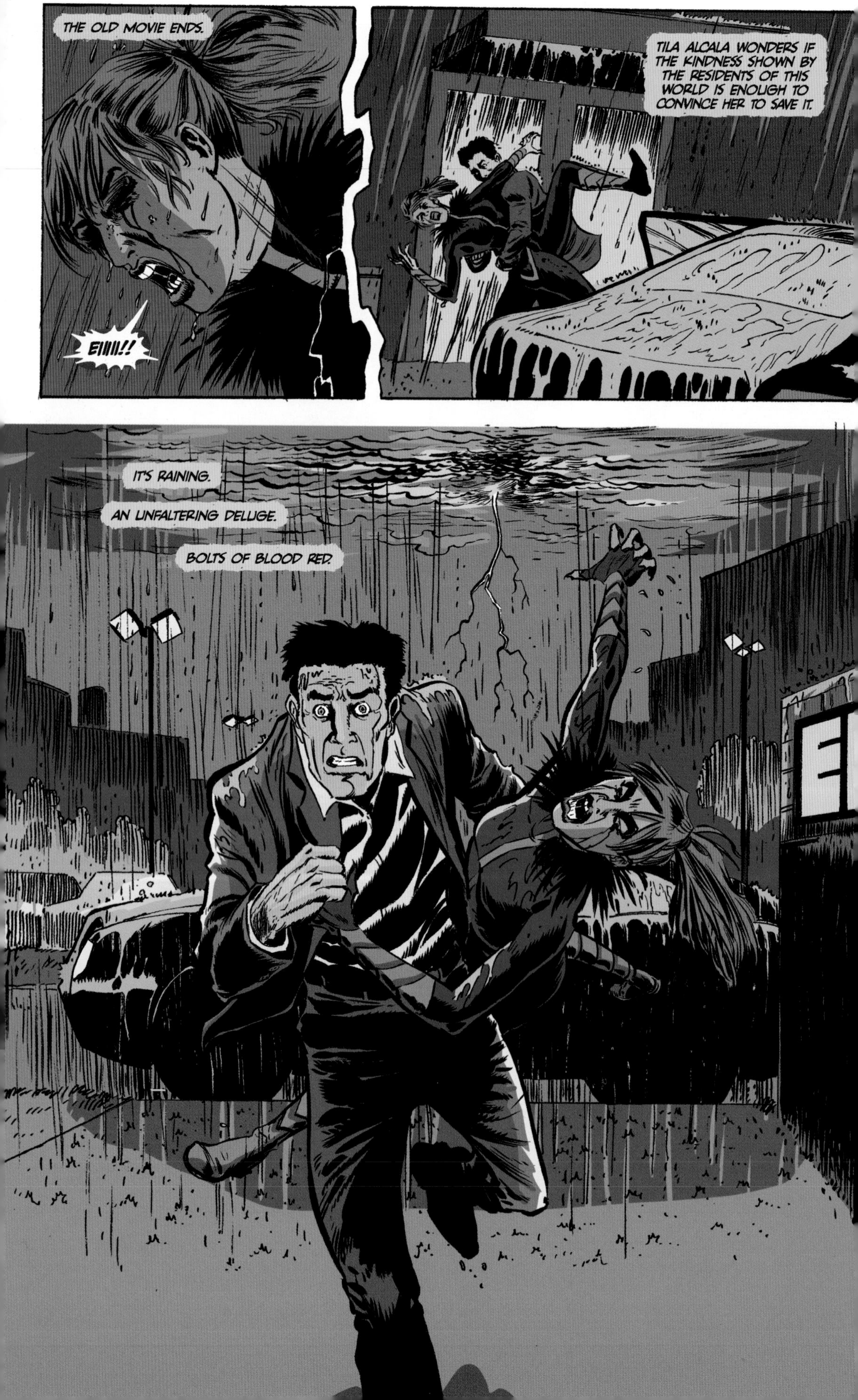
THE OLD MOVIE ENDS.
EIIII!!
TILA ALCALA WONDERS IF THE KINDNESS SHOWN BY THE RESIDENTS OF THIS WORLD IS ENOUGH TO CONVINCE HER TO SAVE IT.
IT'S RAINING.
AN UNFALTERING DELUGE.
BOLTS OF BLOOD RED.

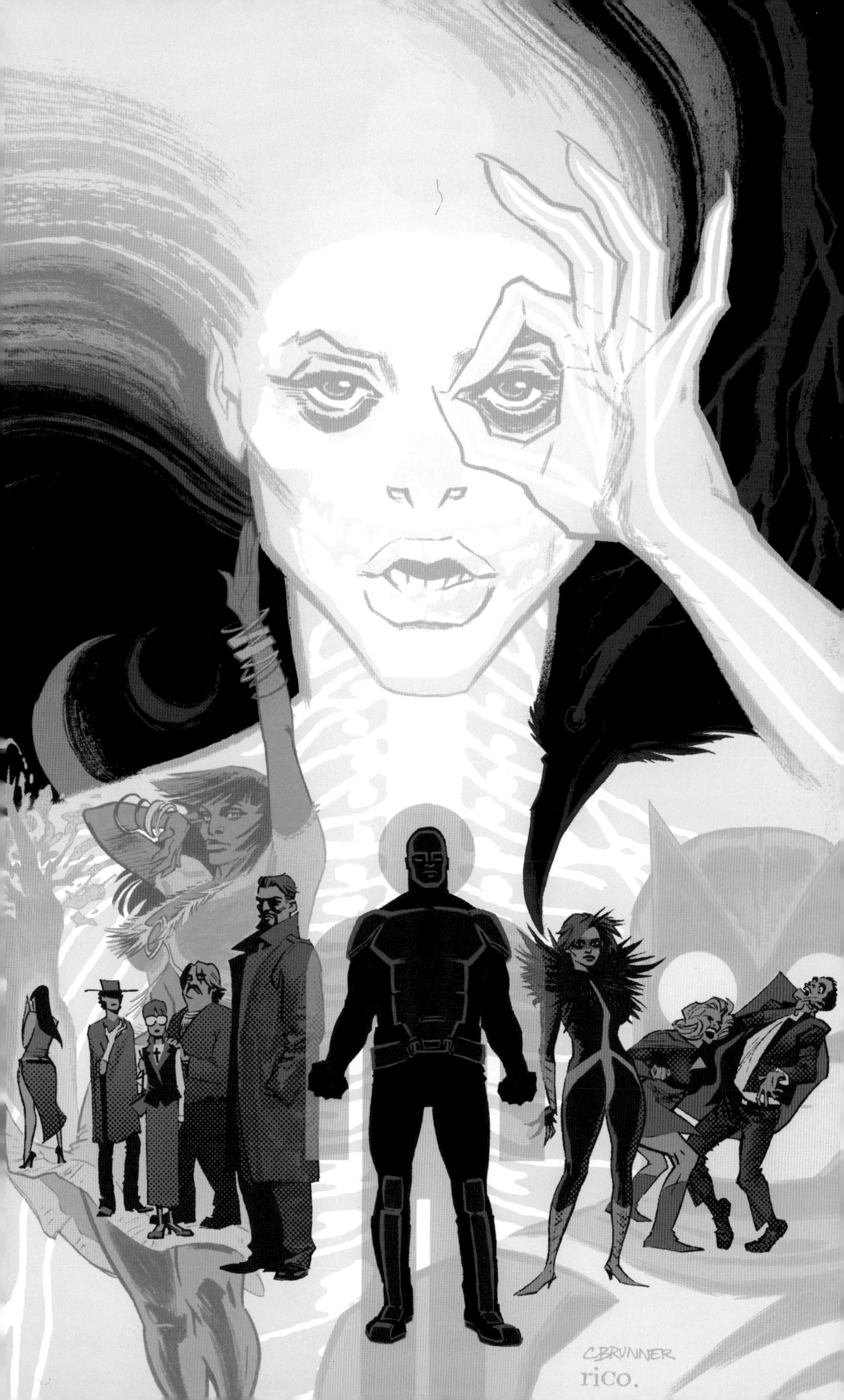

C.BRUNNER
rico.

SUNDOWNERS™ 5

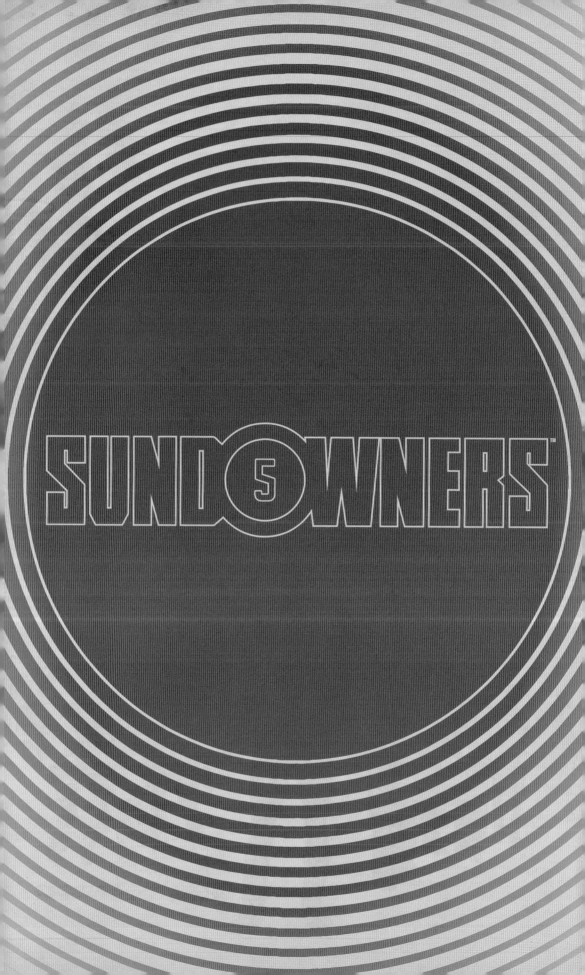

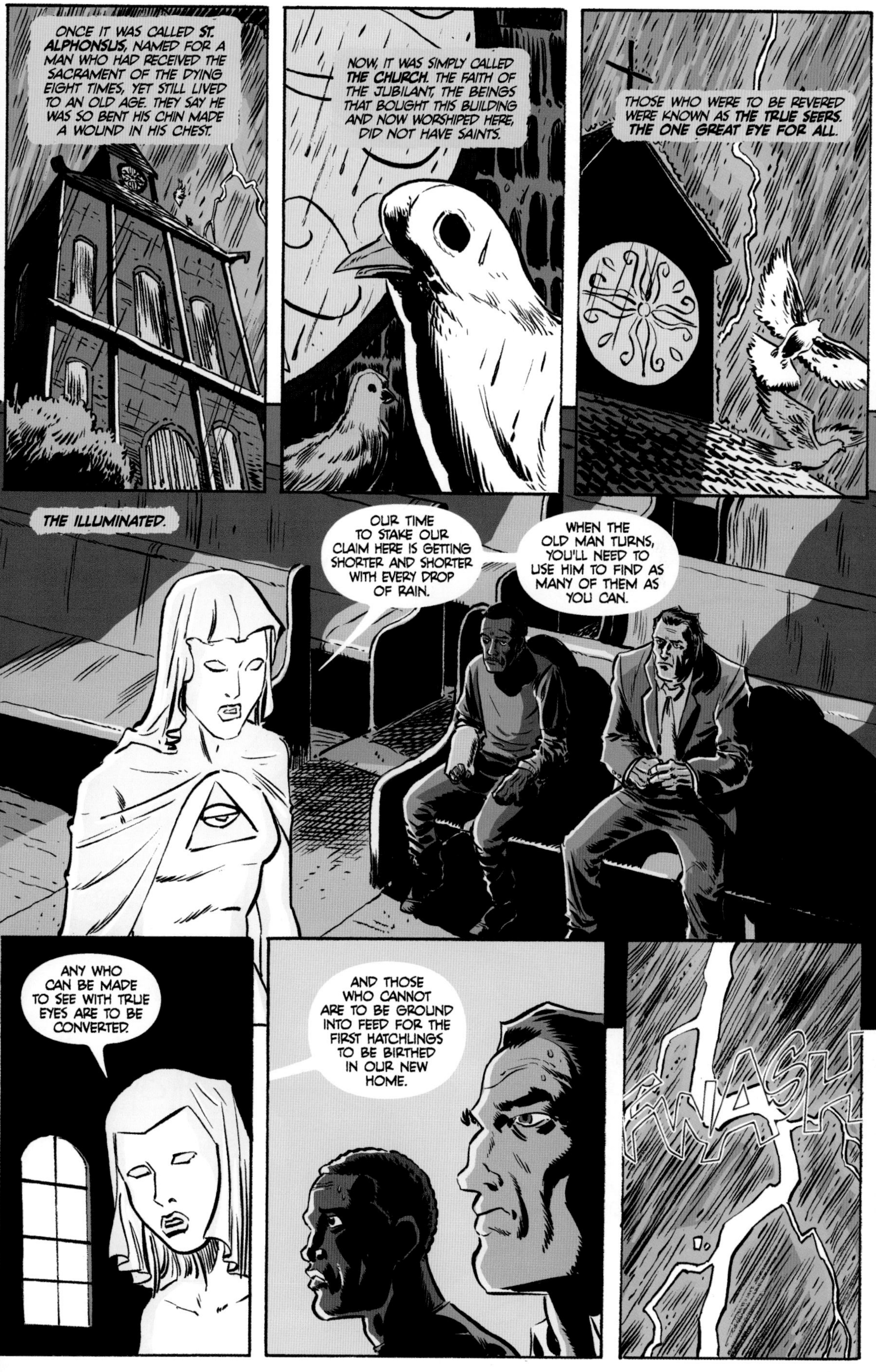
ONCE IT WAS CALLED ST. ALPHONSUS, NAMED FOR A MAN WHO HAD RECEIVED THE SACRAMENT OF THE DYING EIGHT TIMES, YET STILL LIVED TO AN OLD AGE. THEY SAY HE WAS SO BENT HIS CHIN MADE A WOUND IN HIS CHEST.
NOW, IT WAS SIMPLY CALLED THE CHURCH. THE FAITH OF THE JUBILANT, THE BEINGS THAT BOUGHT THIS BUILDING AND NOW WORSHIPED HERE, DID NOT HAVE SAINTS.
THOSE WHO WERE TO BE REVERED WERE KNOWN AS THE TRUE SEERS. THE ONE GREAT EYE FOR ALL.
THE ILLUMINATED.
OUR TIME TO STAKE OUR CLAIM HERE IS GETTING SHORTER AND SHORTER WITH EVERY DROP OF RAIN.
WHEN THE OLD MAN TURNS, YOU'LL NEED TO USE HIM TO FIND AS MANY OF THEM AS YOU CAN.
ANY WHO CAN BE MADE TO SEE WITH TRUE EYES ARE TO BE CONVERTED.
AND THOSE WHO CANNOT ARE TO BE GROUND INTO FEED FOR THE FIRST HATCHLINGS TO BE BIRTHED IN OUR NEW HOME.
FWASH

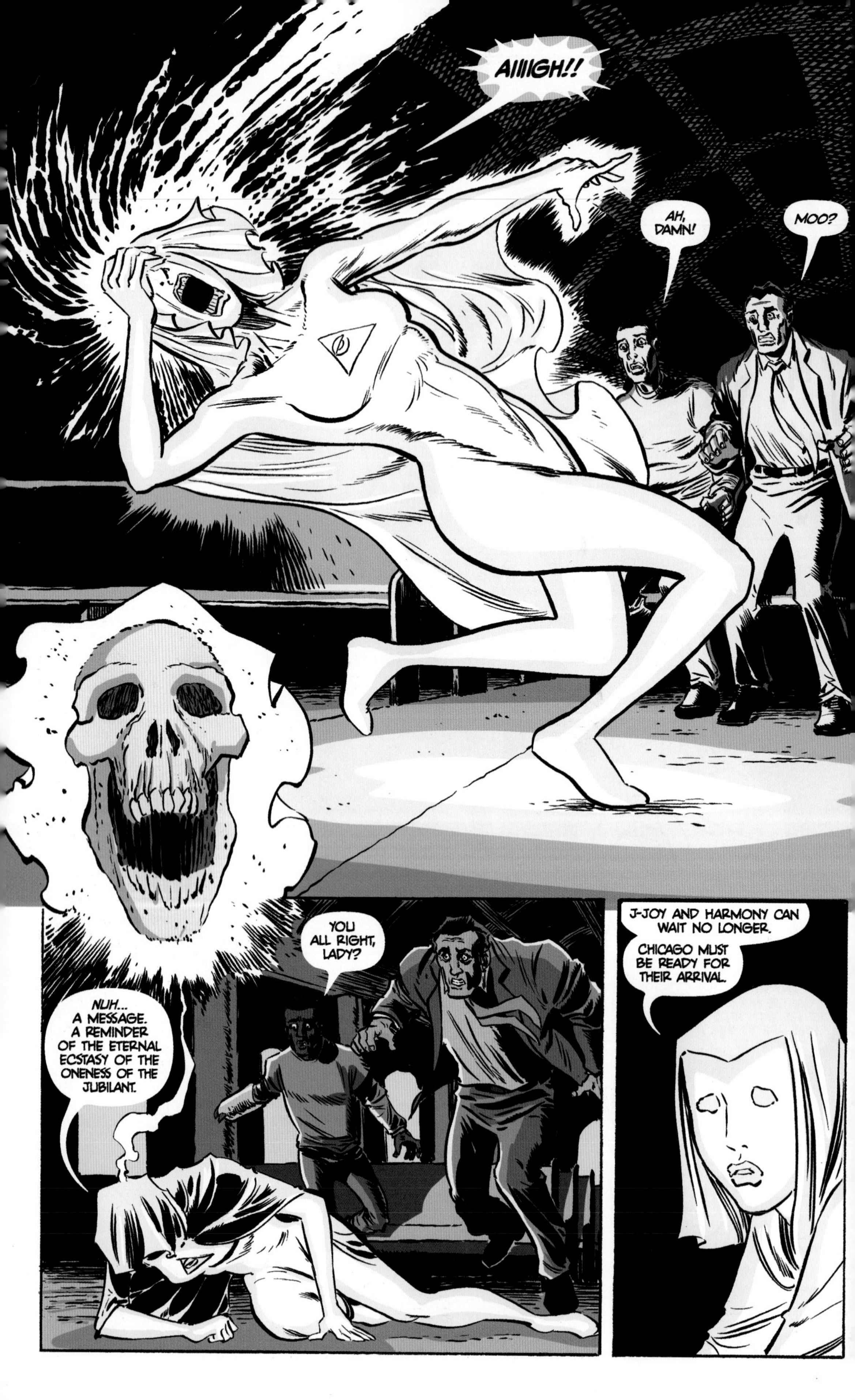

AIIIIGH!!
AH, DAMN!
MOO?
YOU ALL RIGHT, LADY?
NUH... A MESSAGE. A REMINDER OF THE ETERNAL ECSTASY OF THE ONENESS OF THE JUBILANT.
J-JOY AND HARMONY CAN WAIT NO LONGER.
CHICAGO MUST BE READY FOR THEIR ARRIVAL.

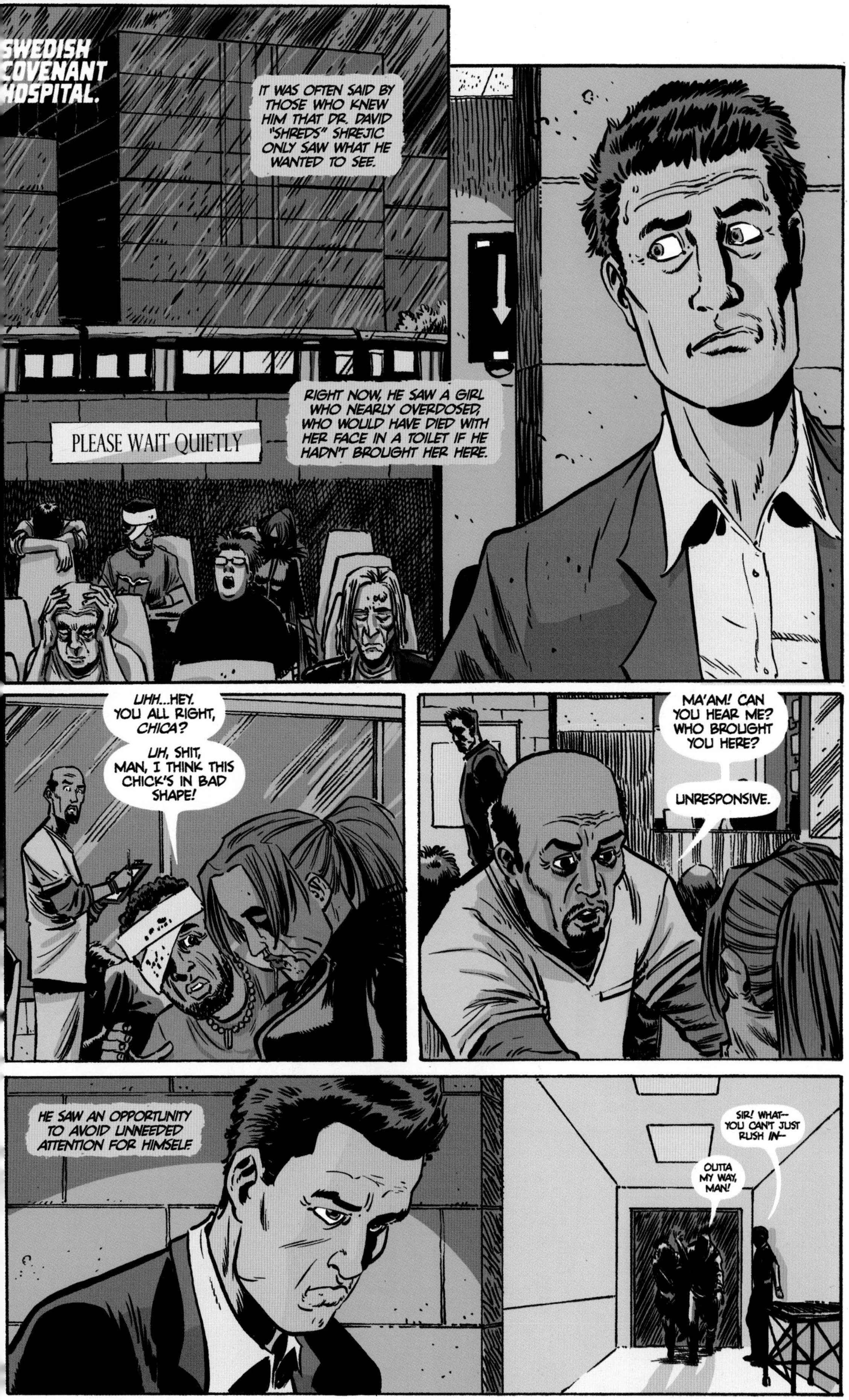
SWEDISH COVENANT HOSPITAL.
IT WAS OFTEN SAID BY THOSE WHO KNEW HIM THAT DR. DAVID "SHREDS" SHREJIC ONLY SAW WHAT HE WANTED TO SEE.
PLEASE WAIT QUIETLY
RIGHT NOW, HE SAW A GIRL WHO NEARLY OVERDOSED, WHO WOULD HAVE DIED WITH HER FACE IN A TOILET IF HE HADN'T BROUGHT HER HERE.
UHH...HEY. YOU ALL RIGHT, CHICA?
UH, SHIT, MAN, I THINK THIS CHICK'S IN BAD SHAPE!
MA'AM! CAN YOU HEAR ME? WHO BROUGHT YOU HERE?
UNRESPONSIVE.
HE SAW AN OPPORTUNITY TO AVOID UNNEEDED ATTENTION FOR HIMSELF.
SIR! WHAT-- YOU CAN'T JUST RUSH IN--
OUTTA MY WAY, MAN!

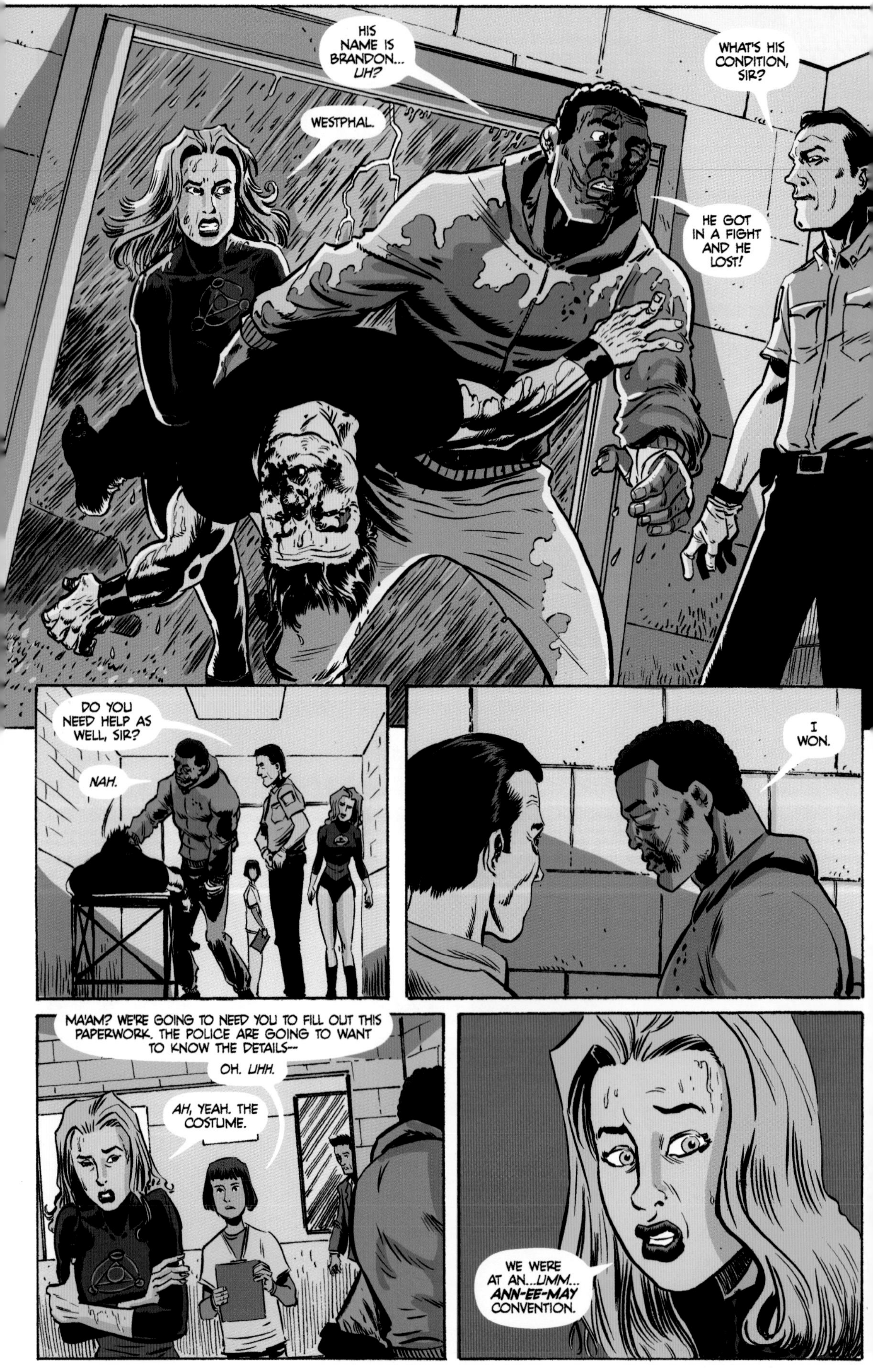
HIS NAME IS BRANDON... UH?
WESTPHAL.
WHAT'S HIS CONDITION, SIR?
HE GOT IN A FIGHT AND HE LOST!
DO YOU NEED HELP AS WELL, SIR?
NAH.
I WON.
MA'AM? WE'RE GOING TO NEED YOU TO FILL OUT THIS PAPERWORK. THE POLICE ARE GOING TO WANT TO KNOW THE DETAILS--
OH. UHH.
AH, YEAH. THE COSTUME.
WE WERE AT AN...UMM... ANN-EE-MAY CONVENTION.

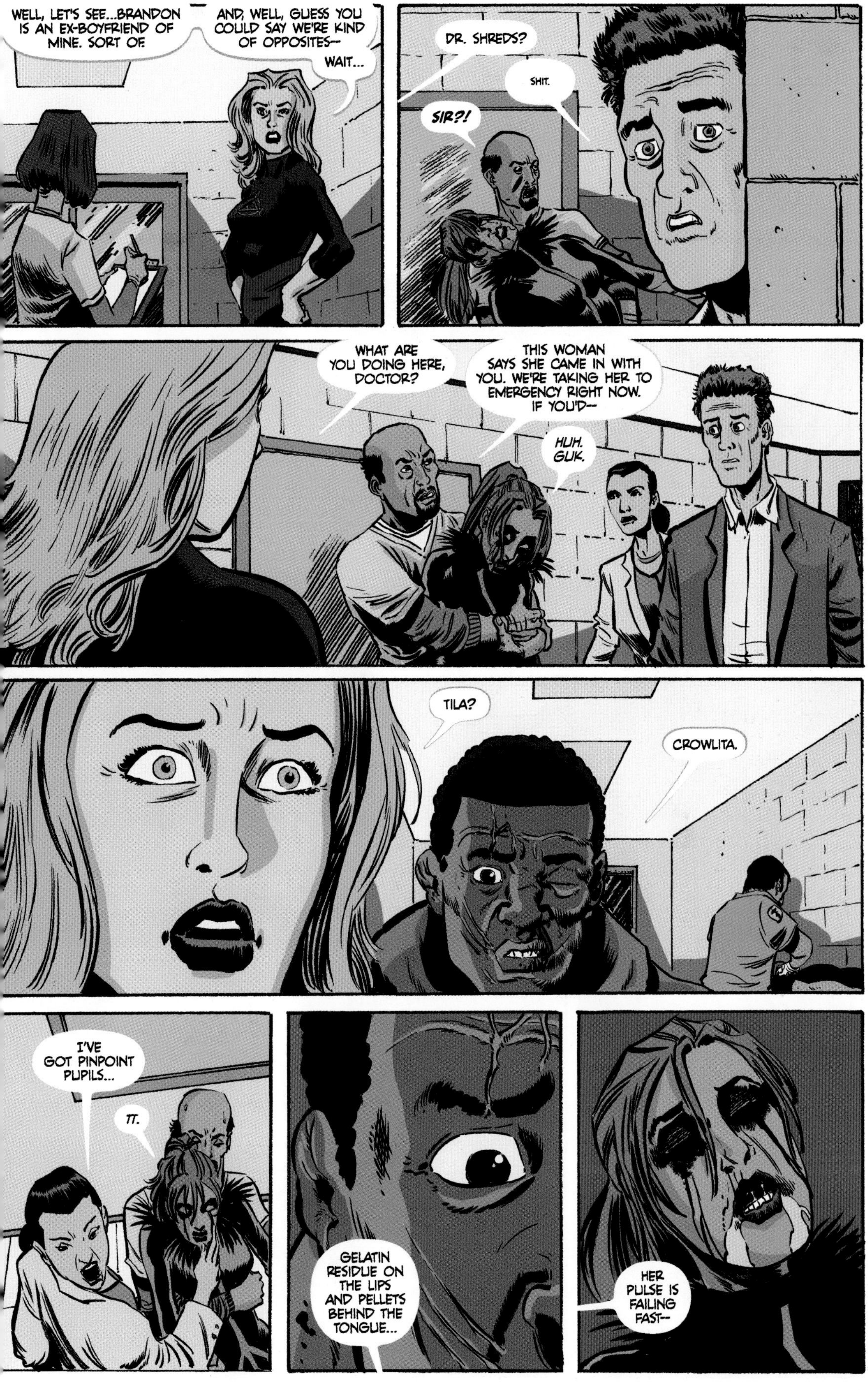
WELL, LET'S SEE...BRANDON IS AN EX-BOYFRIEND OF MINE. SORT OF.
AND, WELL, GUESS YOU COULD SAY WE'RE KIND OF OPPOSITES--
WAIT...
DR. SHREDS?
SHIT.
SIR?!
WHAT ARE YOU DOING HERE, DOCTOR?
THIS WOMAN SAYS SHE CAME IN WITH YOU. WE'RE TAKING HER TO EMERGENCY RIGHT NOW. IF YOU'D--
HUH. GUK.
TILA?
CROWLITA.
I'VE GOT PINPOINT PUPILS...
TT.
GELATIN RESIDUE ON THE LIPS AND PELLETS BEHIND THE TONGUE...
HER PULSE IS FAILING FAST--

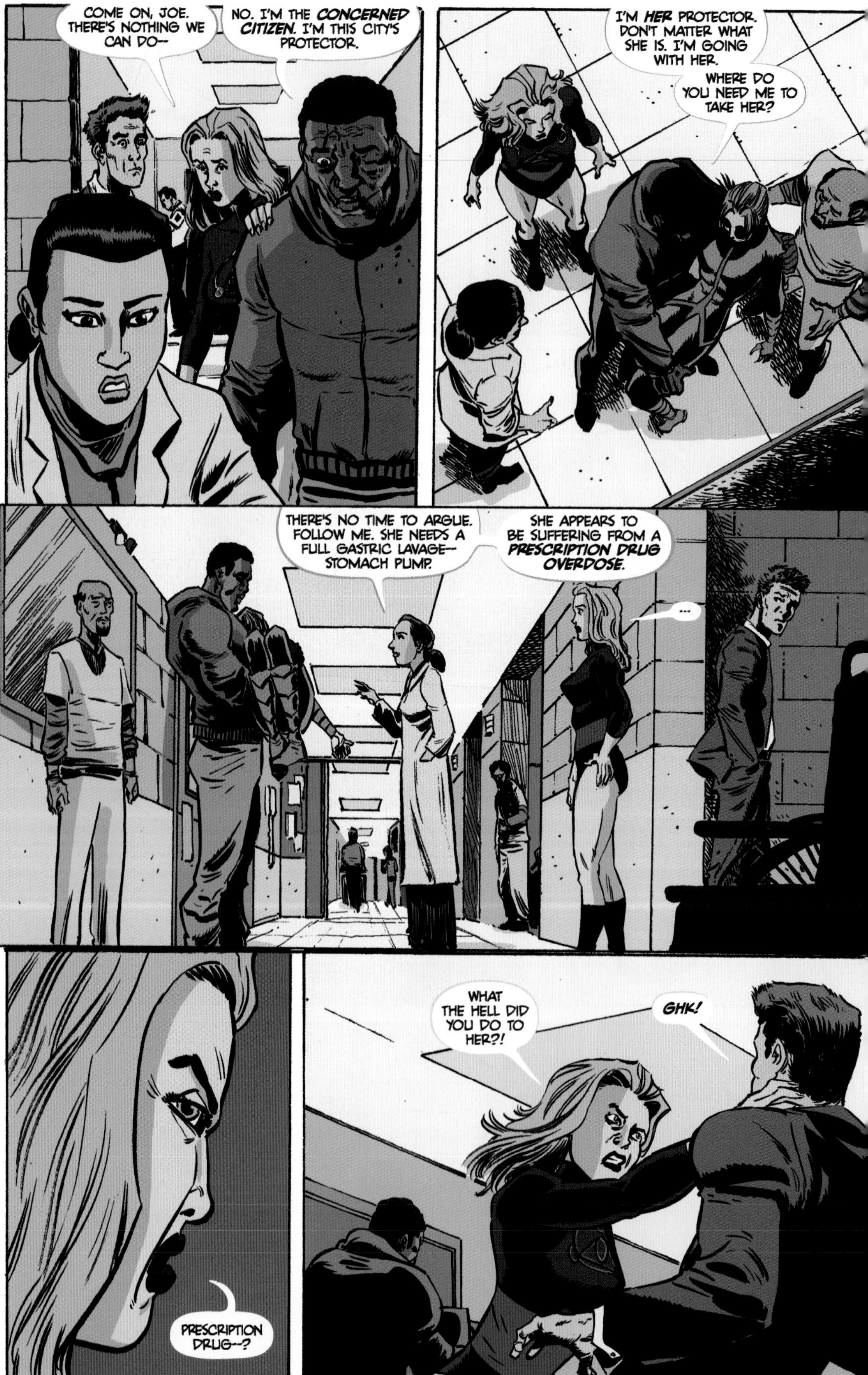

COME ON, JOE. THERE'S NOTHING WE CAN DO--
NO. I'M THE CONCERNED CITIZEN. I'M THIS CITY'S PROTECTOR.
I'M HER PROTECTOR. DON'T MATTER WHAT SHE IS. I'M GOING WITH HER.
WHERE DO YOU NEED ME TO TAKE HER?
THERE'S NO TIME TO ARGUE. FOLLOW ME. SHE NEEDS A FULL GASTRIC LAVAGE-- STOMACH PUMP.
SHE APPEARS TO BE SUFFERING FROM A PRESCRIPTION DRUG OVERDOSE.
...
PRESCRIPTION DRUG--?
WHAT THE HELL DID YOU DO TO HER?!
GHK!

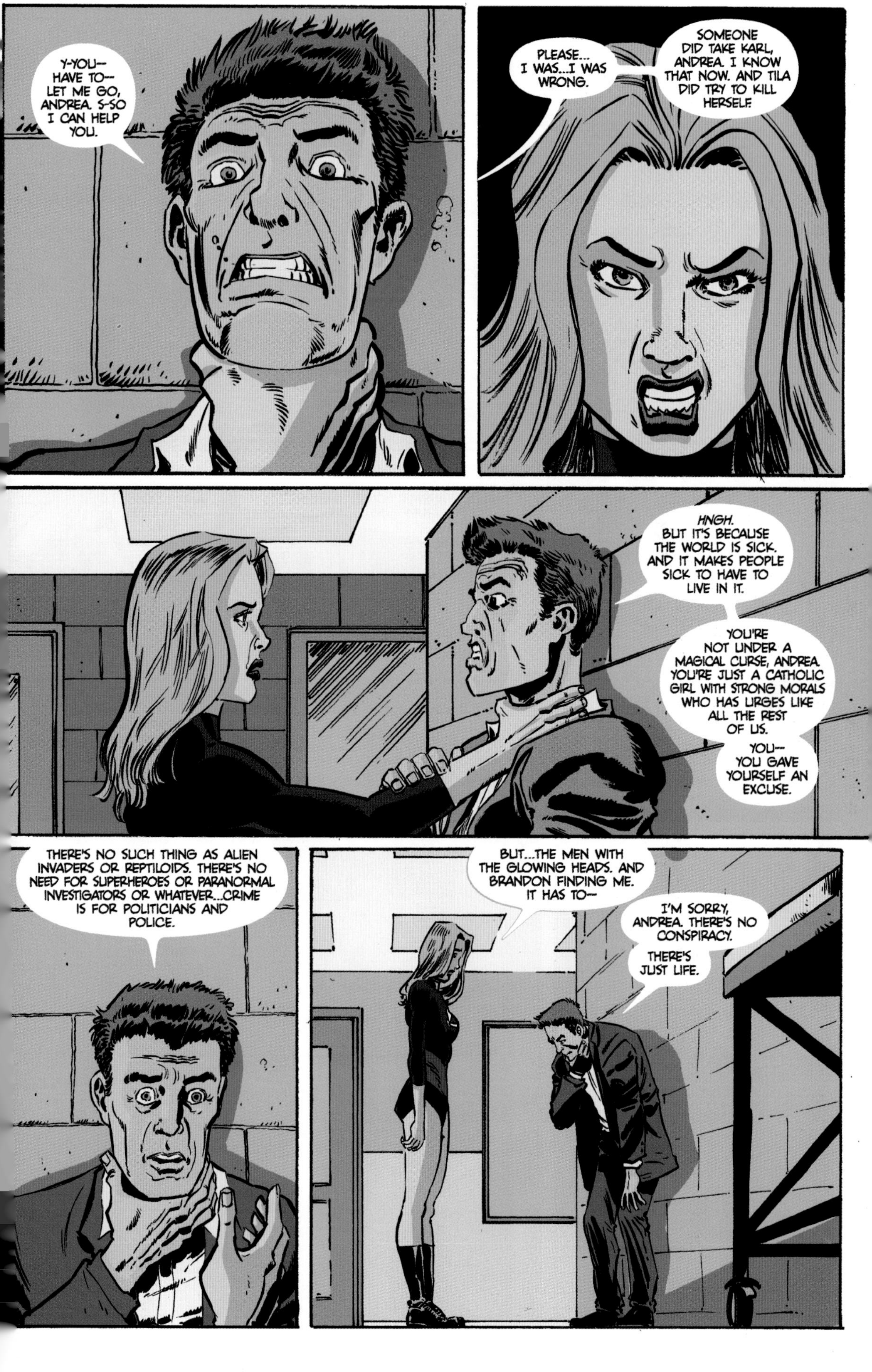
Y-YOU--
HAVE TO--
LET ME GO,
ANDREA. S-SO
I CAN HELP
YOU.
PLEASE...
I WAS...I WAS
WRONG.
SOMEONE
DID TAKE KARL,
ANDREA. I KNOW
THAT NOW. AND TILA
DID TRY TO KILL
HERSELF.
HNGH.
BUT IT'S BECAUSE
THE WORLD IS SICK.
AND IT MAKES PEOPLE
SICK TO HAVE TO
LIVE IN IT.
YOU'RE
NOT UNDER A
MAGICAL CURSE, ANDREA.
YOU'RE JUST A CATHOLIC
GIRL WITH STRONG MORALS
WHO HAS URGES LIKE
ALL THE REST
OF US.
YOU--
YOU GAVE
YOURSELF AN
EXCUSE.
THERE'S NO SUCH THING AS ALIEN
INVADERS OR REPTILOIDS. THERE'S NO
NEED FOR SUPERHEROES OR PARANORMAL
INVESTIGATORS OR WHATEVER...CRIME
IS FOR POLITICIANS AND
POLICE.
BUT...THE MEN WITH
THE GLOWING HEADS. AND
BRANDON FINDING ME.
IT HAS TO--
I'M SORRY,
ANDREA. THERE'S NO
CONSPIRACY.
THERE'S
JUST LIFE.

COPS.

A MAN BEATEN NEARLY TO DEATH AND AN OD'D TEENAGER IN A FETISH OUTFIT? YOU'RE DAMN RIGHT I MADE SURE THERE WERE COPS.

I HOPE YOU'RE IN THE MOOD TO ANSWER SOME QUESTIONS.

2121

POLICE DON'T LIKE ME, AND I DON'T LIKE POLICE, 'LITA.

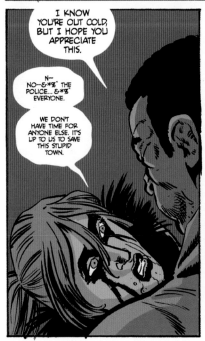

I KNOW YOU'RE OUT COLD, BUT I HOPE YOU APPRECIATE THIS.

N— NO—&*%˘ THE POLICE... &*% EVERYONE.

WE DON'T HAVE TIME FOR ANYONE ELSE. IT'S UP TO US TO SAVE THIS STUPID TOWN.

YOU. ME. ANDREA. AND KARL.

THE ONES WITH THEIR &*%$% EYES OPEN.

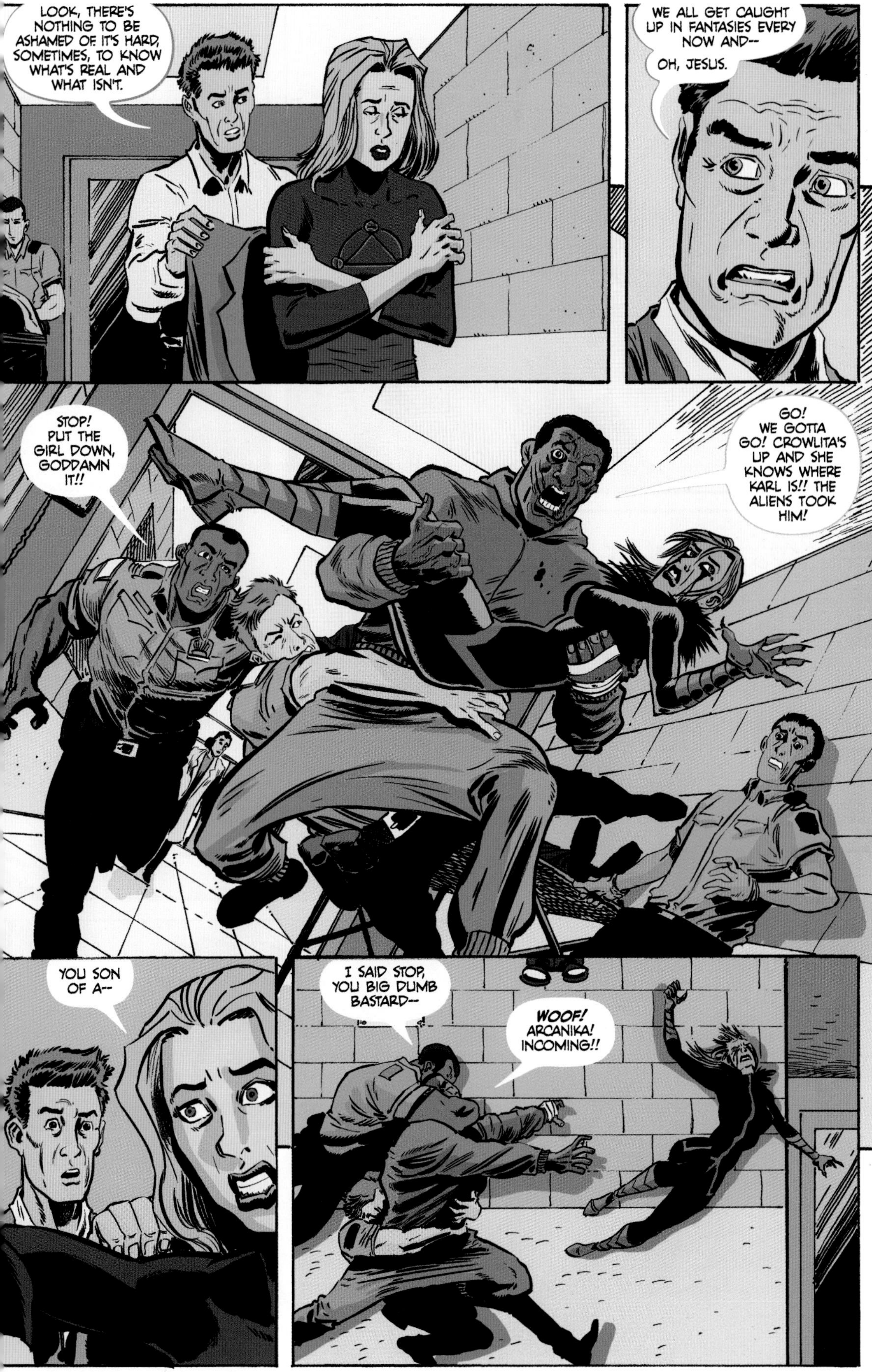

LOOK, THERE'S NOTHING TO BE ASHAMED OF. IT'S HARD, SOMETIMES, TO KNOW WHAT'S REAL AND WHAT ISN'T.
WE ALL GET CAUGHT UP IN FANTASIES EVERY NOW AND--
OH, JESUS.
STOP! PUT THE GIRL DOWN, GODDAMN IT!!
GO! WE GOTTA GO! CROWLITA'S UP AND SHE KNOWS WHERE KARL IS!! THE ALIENS TOOK HIM!
YOU SON OF A--
I SAID STOP, YOU BIG DUMB BASTARD--
WOOF! ARCANIKA! INCOMING!!

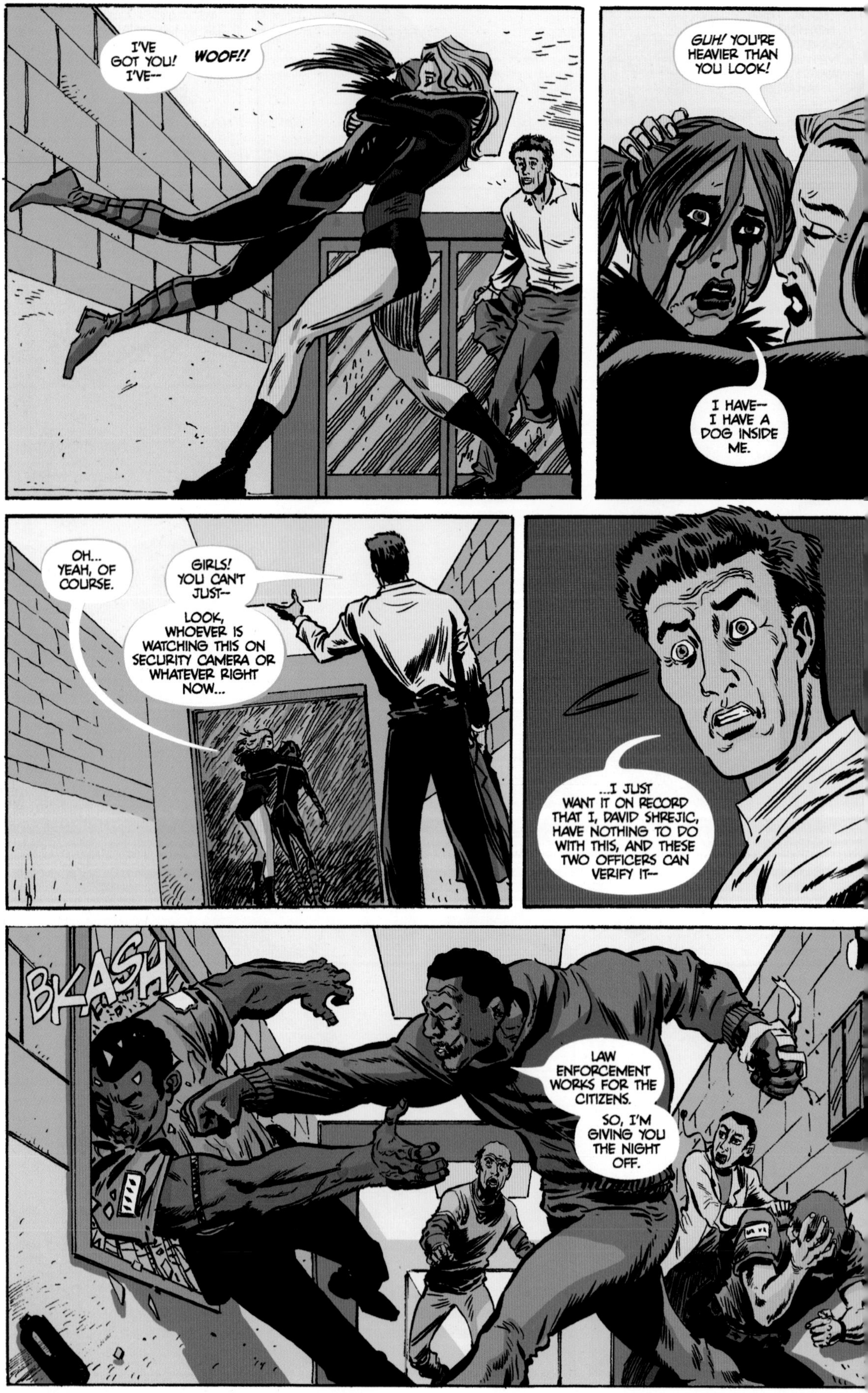
I'VE GOT YOU! I'VE--
WOOF!!
GUH! YOU'RE HEAVIER THAN YOU LOOK!
I HAVE-- I HAVE A DOG INSIDE ME.
OH... YEAH, OF COURSE.
GIRLS! YOU CAN'T JUST--
LOOK, WHOEVER IS WATCHING THIS ON SECURITY CAMERA OR WHATEVER RIGHT NOW...
...I JUST WANT IT ON RECORD THAT I, DAVID SHREJIC, HAVE NOTHING TO DO WITH THIS, AND THESE TWO OFFICERS CAN VERIFY IT--
BKASH
LAW ENFORCEMENT WORKS FOR THE CITIZENS.
SO, I'M GIVING YOU THE NIGHT OFF.

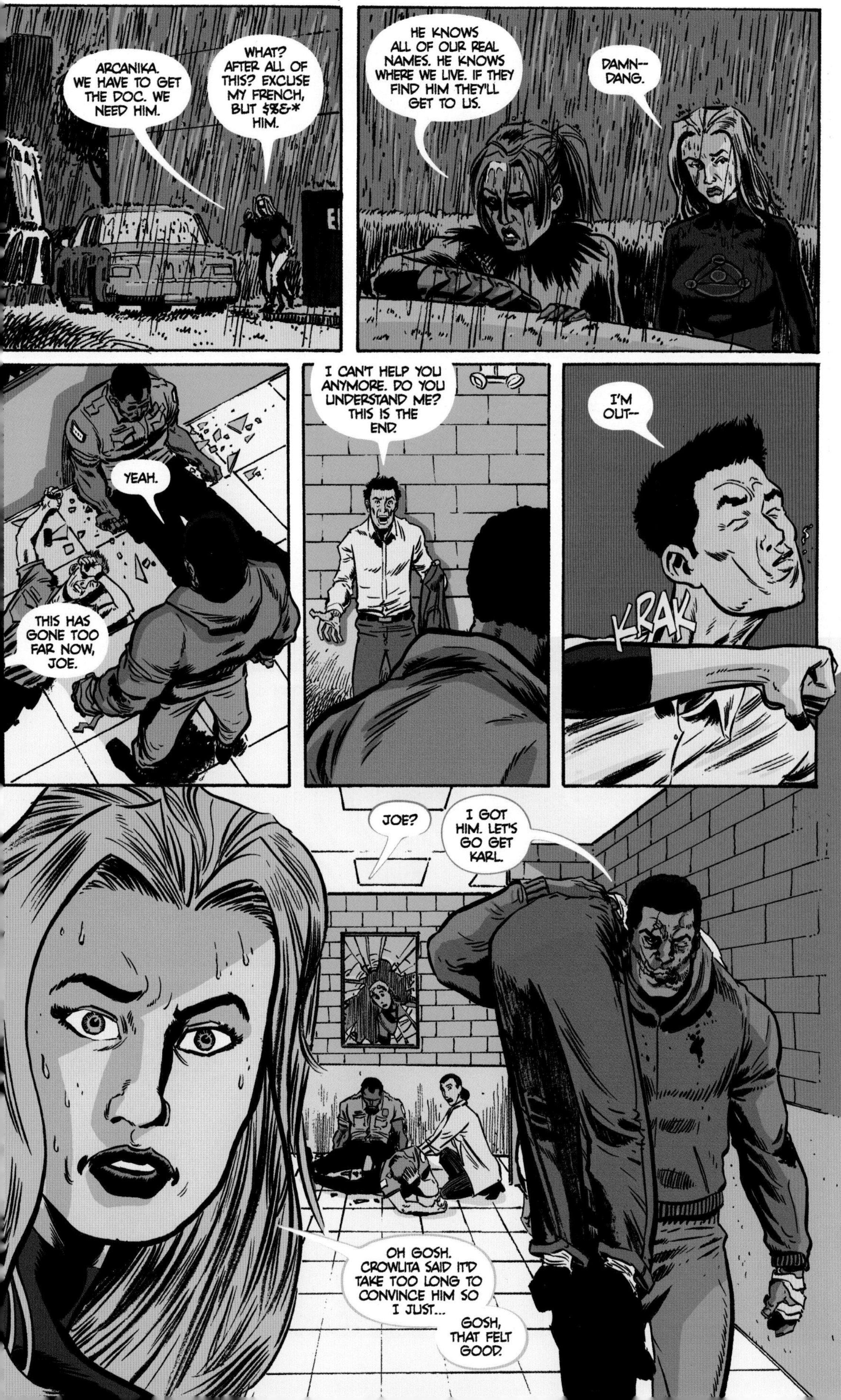
ARCANIKA. WE HAVE TO GET THE DOC. WE NEED HIM.
WHAT? AFTER ALL OF THIS? EXCUSE MY FRENCH, BUT $%&* HIM.
HE KNOWS ALL OF OUR REAL NAMES. HE KNOWS WHERE WE LIVE. IF THEY FIND HIM THEY'LL GET TO US.
DAMN--DANG.
YEAH.
THIS HAS GONE TOO FAR NOW, JOE.
I CAN'T HELP YOU ANYMORE. DO YOU UNDERSTAND ME? THIS IS THE END.
I'M OUT--
KRAK
JOE?
I GOT HIM. LET'S GO GET KARL.
OH GOSH. CROWLITA SAID IT'D TAKE TOO LONG TO CONVINCE HIM SO I JUST...
GOSH, THAT FELT GOOD.

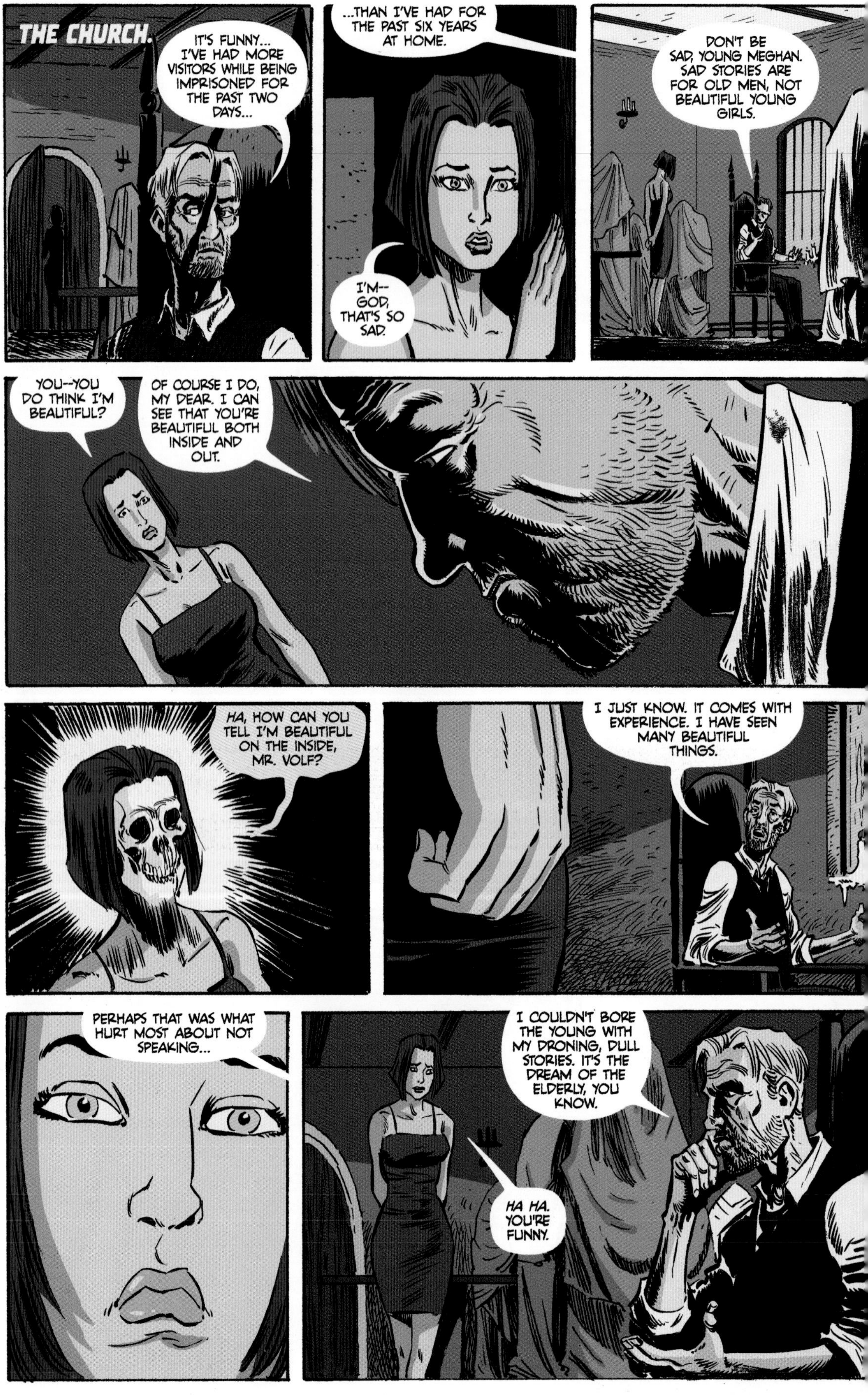
THE CHURCH.
IT'S FUNNY... I'VE HAD MORE VISITORS WHILE BEING IMPRISONED FOR THE PAST TWO DAYS...
...THAN I'VE HAD FOR THE PAST SIX YEARS AT HOME.
I'M-- GOD, THAT'S SO SAD.
DON'T BE SAD, YOUNG MEGHAN. SAD STORIES ARE FOR OLD MEN, NOT BEAUTIFUL YOUNG GIRLS.
YOU--YOU DO THINK I'M BEAUTIFUL?
OF COURSE I DO, MY DEAR. I CAN SEE THAT YOU'RE BEAUTIFUL BOTH INSIDE AND OUT.
HA, HOW CAN YOU TELL I'M BEAUTIFUL ON THE INSIDE, MR. VOLF?
I JUST KNOW. IT COMES WITH EXPERIENCE. I HAVE SEEN MANY BEAUTIFUL THINGS.
PERHAPS THAT WAS WHAT HURT MOST ABOUT NOT SPEAKING...
I COULDN'T BORE THE YOUNG WITH MY DRONING, DULL STORIES. IT'S THE DREAM OF THE ELDERLY, YOU KNOW.
HA HA. YOU'RE FUNNY.

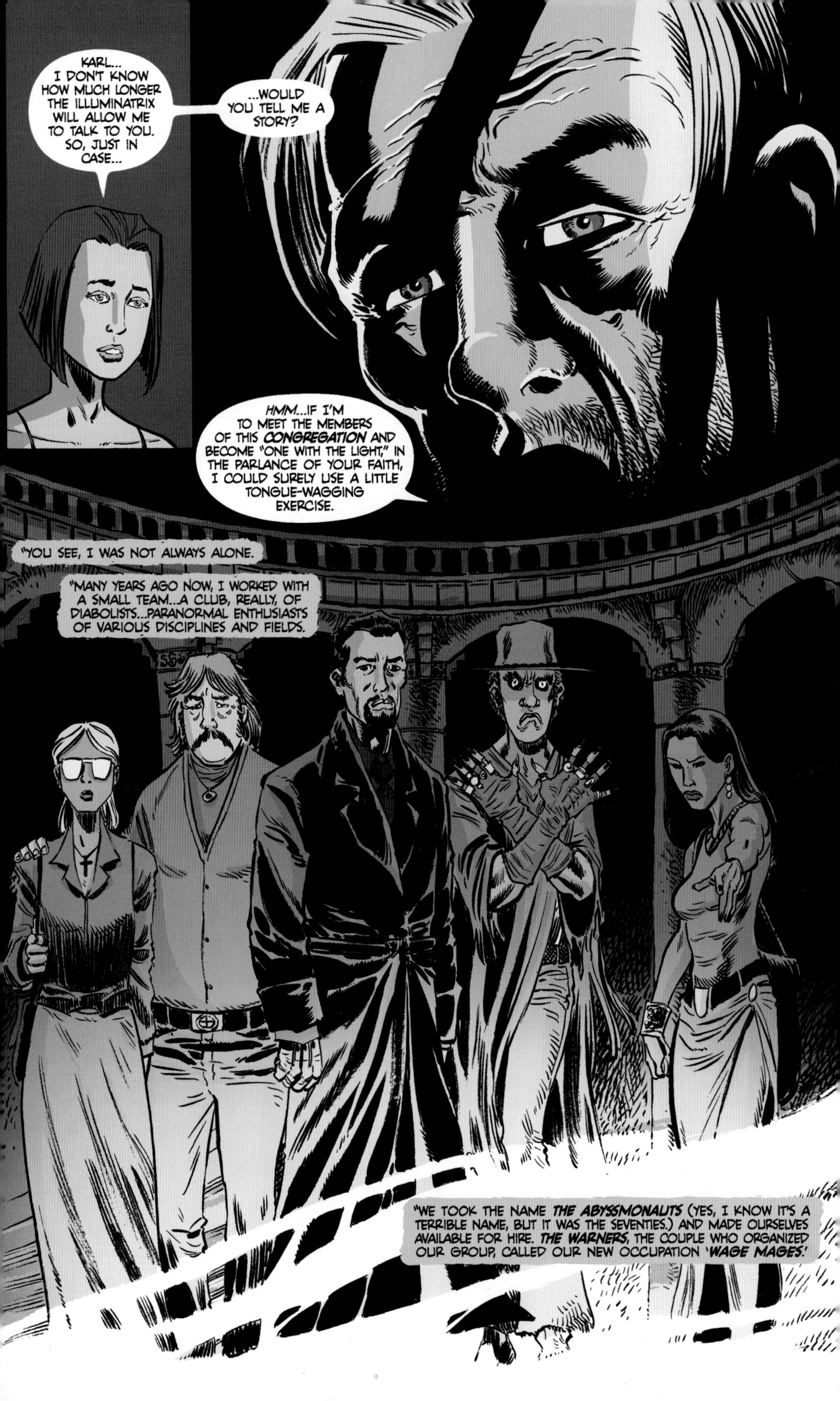
KARL... I DON'T KNOW HOW MUCH LONGER THE ILLUMINATRIX WILL ALLOW ME TO TALK TO YOU. SO, JUST IN CASE...
...WOULD YOU TELL ME A STORY?
HMM...IF I'M TO MEET THE MEMBERS OF THIS CONGREGATION AND BECOME "ONE WITH THE LIGHT," IN THE PARLANCE OF YOUR FAITH, I COULD SURELY USE A LITTLE TONGUE-WAGGING EXERCISE.
"YOU SEE, I WAS NOT ALWAYS ALONE.
"MANY YEARS AGO NOW, I WORKED WITH A SMALL TEAM...A CLUB, REALLY, OF DIABOLISTS...PARANORMAL ENTHUSIASTS OF VARIOUS DISCIPLINES AND FIELDS.
"WE TOOK THE NAME THE ABYSSMONAUTS (YES, I KNOW IT'S A TERRIBLE NAME, BUT IT WAS THE SEVENTIES.) AND MADE OURSELVES AVAILABLE FOR HIRE. THE WARNERS, THE COUPLE WHO ORGANIZED OUR GROUP, CALLED OUR NEW OCCUPATION 'WAGE MAGES.'

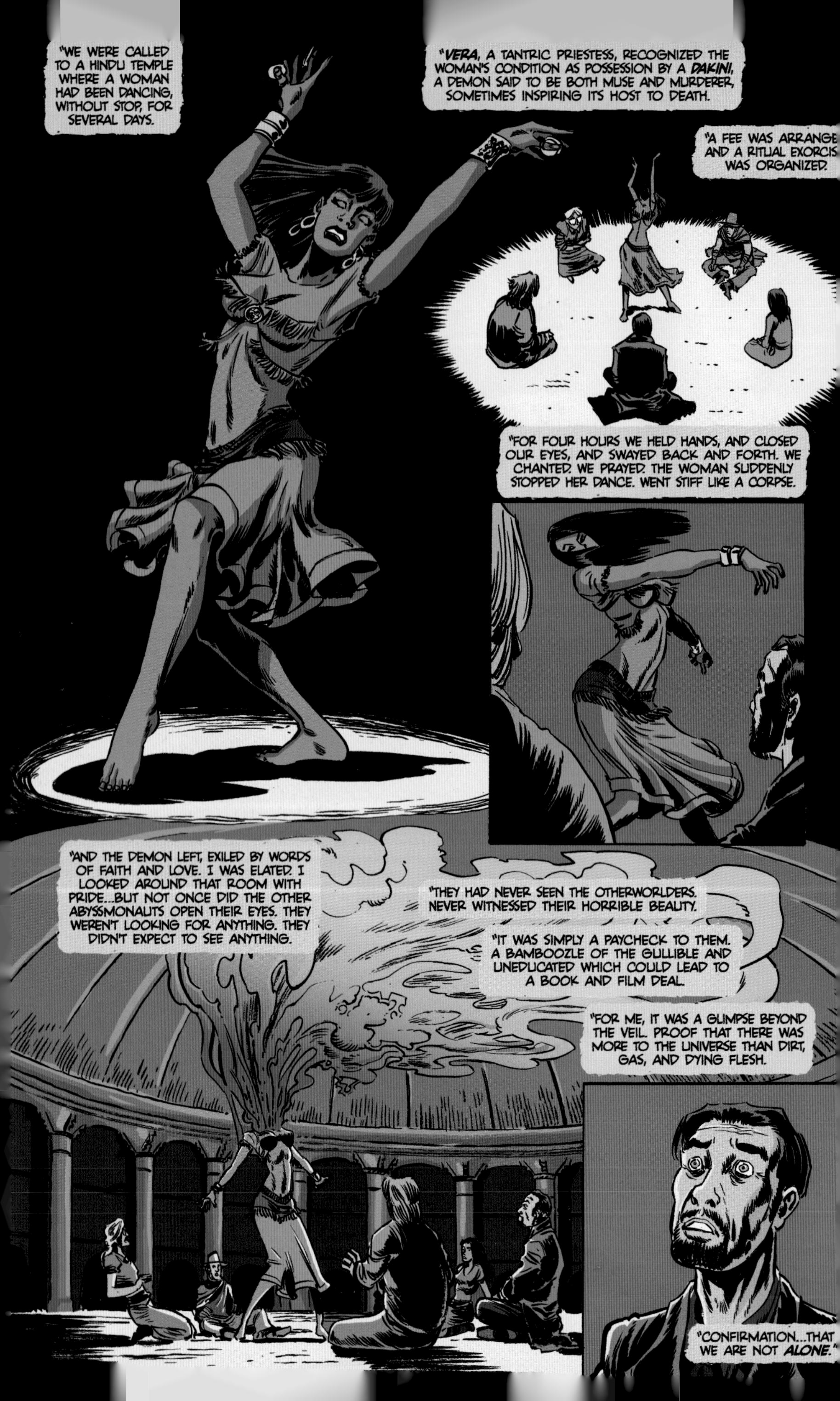

"WE WERE CALLED TO A HINDU TEMPLE WHERE A WOMAN HAD BEEN DANCING, WITHOUT STOP, FOR SEVERAL DAYS.
"VERA, A TANTRIC PRIESTESS, RECOGNIZED THE WOMAN'S CONDITION AS POSSESSION BY A DAKINI, A DEMON SAID TO BE BOTH MUSE AND MURDERER, SOMETIMES INSPIRING ITS HOST TO DEATH.
"A FEE WAS ARRANGE AND A RITUAL EXORCIS WAS ORGANIZED.
"FOR FOUR HOURS WE HELD HANDS, AND CLOSED OUR EYES, AND SWAYED BACK AND FORTH. WE CHANTED. WE PRAYED. THE WOMAN SUDDENLY STOPPED HER DANCE. WENT STIFF LIKE A CORPSE.
"AND THE DEMON LEFT, EXILED BY WORDS OF FAITH AND LOVE. I WAS ELATED. I LOOKED AROUND THAT ROOM WITH PRIDE...BUT NOT ONCE DID THE OTHER ABYSSMONAUTS OPEN THEIR EYES. THEY WEREN'T LOOKING FOR ANYTHING. THEY DIDN'T EXPECT TO SEE ANYTHING.
"THEY HAD NEVER SEEN THE OTHERWORLDERS. NEVER WITNESSED THEIR HORRIBLE BEAUTY.
"IT WAS SIMPLY A PAYCHECK TO THEM. A BAMBOOZLE OF THE GULLIBLE AND UNEDUCATED WHICH COULD LEAD TO A BOOK AND FILM DEAL.
"FOR ME, IT WAS A GLIMPSE BEYOND THE VEIL. PROOF THAT THERE WAS MORE TO THE UNIVERSE THAN DIRT, GAS, AND DYING FLESH.
"CONFIRMATION...THAT WE ARE NOT ALONE."

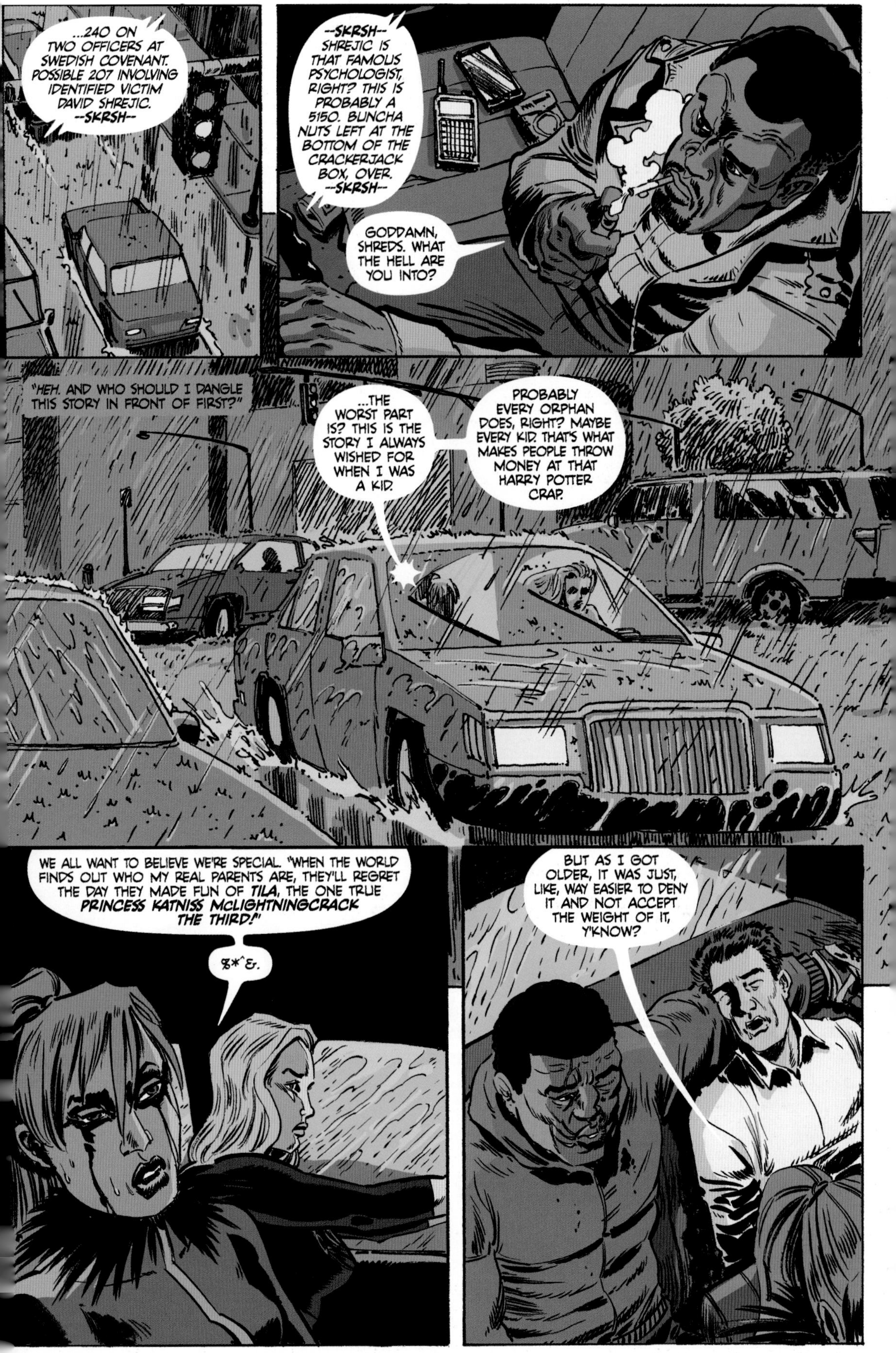
...240 ON TWO OFFICERS AT SWEDISH COVENANT. POSSIBLE 207 INVOLVING IDENTIFIED VICTIM DAVID SHREJIC. --SKRSH--
--SKRSH-- SHREJIC IS THAT FAMOUS PSYCHOLOGIST, RIGHT? THIS IS PROBABLY A 5150. BUNCHA NUTS LEFT AT THE BOTTOM OF THE CRACKERJACK BOX, OVER. --SKRSH--
GODDAMN, SHREDS. WHAT THE HELL ARE YOU INTO?
"HEH. AND WHO SHOULD I DANGLE THIS STORY IN FRONT OF FIRST?"
...THE WORST PART IS? THIS IS THE STORY I ALWAYS WISHED FOR WHEN I WAS A KID.
PROBABLY EVERY ORPHAN DOES, RIGHT? MAYBE EVERY KID. THAT'S WHAT MAKES PEOPLE THROW MONEY AT THAT HARRY POTTER CRAP.
WE ALL WANT TO BELIEVE WE'RE SPECIAL. "WHEN THE WORLD FINDS OUT WHO MY REAL PARENTS ARE, THEY'LL REGRET THE DAY THEY MADE FUN OF TILA, THE ONE TRUE PRINCESS KATNISS McLIGHTNINGCRACK THE THIRD!"
%*^&.
BUT AS I GOT OLDER, IT WAS JUST, LIKE, WAY EASIER TO DENY IT AND NOT ACCEPT THE WEIGHT OF IT, Y'KNOW?

I MEAN, WHY NOT BLAME THAT FEELING OF "OTHERNESS" AND "ALIENATION" ON BEING A WEIRDO, RATHER THAN, Y'KNOW... ACTUALLY BEING A STRANGE VISITOR FROM ANOTHER PLANET TASKED WITH TEACHING WARRIOR-SHAMAN INSURGENTS?

&%@.
I'M IN DENIAL ABOUT MY *INHUMANITY*. I'M *SUPERMAN IN THE CLOSET*.

I *WAS*, ANYWAY.

BUT I CAN'T DENY IT ANYMORE. NOT AFTER THE VISIONS. AFTER THE RED LIGHTNING.

DOCTORS ALWAYS TRIED TO BLAME THE THINGS I'VE SEEN ON THE DRUGS. BUT THE DRUGS WEREN'T THE CAUSE. THEY WERE THE CURE. REALITY-AVERSION THERAPY.

WHAT I SAW WAS THE REALEST THING I'VE EVER SEEN. IT WASN'T LIKE ANY TRIP YOU CAN GET FROM MAXING OUT A CREDIT CARD AT WALGREENS.

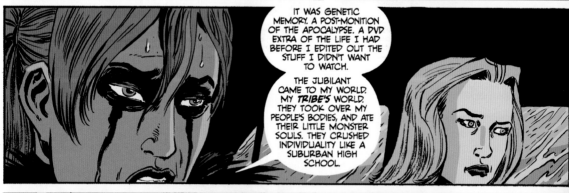

IT WAS GENETIC MEMORY. A POST-MONITION OF THE APOCALYPSE. A DVD EXTRA OF THE LIFE I HAD BEFORE I EDITED OUT THE STUFF I DIDN'T WANT TO WATCH.

THE JUBILANT CAME TO MY WORLD. MY *TRIBE'S* WORLD. THEY TOOK OVER MY PEOPLE'S BODIES, AND ATE THEIR LITTLE MONSTER SOULS. THEY CRUSHED INDIVIDUALITY LIKE A SUBURBAN HIGH SCHOOL.

AND IF WE DON'T STOP THEM, THEY'LL BOWL OVER THIS ENTIRE PLANET AND LEAVE NOTHING BUT A BIG SMEAR OF ALIEN SNAIL SLIME.

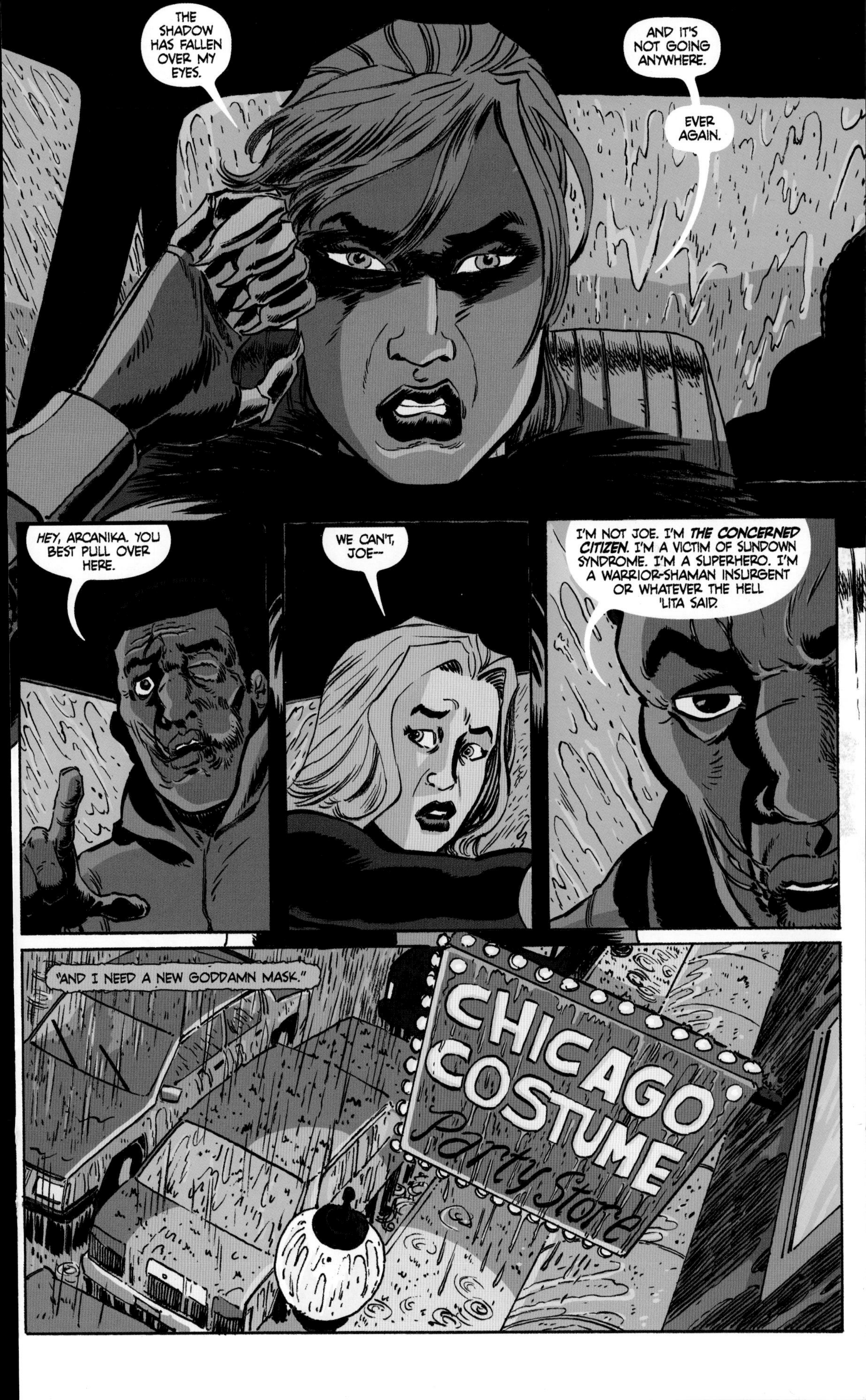

THE SHADOW HAS FALLEN OVER MY EYES.
AND IT'S NOT GOING ANYWHERE.
EVER AGAIN.
HEY, ARCANIKA. YOU BEST PULL OVER HERE.
WE CAN'T, JOE--
I'M NOT JOE. I'M THE CONCERNED CITIZEN. I'M A VICTIM OF SUNDOWN SYNDROME. I'M A SUPERHERO. I'M A WARRIOR-SHAMAN INSURGENT OR WHATEVER THE HELL 'LITA SAID.
"AND I NEED A NEW GODDAMN MASK."
CHICAGO COSTUME
Party Store

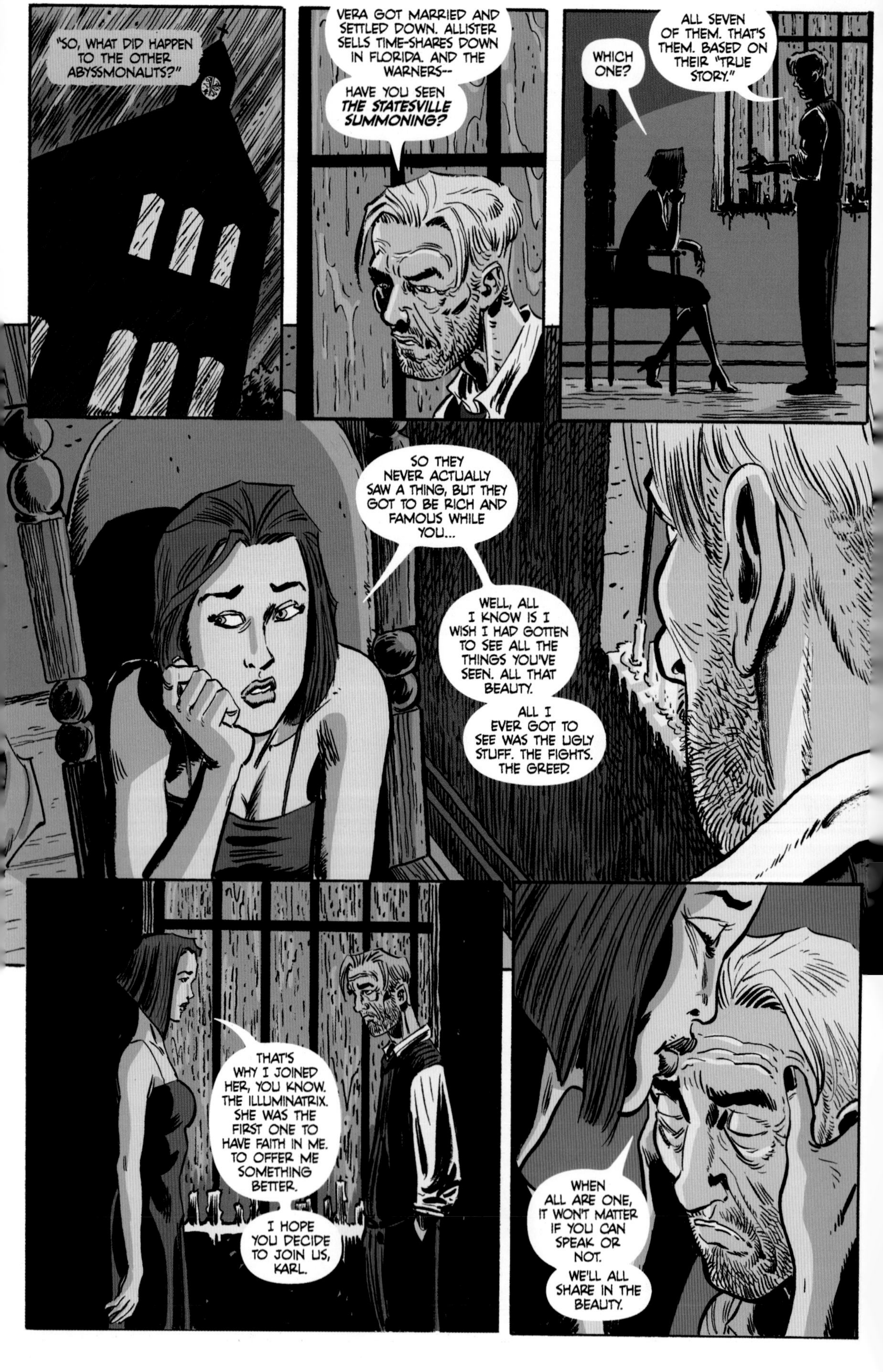
"SO, WHAT DID HAPPEN TO THE OTHER ABYSSMONAUTS?"
VERA GOT MARRIED AND SETTLED DOWN. ALLISTER SELLS TIME-SHARES DOWN IN FLORIDA. AND THE WARNERS--
HAVE YOU SEEN *THE STATESVILLE SUMMONING?*
WHICH ONE?
ALL SEVEN OF THEM. THAT'S THEM. BASED ON THEIR "TRUE STORY."
SO THEY NEVER ACTUALLY SAW A THING, BUT THEY GOT TO BE RICH AND FAMOUS WHILE YOU...
WELL, ALL I KNOW IS I WISH I HAD GOTTEN TO SEE ALL THE THINGS YOU'VE SEEN. ALL THAT BEAUTY.
ALL I EVER GOT TO SEE WAS THE UGLY STUFF. THE FIGHTS. THE GREED.
THAT'S WHY I JOINED HER, YOU KNOW. THE ILLUMINATRIX. SHE WAS THE FIRST ONE TO HAVE FAITH IN ME. TO OFFER ME SOMETHING BETTER.
I HOPE YOU DECIDE TO JOIN US, KARL.
WHEN ALL ARE ONE, IT WON'T MATTER IF YOU CAN SPEAK OR NOT.
WE'LL ALL SHARE IN THE BEAUTY.

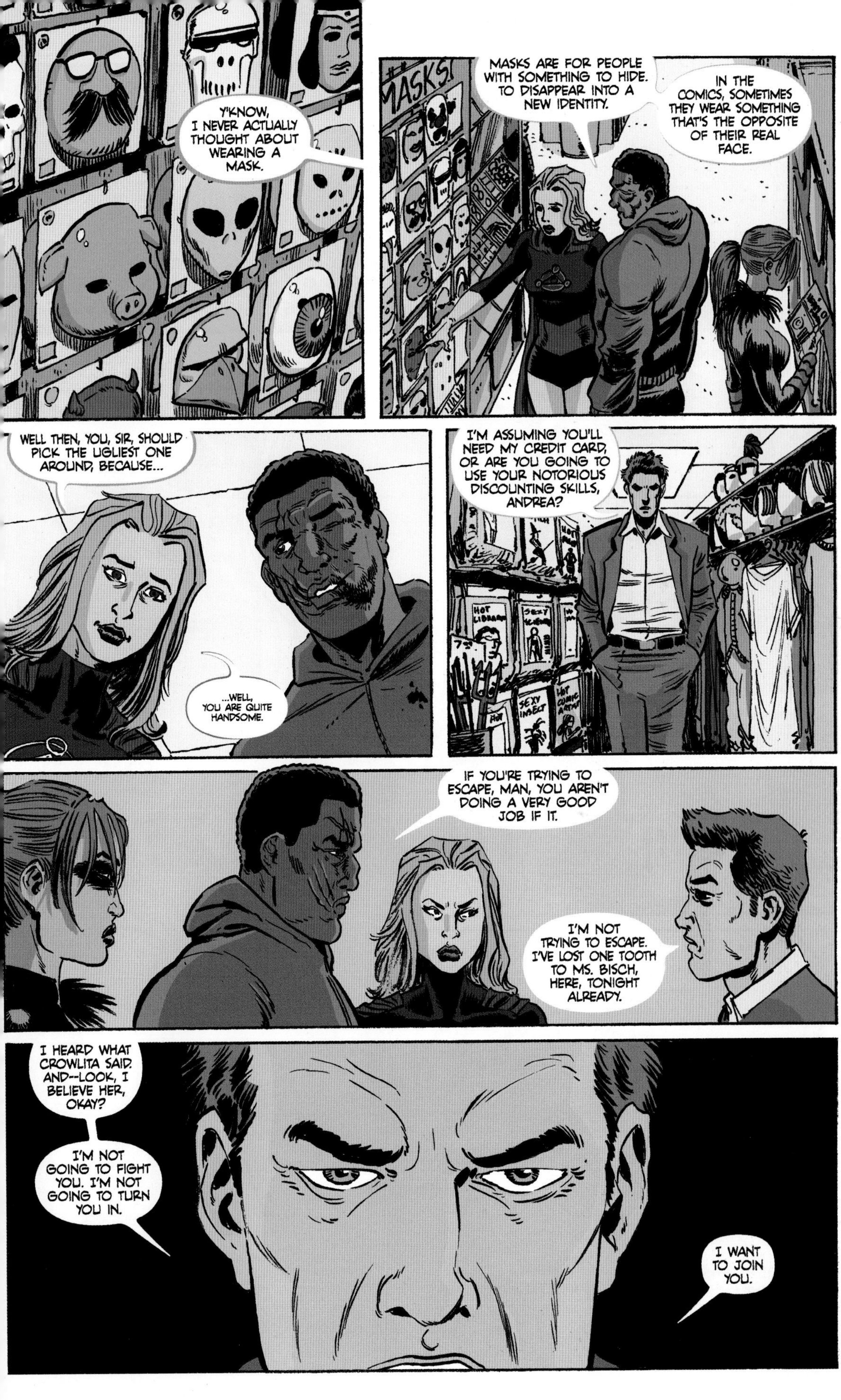
Y'KNOW, I NEVER ACTUALLY THOUGHT ABOUT WEARING A MASK.
MASKS
MASKS ARE FOR PEOPLE WITH SOMETHING TO HIDE. TO DISAPPEAR INTO A NEW IDENTITY.
IN THE COMICS, SOMETIMES THEY WEAR SOMETHING THAT'S THE OPPOSITE OF THEIR REAL FACE.
WELL THEN, YOU, SIR, SHOULD PICK THE UGLIEST ONE AROUND, BECAUSE...
...WELL, YOU ARE QUITE HANDSOME.
I'M ASSUMING YOU'LL NEED MY CREDIT CARD, OR ARE YOU GOING TO USE YOUR NOTORIOUS DISCOUNTING SKILLS, ANDREA?
IF YOU'RE TRYING TO ESCAPE, MAN, YOU AREN'T DOING A VERY GOOD JOB IF IT.
I'M NOT TRYING TO ESCAPE. I'VE LOST ONE TOOTH TO MS. BISCH, HERE, TONIGHT ALREADY.
I HEARD WHAT CROWLITA SAID. AND--LOOK, I BELIEVE HER, OKAY?
I'M NOT GOING TO FIGHT YOU. I'M NOT GOING TO TURN YOU IN.
I WANT TO JOIN YOU.

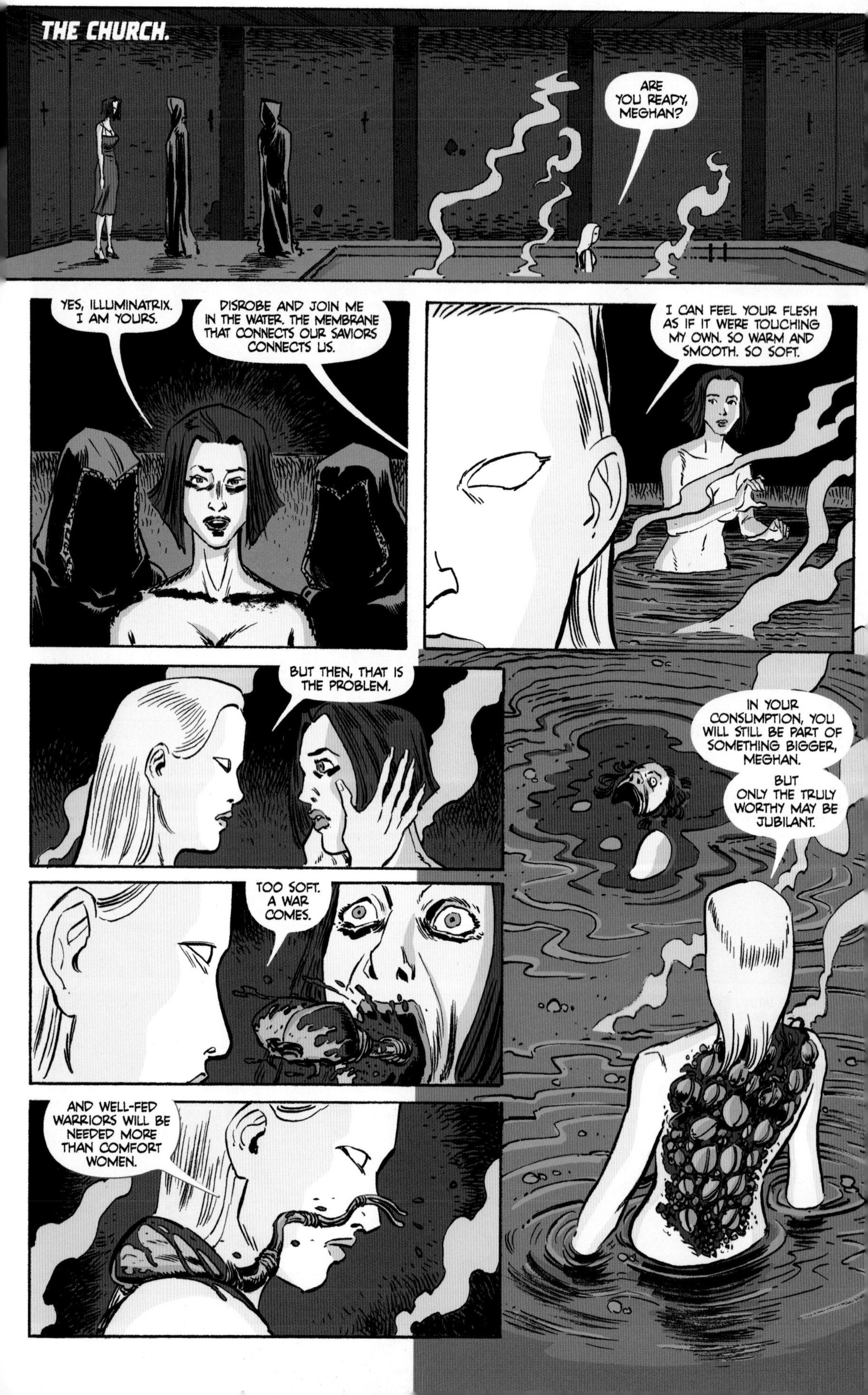
THE CHURCH.
ARE YOU READY, MEGHAN?
YES, ILLUMINATRIX. I AM YOURS.
DISROBE AND JOIN ME IN THE WATER. THE MEMBRANE THAT CONNECTS OUR SAVIORS CONNECTS US.
I CAN FEEL YOUR FLESH AS IF IT WERE TOUCHING MY OWN. SO WARM AND SMOOTH. SO SOFT.
BUT THEN, THAT IS THE PROBLEM.
TOO SOFT. A WAR COMES.
AND WELL-FED WARRIORS WILL BE NEEDED MORE THAN COMFORT WOMEN.
IN YOUR CONSUMPTION, YOU WILL STILL BE PART OF SOMETHING BIGGER, MEGHAN.
BUT ONLY THE TRULY WORTHY MAY BE JUBILANT.

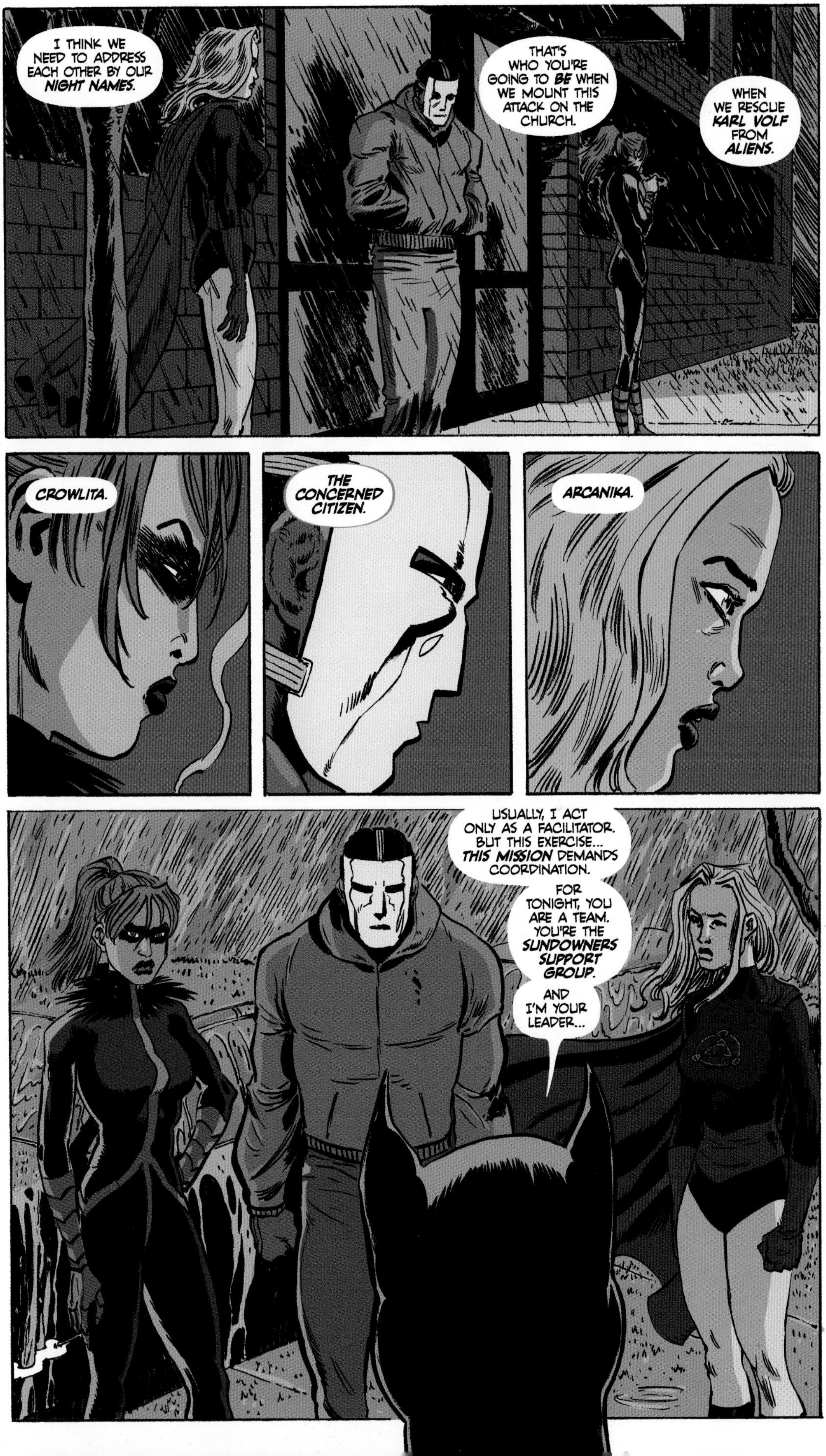
I THINK WE NEED TO ADDRESS EACH OTHER BY OUR NIGHT NAMES.
THAT'S WHO YOU'RE GOING TO BE WHEN WE MOUNT THIS ATTACK ON THE CHURCH.
WHEN WE RESCUE KARL VOLF FROM ALIENS.
CROWLITA.
THE CONCERNED CITIZEN.
ARCANIKA.
USUALLY, I ACT ONLY AS A FACILITATOR. BUT THIS EXERCISE... THIS MISSION DEMANDS COORDINATION.
FOR TONIGHT, YOU ARE A TEAM. YOU'RE THE SUNDOWNERS SUPPORT GROUP.
AND I'M YOUR LEADER...

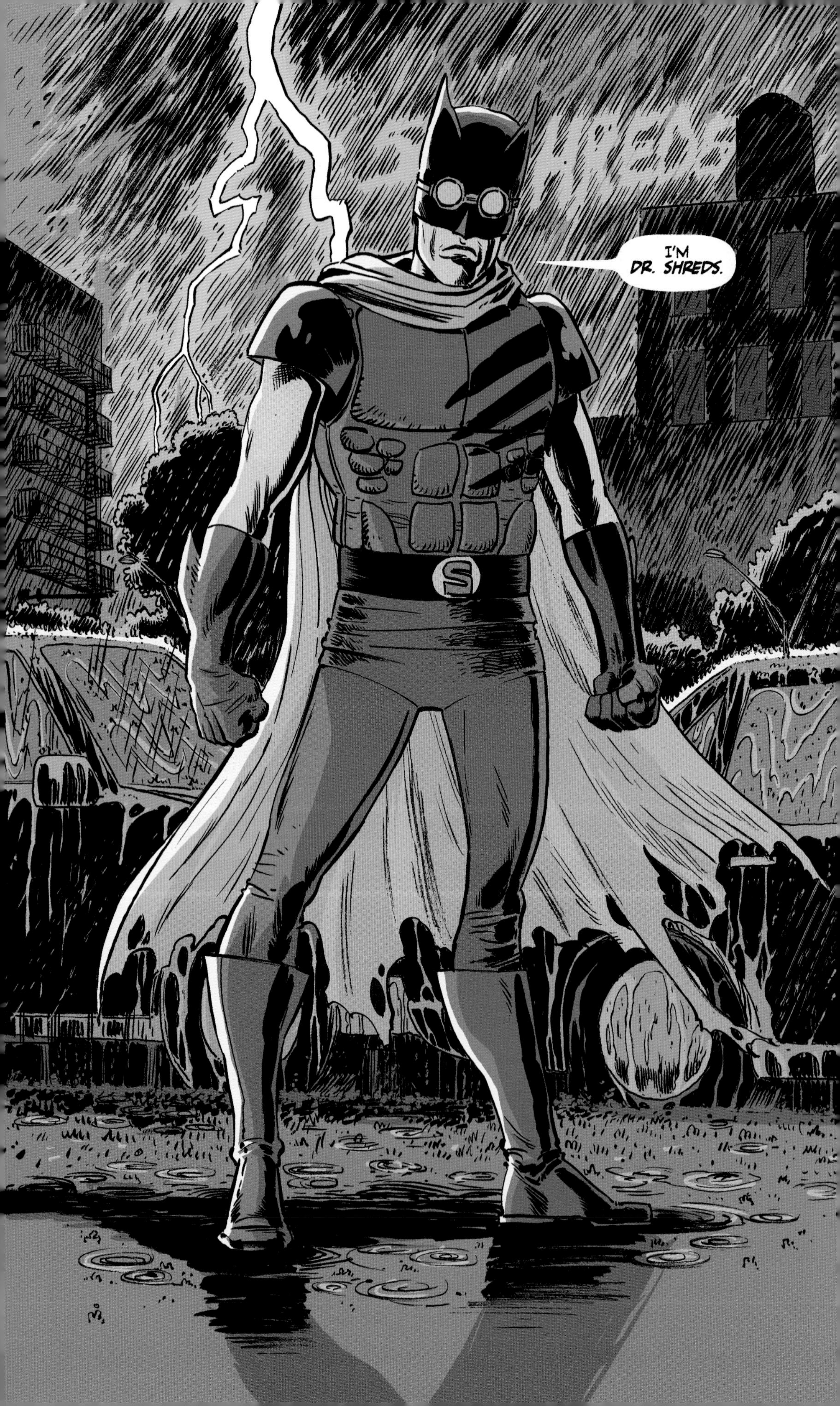
I'M DR. SHREDS.

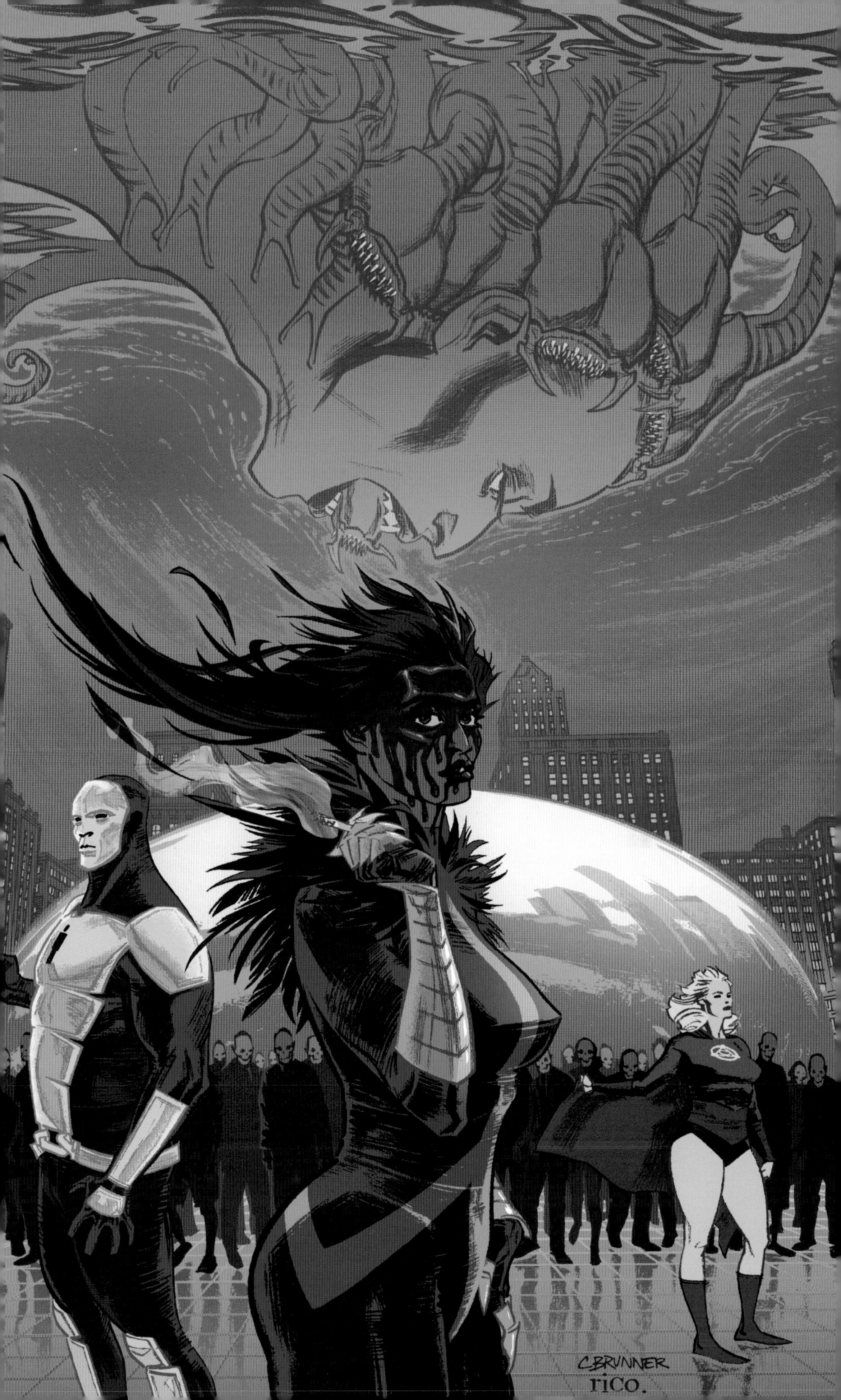
C.BRUNNER
rico.

SUNDOWNERS™ 6

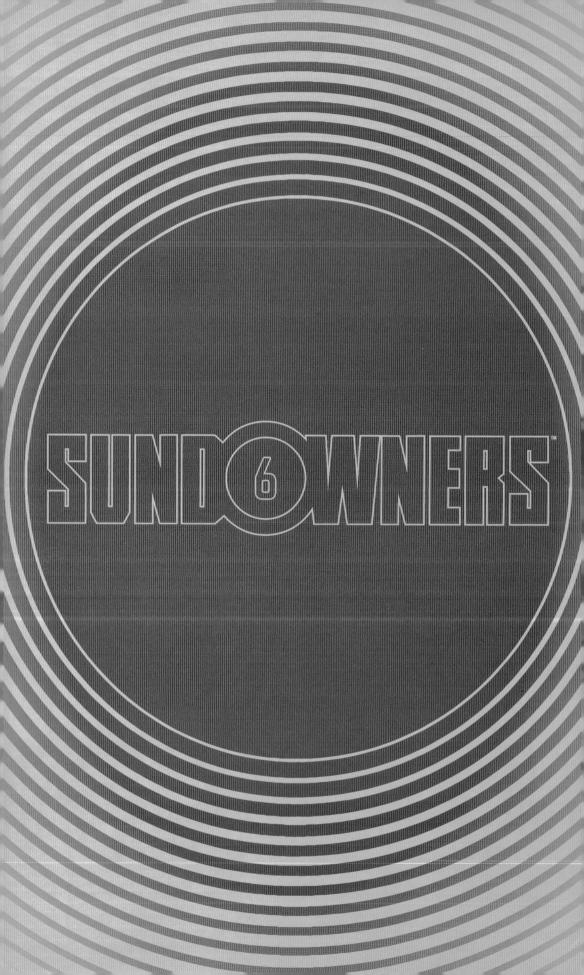

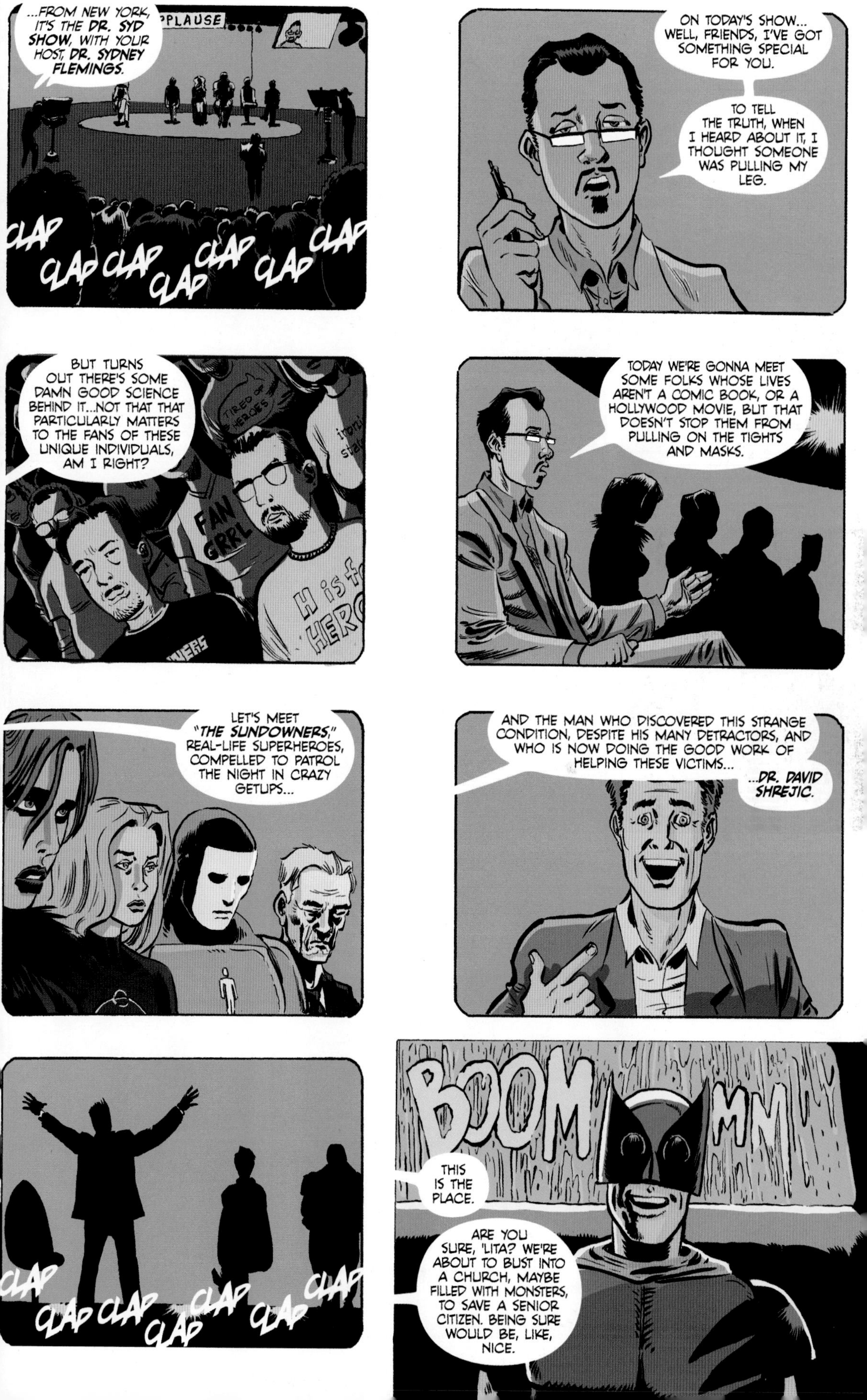
PPLAUSE
...FROM NEW YORK, IT'S THE DR. SYD SHOW, WITH YOUR HOST, DR. SYDNEY FLEMINGS.
CLAP CLAP CLAP CLAP CLAP CLAP CLAP
ON TODAY'S SHOW... WELL, FRIENDS, I'VE GOT SOMETHING SPECIAL FOR YOU.
TO TELL THE TRUTH, WHEN I HEARD ABOUT IT, I THOUGHT SOMEONE WAS PULLING MY LEG.
BUT TURNS OUT THERE'S SOME DAMN GOOD SCIENCE BEHIND IT...NOT THAT THAT PARTICULARLY MATTERS TO THE FANS OF THESE UNIQUE INDIVIDUALS, AM I RIGHT?
TIRED OF HEROES
FAN GRRL
TODAY WE'RE GONNA MEET SOME FOLKS WHOSE LIVES AREN'T A COMIC BOOK, OR A HOLLYWOOD MOVIE, BUT THAT DOESN'T STOP THEM FROM PULLING ON THE TIGHTS AND MASKS.
LET'S MEET "THE SUNDOWNERS," REAL-LIFE SUPERHEROES, COMPELLED TO PATROL THE NIGHT IN CRAZY GETUPS...
AND THE MAN WHO DISCOVERED THIS STRANGE CONDITION, DESPITE HIS MANY DETRACTORS, AND WHO IS NOW DOING THE GOOD WORK OF HELPING THESE VICTIMS...
...DR. DAVID SHREJIC.
CLAP CLAP CLAP CLAP CLAP CLAP CLAP
BOOM
MM
THIS IS THE PLACE.
ARE YOU SURE, 'LITA? WE'RE ABOUT TO BUST INTO A CHURCH, MAYBE FILLED WITH MONSTERS, TO SAVE A SENIOR CITIZEN. BEING SURE WOULD BE, LIKE, NICE.

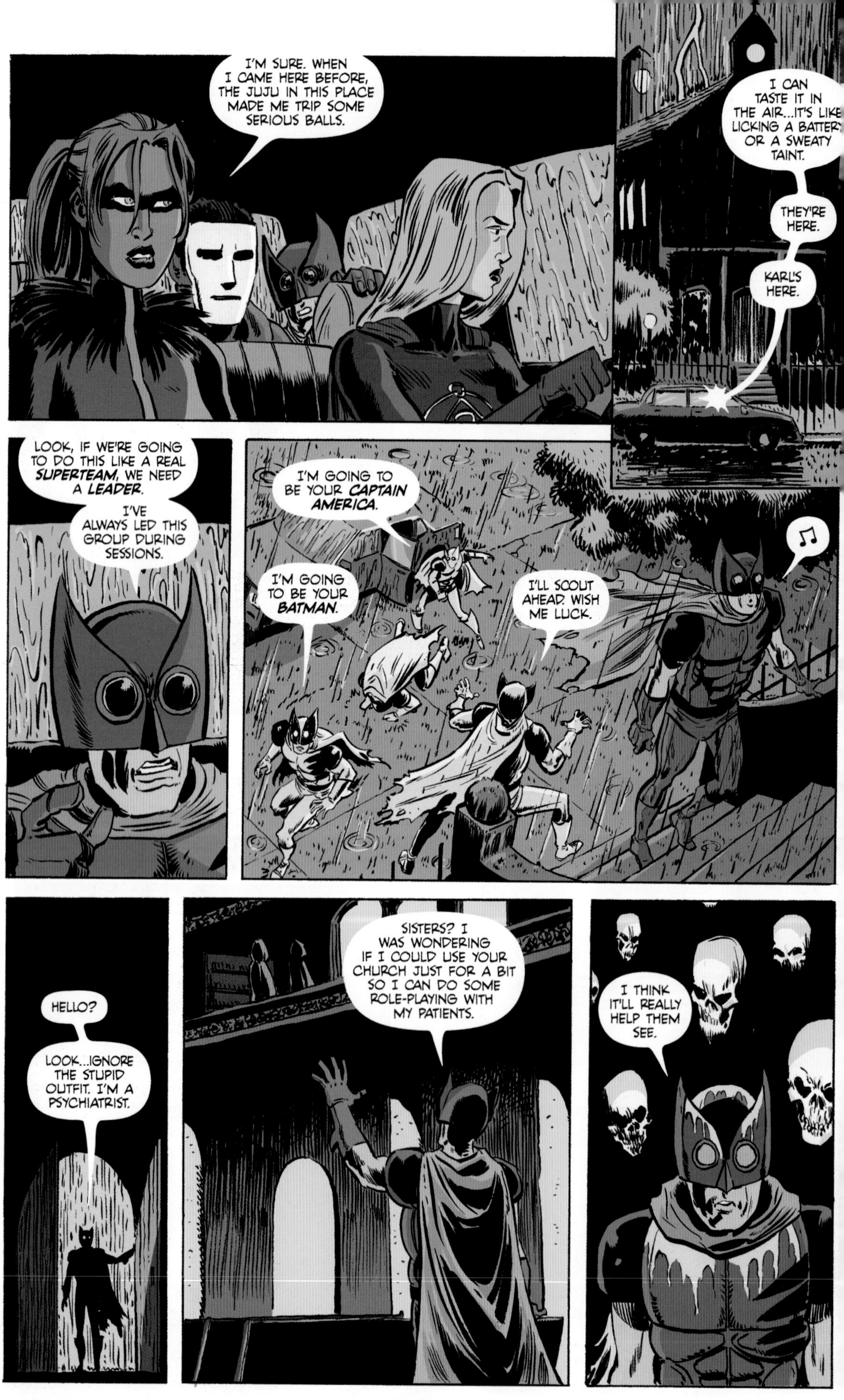
I'M SURE. WHEN I CAME HERE BEFORE, THE JUJU IN THIS PLACE MADE ME TRIP SOME SERIOUS BALLS.
I CAN TASTE IT IN THE AIR...IT'S LIKE LICKING A BATTERY OR A SWEATY TAINT.
THEY'RE HERE.
KARL'S HERE.
LOOK, IF WE'RE GOING TO DO THIS LIKE A REAL SUPERTEAM, WE NEED A LEADER.
I'VE ALWAYS LED THIS GROUP DURING SESSIONS.
I'M GOING TO BE YOUR CAPTAIN AMERICA.
I'M GOING TO BE YOUR BATMAN.
I'LL SCOUT AHEAD. WISH ME LUCK.
♫
HELLO?
LOOK...IGNORE THE STUPID OUTFIT. I'M A PSYCHIATRIST.
SISTERS? I WAS WONDERING IF I COULD USE YOUR CHURCH JUST FOR A BIT SO I CAN DO SOME ROLE-PLAYING WITH MY PATIENTS.
I THINK IT'LL REALLY HELP THEM SEE.

TILA?

THE **SUNDOWNERS** GROUP.

THEY CAME FOR ME. THE CRAZY, WONDERFUL BASTARDS...

OH... NO.

TILA! YOU HAVE TO GET OUT-- *ONGHK.*

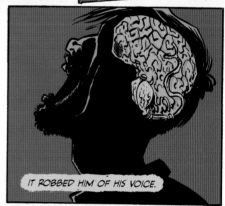

GLK.

SIX YEARS AGO, **KARL VOLF** SUFFERED A MASSIVE STROKE.

IT ROBBED HIM OF HIS VOICE.

A GIFT FROM AN ANGEL GAVE IT BACK TO HIM.

MAYBE, HE THINKS, JUST SO HE COULD EXPERIENCE ITS **LOSS** ALL OVER AGAIN.

YOU. SSSPEAK.

ONLY. WHEN. **THE JUBILANT.** SAY.

UH... SISTERS? LADIES?

IF YOU CAN'T HELP, DO YOU KNOW WHO I SHOULD TALK TO?

CHURCHES ARE ALWAYS ASKING FOR MONEY. I'LL PAY--

AH, WHAT THE--?!

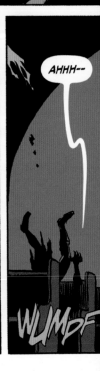

HRRCH!!

AHH!

AHHH--

WUMPF

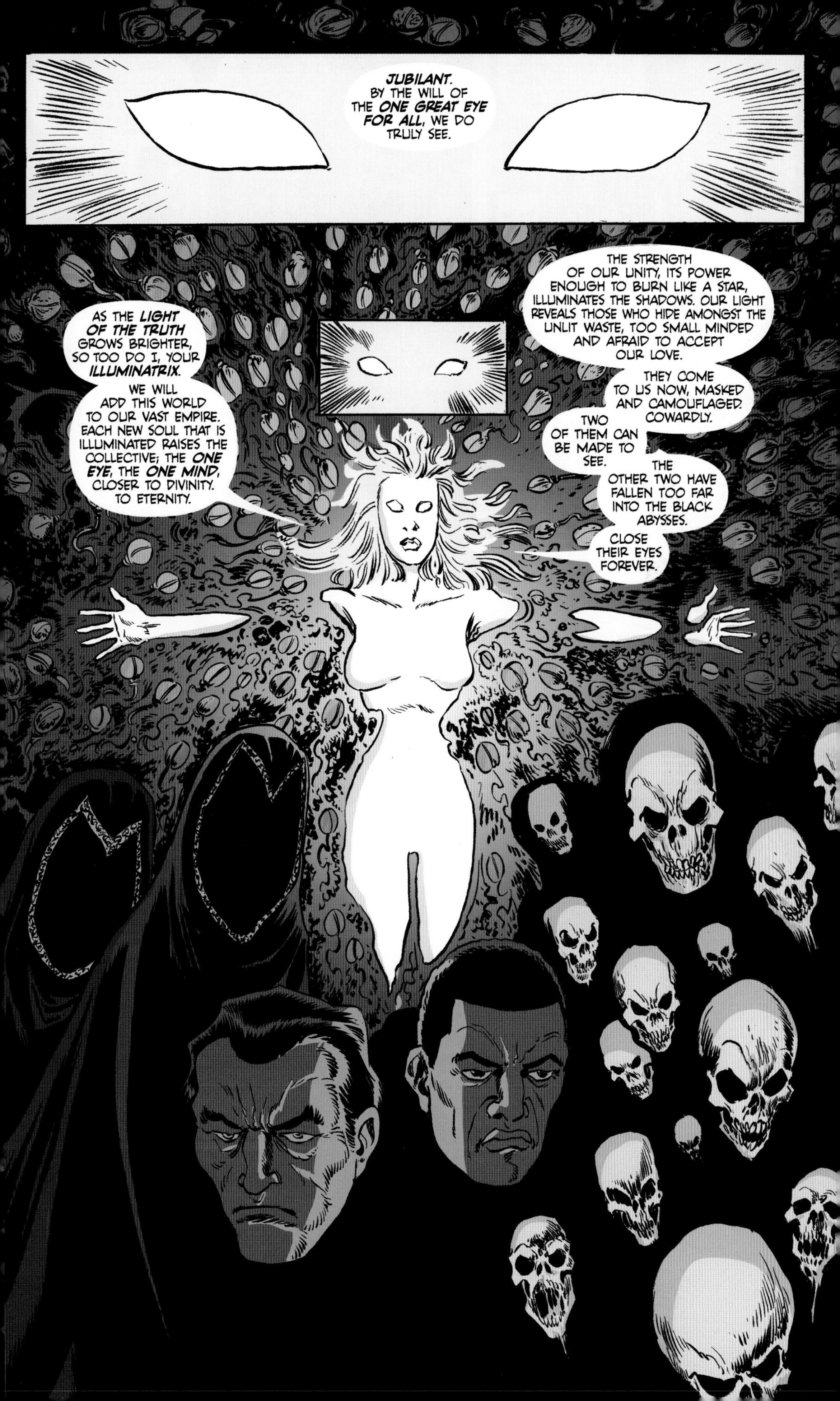

JUBILANT. BY THE WILL OF THE ONE GREAT EYE FOR ALL, WE DO TRULY SEE.
AS THE LIGHT OF THE TRUTH GROWS BRIGHTER, SO TOO DO I, YOUR ILLUMINATRIX.
WE WILL ADD THIS WORLD TO OUR VAST EMPIRE. EACH NEW SOUL THAT IS ILLUMINATED RAISES THE COLLECTIVE; THE ONE EYE, THE ONE MIND, CLOSER TO DIVINITY. TO ETERNITY.
THE STRENGTH OF OUR UNITY, ITS POWER ENOUGH TO BURN LIKE A STAR, ILLUMINATES THE SHADOWS. OUR LIGHT REVEALS THOSE WHO HIDE AMONGST THE UNLIT WASTE, TOO SMALL MINDED AND AFRAID TO ACCEPT OUR LOVE.
THEY COME TO US NOW, MASKED AND CAMOUFLAGED. COWARDLY.
TWO OF THEM CAN BE MADE TO SEE.
THE OTHER TWO HAVE FALLEN TOO FAR INTO THE BLACK ABYSSES.
CLOSE THEIR EYES FOREVER.

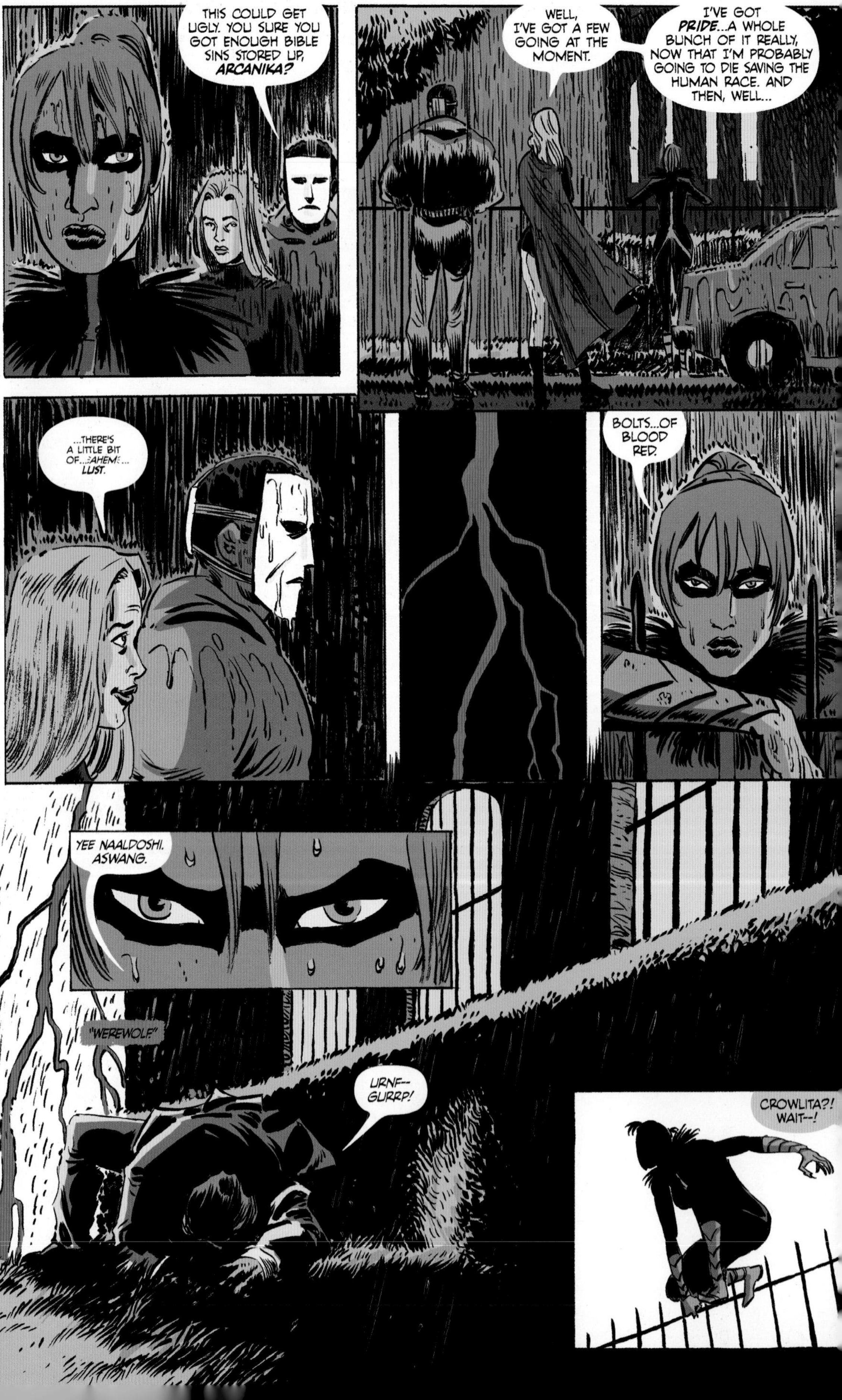
THIS COULD GET UGLY. YOU SURE YOU GOT ENOUGH BIBLE SINS STORED UP, ARCANIKA?
WELL, I'VE GOT A FEW GOING AT THE MOMENT.
I'VE GOT PRIDE...A WHOLE BUNCH OF IT REALLY, NOW THAT I'M PROBABLY GOING TO DIE SAVING THE HUMAN RACE. AND THEN, WELL...
...THERE'S A LITTLE BIT OF...AHEM... LUST.
BOLTS...OF BLOOD RED.
YEE NAALDOSHI. ASWANG.
"WEREWOLF"
URNF-- GURRP!
CROWLITA?! WAIT--!

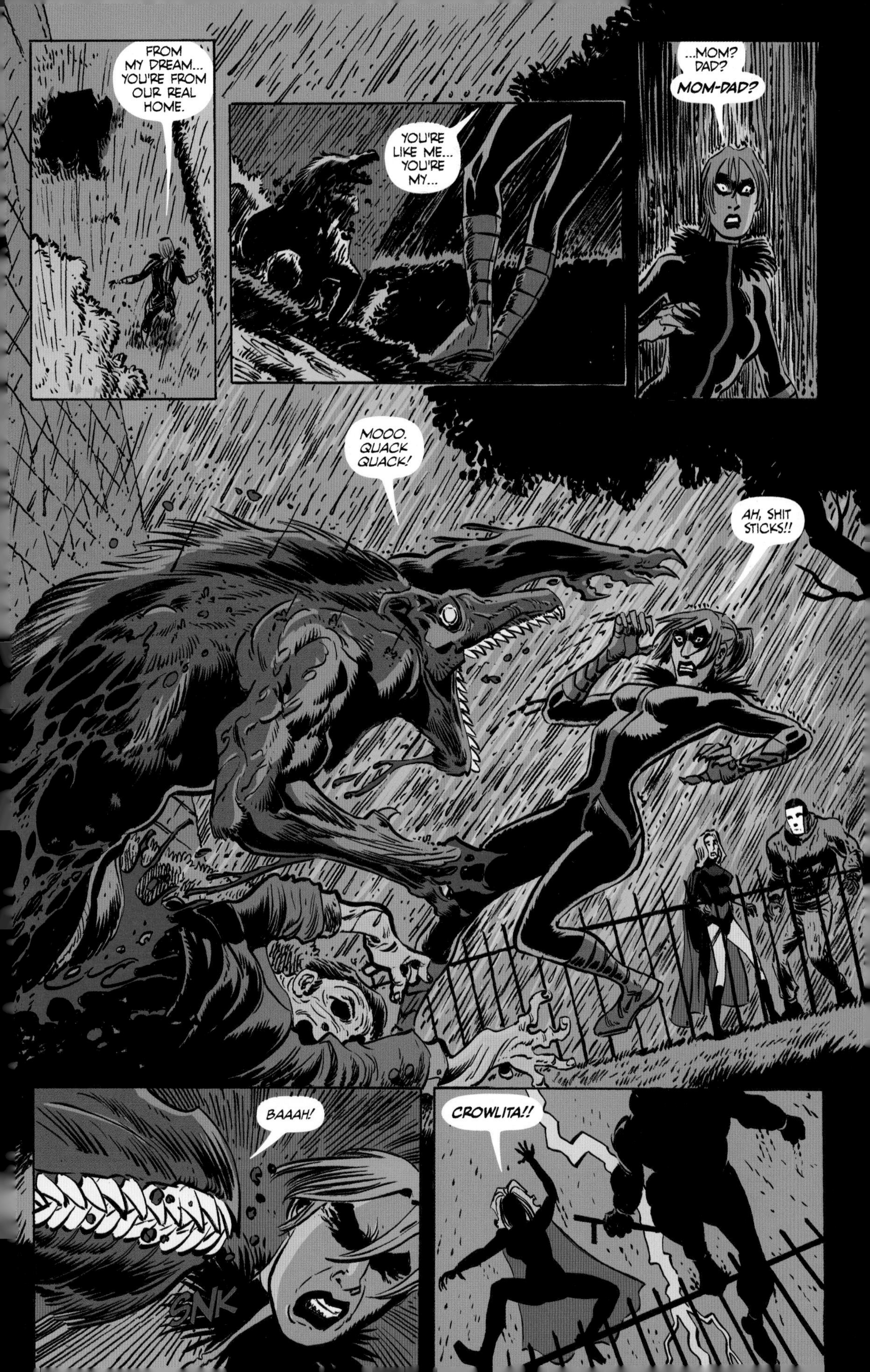
FROM MY DREAM... YOU'RE FROM OUR REAL HOME.
YOU'RE LIKE ME... YOU'RE MY...
...MOM? DAD?
MOM-DAD?
MOOO. QUACK QUACK!
AH, SHIT STICKS!!
BAAAH!
SNK
CROWLITA!!

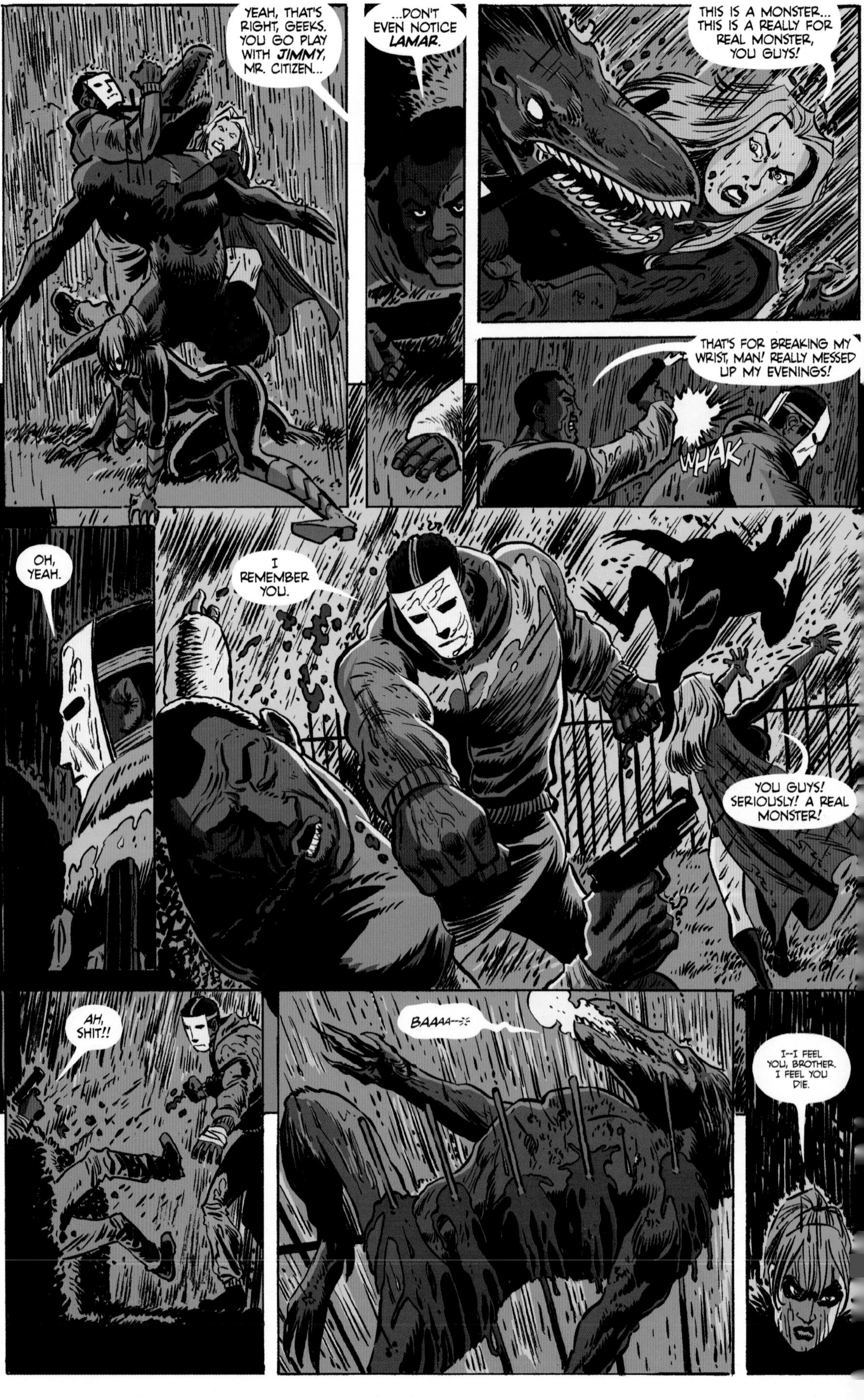
YEAH, THAT'S RIGHT, GEEKS. YOU GO PLAY WITH JIMMY, MR. CITIZEN...
...DON'T EVEN NOTICE LAMAR.
THIS IS A MONSTER... THIS IS A REALLY FOR REAL MONSTER, YOU GUYS!
THAT'S FOR BREAKING MY WRIST, MAN! REALLY MESSED UP MY EVENINGS!
WHAK
OH, YEAH.
I REMEMBER YOU.
YOU GUYS! SERIOUSLY! A REAL MONSTER!
AH, SHIT!!
BAAAA--
I--I FEEL YOU, BROTHER. I FEEL YOU DIE.

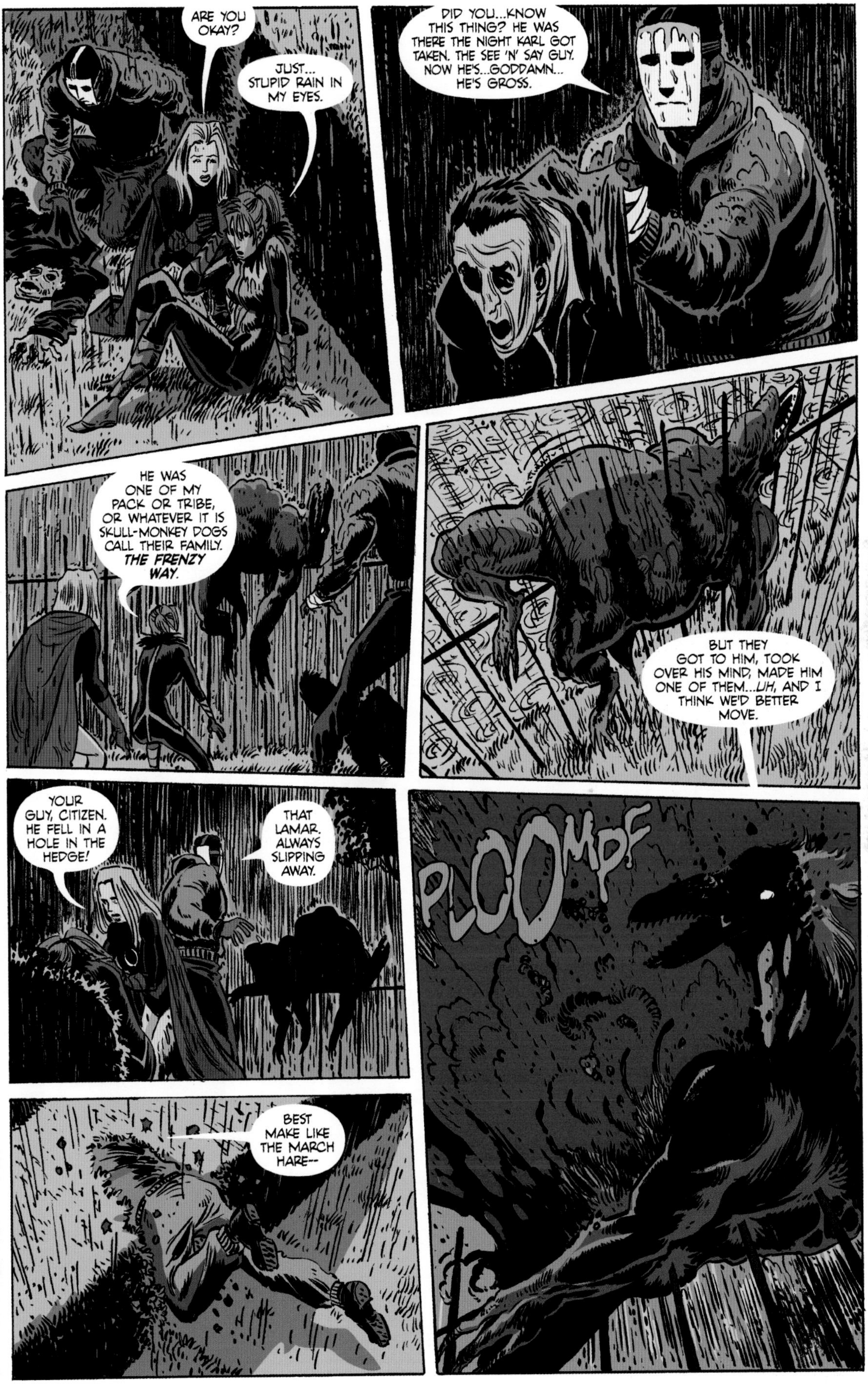

ARE YOU OKAY?
JUST... STUPID RAIN IN MY EYES.
DID YOU...KNOW THIS THING? HE WAS THERE THE NIGHT KARL GOT TAKEN. THE SEE 'N' SAY GUY. NOW HE'S...GODDAMN... HE'S GROSS.
HE WAS ONE OF MY PACK OR TRIBE, OR WHATEVER IT IS SKULL-MONKEY DOGS CALL THEIR FAMILY. THE FRENZY WAY.
BUT THEY GOT TO HIM, TOOK OVER HIS MIND, MADE HIM ONE OF THEM...UH, AND I THINK WE'D BETTER MOVE.
YOUR GUY, CITIZEN. HE FELL IN A HOLE IN THE HEDGE!
THAT LAMAR. ALWAYS SLIPPING AWAY.
BEST MAKE LIKE THE MARCH HARE--
PLOOMPF

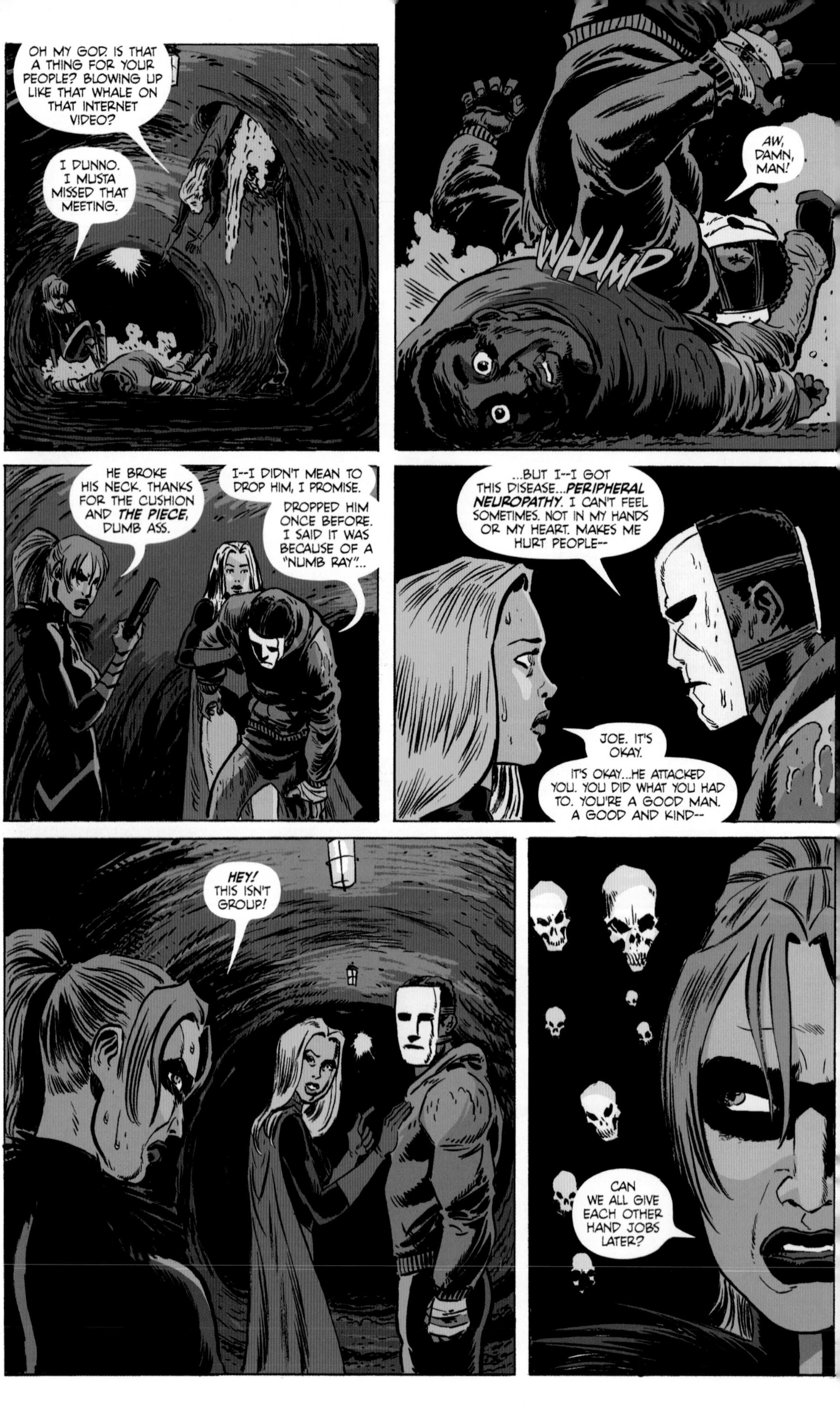
OH MY GOD. IS THAT A THING FOR YOUR PEOPLE? BLOWING UP LIKE THAT WHALE ON THAT INTERNET VIDEO?
I DUNNO. I MUSTA MISSED THAT MEETING.
AW, DAMN, MAN!
WHUMP
HE BROKE HIS NECK. THANKS FOR THE CUSHION AND THE PIECE, DUMB ASS.
I--I DIDN'T MEAN TO DROP HIM, I PROMISE.
DROPPED HIM ONCE BEFORE. I SAID IT WAS BECAUSE OF A "NUMB RAY"...
...BUT I--I GOT THIS DISEASE...PERIPHERAL NEUROPATHY. I CAN'T FEEL SOMETIMES. NOT IN MY HANDS OR MY HEART. MAKES ME HURT PEOPLE--
JOE. IT'S OKAY.
IT'S OKAY...HE ATTACKED YOU. YOU DID WHAT YOU HAD TO. YOU'RE A GOOD MAN. A GOOD AND KIND--
HEY! THIS ISN'T GROUP!
CAN WE ALL GIVE EACH OTHER HAND JOBS LATER?

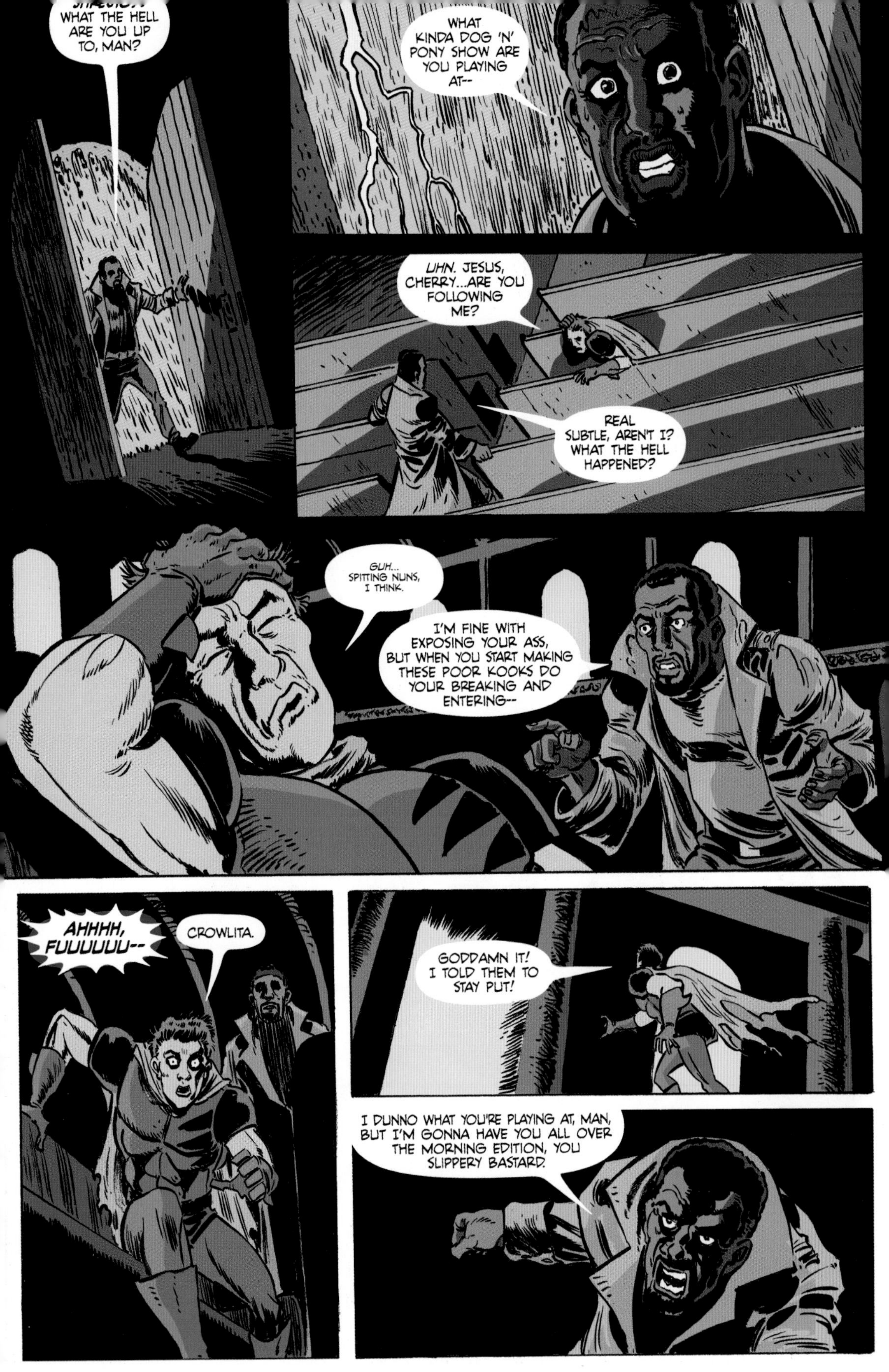

WHAT THE HELL ARE YOU UP TO, MAN?
WHAT KINDA DOG 'N' PONY SHOW ARE YOU PLAYING AT--
UHN. JESUS, CHERRY...ARE YOU FOLLOWING ME?
REAL SUBTLE, AREN'T I? WHAT THE HELL HAPPENED?
GUH... SPITTING NUNS, I THINK.
I'M FINE WITH EXPOSING YOUR ASS, BUT WHEN YOU START MAKING THESE POOR KOOKS DO YOUR BREAKING AND ENTERING--
AHHHH, FUUUUUU--
CROWLITA.
GODDAMN IT! I TOLD THEM TO STAY PUT!
I DUNNO WHAT YOU'RE PLAYING AT, MAN, BUT I'M GONNA HAVE YOU ALL OVER THE MORNING EDITION, YOU SLIPPERY BASTARD.

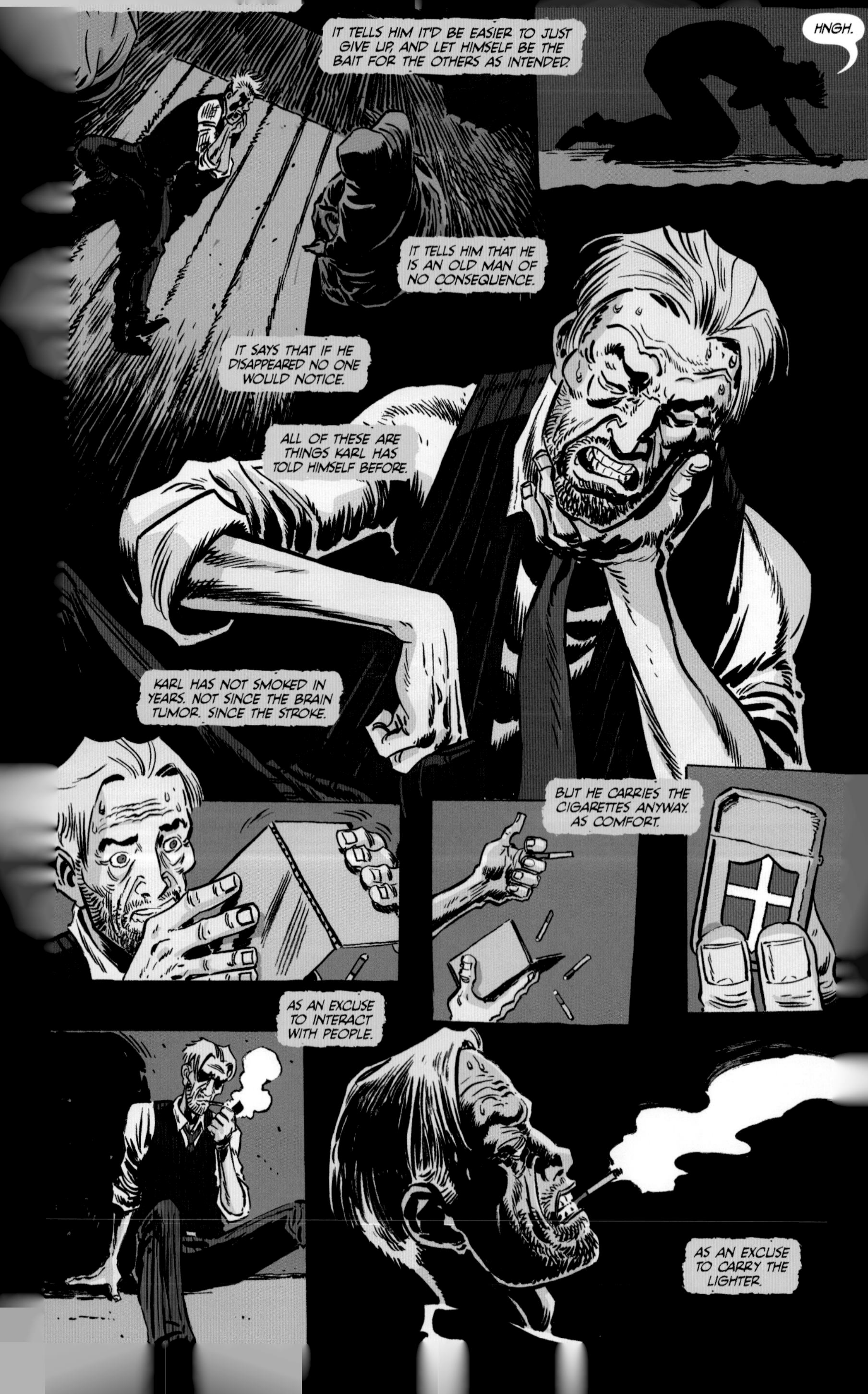
IT TELLS HIM IT'D BE EASIER TO JUST GIVE UP, AND LET HIMSELF BE THE BAIT FOR THE OTHERS AS INTENDED.
HNGH.
IT TELLS HIM THAT HE IS AN OLD MAN OF NO CONSEQUENCE.
IT SAYS THAT IF HE DISAPPEARED NO ONE WOULD NOTICE.
ALL OF THESE ARE THINGS KARL HAS TOLD HIMSELF BEFORE.
KARL HAS NOT SMOKED IN YEARS. NOT SINCE THE BRAIN TUMOR. SINCE THE STROKE.
BUT HE CARRIES THE CIGARETTES ANYWAY. AS COMFORT.
AS AN EXCUSE TO INTERACT WITH PEOPLE.
AS AN EXCUSE TO CARRY THE LIGHTER.

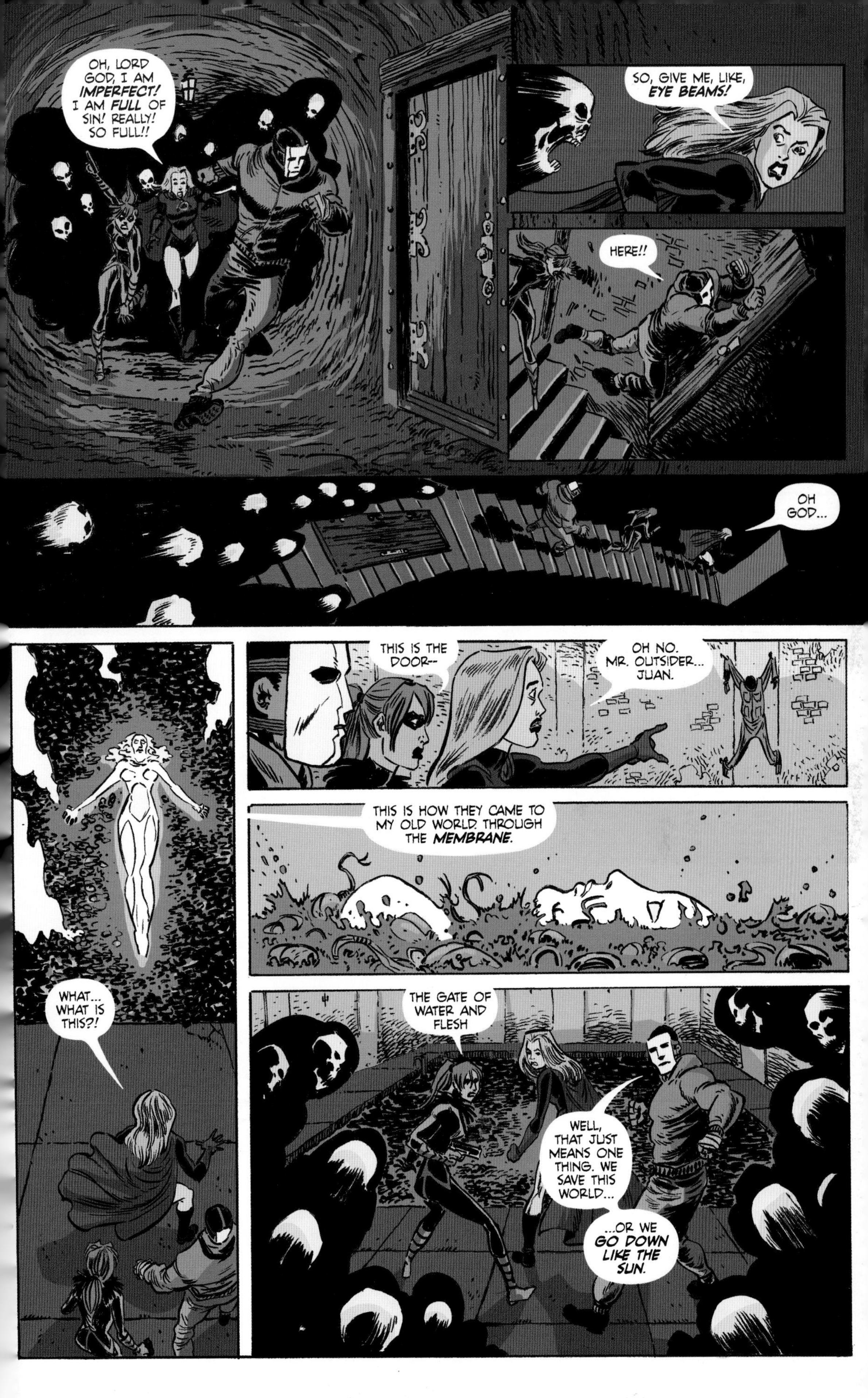
OH, LORD GOD, I AM IMPERFECT! I AM FULL OF SIN! REALLY! SO FULL!!
SO, GIVE ME, LIKE, EYE BEAMS!
HERE!!
OH GOD...
WHAT... WHAT IS THIS?!
THIS IS THE DOOR--
OH NO. MR. OUTSIDER... JUAN.
THIS IS HOW THEY CAME TO MY OLD WORLD. THROUGH THE MEMBRANE.
THE GATE OF WATER AND FLESH
WELL, THAT JUST MEANS ONE THING. WE SAVE THIS WORLD...
...OR WE GO DOWN LIKE THE SUN.

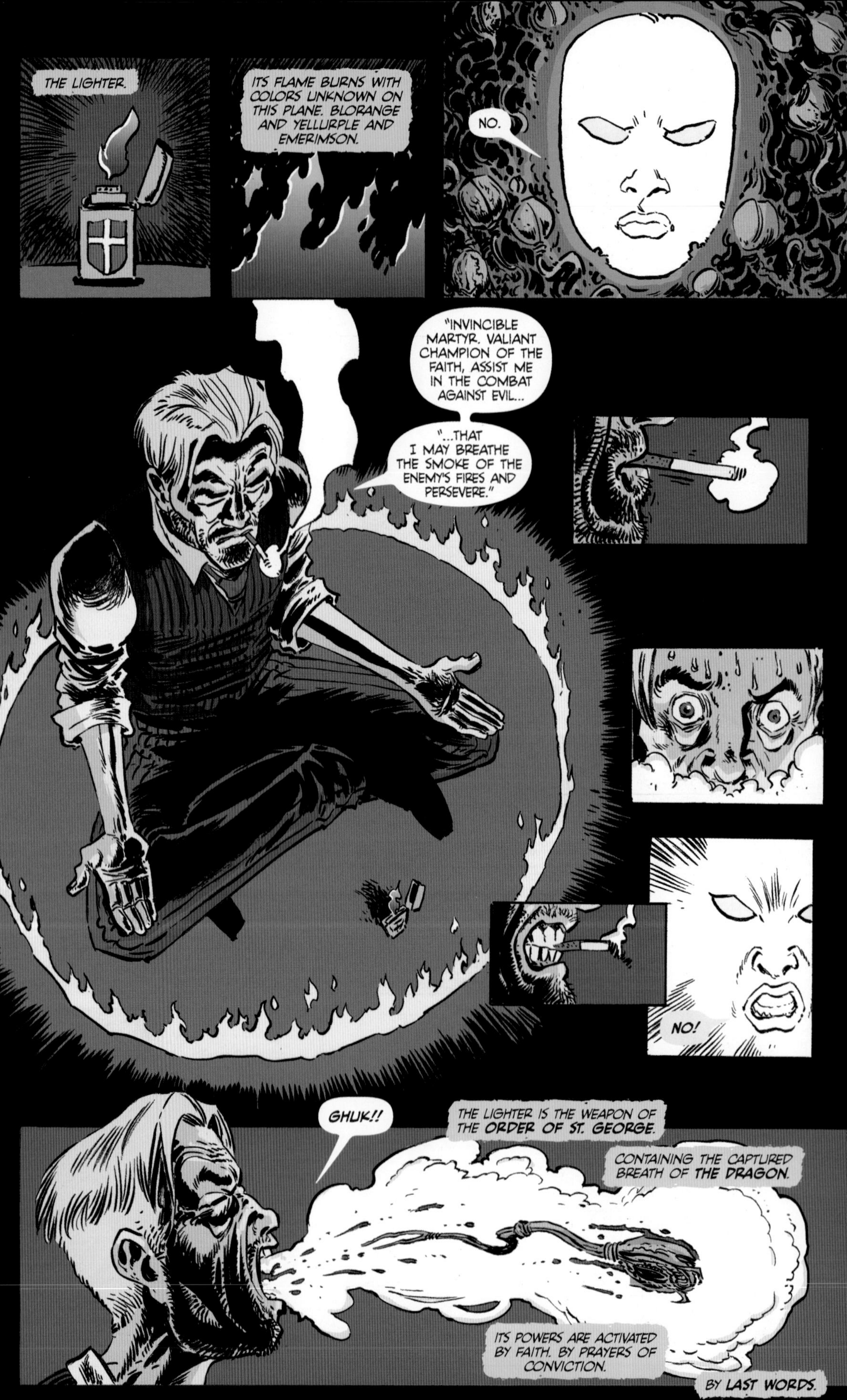
THE LIGHTER.
ITS FLAME BURNS WITH COLORS UNKNOWN ON THIS PLANE. BLORANGE AND YELLURPLE AND EMERIMSON.
NO.
"INVINCIBLE MARTYR. VALIANT CHAMPION OF THE FAITH, ASSIST ME IN THE COMBAT AGAINST EVIL...
"...THAT I MAY BREATHE THE SMOKE OF THE ENEMY'S FIRES AND PERSEVERE."
NO!
GHUK!!
THE LIGHTER IS THE WEAPON OF THE ORDER OF ST. GEORGE.
CONTAINING THE CAPTURED BREATH OF THE DRAGON.
ITS POWERS ARE ACTIVATED BY FAITH. BY PRAYERS OF CONVICTION.
BY LAST WORDS.

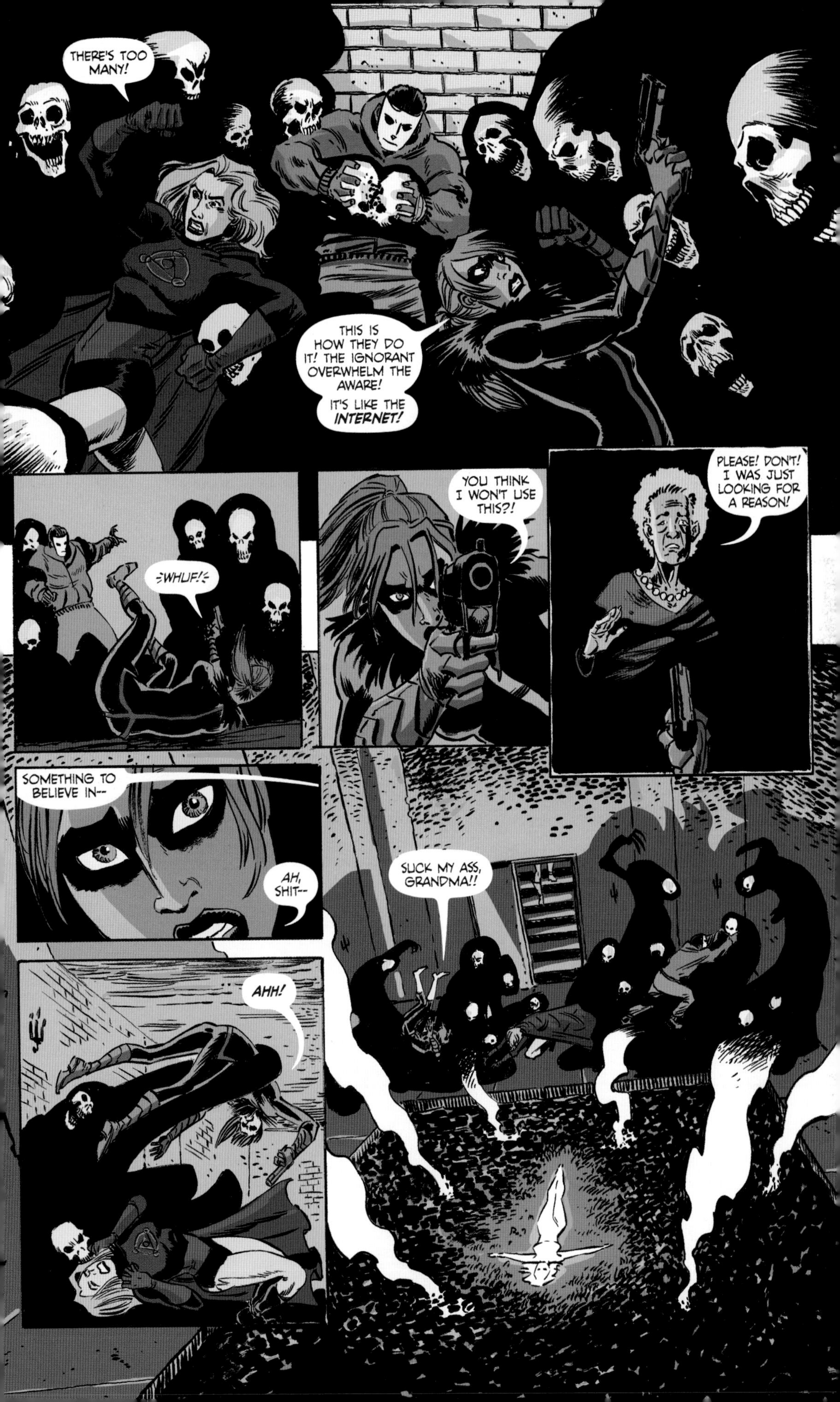

THERE'S TOO MANY!
THIS IS HOW THEY DO IT! THE IGNORANT OVERWHELM THE AWARE!
IT'S LIKE THE *INTERNET!*
=WHUF!=
YOU THINK I WON'T USE THIS?!
PLEASE! DON'T! I WAS JUST LOOKING FOR A REASON!
SOMETHING TO BELIEVE IN--
AH, SHIT--
SUCK MY ASS, GRANDMA!!
AHH!

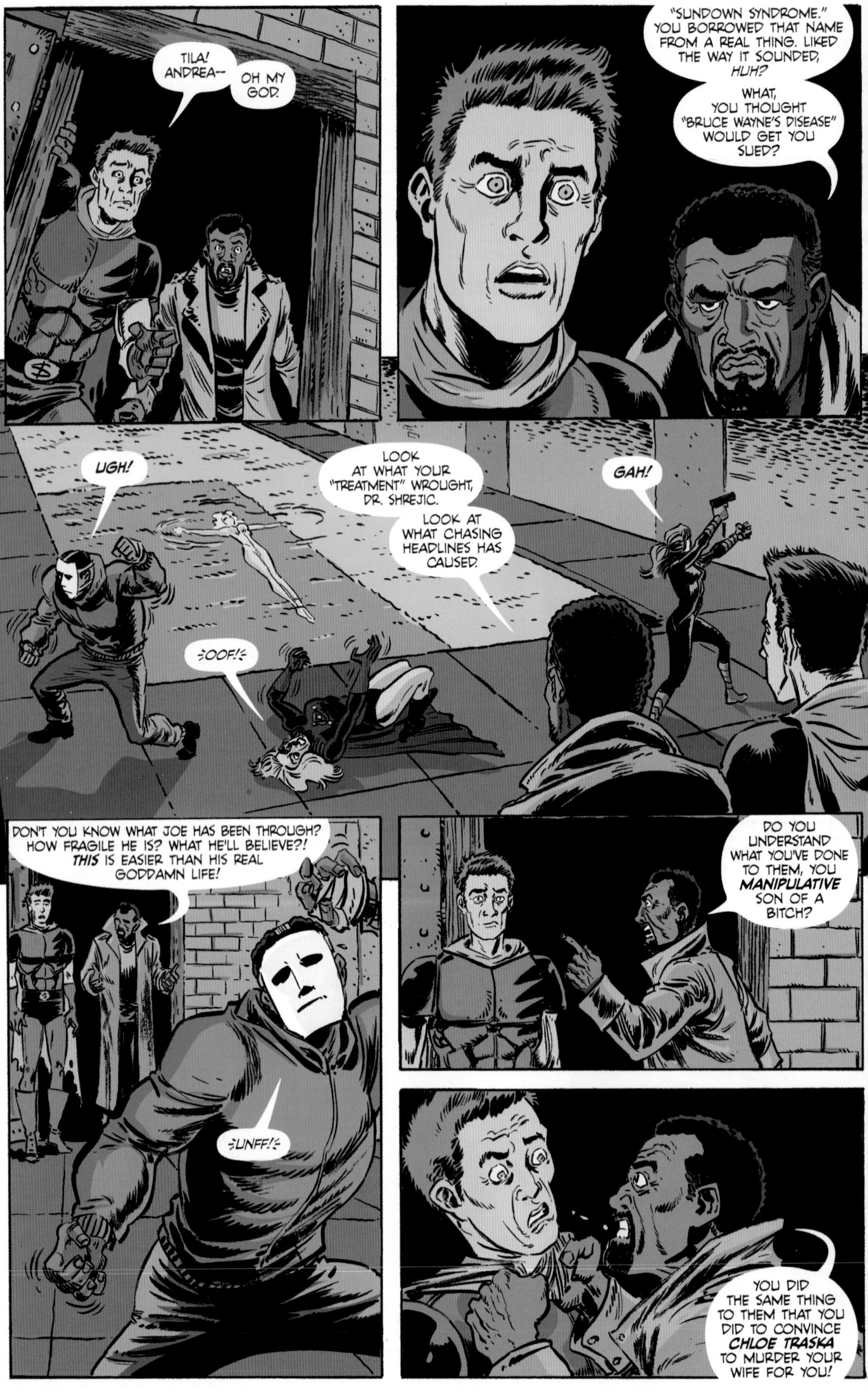
TILA! ANDREA--
OH MY GOD.
"SUNDOWN SYNDROME." YOU BORROWED THAT NAME FROM A REAL THING. LIKED THE WAY IT SOUNDED, HUH?
WHAT, YOU THOUGHT "BRUCE WAYNE'S DISEASE" WOULD GET YOU SUED?
UGH!
LOOK AT WHAT YOUR "TREATMENT" WROUGHT, DR. SHREJIC.
LOOK AT WHAT CHASING HEADLINES HAS CAUSED.
GAH!
OOF!
DON'T YOU KNOW WHAT JOE HAS BEEN THROUGH? HOW FRAGILE HE IS? WHAT HE'LL BELIEVE?! THIS IS EASIER THAN HIS REAL GODDAMN LIFE!
UNFF!
DO YOU UNDERSTAND WHAT YOU'VE DONE TO THEM, YOU MANIPULATIVE SON OF A BITCH?
YOU DID THE SAME THING TO THEM THAT YOU DID TO CONVINCE CHLOE TRASKA TO MURDER YOUR WIFE FOR YOU!

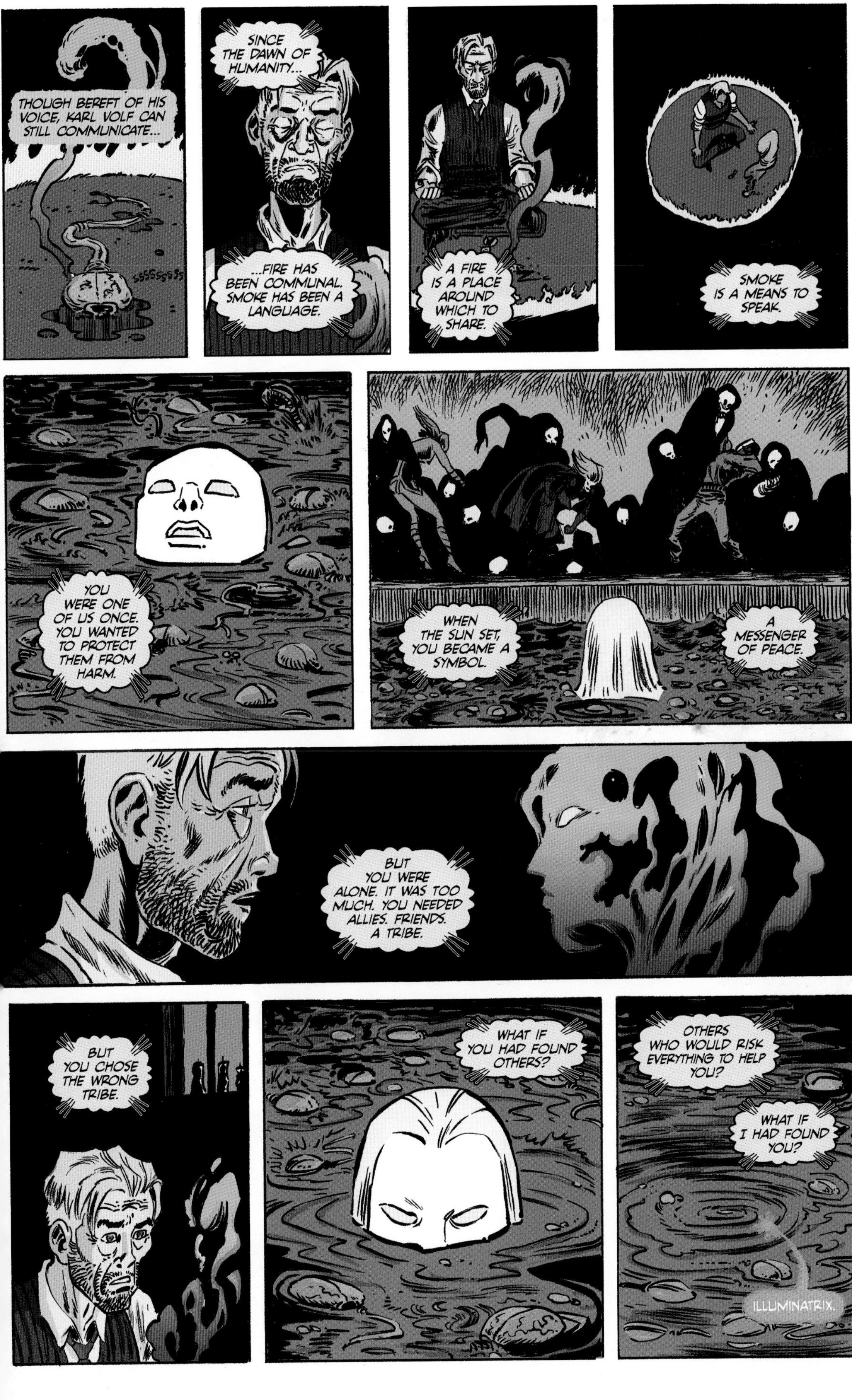
THOUGH BEREFT OF HIS VOICE, KARL VOLF CAN STILL COMMUNICATE...
SSSSSSSSS
SINCE THE DAWN OF HUMANITY...
...FIRE HAS BEEN COMMUNAL. SMOKE HAS BEEN A LANGUAGE.
A FIRE IS A PLACE AROUND WHICH TO SHARE.
SMOKE IS A MEANS TO SPEAK.
YOU WERE ONE OF US ONCE. YOU WANTED TO PROTECT THEM FROM HARM.
WHEN THE SUN SET, YOU BECAME A SYMBOL.
A MESSENGER OF PEACE.
BUT YOU WERE ALONE. IT WAS TOO MUCH. YOU NEEDED ALLIES. FRIENDS. A TRIBE.
BUT YOU CHOSE THE WRONG TRIBE.
WHAT IF YOU HAD FOUND OTHERS?
OTHERS WHO WOULD RISK EVERYTHING TO HELP YOU?
WHAT IF I HAD FOUND YOU?
ILLUMINATRIX.

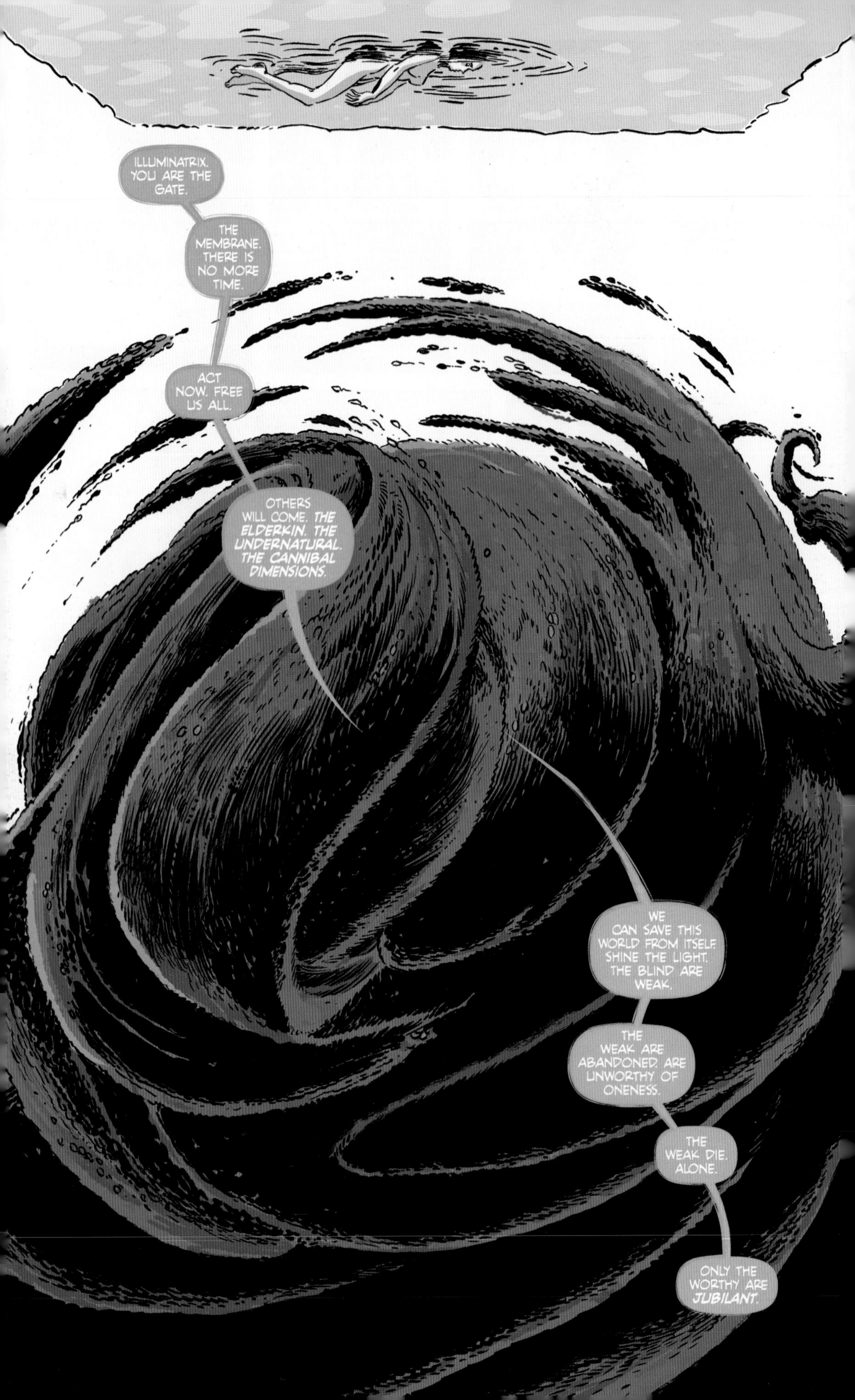
ILLUMINATRIX. YOU ARE THE GATE.
THE MEMBRANE. THERE IS NO MORE TIME.
ACT NOW. FREE US ALL.
OTHERS WILL COME. *THE ELDERKIN. THE UNDERNATURAL. THE CANNIBAL DIMENSIONS.*
WE CAN SAVE THIS WORLD FROM ITSELF. SHINE THE LIGHT. THE BLIND ARE WEAK.
THE WEAK ARE ABANDONED. ARE UNWORTHY OF ONENESS.
THE WEAK DIE. ALONE.
ONLY THE WORTHY ARE *JUBILANT*.

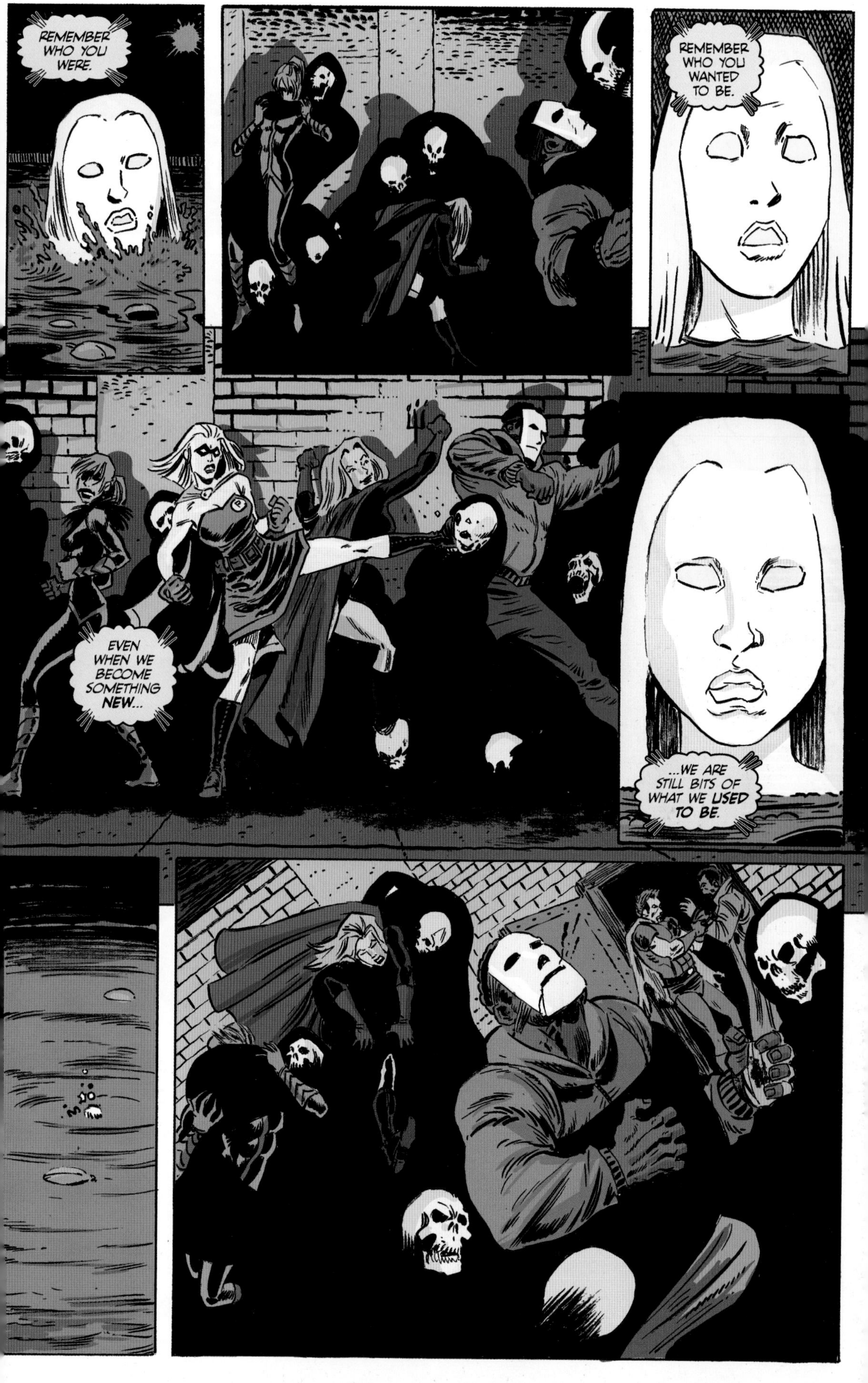
REMEMBER WHO YOU WERE.
REMEMBER WHO YOU WANTED TO BE.
EVEN WHEN WE BECOME SOMETHING NEW...
...WE ARE STILL BITS OF WHAT WE USED TO BE.

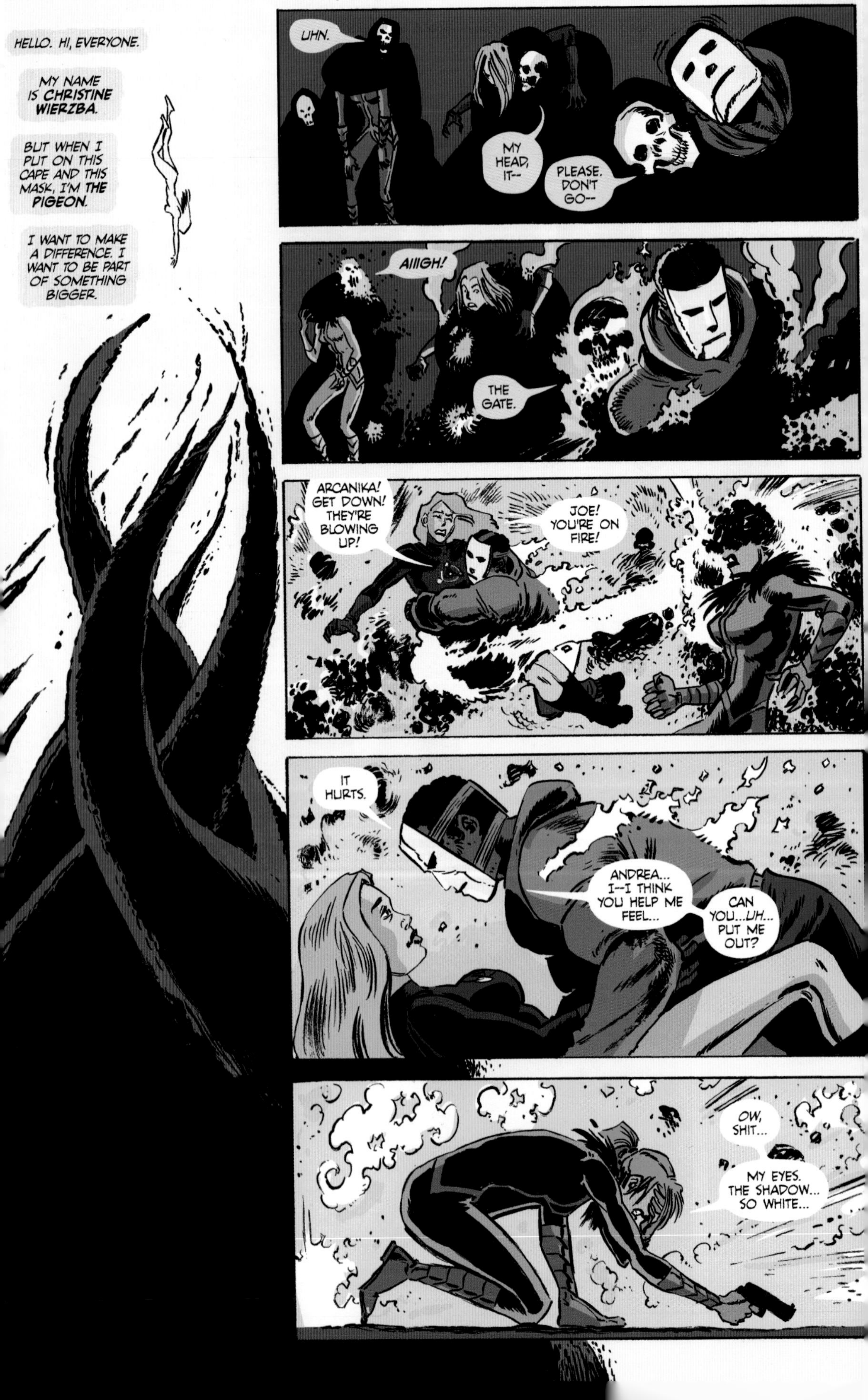
HELLO. HI, EVERYONE.
MY NAME IS **CHRISTINE WIERZBA**.
BUT WHEN I PUT ON THIS CAPE AND THIS MASK, I'M **THE PIGEON**.
I WANT TO MAKE A DIFFERENCE. I WANT TO BE PART OF SOMETHING BIGGER.
UHN.
MY HEAD, IT--
PLEASE. DON'T GO--
AIIIGH!
THE GATE.
ARCANIKA! GET DOWN! THEY'RE BLOWING UP!
JOE! YOU'RE ON FIRE!
IT HURTS.
ANDREA... I--I THINK YOU HELP ME FEEL...
CAN YOU...*UH*... PUT ME OUT?
OW, SHIT...
MY EYES. THE SHADOW... SO WHITE...

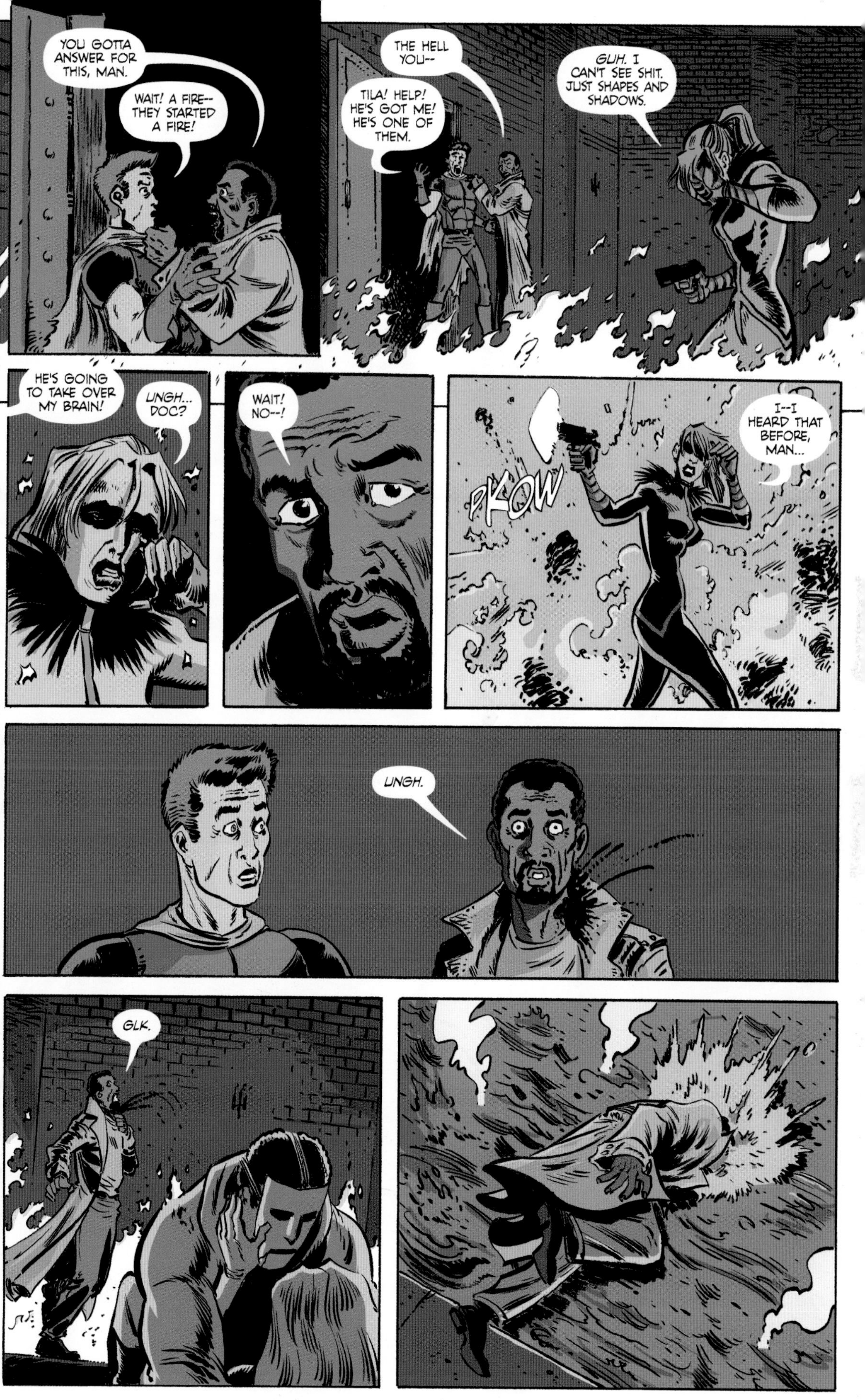
YOU GOTTA ANSWER FOR THIS, MAN.
WAIT! A FIRE-- THEY STARTED A FIRE!
THE HELL YOU--
TILA! HELP! HE'S GOT ME! HE'S ONE OF THEM.
GUH. I CAN'T SEE SHIT. JUST SHAPES AND SHADOWS.
HE'S GOING TO TAKE OVER MY BRAIN!
UNGH... DOC?
WAIT! NO--!
PKOW
I--I HEARD THAT BEFORE, MAN...
UNGH.
GLK.

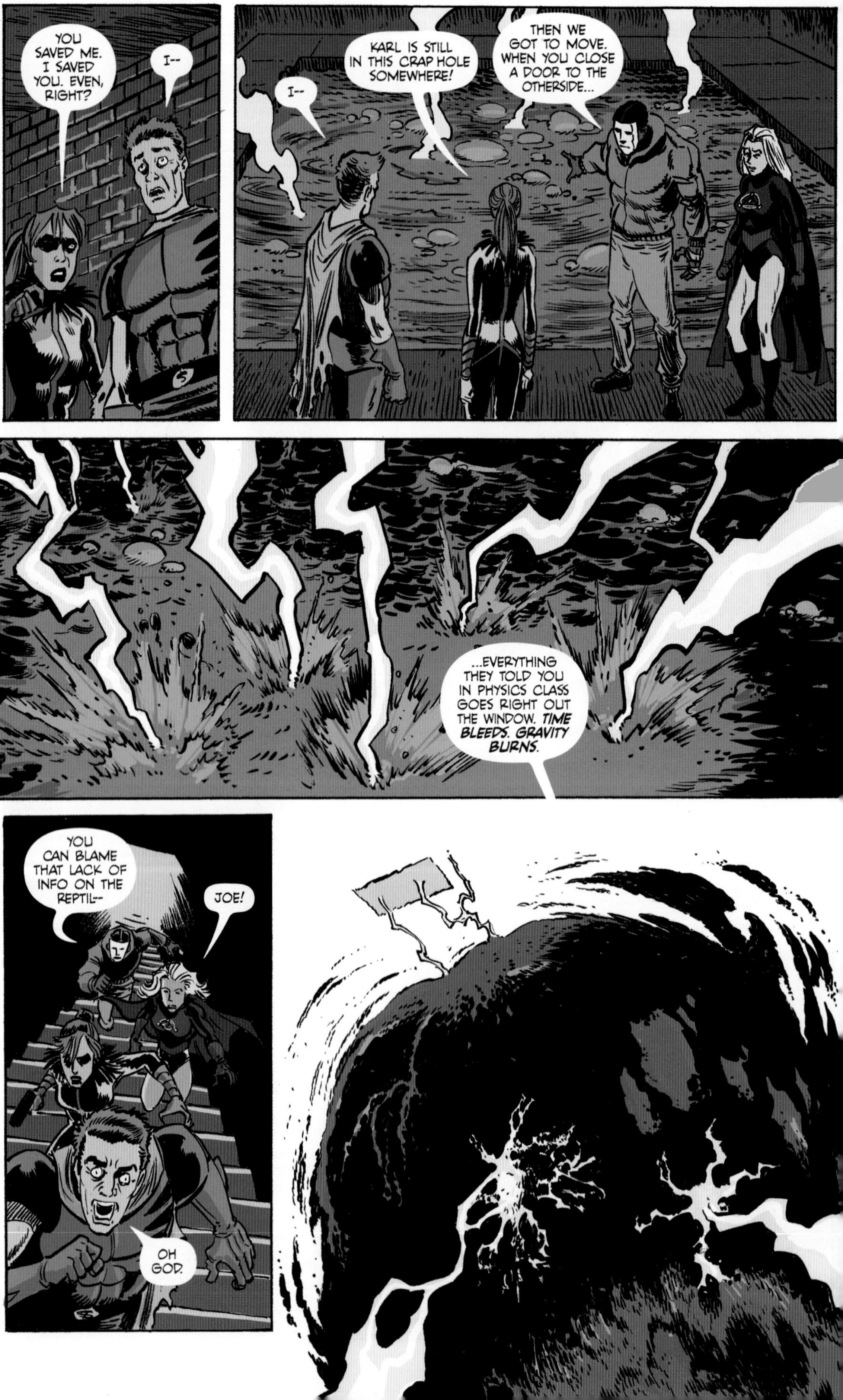

YOU SAVED ME. I SAVED YOU. EVEN, RIGHT?
I--
I--
KARL IS STILL IN THIS CRAP HOLE SOMEWHERE!
THEN WE GOT TO MOVE. WHEN YOU CLOSE A DOOR TO THE OTHERSIDE...
...EVERYTHING THEY TOLD YOU IN PHYSICS CLASS GOES RIGHT OUT THE WINDOW. *TIME BLEEDS. GRAVITY BURNS.*
YOU CAN BLAME THAT LACK OF INFO ON THE REPTIL--
JOE!
OH GOD.

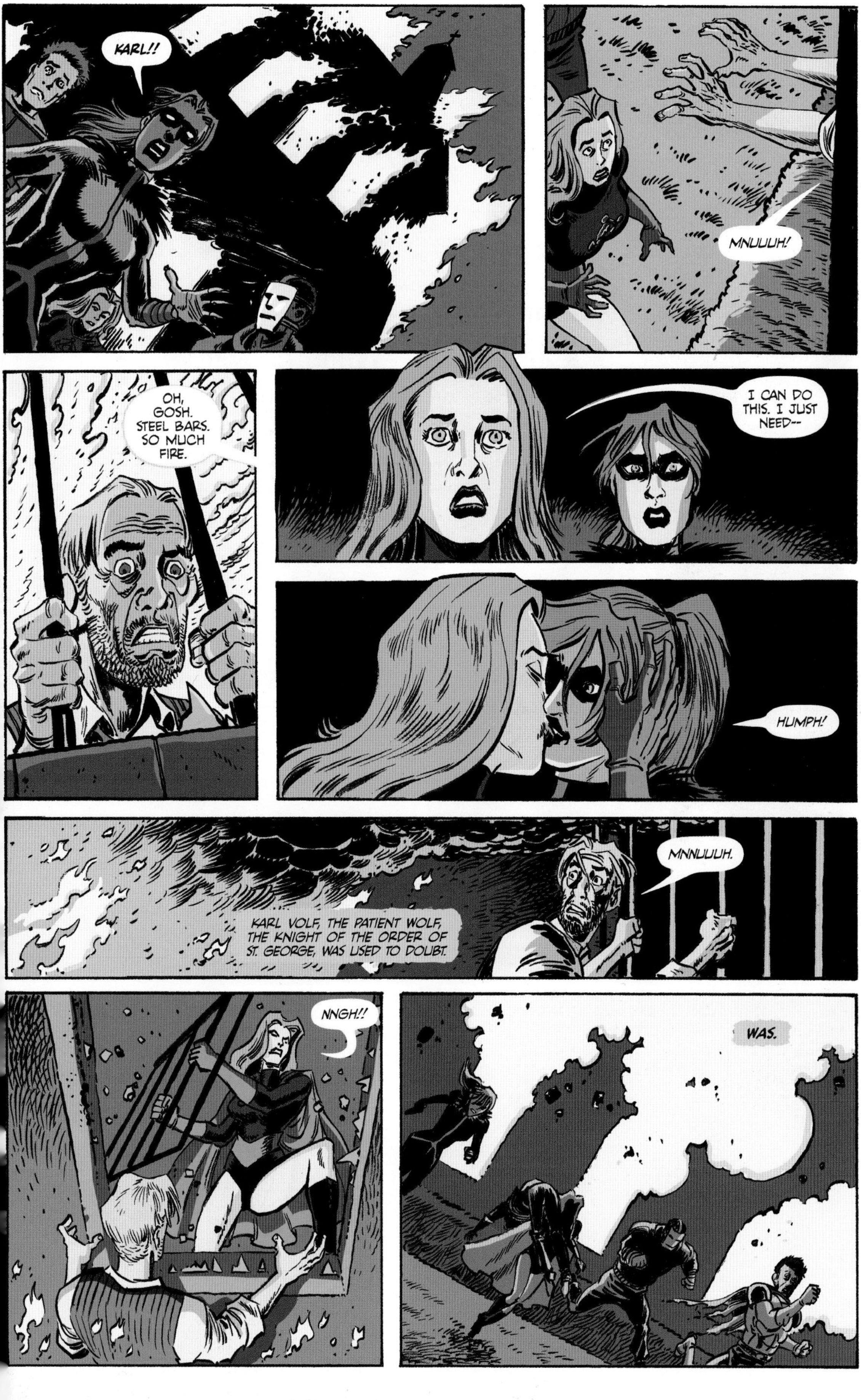
KARL!!
MNUUUH!
OH, GOSH. STEEL BARS. SO MUCH FIRE.
I CAN DO THIS. I JUST NEED--
HUMPH!
KARL VOLF, THE PATIENT WOLF, THE KNIGHT OF THE ORDER OF ST. GEORGE, WAS USED TO DOUBT.
MNNUUUH.
NNGH!!
WAS.

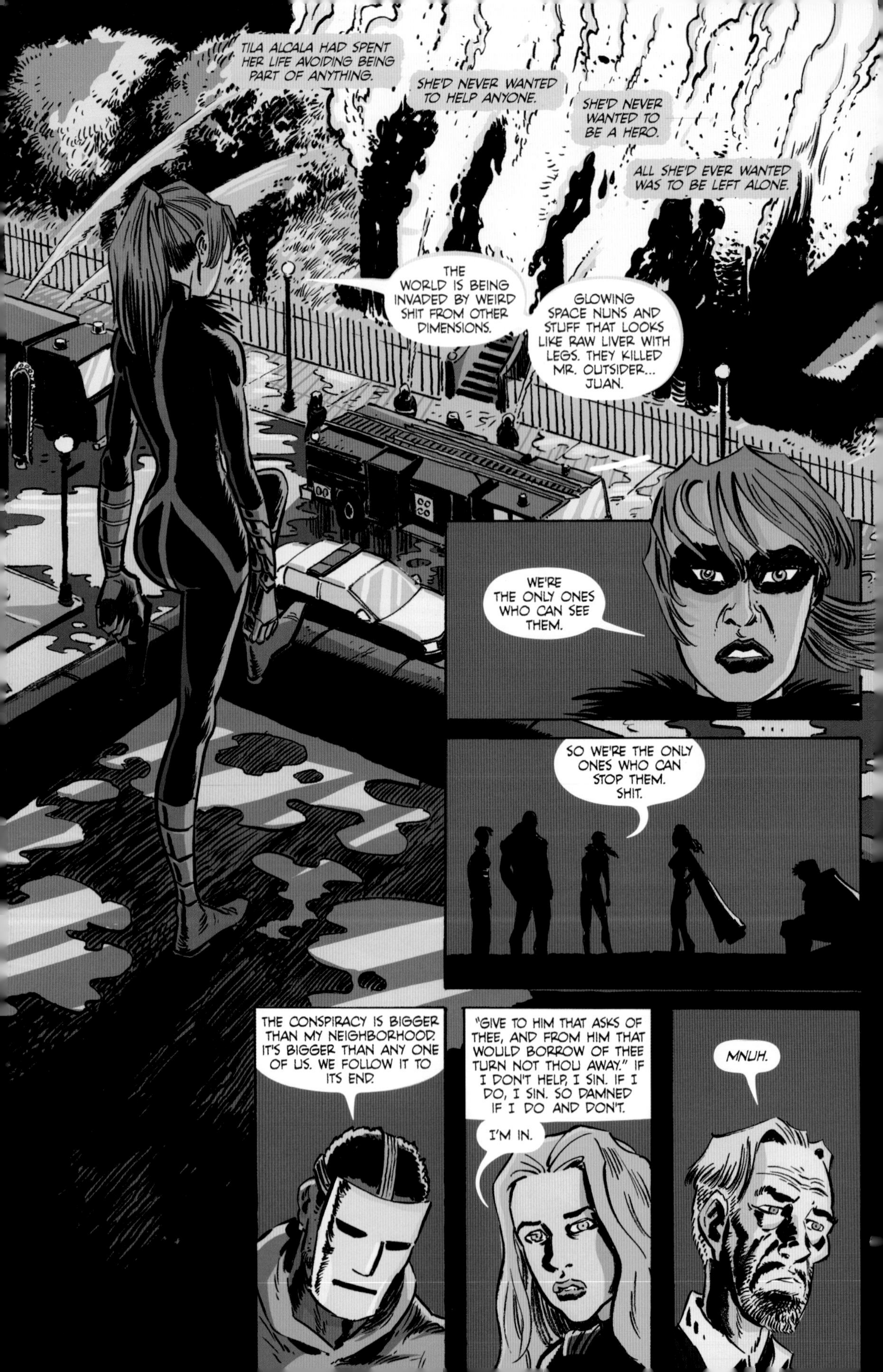
TILA ALCALA HAD SPENT HER LIFE AVOIDING BEING PART OF ANYTHING.
SHE'D NEVER WANTED TO HELP ANYONE.
SHE'D NEVER WANTED TO BE A HERO.
ALL SHE'D EVER WANTED WAS TO BE LEFT ALONE.
THE WORLD IS BEING INVADED BY WEIRD SHIT FROM OTHER DIMENSIONS.
GLOWING SPACE NUNS AND STUFF THAT LOOKS LIKE RAW LIVER WITH LEGS. THEY KILLED MR. OUTSIDER... JUAN.
WE'RE THE ONLY ONES WHO CAN SEE THEM.
SO WE'RE THE ONLY ONES WHO CAN STOP THEM. SHIT.
THE CONSPIRACY IS BIGGER THAN MY NEIGHBORHOOD. IT'S BIGGER THAN ANY ONE OF US. WE FOLLOW IT TO ITS END.
"GIVE TO HIM THAT ASKS OF THEE, AND FROM HIM THAT WOULD BORROW OF THEE TURN NOT THOU AWAY." IF I DON'T HELP, I SIN. IF I DO, I SIN. SO DAMNED IF I DO AND DON'T.
I'M IN.
MNUH.

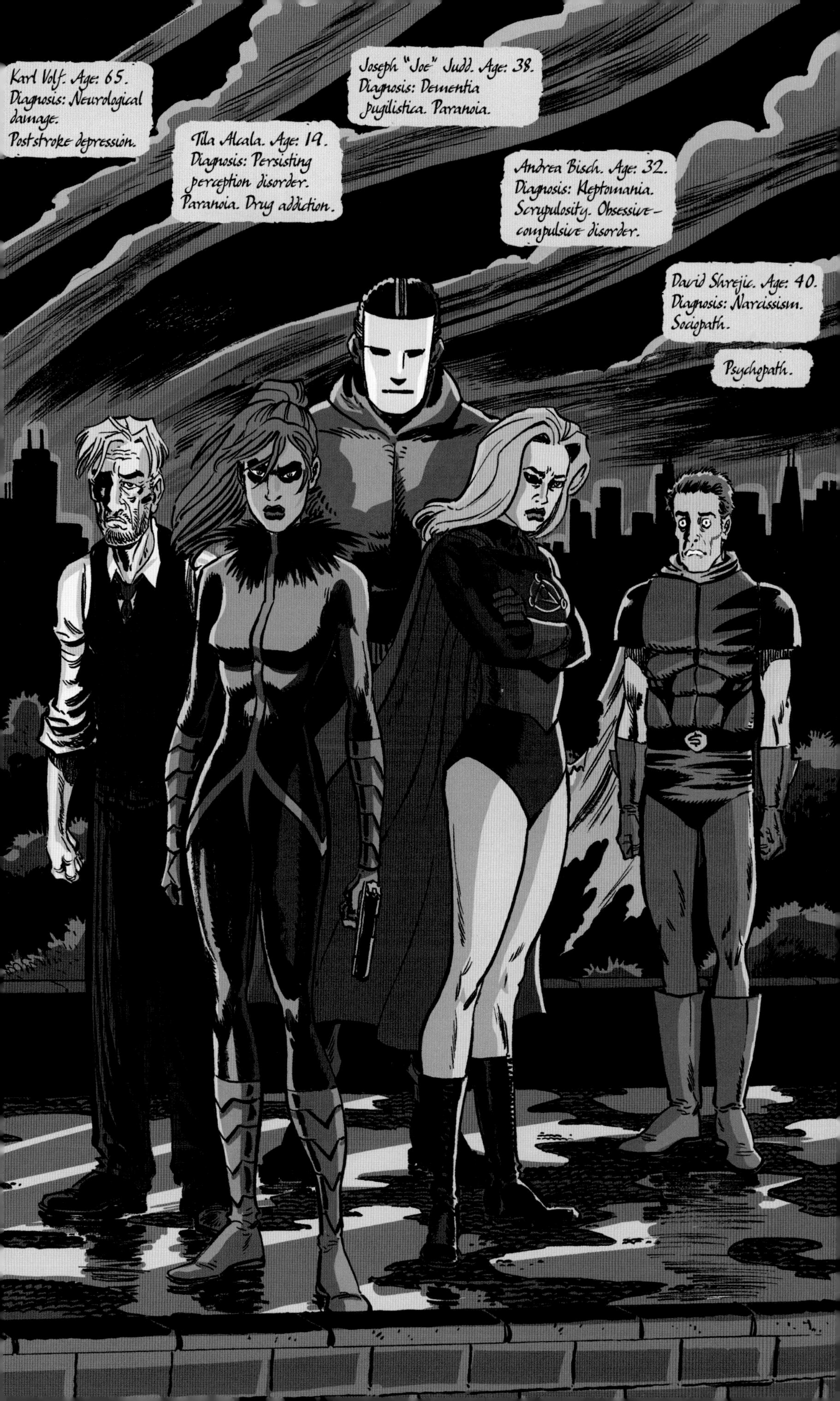

Karl Volf. Age: 65. Diagnosis: Neurological damage. Poststroke depression.
Tila Alcala. Age: 19. Diagnosis: Persisting perception disorder. Paranoia. Drug addiction.
Joseph "Joe" Judd. Age: 38. Diagnosis: Dementia pugilistica. Paranoia.
Andrea Bisch. Age: 32. Diagnosis: Kleptomania. Scrupulosity. Obsessive-compulsive disorder.
David Shrejic. Age: 40. Diagnosis: Narcissism. Sociopath.
Psychopath.

SKETCHBOOK

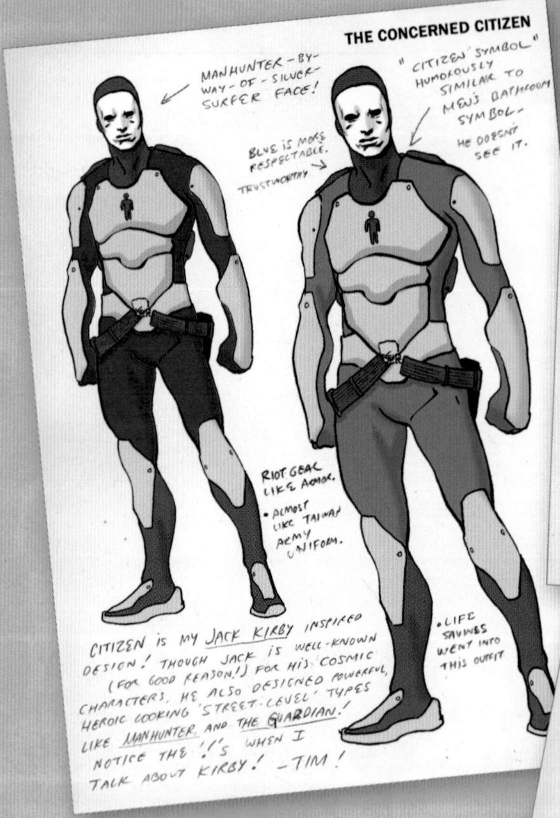
THE CONCERNED CITIZEN
MANHUNTER-BY-WAY-OF-SILVER-SURFER FACE!
"CITIZEN SYMBOL" HUMOROUSLY SIMILAR TO MEN'S BATHROOM SYMBOL- HE DOESN'T SEE IT.
BLUE IS MORE RESPECTABLE. TRUSTWORTHY.
RIOT GEAR LIKE ARMOR.
• ALMOST LIKE TAIWAN ARMY UNIFORM.
• LIFE SAVINGS WENT INTO THIS OUTFIT
CITIZEN IS MY JACK KIRBY INSPIRED DESIGN! THOUGH JACK IS WELL-KNOWN (FOR GOOD REASON!) FOR HIS COSMIC CHARACTERS, HE ALSO DESIGNED POWERFUL, HEROIC LOOKING 'STREET-LEVEL' TYPES LIKE MANHUNTER AND THE GUARDIAN! NOTICE THE '!'S WHEN I TALK ABOUT KIRBY! -TIM!

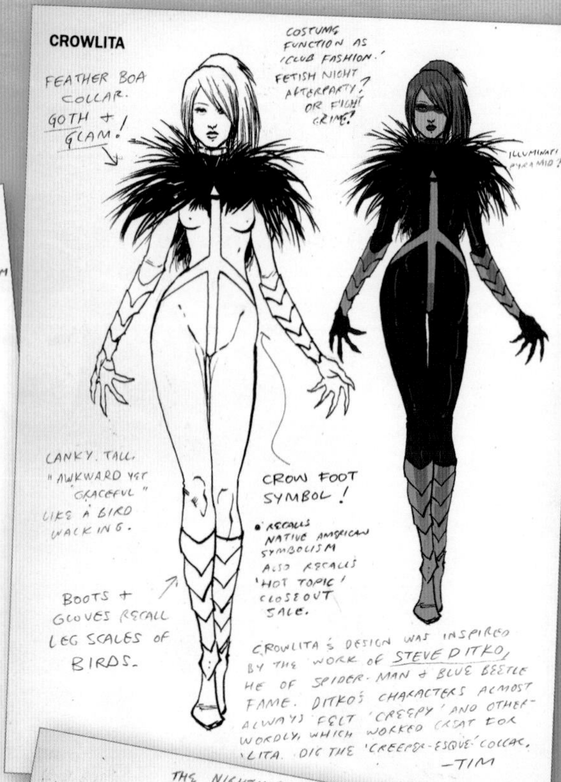
CROWLITA
FEATHER BOA COLLAR. GOTH + GLAM!
COSTUME FUNCTION AS 'CLUB FASHION.' FETISH NIGHT AFTERPARTY? OR FIGHT GRIME?
ILLUMINATI PYRAMID?
LANKY. TALL. "AWKWARD YET GRACEFUL" LIKE A BIRD WALKING.
CROW FOOT SYMBOL!
• RECALLS NATIVE AMERICAN SYMBOLISM ALSO RECALLS 'HOT TOPIC' CLOSEOUT SALE.
BOOTS + GLOVES RECALL LEG SCALES OF BIRDS.
CROWLITA'S DESIGN WAS INSPIRED BY THE WORK OF STEVE DITKO, HE OF SPIDER-MAN & BLUE BEETLE FAME. DITKO'S CHARACTERS ALMOST ALWAYS FELT 'CREEPY' AND OTHER-WORDLY, WHICH WORKED GREAT FOR 'LITA. DIG THE 'CREEPER-ESQUE' COLLAR. -TIM

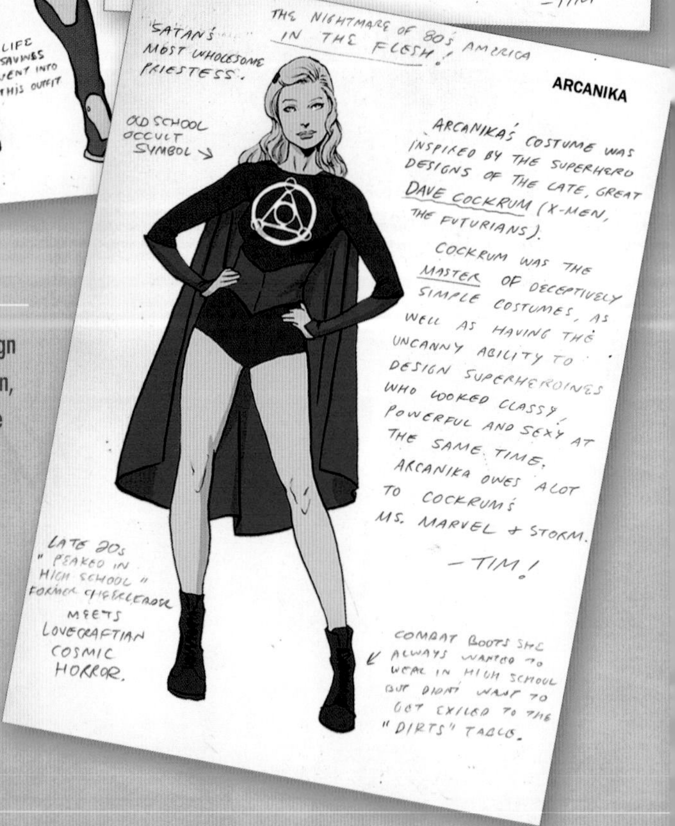
SATAN'S MOST WHOLESOME PRIESTESS.
THE NIGHTMARE OF 80'S AMERICA IN THE FLESH!
ARCANIKA
OLD SCHOOL OCCULT SYMBOL
ARCANIKA'S COSTUME WAS INSPIRED BY THE SUPERHERO DESIGNS OF THE LATE, GREAT DAVE COCKRUM (X-MEN, THE FUTURIANS).
COCKRUM WAS THE MASTER OF DECEPTIVELY SIMPLE COSTUMES, AS WELL AS HAVING THE UNCANNY ABILITY TO DESIGN SUPERHEROINES WHO LOOKED CLASSY, POWERFUL AND SEXY AT THE SAME TIME.
ARCANIKA OWES ALOT TO COCKRUM'S MS. MARVEL + STORM.
-TIM!
LATE 20s "PEAKED IN HIGH SCHOOL" FORMER CHEERLEADER MEETS LOVECRAFTIAN COSMIC HORROR.
COMBAT BOOTS SHE ALWAYS WANTED TO WEAR IN HIGH SCHOOL BUT DIDN'T WANT TO GET EXILED TO THE "DIRTS" TABLE.

TIM: I think most modern comic book superhero design is trying too hard to parallel film superhero design, which makes for a lot of characters who look like crap on a page. The greats knew that superheroes in a comic had to be distinct, identifiable, and easy to draw a bunch of times, as well as looking awesome in two dimensions. So, with the Sundowners, I tried to pay homage to the best comic book superhero designers with each character.

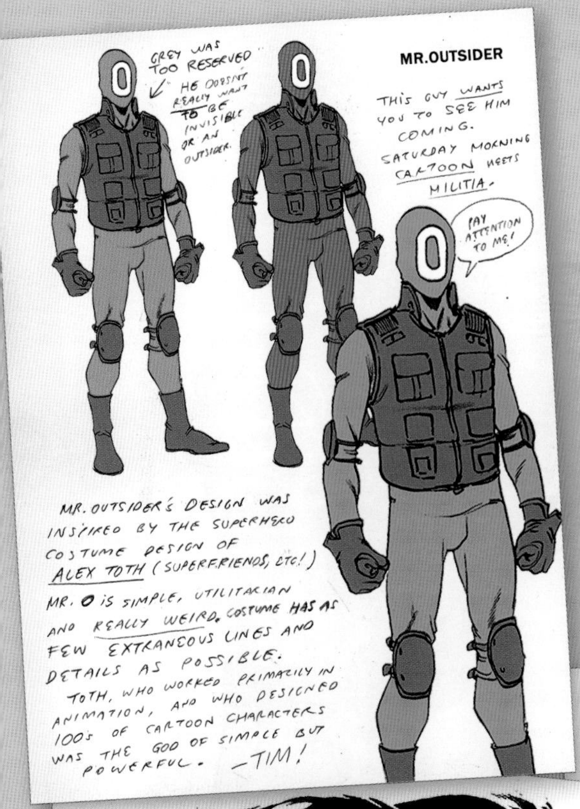

MR.OUTSIDER
GREY WAS TOO RESERVED
HE DOESN'T REALLY WANT TO BE INVISIBLE OR AN OUTSIDER.
THIS GUY WANTS YOU TO SEE HIM COMING.
SATURDAY MORNING CARTOON MEETS MILITIA.
PAY ATTENTION TO ME!
MR. OUTSIDER'S DESIGN WAS INSPIRED BY THE SUPERHERO COSTUME DESIGN OF ALEX TOTH (SUPERFRIENDS, ETC!)
MR. O IS SIMPLE, UTILITARIAN AND REALLY WEIRD. COSTUME HAS AS FEW EXTRANEOUS LINES AND DETAILS AS POSSIBLE.
TOTH, WHO WORKED PRIMARILY IN ANIMATION, AND WHO DESIGNED 100'S OF CARTOON CHARACTERS WAS THE GOD OF SIMPLE BUT POWERFUL. —TIM!

TIM: The Concerned Citizen is a Jack Kirby character, Crowlita is an homage to Steve Ditko, Arcanika is a love letter to Dave Cockrum, and Mr. Outsider is me riffing on the great Alex Toth. Karl Volf . . . Well, he's not exactly a superhero, but his design is based on a dapper old guy I met at a bar in San Francisco.

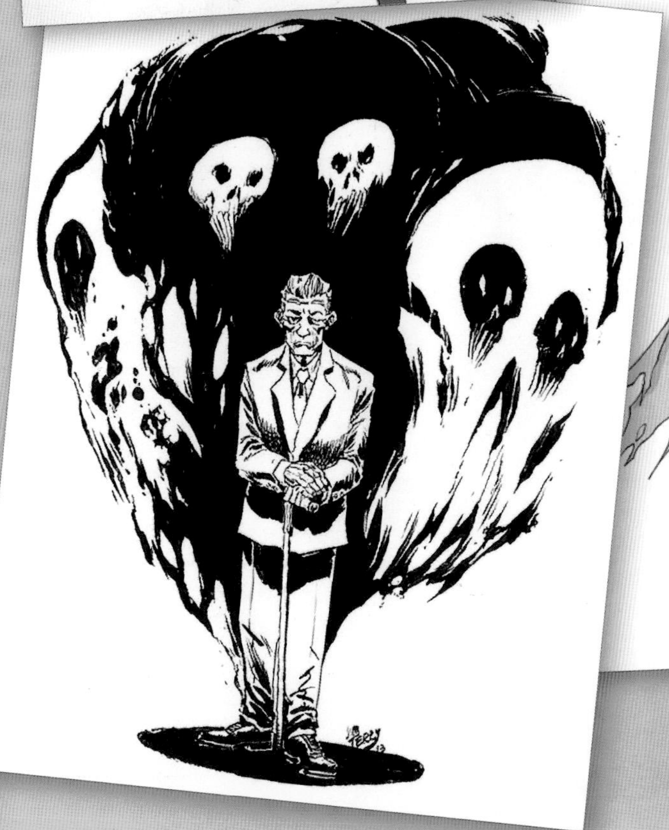

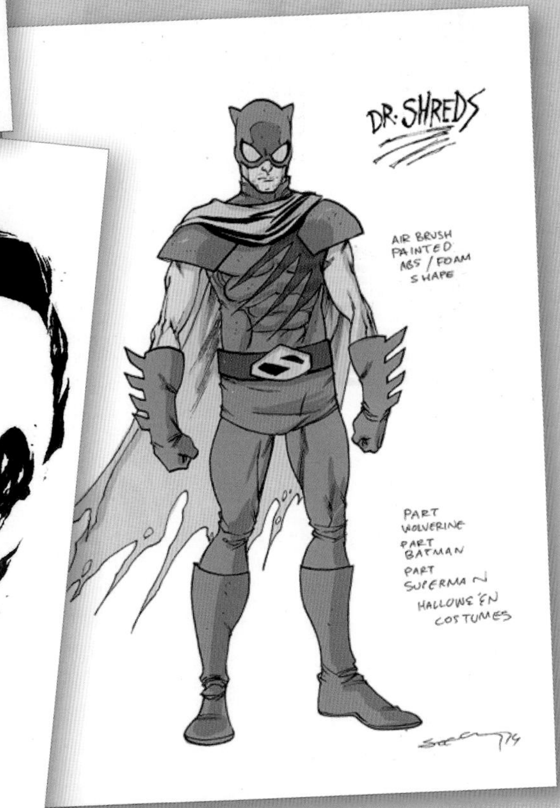

DR. SHREDS
AIR BRUSH PAINTED ABS / FOAM SHAPE
PART WOLVERINE
PART BATMAN
PART SUPERMAN
HALLOWE'EN COSTUMES

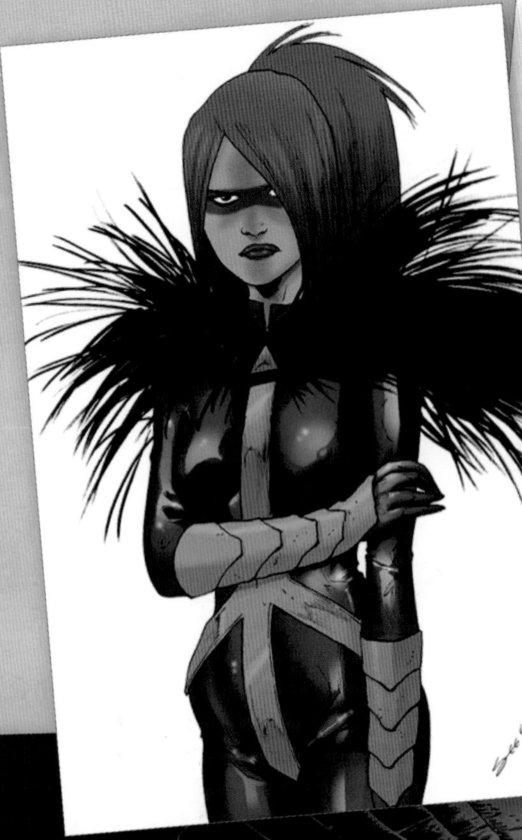

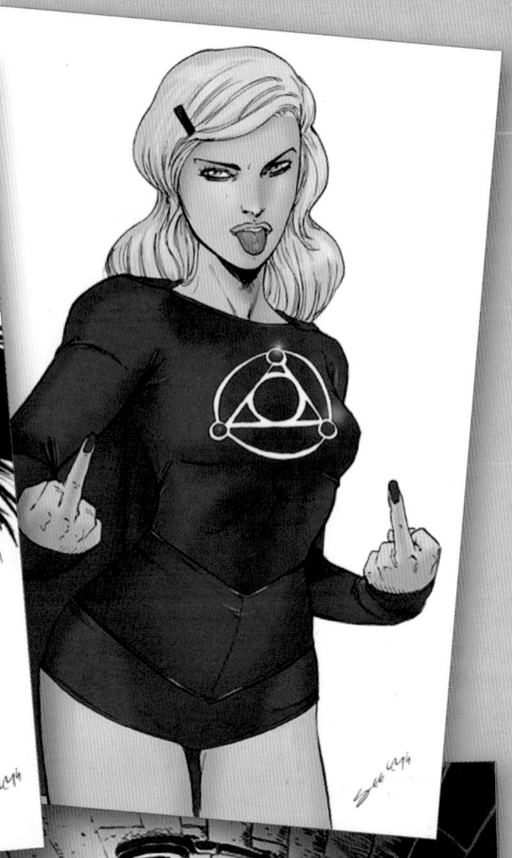

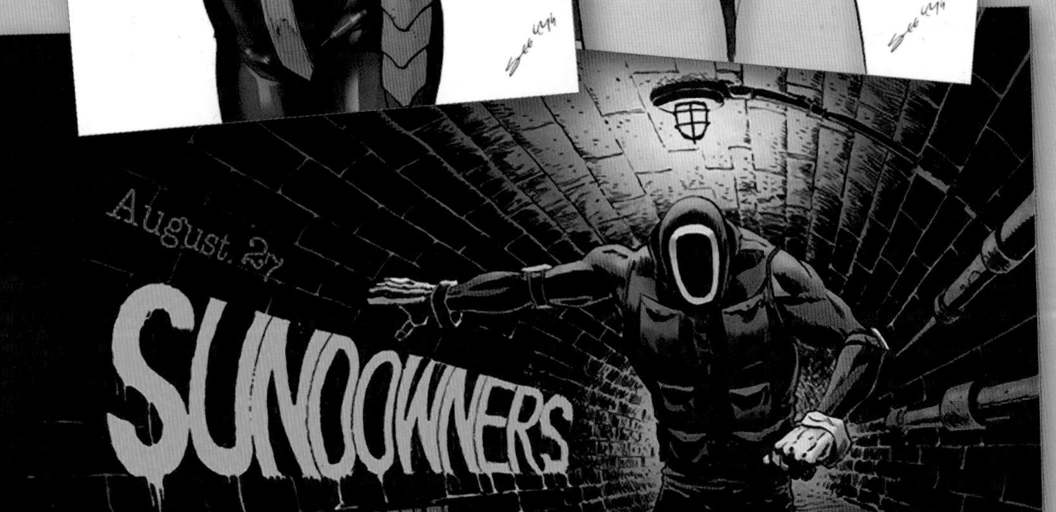
August 27
SUNDOWNERS
TIM SEELEY
JIM TERRY

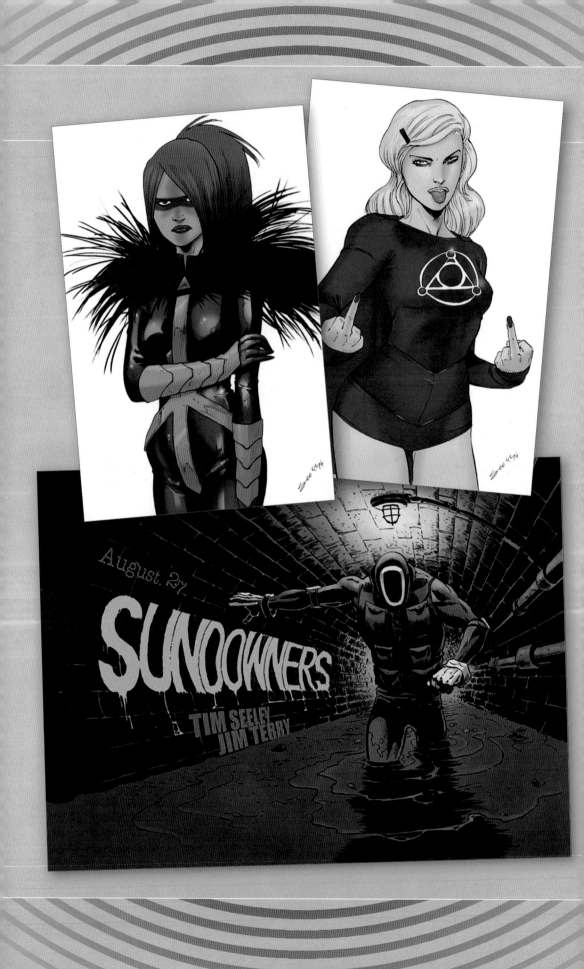